Saigon: A Hi

NGHIA M. VO

McFarland & Company, Inc., Publishers

Jefferson, North Carolina, and London

LIBRARY OF CONGRESS CATALOGUING-IN-PUBLICATION DATA

Vo, Nghia M., 1947–
    Saigon : a history / Nghia M. Vo.
      p.   cm.
    Includes bibliographical references and index.

    ISBN 978-0-7864-6466-1
    softcover : 50# alkaline paper ∞

    1. Ho Chi Minh City (Vietnam)—History. I. Title.
DS559.93.S2V6   2011
959.7'7—dc23   2011029507

BRITISH LIBRARY CATALOGUING DATA ARE AVAILABLE

Front cover image © 2011 Shutterstock

Manufactured in the United States of America

*McFarland & Company, Inc., Publishers
  Box 611, Jefferson, North Carolina 28640
  www.mcfarlandpub.com*

Saigon

Also by Nghia M. Vo
and from McFarland

*The Viet Kieu in America: Personal Accounts of
Postwar Immigrants from Vietnam* (2009)

*The Vietnamese Boat People,
1954 and 1975–1992* (2006)

*The Bamboo Gulag: Political Imprisonment in
Communist Vietnam* (2004)

Table of Contents

Preface

Saigon, once known as the "pearl of the Orient," was born as Baigaur (though we are not sure exactly when), the southernmost Champa[1] village on the Donnai River (present-day Đồng Nai). She became the Khmer[2] Prey Nokor (a village in the forest) after the Khmers invaded Champa in 1190. For more than five centuries, she languished among the dense forests of the Donnai River basin like a virgin waiting to be claimed.

The Chúa Nguyễn,[3] rulers of what is present-day central Vietnam, recognized Saigon's riches beneath the inhospitable and torrid tropical weather. They snatched her from the Khmers in 1698. What started as a colonization process ended up as fratricidal infighting for the control of Saigon and the Mekong Delta. In the process, the Vietnamese beat "several European powers to the punch on several occasions."[4] From 1788 to 1802, Nguyễn Ánh made Saigon his capital, and from there spearheaded a relentless fight to recover his usurped kingdom and its city, Huế. The increased local and regional commercial traffic with other southeastern Asian ports swelled his coffers and allowed him to carry his battles northwards to Huế and Hà Nội. After his victory in 1802, he returned to Huế and relegated Saigon to a secondary role.

The Mekong Delta was swampy and inhospitable because of the presence of voracious mosquitoes that transmitted disabling and often fatal infectious diseases, such as malaria and Dengue hemorrhagic fever.[5] It was also infested with crocodiles and other dangerous wild animals. The steamy tropical heat not only disturbed locals, but also potential visitors and colonists. All these conditions help to explain Saigon's rather slow growth until after the 19th century.

On the other hand, Saigon was a nice inland port well-protected from the forces of nature, including the often violent monsoons that battered the region from May until October. A nice transit area, she allowed easy access to the riches of the Mekong Delta: its rice basket, its various tropical fruits, and its fish and shrimp farms. The Đồng Nai River and the much larger Mekong River had been for centuries thriving waterways that allowed easy communication and commerce with Cambodia and Laos, and the seaports of Thailand, Malaysia, Indonesia and China. Well-sheltered from floods and weather, Saigon was once thought to be too far inland to be an active commercial port.

But once the marshlands had been drained and the surrounding forests taken down, mosquitoes and diseases markedly decreased and Saigon's population rapidly soared.

Saigon, the city, had seen her share of historic, heroic, and bloody battles—battles that were waged by different armies at different times in history to conquer her not only because she was the seductress on the Saigon River, but because she was also the soul, the economic engine of the delta, and perhaps of the whole country.

Vietnamese and Siamese fought for the control of Saigon and the Mekong Delta in the early 18th century. They waged three major battles before settling the fate of Saigon (chapter 1). It was there that the Nguyễn Ánh and Tây Sơn forces waged their fiercest battles that ended up with the 1782 slaughter of tens of thousands of Saigonese. Although the city changed hands four different times, Nguyễn Ánh eventually prevailed and reunified the whole country under his leadership (chapter 2). It was there, in 1835, that the Minh Mạng's army—to reassert its control over the South—slaughtered more than 2,000 of Lê Văn Khôi's followers and razed the Saigon/Gia Định citadel in order to bring the semi-autonomous Saigon back under its rule (chapter 3). The French took over Saigon in 1859, blew up the rebuilt citadel, and established the first colony of their Indochinese Empire. The fall of Kỳ Đồng opened the Mekong Delta to the French colonists (chapter 4). From Saigon, the French carved out their Indochinese colonial empire. It was there that Nguyễn An Ninh spearheaded his political attacks against the French who eventually sent him to his demise in the Côn Sơn Island jail 80 miles away. It was there that the Cao Đài and Hòa Hảo religious sects were born before waging war against the French (chapter 5). It was in Saigon that the Japanese established their military base with the goal of conquering Southeast Asia. Bảo Đại temporarily made Saigon the capital of the State of Vietnam (chapter 6). The new prime minister (and later president), Ngô Đình Diệm, fought in 1955 against the various religious sects and met his violent demise there (chapter 7). The city bore witness to the Buddhist insurrection under the generals' rule (chapter 8). She was then violently attacked by the Việt Cộng in 1968—the Tết tragedy that led to the withdrawal of the American forces (chapter 9).

After the tragic 1975 fall of Saigon, the Saigonese bravely resisted collectivization of agriculture and nationalization of urban commerce imposed by an oppressive communist regime. Resistance was also manifested by the diaspora of millions of boat people—the majority originating from Saigon—who resettled worldwide (chapter 10). Southern resistance, in the end, spearheaded a perestroika-type economic renovation and the revival of the economy. If Saigon lost the war, she eventually won the peace. By "liberating" the North from its unhealthy socialist economics, Saigon single-handedly chartered a new economic course that lifted the country out of its economic doldrums (chapter 11). Without her, Vietnam, economically, would have been another

Cuba or North Korea. As for southerners who could not tolerate the communist regime, they went on to build many enclaves abroad, which were called "Little Saigons" to remind them of the lost homeland and the city they loved very much (chapter 12).

In addition to the historic, economic, and political events that had repercussions as far-reaching as Washington, Paris, and other western cities, the city had her share of tragedies. When the Siamese, the Tây Sơn, the Nguyễn lords, the French, the Japanese, the Americans, and the communists brought their armies to Saigon, her sons and daughters suffered. But they have always gone back to rebuild their city and livelihoods.

Violently pursued and conquered, Saigon saw many of her conquerors leave her for Huế or Hà Nội. Only the French found Saigon attractive enough to make her their jewel of the Orient, the capital of the Cochinchinese colony.[6] She later bloomed and became the capital of the southerners. The richness of the lands and the freedom they had enjoyed for many centuries made the southerners different from northerners. Saigon, with her *laissez-faire*, benevolent, and commerce-oriented attitude has produced a unique heterogeneous Vietnamese culture with characteristic southern flavors.[7] One Việt Kiều recently commented, "I breathe better once I arrive to Saigon from Hà Nội. Life is much easier in Saigon than its northern counterpart."[8]

From the historical point of view, Saigon has never pretended to be like Hà Nội, the cradle of Vietnamese history, or Huế, the 19th-century imperial city of the Nguyễn dynasty. She limped along but came of age when French and Americans poured billions of francs and dollars to shore her up. She made history because beneath her muddy and provincial veil, she had always been an important economic, cultural and political center. All the roads in Vietnam eventually led to Saigon, which was, and is, the dynamic "engine" of the Vietnamese economy. Since the 17th century, the Nguyễn had exploited the riches of the Mekong Delta to pay tribute to Hà Nội and to feed the impoverished people of central Vietnam. The same process repeated itself in the 19th century under the French and again after 1975, when the looted riches of South Vietnam ended up feeding the economically-wasted communist North. In 2007, if Saigon alone contributed 20 percent to the national budget's revenue,[9] the South brought in more than half of the nation's revenue.

Not too many important cities in the world had been that frequently conquered and then neglected; maybe this was because few people had realized her importance and strategic location. Saigon, despite her newcomer status, is rich in economic achievements, history, bloody battles, wars, pain and suffering. She was at the center of many historic events that descended on the country from the 17th century onward. By 2006, she was the largest city in the country, with 6.8 million counted and a few million unregistered inhabitants.

Born in the forests and raised among swampy and lush lands of the delta, she was resilient and free in spirit. Looking outward across the ocean, she searched for modernity, which manifested itself in the forms of trade, commerce, and freedom. Striving for independence since the early stages of her birth, she fought against outsiders: the Thais, the Tây Sơn, the French, the Japanese, the communists, before falling under their rule. She yearned to be free to pursue her agenda: freedom and trade. This turned out to be a tall order and on many occasions she has paid dearly for her stance.

Her free spirit makes her attractive, captivating, and challenging. She is also indomitable, resilient, and unique. Growing by leaps and bounds once left to herself, she is also the seductress on the Mekong, the underestimated nymph that outsiders often misunderstand. By transforming the marshlands of the Mekong Delta into rice farms and by engaging in regional trade, the Vietnamese transformed Saigon into a political and military powerhouse that competed with existing states. Competition eventually led to wars with accompanying successes and failures from which Saigon had to extricate herself.

Bùi Diễm felt it was his "duty not only to the hundreds of thousands of South Vietnamese who died on the battlefield in our struggle for independence and freedom, but also to the millions of others" to write his *In the Jaws of History*.[10] And there is no loftier goal than to write about the South Vietnamese's struggle for identity, independence, and freedom. History is complex and nothing is more complex than the history of Vietnam, especially when officials from the present government have been trying for the last three decades to rewrite it to suit their goals.[11]

Luckily, some American and Vietnamese historians like O.W. Wolters, John K. Whitmore, Keith Taylor, Neil Jamieson, Mark Moyar, A.J. Dommen, Bùi Diễm, Huỳnh Sanh Thông, Lewis Sorley, Andrew Wiest, George Dutton, Li Tana and others who, looking at the issue from a different angle, have shown us inspiring and important details about Vietnamese history. It is my hope to also contribute something to that history so that views can be clearer and less skewed, limited, or one-sided than before. I am deeply thankful to the scholars of Vietnamese history who have tried their best to provide us with an impartial look at South Vietnam.

Saigon and the South are not the imagined Vietnam described by Frances FitzGerald—an image born from her readings of old French textbooks—where the Vietnamese were reduced to passivity by their lack of history.[12] Templer once disagreed with her: "Her ideas, presented in a ringing, authoritative tone but with only the sparsest evidence, say little about the Vietnamese."[13] Instead, this is another Vietnam where the people were "traveling, trading, migrating, conquering, fleeing, expanding, and exploring."[14] This is the truly dynamic Vietnam where people carved a city out of the forests and the marshes and built a new nation. This is the Vietnam few people knew about: a rugged and rough but lively, dynamic, and hard-working city carved out of the rich and forested swamps of the South.

A few words about the author's connection to Saigon may be appropriate. Saigon was the city where I was born, grew up, and was educated: a city where I spent more than two decades of my life. I witnessed her rise and fall on many occasions: the French leaving in 1954-55, the Americans coming in 1963 and leaving a decade later, the South Vietnamese leaving in 1975. I witnessed the Buddhist revolt, the many military insurrections, President Diem's killing, the Tet Offensive, the American military surge, President Thieu's rise and fall. I saw the sleepy French town metamorphosed into an American city with its thousands of television antennas surging above tile, steel, or straw roofs, its bars and girls, its fortified high rise buildings and unguarded slums, military police at main corners of the city ready to catch draft evaders. It was a city full of energy that knew how to play, buy, sell, and trade but never thought about her future. It was a city where military personnel, spies, journalists, adventurers, and simple people, rich and poor, lived, coexisted, fought, and tried to survive.

It is, therefore, a privilege for me to dedicate this work to the soldiers, Vietnamese and allied, who fought to preserve this bastion of freedom against the Red Tide; to the Vietnamese in general, and to the South Vietnamese in particular, the pioneers who have struggled and suffered so much to build Saigon from the swamplands of the Mekong Delta, to preserve, rebuild, and make her into a viable and respectable city in Southeast Asia; to her friends, French, American, and other, who have contributed to the historical knowledge of this city. My thanks to Lien Huong Fiedler who has helped me locate rare books about Saigon and Vietnam from the excellent collection of the Library of Congress in Washington, DC.

When I embarked on this project almost a decade ago, I thought it was a simple topic. I was wrong. I ended up in so many valleys and hills, recesses and dead ends, as well as breakthroughs in history, that it finally took me longer than expected to complete the project. It has been, however, an exhilarating voyage from which I have learned a lot. I hope you will find this voyage into the history of Saigon and South Vietnam as fascinating and stimulating as I have. I also believe the city deserves to have her name of *Saigon* back.

Saigon, the Jewel of the Orient,
Saigon, the Seductress on the Mekong,
Saigon, the hard-working, ebullient, irrepressible City on the *Saigon* River.

Saigon has been known as Saigon since 1698 in textbooks, novels, documents, and films. It has also been known as Gia Định Thành, Đồng Nai, Bến Nghé, Bến Thành, Prey Nokor, Baigur, and recently Hồ Chí Minh City. More about these names and their origins can be found in the table on page 8. To avoid confusion, I have opted to refer to the city by just one name throughout the text that follows. Since, for some 300 years, she was known as Saigon, I have chosen to refer to her as Saigon, the name by which I have always known her.

A brief note about Vietnamese names is in order. Following the Chinese tradition, they begin with the family names followed by the middle names, and end with the given name. This way of writing names is the reverse of the one used in western countries and was based on a Confucian tradition of respect for forefathers. People never call Mr. Nguyễn Văn Học, for example, by Mr. Nguyễn (family name), but rather by Mr. Học. In this book, we will follow this established tradition so as not to confuse the readers. After 1975, when the Vietnamese moved overseas, most westernized their names to follow state regulations. Mr. Nguyễn Văn Học has thus become Mr. Học Văn Nguyễn. Only in this situation, have we used the westernized version of the name.

Although there have been some territorial overlaps between the three major designated Vietnamese regions under the various political regimes, they did not vary a lot over the centuries. In order not to confuse the readers, we have simply used South, Central, and North Vietnam instead of the more esoteric names noted in table II.

1

The Riverine Trading Post (1698–1777)

The shroud of obscurity that bathed the origins of Prey Nokor/Saigon could only suggest her limited importance to the political entities that controlled the region before the 17th century. A look at the map of Southeast Asia reveals no major political center in the Mekong Delta in the 16th and early 17th centuries despite its active commerce.[1] In spite of her unique location on the waterways of the Mekong Delta, she was probably too far inland to be a valuable and important trading post. Besides, she had to compete with other local riverine ports known for their special products or functions: Sóc Trăng (red salt), Cà Mau (dried and live fish), Hà Tiên (regional port), Rạch Giá (white wax market), and Sa Đéc (iron market). Her surrounding area, sparsely populated, underdeveloped and covered with insalubrious swamps and forests of kapok trees did not immediately lend itself to urban growth.[2]

For various reasons, Saigon's growth did not take off for many centuries until after the arrival of the Vietnamese and Chinese who, respectively, intensified rice culture and commercial trade. Nguyễn Ánh consolidated her role by making the town his administrative and political center.

From Prey Nokor to Gia Định/Saigon

Saigon most likely began as Baigaur, a Cham village before the 11th century CE. Being the southernmost village of the Cham empire, which stretched from Hoành Sơn (close to present-day Quảng Trị) in the north to the northern border of the Mekong River in the south, Baigaur's importance was negligible. For the Chams, who had a series of important seaports—Indrapura (Đà Nẵng), Vijaya (Qui Nhơn), Kauthara (Nha Trang), Panduranga (Phan Rang)—along the long coastline facing the South China Sea, Baigaur was only an isolated trading post with connection to the hinterland.[3] And the latter was very rich in red salt, dry wax, dried and live fish, buffaloes, and rice.

It is possible that Baigaur in turn became the Khmer Prey Nokor when

7

the Khmers defeated the Chams and sacked their capital Vijaya in 1145 CE.[4] The Khmer (Cambodian) kingdom at that time was huge and encompassed present-day Malaysia, Thailand, Cambodia and South Vietnam. By the 14th century, Prey Nokor was a known trading post throughout Southeast Asia.[5] Ships from China, Malaysia and India stopped there for trade, feeling well-protected from monsoon storms and probably from Cham pirates who patrolled the present-day central Vietnam coastline. Land roads connected Prey Nokor northward to Phú Xuân (Huế), westward to Cambodia and southwest to Châu Đốc and Hà Tiên. The city's commercial role slowed down for a certain time before picking up again in the late 17th century.

The original village stood on a bend of the Saigon River and was limited on the northern side by the Thị Nghè arroyo (creek) and the Bến Nghé (Chinese) arroyo to the south. Louis Malleret, a 20th-century archeologist, localized it in a rectangle bounded by Gò Vấp and Thị Nghè in the east, Bà Điểm to the north, Phú Lâm to the west and the Chinese arroyo to the south.[6] Because she was controlled by various political entities, Saigon had, therefore, assumed different names at various periods in history.

Influence	Names
Cham (?)	Baigaur
Khmer (?1100–1698)	Prey Nokor
Vietnamese (1698–1859)	Gia Định, Đồng Nai, Bến Nghé, Bến Thành Saigon
French (1862–1954)	Saigon
Vietnamese Nationalists (1954–1975)	Saigon
Vietnamese Communists (1976–?)	Hồ Chí Minh City (HCMC)

Table I. Saigon's Names Under Various Regimes

Although the Vietnamese had already lived around Prey Nokor by 1620, the chúa (lords) Nguyễn officially controlled it only in 1698 by annexing over 1,000 square miles of land and dividing it into administrative regions.[7] They renamed it Gia Định Thành from the Malaysian "ya" (water, river, stream) and "digin" (cool and clear): the city of the clear and cool river.[8] The Saigon River (as well as the nearby Đồng Nai River, East and West Vàm Cỏ Rivers) was clearer in color and cooler than the Mekong River. The area was underpopulated: by the beginning of the 18th century, only about 40,000 Vietnamese families or 200,000 people[9] lived in the New South (Nam Bộ or Cochinchina).[10]

Names	South Vietnamese	North Vietnamese	French	Modern
Đàng Trong	Miền Nam	Nam Bộ	Cochinchina	South Vietnam
Đàng Trong	Miền Trung	Trung Bộ	Annam	Central Vietnam
Đàng Ngoài	Miền Bắc	Bắc Bộ	Tonkin	North Vietnam

Table II. Names of Different Regions of Vietnam According to Different Groups

The village derived its name, "prey" (forest) and "nokor" (city, land), from Sanskrit "nagara." The appellation seemed to imply there once had been a "city or village in the forests" due to the dense vegetations that surrounded it. How and when the name of Prey Nokor became Saigon is still debated today. Archeological findings in the 1940s revealed a wall and other Khmer artifacts in Phú Lâm, suggesting the presence of a settlement, although there was not enough evidence to prove or discard the name of a "kingdom in the forest."[11]

According to Chinese-Vietnamese etymology, "sai" in Chinese means firewood or twigs while "gon" is equivalent to cotton stick or pole. Saigon could thus designate the many cotton trees that grew around the village. The name could also come from the Cantonese name of Cholon (or Di An, the Chinese section of Saigon) or Tai Ngon (or embankment).[12] The Chinese pronunciation was Tin Gan, Tai Ngon or Tai Gon.

If we believe the Chinese etymology, the original Saigon was used to designate the western or Chinese section of the town.[13] The eastern or Vietnamese section was known as Bến Nghé or Pen Ghé. The French in 1862 incorrectly used Saigon to designate both the Vietnamese and Chinese settlements. The name of Saigun (sic) was already well-known and in use when John Crawfurd visited it in 1820.[14]

The plethora of names used during the Vietnamese period (1698–1859) points to the possibility that the central government of Huế either ignored its local names or tried to impose its own name (Gia Định) to the village. And, because of the presence of the citadel, which was first built in 1790, the village had also been called Bến Thành (Quay of the Citadel). A market was set up in the area and soon became known as the Bến Thành Market (Central Market), which is still present today. Local people also called the village Đồng Nai or Deerfield for the large deer population that roamed in the area. Deer were still encountered within the town limits when the French laid down the foundations of their new city there.

Bến Nghé (Buffalo Quay)—at the confluence of the Thị Nghè and Chinese arroyos—was known for its buffalo trade. Through the quay, which had been present since the days the Khmers controlled the village, the Vietnamese had direct access to buffalo, which were needed for field-work. Many of the draft animals came from Thailand by way of Cambodia: They were "one of the significant goods [exported] from Northeastern Siam to Cambodia." This busy regional trade became essential for large-scale commercial cultivation of rice in the Mekong Delta in the late 18th century,[15] which in turn opened up the region economically and commercially. As Trịnh Hoài Đức put it, "Land in Biên Hòa needs buffaloes to cultivate it. Such land could yield one hundred *hoc* of rice for one *hoc* of seeds planted."[16] It was therefore common for rich owners to own 200 to 300 oxen and buffalo each in the late 18th century. As late as the 1950s, each 40,000 of the 70,000 oxen exported from Takeo and

Pong Tom went to the Saigon-Cholon area along with all of their 10,000 buffaloes.[17] By the time the French arrived, Bến Nghé was not a large or compact
settlement, but a conglomeration of 40 villages along the Bến Nghé arroyo
and the citadel.[18]

The name Thị Nghè Arroyo derived from Lady Thị Nghè. The daughter
of Văn Trường Hậu, she married a man of letters who was employed in the
provincial administration and bore the title of ông nghè (holder of the bac-
calaureate or graduate). Since he had to cross the channel every day to go to
work, she made it easy for him by building a bridge. Locals baptized the bridge
after her and called it Cầu Thị Nghè (bridge of Madame the Graduate). The
arroyo was given the same name.[19]

When the Chinese, with chúa Nguyễn's approval, arrived in the Mekong
Delta in 1690, they built two settlements, one in Biên Hòa and the other in Mỹ
Tho. A third and smaller group gathered on the western side of Prey Nokor/Gia
Định and called it Di An. The latter lay at the intersection of waterways leading
to Biên Hoa, Phnom Penh, and the lower Mekong Delta, an excellent area for
riverine trade.[20] Di An, in the beginning, was smaller than the Biên Hòa or Mỹ
Tho settlements. When the Tây Sơn attacked Gia Định in 1778, the Chinese
in Biên Hòa relocated to Di An to come under the protection of Vietnamese
troops.

Most of the commerce took place in Di An as local and foreign junks
preferred to dock, load and unload there, rather than in Bến Nghé, the Vietnamese side of the town. Big shops were built in brick along the Chinese
arroyo and rented out to the Chinese from China who came once a year on sea
junks to sell their merchandise either wholesale or retail. Close by was the
Cầu đường (sugar bridge), where candied sugar, bars of sugar, and other sugary
products were sold. Blacksmiths and makers of iron wire sold their wares at
the *Lò rèn* market. In the 18th century, the Nguyễn built large storage centers
in Di An to accommodate the growing trade. As commerce grew, Di An became
known as Chợ Lớn (the great market); the name was officially recognized in
1801.[21]

Roland Dorgeles wrote: "Everything has its price in Chợ Lớn and is
bought or sold. Even the mud. Since they are obliged to live on mud-flats,
they have become venders of mud—two piasters the cubic meter—for filling
in! They sell anything; they would sell the water of the canals if they found
buyers; they would sell the air."[22]

Chợ Quán, which comprised the villages of Tân Kiêng, Nhơn Giang, and
Bình Yên, sat midway between Chợ Lớn and Bến Nghé. It derived its name
from the presence of markets (chợ) and inns (quán). A hospital was also built
in the area.[23] By 1860, the area was lush with vegetation. On the right of
the pathway that led to Chợ Quán was a full-grown bamboo hedge and on
its left a rice field with a deep pool in the middle of which buffalo bathed.
Chợ Quán was hidden behind rows of orange and pomelo trees that clustered

around the houses. Scattered houses were separated by hedges of cactus or bamboo.[24]

Before 1860, there was a Khmer settlement on the northwest end of Prey Nokor (Phú Lâm). The Phú Lâm area was adjacent to Gò Vắp and Bien Hòa.[25] These were elevated lands, favored by the Khmers. As animosity between the native Khmers and the Vietnamese settlers grew, the Chinese settlement of Di An served as a buffer zone between the Vietnamese and Khmer settlements. The Khmers, facing the rapid influx of the Vietnamese, retreated further inland toward Tây Ninh, at the foot of the Bà Đen Mountain, leaving the town to the Vietnamese and Chinese.

The Khmer (Phú Lâm), Chinese (Di An), and Vietnamese (Bến Nghé) settlements were at that time linked together more by waterways, canals, and rivers than by roads. Roads and bridges were few at the time, rendering communication difficult. People moved around by boats or sampans, which were also known as xuồng ba lá.[26]

By 1772, Gia Định/Saigon had become a city walled-off from the countryside—more figuratively than literally—with local markets and storage centers located in Chợ Lớn. Inside the town lived mandarins, soldiers, merchants, factory workers, Chinese, and some foreigners. They were different from the peasants, the real workers who lived in the surrounding countryside. All these settlers, inside and outside Saigon, however, soon distinguished themselves from northerners by their individualism, sense of adventure, and openness towards foreigners—newly acquired characteristics of southerners.[27] Although the distance between Hà Nội and Saigon was only 700 miles, the trip through dense tropical forests, tall mountains, and wild rivers was a challenge for most people at that time. By the time they reached their destination, they became changed people. If it took trained and healthy young soldiers three to six months in the 1960s to cover the Hồ Chí Minh Trail, the trail the communists used to infiltrate the South from the North during the war, it would have probably taken one full year during the 17th and 18th centuries to complete the road trip.

From 1788 to 1801, Gia Định became Nguyễn Ánh's administrative and military center, the place from which he waged a war to recover his throne in Huế. He was the first person "to organize Nam Bộ as a region capable of participating successfully in war and politics among Vietnamese speakers."[28] From then on, names such as "Gia Định people," "Gia Định soldiers," and "Gia Định land," began appearing in the history of Vietnam.[29] He elevated the town to Gia Định kinh or capital of the empire in 1790. And for more than a decade, Saigon reached her apogee: this was where Nguyễn Ánh received foreign dignitaries, prelates, and fulfilled his government duties. This was the soul of the Nguyễn Empire, which also controlled Cambodia and Laos.

To have a building that harmonized with his title and influence, he had a citadel built in town with his own residence inside it. This was a massive project that required a lot of manpower: 30,000 people whom Nguyễn Ánh requisitioned locally. The Saigonese had never seen or imagined such a grandiose building. Unhappy with the new burden, many rebelled against the government. Having barely recovered from the long wars against the Siamese and Tây Sơn, they were forced to sacrifice their work and livelihood for another ambitious building project. Not only were they taken away from their own land, they were also displaced to make way for the new towering building.

Once the project was completed, the presence of the citadel also polarized the town into Bến Nghé, a Vietnamese administrative center, and Chợ Lớn, a Chinese commercial emporium. Although diversification had occurred, that polarization still persists today.

Once Nguyễn Ánh had won the war and moved to Huế in 1802, the town was demoted to Gia Định thành—citadel of Gia Định—and became the residence of the governor general. In 1835, after the Lê Văn Khôi revolt was suppressed, it was downgraded to a province town.[30]

It was not until the French conquered it that Gia Định came back to life. Although they controlled the town since 1859, the French took three long years to make up their mind about its name. They finally called it Saigon, which had always been a popular name with the locals. Phonetically, for a western tongue Saigon was easier to pronounce than Gia Định, Bến Nghé, Bến Thành, Đồng Nai, or Prey Nokor. The name Saigon stuck to the town until 1975. Di An or Chợ Lớn was incorporated into Saigon proper under the Diệm government in the 1950s.

It is interesting to note that while the Vietnamese populated Saigon, the Chinese gave her her unique name, and the French officially used her as the capital of Cochinchina. Saigon and the Mekong Delta, therefore, seemed to be a place where diversity worked at its best. No one owned it, although everyone had a say in it. Diversity, however, could work both ways—for or against the town/city. In the end, this diversity, which for centuries was the strength behind the transformation of a village in the forest into a mega-city, tore it apart and caused its downfall. Saigon, therefore, is the product of millions of people, big or small, who had contributed sweat and blood to its building and expansion.

After the revolution, new districts were added to Saigon proper, which took the name of Hồ Chí Minh City. The name of Saigon remains popular with its inhabitants—the Tân Sơn Nhứt airport, for instance, is known as SGN for Saigon—and many still refer to the city as Saigon.

From a sleepy fishing village, Prey Nokor/Saigon in time became an important commercial and trade center. All it needed were people (Vietnamese), product (rice), and means (trade, boat-building). These needs would be fulfilled toward the end of the 18th century when all these factors came together almost at the same time.

Nam Tiến (Southern Expansion)

The root of the creation of the đàng trong was nam tiến. South Vietnam would not have existed had it not been fed by a relentless movement of Vietnamese southwards. As its economic value rose, more people poured into this region looking to build a new life. Had the Vietnamese not settled the region, it would have either remained in the hands of the Khmers or fallen under the control of the aggressive Siamese. The Vietnamese eventually prevailed and đàng trong turned out to be the best military and economic achievement in Vietnam during the 18th century.

Đại Việt, as Vietnam was called in the 15th and 16th centuries, roughly corresponded to present-day North Vietnam with the capital at Thăng Long (Hà Nội). It was ruled by the Lê dynasty beginning in 1428, although their authority had been declining from the mid–16th century onward. The Lê king was assisted, or rather controlled, by chúa (lords), Trịnh and Nguyễn, who had been competing for the post of regent.

When Trinh Kiểm became regent of the Lê king, his brother-in-law Nguyễn Hoàng immediately realized the Trịnh and Nguyễn houses were headed toward confrontation. He wisely asked the advice of sage Nguyễn Bỉnh Khiêm (1491–1585), who told him the future would be better for him in the south: "Hoành Sơn nhất đái, vạn đại dung thân" (in the region of Hoành Sơn is room to stand for thousands of generations).[31]

Heeding the advice of the sage, he asked his sister, who was Trịnh Kiểm's wife, to suggest to her husband to send him away as military commander of the distant frontier region of Thuận Hóa (present-day Quảng Trị). Trịnh Kiểm, seeing the chance to get rid of a rival, immediately agreed. He, however, did not know he had bestowed to Nguyễn Hoàng a kingdom, which in time would compete with Thăng Long. Nguyễn Hoàng, in fact, did not know it either, although he took a big, almost desperate gamble. His main goal was to steer clear of his brother-in-law.

In 1558 he headed for Thuận Hoá, where he was, as a matter of fact, downgraded to a lowly governor of an un-glamorous region: an arid and mountainous region that could not even feed its own people. It was a place where criminals were banished and political dissidents sought refuge. A frontier region and a buffer zone between the Vietnamese and the Chams, it also witnessed constant military excursions from one side or another.

Nguyễn Hoàng, taking his job seriously, became an efficient administrator who dutifully paid taxes to the northern Trịnh-Lê. Although he returned to the north to help King Lê on two different occasions, he only severed his ties with the court in 1602 in order to devote his time fully to the building of the south. After his death in 1613, his successors continued to expand southwards toward the lands of the Chams and Khmers.

His son Nguyễn Phúc Nguyên (Chúa Sãi) in 1620 stopped sending the yearly required tribute to the Thăng Long government. Upset, the Lê-Trịnh northern rulers launched a 45-year war against the southern Nguyễn. The latter accused the Trịnh of usurping the authority of the Lê; the Trịnh accused the Nguyễn of rebellion and of not paying the required tribute. This first north-south war (1627–1672) was reminiscent of the most recent communist war in Vietnam (1954–1975). The north (đàng ngoài) made seven different attempts to invade the south (đàng trong); all attempts were repulsed despite the fact that the northern army was well-organized, combat-tested and three to four times larger than the south's.[32] Knowing their weakness, the Nguyễn in 1630 had a double defensive wall built at Đồng Hới in the province of Quảng Bình at the isthmus dividing đàng ngoài and đàng trong, where they positioned modern cannons to keep northern soldiers away.[33] The wall also prevented any cultural and economical exchange between north and south.

The north finally gave up in 1672 and peace lasted for more than a century. Thus, for more than two centuries (1600–1802), north and south had evolved separately without exchanging commerce or trade. Westerners often were not aware of this physical separation, which ultimately affected the culture and behavior of northerners and southerners. Nam tiến, however, was not a linear progression. It took 82 years for the pioneers to go from Phú Yên to Phan Thiết and about six decades to move from Gia Định to the Mekong Delta. As the Vietnamese penetrated through the densely-populated Cham regions of central Vietnam and the Khmer populated Prey Nokor, they faced stiff resistance from the natives, which resulted in recurrent insurrections and fights between pioneers and natives.

By the end of the 17th century, the Chams were reduced to the two provinces of Phan Rang and Phan Ri (Panduranga). The Vietnamese continued to move southward and took over Bà Rịa (1658) and the provinces of Gia Định (1698), Mỹ Tho and Vĩnh Long (1731) and Sóc Trăng (1747). Progression became slower as the pioneers closed down on the delta. Luckily, there was no major bloody confrontation as the Khmers voluntarily withdrew westward to Tây Ninh. The pioneers just leapfrogged the contested areas and moved further south or west as evidenced by the presence of a Vietnamese settlement in Phnom Penh[34] and another one in Siam during that period.

There were 20,000 to 40,000 Vietnamese in Gia Dinh-Saigon by 1710.[35]

The Siamese conquered and ruled the Khmer city of Angkor from 1353 to 1357. They again invaded Cambodia in 1394. Under these foreign assaults, the Khmers decided to abandon Angkor in 1431 and to move to the present-day city of Phnom Penh.[36] Feeling threatened again in the early part of the 17th century, the Khmer king Chey Chettha II turned to the Huế government for protection by taking a Nguyễn princess in marriage in 1618. In exchange, the chúa Nguyễn established a tax-collecting office in Prey Nokor in 1623. With the number of these offices multiplying, the Nguyễn were able to not only protect their citizens, but also to assess the riches of Cambodia. In 1674,

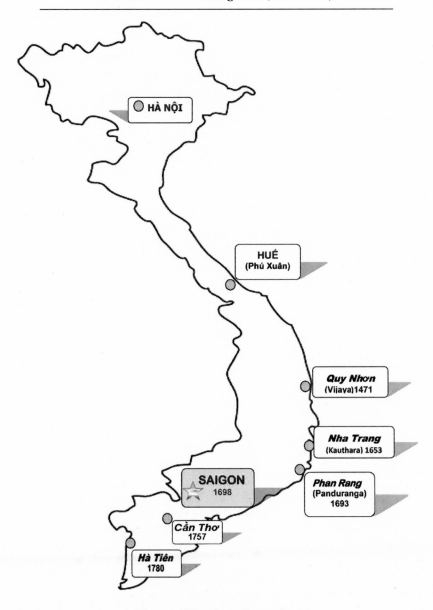

Vietnam's Southern Expansion.

they intervened again to solve a Khmer dynastic quarrel pitting two brothers against each other for the throne. Both of them ended up paying tribute to Huế.[37]

The new frontier, however, was not free of tensions, especially with Vietnamese and Chinese migrants living amidst the Khmers and impinging on their properties. Alliances easily shifted depending on political or commercial associations. The Chinese in Mỹ Tho had allied themselves with the Vietnamese to fight against the Khmers. In 1688, failing to take control of the Mekong shipping lanes from Saigon to Phnom Penh, they turned to piracy. The Vietnamese army had to intervene to control them.

In 1698, the Vietnamese established the Gia Định prefecture in the Đồng Nai region with two military centers: Trấn Biên (close to Biên Hòa) and Phiên Trấn (present-day Saigon). They organized the Chinese into the Long Hà commune in Biên Hòa and the Minh Hương commune in Saigon. A third military center, called Long Hồ camp, was opened in 1732 in Cái Bè across from modern Vĩnh Long. This was topped by the creation of the office of the *Kinh Lược Cao Man* (royal delegate for Cambodia) in 1753 in Saigon with a commanding army corps in Bình Khánh (Khánh Hòa), Bình Thuận, Trấn Biên (Biên Hòa), Phiên Trấn (Gia Định), and Long Hồ (Cái Bè). Saigon for the first time became the political and military center of the eastern water frontier.

In 1755, the Vietnamese established a military base in Mỹ Tho and expanded westwards to Tây Ninh and southwards to Trà Vinh and Ba Thác (currently Trà Vinh and Sóc Trăng). By the late 1750s, Vietnamese-controlled territory on the western water frontier abutted Mạc Thiên Tứ's Chinese kingdom of Hà Tiên. The Mạc had been the Nguyễn's vassals since 1708.[38]

In 1771, the Huế court dispatched General Nguyễn Cửu Đàm to control a Siamese invasion. After danger was averted, Đàm returned to Saigon where he had an eight-kilometer-long earth wall built to protect the western and southern sides of the town.[39]

A New Way of Being Vietnamese

Settlers came to the delta either as individuals, isolated families, or as part of a military đồn điền (settlement). The move could be voluntary or forced. Trying to get away from war tribulations, economic misery, and the oppression of a strict Confucian northern society, these voluntary migrants looked for a better living environment.[40] The đồn điền allowed the anchoring as well as expansion of Vietnamese communities throughout the Mekong Delta. The protective and stabilizing force of the soldiers expanded the authority of the chúa Nguyễn. Troops worked part time as soldiers and the rest of the day as pioneer farmers. Communities were then populated with settlers. They were given generous inductions like keeping the lands they had worked on and not paying taxes for the first three years. In many places, they did not pay any tax at all because of poor or nonexistent administration.

Of course, there were also misfits, adventurers, convicts, and prisoners of war within this group. To rapidly populate the new frontier, forced migration was also used. Thousands of captured northern soldiers in 1648 were eventually resettled as pioneers in Phú Yên province. Soldiers were divided into villages, 50 to each village, given half a year's supplies, and told to seek livelihoods as farmers or settlers. Villagers caught in the middle of the war zones were also forced to resettle—a characteristic of Southeast Asian warfare at the time. Many of these uprooted people became unhappy because of the forced displacement and later joined the rebellion against the Nguyễn rulers; such was the case of the great grandfather of the later Tây Sơn rebel brothers.[41]

The 17th-century đàng trong functioned like a large military camp. Conscription was very strict: "A man will lose his head if he is found trying to avoid being a soldier." A recruiting officer would also lose his head if he accepted a substandard conscript.[42] Young men were not allowed to return to their villages until they were 60 years old, although married soldiers could live with their wives in military quarters. The army (quân) and the people (dân) were regarded as one self-sufficient unit: quân dân.[43] By drafting most men in the country, the army had at its disposition qualified craftsmen, dye-workers, and shoemakers who could help the villagers it supervised. Many were part-time soldiers and settlers. A handkerchief tied about the head, somewhat in the shape of a turban, and a loose smock frock with a pair of trousers, constituted the dress of a soldier at the time.[44] Individuals, families, villages, and military units were liable to move from one place to another to fill up newly conquered regions or to accept new assignments.

To provide an alternative to the northern culture and the Cham environment, the Nguyễn lords initiated new rules. They adopted Mahayana Buddhism as national religion to which they added a few indigenous spirits to make it more appealing to pioneers and local people—a hybrid religious system that "bestowed moral legitimacy on Nguyễn authority in *đàng trong.*"[45] Mahayana Buddhism, they thought, would provide better moral support and spiritual comfort than the stern northern Confucianism. It would also blend more easily in a Cham polytheist environment. They therefore built many pagodas—400 in the region of Huế-Phú Xuân alone—to support the new faith. The royal family also got involved in religion. In 1695, chúa Nguyễn Phúc Chu, his mother, his queen, and all the members of the royal family converted to Buddhism on Buddha's anniversary. Three days later, high court officials were also converted. A few days later, 1400 people did the same thing.[46]

The Thiên Mụ pagoda built in 1601 in Huế replaced a previous Cham temple, which stood on a hill known for having great-spirit potency. By building a pagoda to a spirit that was not yet recognized by the northern Lê court, Nguyễn Hoàng wanted to express his disconnection with that court. By building it on the site of a previous Cham temple, he intended to notify the native Chams of a governmental change and of his takeover of the south. The Cham goddess Po Nagar was adopted and thoroughly Vietnamized into Thiên-Y-A-Na. Her polyandry and the large number of her offspring were no longer mentioned in order to comply with Vietnamese beliefs. She devoted her time to instruct people and used her supernatural powers to garner respect. Over the centuries, she has been worshiped as a deity and has acquired a Vietnamese name, "Bà Chúa Ngọc" (the Lady Princess Pearl), in central Vietnam[47] and "Bà Chúa Sứ" (the Goddess of the Realm) in the Mekong Delta.[48] She has not only metamorphosed into a Vietnamese deity, but has also acquired a regional identity.

The pioneers adapted many local traditions as their own. They learned to eat raw food (gỏi) and to wrap their hair in a piece of cloth (đội khăn) following the Cham culture. They consumed mắm nêm, a fermented fish sauce, which turned out to be Cham in origin. Following rigid Confucian rules, they wore dark-colored or brown clothes but were attracted to the strange Cham culture with its ornate temple towers and its unusual goddesses. They soon picked up the lively colors of the Cham dresses. The áo dài, the Vietnamese tunic slit on both sides from the waist down, was also an adaptation of the Cham dress, which was different from the northern áo tứ than, a four-piece dress.[49] The bà ba, a button-up, long-sleeved shirt, was of Chinese origin. The ghe bầu—riverine boat—which was an adaptation of the Malay prahu, was borrowed from the Chams.

The end result was an immersion into native culture as well as assimilation of native people and culture, whichever worked best. If assimilation was not particularly traumatic for the Khmers, it was painful and bloody for the Chams, who submitted to the Huế court only in the 19th century. In order to remain in good grace with the spirits of the land, the Vietnamese made a symbolic reparation with yearly offerings. On the occasion of Lễ cúng chủ đất củ (offering to the former lord of the land), they burned gold or silver paper money to repay the "former" lord for the land rent. That tradition continued on into the late 19th century. One such ceremony in 1879 in Chợ Lớn was said to have lasted one full week.[50]

The South for the pioneers was a new world that exposed them to high-volume commercial rice culture. The imported northern plow, which was light, had to be reshaped to withstand the hard southern soil; the latter, which had been rarely plowed, was still virgin and covered with thick grass. To the Cham plow they added a follicle to adjust its angle and in the process made a new style of plow. They picked up trade business from the Chinese and got involved in local and then regional river trade. They intermingled with the Khmers, Chams and Chinese to form a pluralistic, multiracial culture unique to this region. As a result, they became more open to foreign cultures than Northerners. Within this environment, they were exposed to a variety of religions: Buddhism, Islam, Hinduism, and later, Catholicism. Islam and Hinduism came from the Chams and Khmers, Catholicism from European priests, while Buddhism had been propped up as the religion of the state. Although many Khmer pagodas and Cham mosques were built during that period, most of them did not stand the test of time. Only recent buildings are part of modern Saigon's architecture. The Chandaransay Khmer temple built in Saigon in the late 1940s presently serves the local Khmer community; it is also a school teaching religious studies.[51] The Central Mosque, built in 1931, replaced an older mosque from the 19th century. The Moslem Mariamman Temple was also built in the 19th century.[52] Northerners, less, or not at all, exposed to Islam and Hinduism, remained under strong Confucian influence.

In the land-scarce northern Red River Delta, inward-looking peasants positioned themselves within the village's system in order to control the limited communal resources and the periodic redistribution of land between renters. Landless peasants worked on communal lands as renters. Without land, they would go hungry; moving to another village to look for a job would involve loss of seniority and a drop in ranking and privilege at the new place. Therefore, moving away would have been worse than staying put.

In đàng trong, where land was easily available, peasants were no longer bound to restrictive village ranking for they could move on and try their luck somewhere else.[53] Being free to choose the location and type of work rendered them more inventive and open to risk-taking. Besides, the Mekong Delta was endowed with fertile soil, abundant rainfall, plentiful waterways and moderate temperatures. The natural abundance of the delta created a disposition toward openness, immediate gratification of desires, and lack of concerns for the tomorrow.[54] Southerners were also noted to be liberal and generous as food and resources were abundant and easily accessible. Two western travelers recounted the following stories centuries apart. In 1620 Christoforo Borri witnessed a Portuguese merchant begging a poor southern fisherman, who just came back from a fishing trip, for some fish. The fisherman, without argument, handed him a whole pannier of fish.[55] In 1972, Neil Jamieson met a former village chief as he passed through a village. The former chief invited Neil for a drink. Soon, many of the chief's followers joined the group. Later, probably prompted by his acquaintances, the new village chief showed up accompanied by his friends. The current and former village chiefs vied with each other in trying to buy drinks and food for the entire crowd. Each tried to be more generous than the other and food and drinks soon piled up on the tables.[56] These scenes were frequently noted throughout the south, where people generously wined and dined their guests and friends without thinking about the day after.

The two-century social and political segregation explained the differences between northerners and southerners in many respects. These differences were eventually deep enough to evolve into "*a new way of being Vietnamese.*"[57] The old-fashioned northern culture had to make place for the new southern culture.

Other Political and Religious Entities

Present-day central and south Vietnam were formerly occupied by the Chams and Khmers respectively, whose central governments gradually lost power in the 17th and 18th centuries to the newly arriving Vietnamese. These pioneers, along with the Chinese and missionaries, forever changed the identity of the Mekong Delta and transformed it into a new political and economic center. This was a region of mixed ethnicities that was powered by trade along the waterways of the Mekong Delta.

A. CHAMPA AND THE CHAMS

It is not known when Champa first appeared on the Indochinese map because of the scarcity of historical data in that region between the second to sixth centuries. The presence of tribes around Lin-Yi (present-day Huế region) was noted by the Chinese in A.D. 192 These tribes, who are of Malay stock, came in direct contact in the north with the Vietnamese who were then dominated by the Chinese. Vietnam was just a small principality localized around the Red River Delta. As the Lin-Yi tribes continued to expand northward toward Hoành Sơn (Gates of Annam) in the third century, they met serious resistance from the Vietnamese. They also moved southward and engulfed other Hinduized communities (Champa) to the south. Lin-Yi and Champa merged into one single entity sometime between the second and sixth centuries A.D. By the fourth century, the Chams were known to build houses of fired brick and to use the custom of cremating the dead.

The Chams' first known capital was located at Trà Kiều (Đà Nẵng). Close by was the religious center of Mỹ Sơn, a center for the propagation of Hinduism since the fourth century. They converted to Islam somewhere around the tenth or 11th centuries. It is assumed that Islam came to Indochina between 600 and 900 CE. Presently, 80 to 85 percent of the Chams are Moslem (Cham Bani), while the rest are Hindu (Balamon). The two groups, although they share the same heritage and live in the Mekong Delta, do not intermarry.

By the seventh century, the Chams had moved down the coastline all the way to Nha Trang. For 200 years from the eighth century onward, the Cham civilization reached its zenith and the Chams controlled a large swath of land from Hoành Sơn in the north to the Đồng Nai basin in the south. Baigur stood at their southernmost boundary. Champa was composed of five principalities: Indrapura, Amaravati, Vijaya, Kauthara, and Panduranga.[58] It was a confederation that included not only the lowland Chams but also highlanders like the Rhade, Jarai, Curu, Roglai, Mnong and Stieng.

Sandwiched between the Vietnamese to the north and the Khmers to the south, Champa hardly knew peace and was forced to constantly wage war against one country or another.

B. CAMBODIA AND THE KHMERS

The Khmers are part of the Mon-Khmer group that eventually migrated into the Indochinese peninsula. The Mon settled in upper Thailand and Burma while the Khmers went further down toward present-day Cambodia and Vietnam. Therefore, the Khmers physically resembled the Thais and Laotians.

The Khmer kingdom began in the eighth century CE when it took over other nearby political entities (Funan, Chenla).[59] Its civilization peaked from the ninth to the 14th centuries with the building of the magnificent Angkor temples. Its kingdom reached from Cambodia proper as far as South Vietnam, part of Thailand, and Malaysia. The Khmers invaded Champa and removed the golden statue from the temple of Po Nagar in Nha Trang in 950 CE. They invaded this country again in 1203 but went into decline in the 15th century.[60] They moved their capital from Angkor to Phnom Penh in 1431.

In 1674, internecine rivalry broke out. Ang Tai, allied to Siam, deposed King Ang Non, who took refuge in Vietnam. The Nguyễn army, at the request of Ang Non, took over Prey Nokor and Oudong (40 kilometers northwest of Phnom Penh). Ang Tai fled and was replaced by Ang Sor, who became the new mountain king. Ang Non, the water king, remained in Prey Nokor. The Khmer kingdom thus became divided into two smaller royalties with present-day Cambodia under Ang Sor and Prey Nokor and the Mekong Delta under Ang Non. Both Ang Sor and Ang Non paid tribute to the Nguyễn.

When Ang Non died in 1690 without a successor, his kingdom came under the control of the Nguyễn.[61] The latter carved out two provinces, Biên Hòa and Gia Định (including Prey Nokor), in 1698 from the defunct lower Khmer kingdom. Prey Nokor became Gia Định—the future Saigon, a Vietnamese administrative and economic center in the Mekong Delta.

C. THE CHINESE

Chinese immigrants came to đàng trong in different waves. They clustered themselves in three main areas: Hội An-Huế on the coastline of central Vietnam, the Mekong Delta and the fishing port of Hà Tiên on the southernmost end of Vietnam. By the late 18th century, they numbered perhaps as many as 30,000, although their exact number is unknown.

The Minh Huong (Ming exiles) first arrived in Đà Nẵng in 1680 asking for political asylum. Being loyalists of the deposed Ming dynasty, they were forced to shave their foreheads and wear a pigtail like the Mongols to avoid decapitation. Although the majority followed the new rule, 3,000 people piled up in more than 50 boats and fled to Vietnam. The chúa Nguyễn, seeing these strong and able-bodied men showing up at his court, feared a potential threat to his kingdom. He immediately sent them far away to the Mekong Delta, which at that time was still under Khmer control. Not only did he get rid of the Chinese, but he also used them to secure a foothold in the delta.

In the Mekong Delta, the exiles either settled in Mỹ Tho or Biên Hòa (Cù Lao Phố) while a smaller group established residence in Di An, west of Prey Nokor. The Nguyễn lord was correct in his assessment of the Chinese: The ones in Mỹ Tho, unable to take control of the commercial river lanes, resorted to ransoming river junks. They openly rebelled against the government in 1688 by siding with the Khmer king. Forced to intervene, the Nguyễn army quashed the rebellion, moved to Phnom Penh and forced the Khmer king into submission.[62] It opened a military camp in Bến Nghé to better control the region. By the time Gia Long became king, many Minh Hương were third generation locals who had long supported the Nguyễn cause.[63] Originally applied to Ming exiles, the term Minh Hương in the mid–19th century came to refer to the offspring of Sino-Viet or Sino-Khmer intermarriage.

Good in trade, they got involved in rice trade and shipping traffic on the Mekong Delta and dominated that market for centuries to come. The Vietnamese or Khmers farmed the land, and the harvested rice was traded around by Chinese merchants. During the war against the Tây Sơn, the Biên Hòa group moved to Di An close to Prey Nokor to continue their business under the protection of the Vietnamese army. Di An was later renamed Chợ Lớn.

The Minh Hương could be further subdivided into the Cantonese Mac of Hà Tiên, the Teochiu followers, the Fujianese, and other groups. The Fujianese arrived in Vietnam early and formed the bulk of the rich merchants. They married with the Vietnamese elite and produced important figures like Trịnh Hoài Đúc, a senior minister and Trần Tiến Thanh, the regent of the Nguyễn dynasty in 1883.[64]

The Thanh Nhân (Qing people), who were subjects of the Qing dynasty, came to Vietnam in the middle to latter part of the 18th century. Since Chinese émigrés were allowed to return to China, they no longer saw the need to integrate into the Vietnamese community. They formed separate enclaves that remained connected to their South Chinese roots and ongoing contacts with clans and secret societies.[65] Despite their wide and tangible differences, the majority of them were connected to the large coastal trading arena. They got involved in the maturing coastal trade between đàng trong and China following the easing of Qing restrictions on their subjects' participation in overseas trade.

The Chinese were far from being a uniform group. The Minh Hương in Biên Hòa and Mỹ Tho did not get along; neither did the Minh Hương and Thanh Nhân. In Hội An, the merchants Tập Đình and Lý Tài raised their own armies and supported the Tây Sơn in 1773 while Đỗ Thành Nhân with his own Chinese army in Gia Định sided with chúa Nguyễn in 1775. Lý Tài, by 1775, had switched to Nguyễn Anh's side.[66]

D. LAOTIANS

There was also a small contingent of Laotians in the Mekong Delta. They lived in modern Bạc Liêu province close to the South China Sea. Although Bạc Liêu has no meaning in Vietnamese, it was derived from the Chinese pronunciation of a Khmer name, Po Leo, meaning "Lao Hill."[67] How the Laotians got all the way to the lower Mekong Delta is difficult to figure out.

The Mekong Delta in the 17th and 18th centuries became a melting pot for all the minorities who lived off the trade on the "water frontier," a "vast riverine network connecting Saigon, Phnom Penh, and the regional cities and countries Bangkok, Malaysia, [and] Canton."[68]

E. THE MISSIONARIES

To prevent confrontation between Spain and Portugal during the discovery of the Indies, in 1493 Pope Alexander VI divided the world with a meridian running 100 leagues west of the Azores. Territories west of that meridian belonged to Spain (West Indies in America) while those east of the line were assigned to Portugal (East Indies in Asia).[69] Missionaries traveling to Asia had to go to Lisbon to swear allegiance to the Portuguese monarch and work under the direction of a Portuguese priest.

Although the first Catholic priest, Portuguese Father Ignation, landed in đàng ngoài in 1533, the Spanish Diego Adverte came in 1596 and Portuguese Cristoforo Borri arrived in 1615. The first Catholic missions were founded in đàng trong in 1615 and in đàng ngoài in 1626 under Portuguese authority.[70] By the mid–17th century, the Dutch, English, and Spanish began challenging the pope's decree by trying to carve out their own spheres of influence. The Dutch seized the port of Malacca from the Portuguese in 1641 and the English took over India and Madagascar.

The two most renowned missionaries were Alexandre de Rhodes and the bishop of Adran. The latter, intimately linked to Nguyễn Ánh, will be discussed in the next chapter.

Alexandre de Rhodes was born in Avignon, France, in 1591, of Jewish parents who were forced to convert to Catholicism by the Inquisition. Rhodes derived from the Provencal word "rode," the small "wheel" that medieval Jews were forced to wear on their clothing for identification.[71] He was sent to work in Japan in 1618 after completing his theological studies. Diverted to Goa and then Malacca, he finally ended up in Macao in 1623. Gifted in languages, he was fluent in French, Italian, Greek, Latin, Hebrew and Portuguese. He eventually learned Vietnamese, Hindu, Japanese, Chinese, and Persian.

In 1624, he was sent to đàng trong along with five other priests. This turned out to be his most illustrious assignment. His gift to the country was the codification of the quốc ngữ or Vietnamese national language, which is still used today. When he landed in đàng trong in 1625, he was frightened upon hearing the Vietnamese language for the first time. It sounded like "the twittering of birds," as he described in his book, *Divers Voyages*, published in Paris in 1653.[72] The Vietnamese at the time used the nôm, a Vietnamese vernacular script based on Chinese characters. The nôm was difficult to learn because it implied knowledge of both Vietnamese and Chinese languages, which only a few lettered men could master. Vietnamese words are monosyllabic and have different meanings depending on the inflection—there are six of them—they were given. Each word, therefore, might have six different meanings. Because common people were usually illiterate, evangelizing was difficult.

The priest set out to study the language with a local boy who taught him all the different intonations. The boy did not understand the priest's language and the priest did not understand the boy's. After three weeks, de Rhodes was able to converse in Vietnamese and the boy in French. He then transcribed the language into the Roman alphabet and by adding diacritics to denote the inflection, he codified the quốc ngữ. His superiors sent him to đàng ngoài, where he stayed from 1627 to 1630, when he was expelled. He returned to đàng trong in 1640 but was jailed and then condemned to death. The Nguyễn lord commuted his sentence and expelled him in 1645.[73]

Back in Europe, de Rhodes submitted to Pope Innocent X in 1649 a plan permitting the ordination of indigenous Asian priests. In 1659 the pope created the Apostolic Vicars for the Asian Missions, who would directly control missionary activity, bypassing the Portuguese. He also allowed de Rhodes to create the Societe des Missions Étrangères, an organization that recruited independent priests, mostly French, who would do missionary work in Vietnam under the supervision of the apostolic vicars. This crucial move allowed France, from that time onward, to carve a religious, and then political, influence on Vietnam. By the late 19th century, French priests had exclusive control of the missionary work in Indochina. The work was helped by de Rhodes' publication in 1615 of the first Latin-Portuguese-Vietnamese dictionary and a Vietnamese grammar using his system of romanized Vietnamese; the quốc ngữ later became the Vietnamese national language. De Rhodes also published the first quốc ngữ catechism, allowing indigenous catechists to help missionaries spread the religion.[74]

The relationship between Vietnamese rulers and missionaries had not always been confrontational or antagonistic—it was even cordial for many decades, especially in the beginning. Rulers gave the missionaries refuge within their courts and some even elevated them to the rank of advisors, doctors, scientists, interpreters, and middlemen for armament purchases. The latter had free access to commoners and even converted a few ladies at the Nguyễn court. But religious differences caused the relationship to turn sour, forcing rulers to jail, expel, or even execute many priests. Missionaries who considered offerings and prostrations before ancestral altars (ancestor worship) to be false worship forbade converts from performing these rituals.[75]

Siamese Wars

By the 18th century, as đàng trong began to assert its military and political power in the Mekong Delta, Siam (Thailand) also emerged as a regional power on the other side of the Gulf of Siam. A conflict between these two regional powers was bound to occur sooner or later. Siam not only tried to control Cambodia, but also had its eyes on the Mekong Delta. It launched three attacks by land and sea through Mang Kham (later renamed Hà Tiên) with territorial expansion in mind. Behind some of these wars was a fight for market dominance in the Gulf of Siam. The initiators were Chinese: the Cantonese Mạc in Hà Tiên and the Teochiu Chinese in Chantaburi and Trat. The Chinese émigrés who settled in regions controlled by đàng trong and Chantaburi, Siam, in the 17th century became wealthy merchants and trade competitors by the 18th century. They in turn influenced their governments, helping them consolidate their commercial empire.

Mạc Cửu, a Chinese from Canton, came to work for the Khmer king in 1690. Fed up with palace infighting, he asked the king to name him governor of Hà Tiên, a village on the Gulf of Siam which he over the years transformed into an important port-state. During the same period, the Teochiu Chinese settled in Chantaburi on the southeastern coast of Siam, which they also transformed into an important trading post. The rise of power and trade of the Hà Tiên Cantonese threatened the interests of the Teochiu Siamese. The latter enlisted the help of the new Siamese king, the half-Teochiu General Taksin, to militarily control the Hà Tiên Cantonese. Taksin can be understood as representing the interests of the Teochiu Chinese in eastern Siam.[76]

The first attack came in 1674. Khmer King Ang Non sought the assistance of the Vietnamese after being ousted from power by his cousin and brother-in-law, King Chey Chettha IV. The Vietnamese forces took Prey Nokor and marched toward the Cambodian capital. Chettha IV, unwilling to cede power, turned to the Siamese for help. A peace settlement allowed Chettha IV to keep the throne while a territory comprised of Prey Nokor and the delta was carved out of the Khmer state for King Ang Non. The new state, although under the control of Ang Non, was in fact a dependency of the Vietnamese Huế court. When Ang Non died in 1690, that state passed under the control of Huế and by 1698 became the provinces of Biên Hòa and Gia Định. The Vietnamese similarly gained control of Mỹ Tho and Vĩnh Long in 1730 and Sa Đéc and Châu Đốc in 1757 through successive power brokering in Cambodia.[77]

The Siamese launched another land attack on Cambodia in 1715 in an attempt to reinstate their protégé on the throne. The Saigon-leaning Khmers pushed the Siamese back. The Siamese returned in force in 1717 using the two-pronged approach by land (50,000 troops) and by sea (20,000 troops) through Hà Tiên. Once the Vietnamese counterattacked and destroyed his smaller vessels, the Siamese minister-commander got cold feet and sailed out of Hà Tiên, leaving his troops behind. The demoralized Siamese army fled, leaving behind dead men and artillery. Hà Tiên, however, lay in ruins.[78]

The third and worst two-pronged Siamese invasion lasted from 1771 to 1773. The Siamese came through Hà Tiên again and bombarded the town for ten days in a row. Hà Tiên's governor, Mạc Thiên Tử, remained defiant and continued to defend the town. Once the bombardment had softened the target, the Siamese went on the attack. Although Mạc Thiên Tử was ready to fight, his entourage carried him away, deciding that the survival of the state depended on that of the prince. The town was taken, pillaged and destroyed; the prince's younger children and concubines were taken prisoners. Badly shaken, Mạc Thiên Tử asked for Saigon's help, but General Khôi, thinking that the attack was limited to Hà Tiên alone, was slow to react. Thiên Tử gathered his small forces and retreated to Châu Đốc, where he put up another resistance against the Siamese. Beaten, he escaped to Tân Châu and came under the protection of local Vietnamese forces.

On the order of the Huế government, General Đàm, replacing General Khôi, gave chase to the main Siamese forces in Cambodia. He pooled 10,000 troops and 30 war junks and sailed up the Mekong River. He defeated the Siamese in a decisive manner on the outskirts of Phnom Penh. Siamese King Phya Tak withdrew his troops and called for peace.

General Đàm brought his forces back to Gia Định in 1772. Since the distance between Gia Định and Phnom Penh was a mere 130 miles and to counter any "belligerent action" by the Siamese, he had a 15-mile-long earthen rampart built to protect the southwest side of the town. Connecting the upper estuaries of the Thị Nghè and Bến Nghé arroyos,[79] the rampart formed a protective shield to the town, which was already protected on its sides by the arroyos, and by the Saigon River on the south. It is ironic to think that the same defensive rampart would be used against the invading French a century later. Situated on the west side of Saigon, the rampart was used to protect the city from the Siamese who arrived from the west. As for the French, who came from the east and had already controlled Saigon, the rampart was used to prevent them from moving further inland and controlling the Mekong Delta.

A peace treaty was finally signed in 1774. The treaty gave the Vietnamese temporary supremacy over the Mekong Delta and beyond. It also gave them new lands in the Mekong Delta.[80] Mạc Thiên Tử, having witnessed his town sacked at least three times and having almost lost his life there, never returned to Hà Tiên again, even after the Siamese had left town in 1773. Hà Tiên, as a trading center, gradually declined, with exports moving toward the port of Gia Định.

The Siamese did come back to the delta one more time when Nguyễn Ánh, defeated by the Tây Sơn, asked Siamese King Rama I for help in 1784. Rama I sent an army which occupied Hà Tiên, Cần Thơ, Châu Đốc, and Sa Đéc. The Tây Sơn, however, defeated the Siamese in Mỹ Tho in 1785. The Siamese left and never returned again.[81]

The year 1785 thus marked the turning point for the Vietnamese, who soon took over total control of the Mekong Delta. The process, however, took almost two centuries—from 1600 to 1785.[82] They had to fend off attacks from the đàng ngoài, the Siamese, and at the same time to subdue the Chams and Khmers. These two centuries, although long, allowed the settling and commercialization of the South and the gradual assimilation of native populations.

* * *

While holding northerners at bay, the South Vietnamese moved into the Mekong Delta after displacing the Chams and Khmers. They controlled the Siamese, who also had their eyes on the delta. Defeating them was the main goal before extensive exploitation of the delta would be possible. Thus, the 17th and early 18th centuries were, for the South Vietnamese, periods of control and stabilization of the delta.

By 1698, the Khmer fishing and trading village of Prey Nokor officially became the Vietnamese Gia Định (Saigon), the administrative and military center of the Nguyễn in the Mekong delta. The seeds had been planted for a major economic and political transformation of the region.

2

Gia Định/Saigon, the Royal Capital (1777–1802)

The costs of territorial expansion into the Mekong Delta, of maintaining an army in Gia Định-Saigon to fight off the Siamese, the loss of revenues from decreased trade, and the building of new palaces in Huế, drained the coffers of the Nguyễn, who were forced to raise new taxes. Regent Trương Phúc Loan, a corrupt minister,[1] worsened the economic woes by diverting money to himself, thereby pushing the peasants to revolt against the Nguyễn.

The Fall of the Nguyễn Lords

By causing the downfall of the Nguyễn, the Tây Sơn rebels forced the latter to retreat to Saigon. The insurrection, starting in central Vietnam, switched to Saigon, which eventually bore the brunt of four separate Tây Sơn attacks. For more than a decade, Saigon became a heavily contested and strategic town, for whoever controlled it eventually controlled the whole country.

As the pioneers moved to the Mekong Delta and began producing rice and pouring money into đàng trong's coffers, Huế, located in the upper section of the southern half of the country, could not keep up administratively and militarily with the rapid expansion. The delta was an unknown territory that had not been fully controlled yet by the mid–18th century. Not only was đàng trong elongated and narrow, there was a small and independent Cham state (Panduranga) between it and the delta. To reach the delta, orders and troops had to navigate around Panduranga. And the far south still belonged to the Khmers. The port of Hà Tiên was then under the control of Chinese Mạc Cửu, although the latter had, in 1708, solicited the protection of the Nguyễn. The land route to Hà Tiên had to go through lands held by the Khmers. And beyond Cambodia, stood the rival Siamese who were ready to jump into the delta.

The Nguyễn generals posted in Gia Định, although they represented the Huế court, ruled as semi-autonomous warlords who had total power in the delta. Any news about Hà Tiên, Siam, and Cambodia had to be filtered through

28

and then relayed by the generals back to Huế. In this setting, the generals could relay anything they felt was important and discard whatever they objected to. Orders from Huế could take many days or weeks to reach Gia Định. By that time, the generals had to improvise and do the best they could under the circumstances. Once orders had been received, the generals could execute or sit on them using one excuse after the other. They were sometimes swayed by Khmer kings for not taking action in exchange for "bribes." In 1689 and 1690, two consecutive chief commanders ignored Huế's orders to attack the Khmer, delaying Nguyễn's advance into an area for about a decade.[2]

Although the Vietnamese grew rice anywhere they settled, large-scale rice trade could not be envisioned until they controlled the delta and took advantage of the riverine trade established by the Chinese. In the meantime, the huge amount of rice produced had economic repercussions in Thuận Hóa and Quảng Nam, the northernmost part of đàng trong. People in these regions soon became dependent on the cheap delta rice instead of working hard on their own land.

Rice thus needed to be transported to the capital Huế for distribution to the northernmost part of the country, but organizing a convoy was not easy. A large number of boats had to be requisitioned at the same time for a trip that could take at least ten days each way. Boat owners would rather get involved in other, more profitable, trades. But the rice traffic was so vital to Huế's economy that the Nguyễn ordered boat owners to transport rice to Thuận Hóa twice a year up to 1714; in exchange, boat owners received tax exemptions and a small sum for expenses. The arrangements turned out to be very unpopular by 1714 and forced the Nguyễn to offer to pay cash for rice cargoes depending on the load and the distance traveled. With state revenues declining in 1760, the Nguyễn reverted back to the earlier compulsory model. Rice soon became the main item shipped in Vietnam's internal trade.[3] Even in the early 19th century, about 2,000 junks were used in rice transportation between Saigon and Huế.

Taxes were not always levied in a uniform manner. In 1768, Huế requisitioned 341 boats to transport rice to Thuận Hóa. Qui Nhơn was ordered to send 93 boats (27 percent) while the rice-producing Gia Định sent only seven boats. These numbers could only suggest Huế's limited administrative control of manpower and resources in the far south. When new taxes were needed to offset the decreasing revenues from declining overseas trade in the 1750s, land taxes were raised on the people in Quảng Nam and in the highlands. Besides, officials were allowed to recoup their salaries, expenses, and perquisites directly from the taxpaying population. This dangerous policy in difficult times would pit personal interests of officials against those of government and taxpayers alike.[4] In some cases, taxpayers had to pay both government and officials' taxes. These harsh measures, which affected the people of Qui Nhơn and Quảng Nam more than other regions, were at the root of the Tây Sơn rebellion.

While expanding south and west the Nguyễn had to wage wars almost in succession against đàng ngoài (1627–1672), the Chams, Khmers, and Siamese (1674–1785), then the Tây Sơn (1772–1802). During the same period, they administered the new land as well as developed rice culture and expanded trade; as a result, they were too busy to lay down an organized administration which would treat people fairly and equitably. Decreased revenues coupled with increased expenses caused them to tax people heavily. The end result was the Tây Sơn rebellion, which eventually toppled their regime.

Their achievement was nonetheless spectacular for they were able to acquire in merely 200 years three fifths of Vietnam's contemporary territory. They had achieved what Nguyễn Bỉnh Khiêm had prophetically predicted to their forefather Nguyễn Hoàng in 1558. The rapid expansion did not allow them to effectively control the south and eventually sealed their downfall. The downfall, although bloody and traumatic, turned out to be the best lesson for the Nguyễn descendants. It was only after they were driven out of the Thuận Hóa-Quảng Nam base and moved to Saigon—the new national center of gravity—that Vietnamese possession of the delta became irreversible.[5]

In the meantime, they had to fight against their toughest rivals yet, the Tây Sơn.

The Tây Sơn Wars

The three brothers Nguyễn Nhạc, Nguyễn Lữ, and Nguyễn Huệ led the revolt against the Nguyễn lords. Born from the Hồ family, they were related to Hồ Quí Ly, the 15th-century regent of the Thăng Long (Hà Nội) court. Between 1653 and 1657, their great grandfather, along with other captive northern soldiers, was transferred to Quảng Nam to be resettled as a pioneer. The pioneers later changed their names to Nguyễn in order to get favors from the Nguyễn lords.

Nguyễn Nhạc, a betel nut trader and a public clerk (tuần biện lại) responsible for colleting taxes, after abusing his position as tax collector, escaped to the Tây Sơn mountains to avoid punishment.[6] He retreated to An Khê—a mountainous region of today's central Vietnam—and gathered around him his brothers, criminals, fugitives, malcontents and Cham nationals; he used the excuse of fighting for the Nguyễn against the despicable regent Loan. This was not a "peasant's movement," but a "provincial revolt," supported by a group of disaffected uplanders.[7] In 1773, using a ruse similar to the Trojan horse,[8] they captured the fort and city of Qui Nhơn. The town merchants supported Nguyễn Nhạc because they wanted an administration favorable to mercantile interests. The local Chinese, severely affected by the downturn of the overseas trade, provided him with manpower and money.

Profiting from the rebellion, đàng ngoài pushed south, captured Huế, and forced king Định Vương to escape to Saigon in 1774 by sea. The latter reorganized his forces with the help of Mạc Thiên Tử, the Chinese governor of Hà Tiên, and Saigon's general Tổng Phúc Hợp. Saigon, the village in the forest, thus became the refuge for the southern king and the setting for many bloody battles between the Nguyễn and the rebels.

Tây Sơn Nhạc ingeniously told his brother Lữ to sail around the country by sea and up the Saigon River to catch general Hợp from behind. The surprise was total and Saigon fell to the Tây Sơn for the first time in the spring of 1776. Mạc Thiên Tử, despite having only 3,000 men left, was quite resolute. He would rather die fighting than switch sides or surrender to the Tây Sơn. In an act of valiant courage, he retook Saigon in July 1776. Định Vương, who had withdrawn to Cần Thơ, returned to Saigon in triumph.

The Tây Sơn then amassed a huge army under the command of Huệ and Lữ and took Saigon for the second time in August 1777. Prince Nguyễn Dương and Định Vương retreated to Cần Thơ under the protection of Mạc Thiên Tử who, despite his age, continued to fight against the Tây Sơn. The rebels defeated Mạc, pursued the remnants of the Nguyễn army and killed Prince Nguyễn Dương in September 1777. They took Định Vương along with the rest of the Nguyễn family and returned to Saigon. On October 18, 1777, with great pomp and pageantry, the Tây Sơn beheaded Định Vương and all his relatives to celebrate their conquest of the South and seal the collapse of the Nguyễn dynasty.[9] Not all was lost, however, for Nguyễn Ánh, a nephew of Định Vương, was able to escape into the marshes and to make his way to Hà Tiên. Saigon's General Đỗ Thành Nhơn rallied the loyalists under the Đồng Sơn army and retook Saigon late in 1777. Nguyễn Ánh used the occasion to reorganize Saigon's administration and train an army.

The Tây Sơn again amassed a large army in the Gia Định area in March 1782, crushed the Nguyễn army by land and sea, and took Saigon by storm. They looted and destroyed the town. More than 20,000 inhabitants were killed in revenge for their support of the Nguyễn. The massacre, which also included 10,000 Chinese from Chợ Lớn, was thought by some to be aimed at destroying the Chinese monopoly on commerce. This was one of the objectives of the Qui Nhơn merchants who had been the main backers of the Tây Sơn rebels from the beginning.[10] Tây Sơn forces pillaged and burned shops and vessels belonging to Chinese merchants and proceeded to kill them systematically. They then threw the corpses into the Saigon River, and for one month, no one dared to eat shrimp or to drink water taken from the river. All the mercantile goods—muslin, silk, tea, perfumes, paper—were removed from Chinese homes and thrown out into the streets, and no one dared to pick them up.[11]

The 1782 Saigon massacre, during which Vietnamese and Chinese—soldiers, civilians and merchants—were killed by the Tây Sơn, provoked a violent split between the Chinese and the Tây Sơn. The reasons behind that gruesome massacre are still debated (revenge against the Chinese for having killed Nhạc's key lieutenant, financial reasons, siding with the Nguyễn), although it appears to have been a reaction to Chinese settlers' actions against the Tây Sơn. This was the largest massacre in Saigon's history. Bodies were buried in mass graves midway between Saigon and Cholon and when the French arrived in 1859, roughly eight decades later, the painful "Plain of Tombs" remained a visible scar of this catastrophe.

John White, who visited the town in 1824, wrote,

> The ground in the northern part of this city serves as a repository of the dead in a space of two miles by about three-fifths of a mile; and this immense cemetery is filled with tombs, built like those of the Chinese in the form of a horseshoe. Its borders are planted, as are many of the streets in the suburbs, with the palmaria trees; they can be compared to, if it is not too daring, to the Boulevards in Paris.[12]

Nguyễn Ánh fled to Phú Quốc while royalists continued to mount guerrilla attacks against the invaders. By October 1782, one of the royalist groups had been able to retake Saigon. However, Tây Sơn Huệ and Lữ descended with another force in March 1783 and completely destroyed the Nguyễn navy. The fleet was critical in transporting manpower and providing artillery support for the troops. Without the fleet, the Nguyễn army folded and Saigon came under the control of the rebels for the fourth time in six years. Nguyễn Ánh not only lost his army and navy, but also his own two sons, princes Mạnh and Điền, to the hands of the enemy.

In January 1785, backed by 20,000 troops and 300 ships provided by the Siamese king, Nguyễn Ánh directed a two-pronged attack on land across Cambodia and by sea through the Gulf of Siam on the southern Vietnamese provinces. However, the Tây Sơn were ready and waited in ambush on the Mekong River close to Mỹ Tho. They trapped and destroyed the Siamese navy and killed most of the troops. This was a devastating blow for the Nguyễn forces and Nguyễn Ánh once again returned to Bangkok empty-handed and depressed.[13]

The Tây Sơn then turned their eyes northwards where they toppled đàng ngoài and defeated the Chinese. Nguyễn Huệ died suddenly in 1792 and Nguyện Nhạc followed him the year after. The Tây Sơn gradually went downhill and were defeated by Nguyễn Ánh in 1802. They had taken the country by storm. In a land besieged by insurrections, theirs was the most successful one. While đàng ngoài could not beat đàng trong in 50 years of war with a well-funded and trained army, they did it in a few years with a collection of untrained and ragtag people. Masters of organization and powerful war strategists, they were able to raise armies to fight against Siam and China. They waged wars and battles against anyone and even amongst themselves. In these chaotic times, they were able to coerce people into their armies and to keep them focused on wars. They could be compared to a hurricane that landed and went away as soon as it touched ground, wreaking havoc on people and country. They were certainly controversial people. If they were victorious in many battles, they also caused major economic damage to the country. With wars going on for three decades, lands remained uncultivated, commerce was nonexistent, disorder and unruliness left people poor, unhappy, and destitute. They were "actors without script ... guided not by long term visions, but by short term expediency."[14] It is not known what would have happened had they not existed. Like tornadoes, they wiped the slate clean so that new things could happen. Without them, there would not have been a Nguyễn Ánh and the Siamese and Chinese would probably have invaded the country. First, Nguyễn Ánh was not in direct line, but three levels removed from the throne. The Tây Sơn, by killing all potential inheritors, pushed him to the forefront to become the next king. Second, in 1785, had they not stopped the Siamese, the latter would have taken control over the entire Mekong Delta, and Saigon would have been a Siamese city. Third, had Tây Sơn Nguyễn Huệ not defeated the Chinese, who were invited by the northern Lê king, they would have taken over North Vietnam.

The Tây Sơn, however, were not innovators or revolutionaries, but political opportunists. They had no master strategy, much less any particular guiding philosophy. They were always parochial in orientation and focus and tended to return to their bases: Nhạc holed up in Cha Bàn and Huệ in Phú Xuân from 1786 and 1792. In addition, the brutal campaigns were less about peasants' desires or objectives than about political ambitions of its leaders. Peasants were fodder for armies, bodies for corvée labor, and sources of supplies and revenues.[15] The Tây Sơn's soldiers were often malnourished. They deserted as quickly as possible, fleeing lack of food and cruel treatment at the hands of the commanders. Those who resisted conscription were decapitated. The talent of the generals was to kill a great many people to make the rest fearful and to obey promptly.[16] Scholars were also forced to serve in the Tây Sơn's administration. One of them who betrayed the chúa Trịnh to the Tây Sơn despite his teacher's advice, explained his rationale by declaring, "I am not as much afraid of my teacher as I am of the rebels, and I do not love the chúa as much as I love myself."[17] Those who refused could choose between suicide or going into hiding.

The short rule of the Tây Sơn over Saigon left devastating effects on the South as well as on the rest of the country. Nguyễn Huệ has been compared to Napoleon. Both lived in the 17th century and were brilliant tacticians who won huge battles against powerful opponents. They led their respective countries through two decades of war. Both were consumed by inordinate ambition and wanted to control their own worlds. They betrayed the revolution that swept them to power by becoming far worse tyrants than the leaders they replaced. Their discreditable acts did not diminish the adulation their followers reserved for them.

Nguyễn Huệ, however, was the better military leader of the two. Despite being roughly schooled, he never lost a battle, overwhelmed greater odds, and achieved victories at a younger age than Napoleon. The latter, besides his military prowess, reformed the French government and administration of justice. Although his conquest was ephemeral, he was the builder of a modern nation. Nguyễn Huệ, on the other hand, was only a military adventurer, whose accomplishments brought nothing more than the success of his personal ambitions.[18]

The battles for Saigon were heavily contested between the Tây Sơn and the Nguyễn loyalists. The Tây Sơn were never able to secure and control the town for a long time because the Nguyễn supporters kept fighting on. When the Tây Sơn finally controlled Saigon in 1884 after attacking it four times, they had to wage another battle against the Siamese the following year before pulling back to central Vietnam and leaving Saigon and the South to Nguyễn Ánh.

Chúa Nguyễn Ánh[19]

After escaping from Saigon in 1777, Nguyễn Ánh met Pigneau de Behaine—a 35-year-old French priest—in the forest of Hòn Đất, close to Hà Tiên. This was a fateful encounter, for had the prince not gone to Hòn Đất, he would not have met the bishop. As for the latter, had he not decided to settle in Hòn Đất, he would not have met the prince.

What transformed a 15-year-old prince—third in line to the throne, chased and ruthlessly hunted down by the Tây Sơn, and now hidden in the forest without army, retinue, or funding—into an empire builder, a leader and unifier of people was the dream of a man who knew he was predestined to run a Vietnam bigger than anyone could ever have imagined. He would relentlessly work under the most adverse conditions for the next 25 years to fulfill that dream.

What transformed a 37-year-old obscure missionary into a kingmaker and empire builder was the dream of a man who aspired to build a Catholic empire in the East. His encounter with Nguyễn Ánh crystallized his dream and drove him into feverish action. From then on, he attached himself to the service of Nguyễn Ánh, thinking that by helping the prince recover his throne, he would realize his own dream.

Nguyễn Ánh thus lived in the Hà Tiên forest for more than two months. As the Tây Sơn rebels began to close in, Pigneau helped the prince escape to Pulo Panjang, one of the islands in the Gulf of Siam.[20]

Nguyễn Ánh met Pigneau again at a missionary college in Saigon in 1779 and occasionally attended the bishop's sermons during his stay in Saigon. He tried to cooperate with the bishop, who could help him with military support and administration. Pigneau, on the other hand, hoped to receive the king's support for his missionary enterprise. The two men, however, disagreed on the issue of ancestor worship although they tried to compromise with each other. With Nguyễn Ánh's tolerance of religious freedom, Christianity continued to spread in Gia Định.

The pair met again in Thailand in 1785 following Nguyễn Ánh's defeat at the hands of the Tây Sơn. The desperate Ánh entrusted his son prince Cảnh to the bishop and gave him permission to negotiate with French King Louis XVI.[21] For four years, Pigneau lobbied for the king's help to little avail, causing him to return to Pondicherry bitter and disappointed.

In the meantime, Nguyễn Ánh did not sit idle. He raised another army and landed on Vietnamese soil in June 1788. As the Tây Sơn brothers fought among themselves, Nhạc pulled some troops out of Saigon to reinforce his city of Qui Nhơn. Nguyễn Ánh's army moved northward and captured Cần Thơ. The people, upon hearing his return, joined his troops. Mỹ Tho fell to Nguyễn Ánh's camp. The governor of Saigon, Tây Sơn Nguyễn Lữ, fled, allowing Nguyễn Ánh to return in triumph in the city on September 7, 1788.[22]

Problems of succession arose when the last Nguyễn, King Võ, passed away in 1765. The death of the crown prince soon after raised the question of royal legitimacy as some opted for one prince and another group chose another person. When Nguyễn Ánh first arrived in Saigon in 1775, he was 13 years of age. When the two other pretenders were killed by the Tây Sơn in 1777, his chances improved, although without a supporter and a power base, he did not carry a lot of weight among the powerful southern military commanders. These were the same generals who waged war against the Tây Sơn and decided the affairs of đàng trong since the central government of Huế no longer existed. Đỗ Thành Nhân chased the Tây Sơn away from Saigon in 1776 and 1777, Châu Văn Tiếp did the same thing in 1782, and Võ Tánh in 1783. Although Đỗ Thành Nhân—the most powerful commander—took Nguyễn Ánh under his wings in 1777, he did not treat him deferentially. Nguyễn Ánh bided his time and in 1780, managed to have Nhân killed.[23]

By getting rid of Nhân, Nguyễn Ánh took over his army and directly commanded the soldiers, although many of them found the killing unnecessary. They left and formed individual military groups, which fought against Nguyễn Ánh. They were more loyal to Nhân than to the royal family. As for Châu Văn Tiếp, Ánh was able to secure his submission only in 1800. Võ Tánh did not submit until 1788, although he proved to be a valiant and faithful commander.

Nguyễn Ánh was able to rally around him tired soldiers, fractious generals, doubtful Vietnamese, Chinese, Khmers, Chams, and mercenaries, despite being chased out of town on four different occasions. He, however, had to prove himself before winning the confidence of these fractious military leaders who led the war against the Tây Sơn, the Chinese, and western adventurers and missionaries. Among his subjects, one could count French, Spanish, British, Lao, Chinese and Siamese soldiers, Khmers, Malays, Chams, even Chinese pirates, and hill minorities.

He gave men of talent opportunities to advance under his regime. A Khmer servant, Nguyễn Văn Tôn, defeated the Tây Sơn troops in 1787 and became a general. Despite tending buffaloes in his youth, Lê Văn Duyệt's obscure past did not prevent him from becoming a general in the Gia Định's army. He became Nguyễn Ánh's right-hand man and fought for him not only in the South but also in the North, on land as well as at sea. In 1803, when Nguyễn Ánh, after being enthroned as emperor Gia Long, asked him to remain in Huế to help him build a citadel, Lê Văn Duyệt argued that his men were tired, had fought for many years and just wanted to return south. Instead of being upset, Gia Long simply attempted to persuade further. There was no record of who blinked first, but Duyệt continued to serve his emperor until the latter died in 1820.

Disciples of Võ Trường Toản, a prominent Gia Định's scholar, flocked to Nguyễn Ánh's side and helped him establish a new regime.[24] Nguyễn Ánh created the Công Đồng Thử, the Council of High Officials, to run the affairs of the Gia Định prefecture. Local officials were also appointed. Taxes and mobilization were implemented.

By 1788, Saigon/Gia Dinh was Nguyễn Ánh's stronghold and the only place in the country that had resisted inclusion into Tây Sơn's territory. It was from this powerbase that he would launch his attack to regain control of his kingdom. While the Tây Sơn were never able to hold on to Gia Định and the South for any extended period of time, Nguyễn Ánh succeeded in capturing the economically and strategically valuable region. He drew the support of the Chinese, which was crucial in the retaking of the country. Many reasons have been listed for this success. The chúa Nguyễn were above all the benefactors of the Chinese by allowing them to settle in the area. They arrived in Gia Định 18 months earlier than the rebels and were able to argue their legitimacy to the local population. Besides, the 1782 Saigon massacre caused the Chinese to throw all their support behind the Nguyễn.[25]

The Chinese role was mainly economic: They provided supplies and equipment to Nguyễn Ánh's army. They brought iron, lead, sulfur, which were essential to warfare, to Gia Định in exchange for rice, raw silk, cotton fabric.[26] Nguyễn Ánh's greatest generals, like Nguyễn Văn Nhân, Nguyễn Huỳnh Đức, and Lê Văn Duyệt, headed the administration and later became tổng trấn quân (governor generals). As a result, Chinese traders were protected under Gia Long (1802–1820) and Lê Văn Duyệt (1820–1832). That policy would change under Minh Mạng, who suspected the Chinese of smuggling rice.

With funds the bishop had raised in India, he bought two warships along with 100 cannons and 1,000 European rifles, set sail to Vietnam and arrived in Saigon on July 28, 1789. Nguyễn Ánh welcomed the reinforcements to his small forces. The news that the French had intervened worked as a form of psychological warfare in favor of the prince: resistance faltered and new converts flocked to his side. Nguyễn Ánh, on the other hand, was happy the treaty was annulled, for he took pride in being able to recover his throne by the power of his own arms.[27]

The bishop helped Nguyễn Ánh by handling his correspondence with foreign states—Asian as well as European. He advised him on the establishment of new industries: coal and tar furnaces, gunpowder factories and an arsenal. He introduced silkworm breeding and sugar cane, pepper, and shade tree planting. New bridges were built and old ones repaired. He established military and naval training schools: one was set up in Gia Định, where Puymanel gave instruction on European tactics. This led to the formation of mobile artillery also known as "Flying Dragons," which had devastating effects on the enemy.

In 1789, Puymanel also assisted in the building of the Saigon citadel, which included at its center Nguyễn Ánh's royal palace. This citadel, and 31 others built in the delta during that period, bore European designs but were topped with Chinese-style roofs. The Saigon citadel called "thành bát quái" (Eight Diagrams) was shaped like a lotus flower, which has a strong Vietnamese connotation.[28]

The massive square complex sat on the plateau overlooking the Saigon River. Each side was longer than three city blocks and the outer and inner circumferences measured 3,820 and 2,592 m respectively. The citadel had a double wall with a ditch in between:

The 6.34 m inner wall was built with stones from Biên Hòa. Its base was 36.5 m wide.

The ditch was 6.8 m deep and 75.5 m wide.

The outer earthen rampart had a gentle slope on the outside to make it difficult for assailants to breach the wall.[29]

A hexagonal watchtower with an attached cord-ladder was located 61 meters above the front courtyard of the citadel. The watchman raised a banner during daytime or hung a lit lantern at night to signal alert. There were two gates on each of the four sides of the citadel. Barracks were erected at three of these gates and roofed with red tiles. Wooden bridges connected the outer and inner walls and were later replaced by stone bridges. Besides the king's and queen's palaces, there were many offices, a granary, the treasury office, a warehouse for gold, silver, satin, fabric, a weapons warehouse, and many apartments. The Thái Miếu (royal temple), which sat in the courtyard, was disassembled and moved to Huế in 1801 after Nguyễn Anh's victory.

About a mile from the citadel at the junction of the Bến Nghé arroyo and the Saigon River was the Ba Sơn shipyard, where warships, black- or red-painted were anchored. Outside the citadel were located an elephant park, a gun powder mill, a jailhouse, an embassy to accommodate envoys from other countries, and a customhouse.[30]

Jean Marie d'Ayot was in charge of the building and tactical operation of the navy fleet. He introduced the use of signals and well-directed naval gunfire. The French mercenaries also helped with the acquisition of weapons.

However, the bulk of military tactics and strategy rested on Nguyễn Anh and his generals. There were only four officers and 80 French soldiers who participated in the battles, most of them in support positions. They all returned home after the end of the war except for a few who remained and were elevated to mandarin positions at the Nguyễn court.[31]

The bishop passed away on October 9, 1799, from a tropical fever (possibly malaria) and received a state funeral presided over by Nguyễn Ánh himself. Ánh called the bishop "Master," a title reserved only for a well-respected Confucian man. The procession of 40,000 people was led by the crown price, followed by the king's mother and sister, the queen, his concubines, and his children.[32]

For the last six or seven years, Nguyễn Ánh proceeded cautiously regarding the military. He started seasonal campaigns that began every spring: he would sail north, take a chunk out of enemy land, build forts and leave garrisons to hold them, and then withdraw to the south with the monsoon rains. The process would repeat again each year. His advances were slow, gradual and methodical, but always directed northwards. His actions and techniques did not have the brilliance and the impetuosity of Nguyễn Huệ's: they were based more on practical and logical matters. His genius lay in his steadfastness and perseverance: he was more like an ant-worker than a sprinter.[33]

In Saigon, his schedule was tight. He got up at six and took a cold shower. At seven, he received his mandarins and discussed with them events and state matters of the previous day. He dictated all the orders and then visited the arsenal, ordnance factory and the foundry. His lunch, at 12:00 or 1:00, consisted of rice and dried fish, following which he took a nap from two to five. He gave audience and dealt with state affairs from five until midnight then retired to his chamber to write notes and take a light supper. He then spent an hour with his family before going to bed between two or three. He thus had six hours of sleep during the whole day. He did not drink alcohol or wine and his diet consisted of fish, rice, vegetables and fruit.[34]

The war, on the other hand, continued at a slow pace. In July 1792, Nguyễn Ánh managed to raid Qui Nhơn, the southern Tây Sơn headquarters, and to destroy its fleet. Although the future seemed hopeless, the Tây Sơn still had a strong land army. It was only in March 1799 that Nguyễn Ánh launched another attack by land and sea on Qui Nhơn. Its citadel fell in July 1799. General Võ Tánh, Nguyễn's brother-in-law became the citadel's commander, which was soon besieged by the Tây Sơn's land army. Võ Tánh held on for 17 months before surrendering, but by that time Nguyễn Ánh, bypassing the besieged citadel, had captured Huế, the Tây Sơn's capital.

By the year 1800, Nguyễn Ánh's army was composed of about 140,000 men. Although big by the standards of the times, it was rather small by later standards.

Army	*Men*
24 squadrons of buffalo cavalry	6,000
16 battalions of elephants (200 beasts)	8,000
30 battalions of artillery	15,000
25 regiments of 1,200 each (trained in European manner)	30,000
Infantry with matchlocks, sabres and trained in the ancient manner of combat	42,000
Guards trained in European tactics	12,000
Land forces	**113,000**

Marine	
Artificers in the naval arsenal	8,000
Sailors on ships in the harbor	8,000
Attached to European-built vessels	1,200
Attached to junks	1,600
Attached to 100-row galleys	8,000
In sea service	**26,800**
Total	**139,800**

Table III. Nguyễn Ánh's military forces in 1800[35]

By June 1, 1802, Nguyễn Ánh had reconquered the country the Nguyễn dynasty had lost 25 years before. That was a bittersweet victory for a man who had spent half of his life chasing a dream under overwhelming odds. In a ceremony given in Huế, he officially ascended to the throne under the name of Gia Long or "Prosperity." However, he did not take the title of "emperor," for that would come only many years later after Chinese recognition.[36]

With an army of 140,000 men and sailors, he crossed the Đồng Hới on June 20, 1802. By July 20, he arrived at the city of Thăng Long (Hà Nội) where Canh Thình was caught by his own people and delivered in chains. Thình was taken to Huế where, in front of a large crowd, he was executed. The bones of Quang Trung (Canh Thình's father), his wife, and grandparents, were exhumed and placed in a basket for the soldiers to urinate on before the prisoner's eyes. Then Canh Thình's limbs were attached to four elephants and torn apart. The remains were collected and exhibited at the marketplace until they became putrid.

Although cruel, this type of treatment was not limited to Asia. Ravaillac, King Henri IV's assassin, was torn apart alive by four horses, as was Damiens, the man who attempted to kill Louis XV. The English were no strangers either to this type of wicked revenge: They exhumed Oliver Cromwell's corpse and hung it to the gallows.[37] After 1975, the communists sent 250,000 ARVN soldiers to long-term concentration camps—where thousands died of hunger, mistreatment and lack of medication[38]—and forced three million people to flee overseas aboard un-seaworthy wooden boats, resulting in the death of tens of thousands at sea.[39]

Saigon, an Economic Center in the Water World

Trading business took place in the 16th and 17th centuries between many Asian countries and town-ports in the Mekong Delta. However, it was only in the late 18th century, when Nguyễn Ánh returned to Saigon (in 1788), that the city's trade expanded. What the Vietnamese brought to the area was an intensive rice culture coupled with trade. Under the direction of Nguyễn Ánh, who reorganized and centralized the southern administration, Saigon's role as the main southern port was sealed and from that time onward, most of the goods arrived and were shipped out from there.

The Saigon River was deep enough to accept large Chinese junks. The latter anchored in front of the Cần Giờ village when they arrived at the mouth of the river. They waited one or two days for permission to sail upriver. After the cargo was weighed, foreign vessels had to be towed by local boats in some areas because of the narrowness of the channel and the river was not tidal like the Mekong. The junks would drop anchor in Chợ Lớn, about three miles upriver from the Saigon pier where all transactions took place and the Nguyễn's warehouses were located.[40]

The Water World consisted of two networks intimately linked together. First, the regional network using maritime trading routes connected countries like China, Vietnam, Malaysia and Thailand.[41] Some Chinese junks would make roundtrips to trade exclusively with Vietnam while others visited Malaysia or Siam. The backbone of this network consisted of medium and small-sized-junks rather than larger ones, suggesting a strong local or regional rather than long-distance trade.[42]

Second, the less well-known riverine network managed by local traders served as a collecting and distributing warehouse for the regional network. The main port in Cochinchina was Saigon, which was connected by secondary ports: Mỹ Tho, Vĩnh Long, Sa Đéc, Châu Đốc, Hà Tiên, Rạch Giá, Cà Mau, and Sốc Trăng.[43] The Khmer names of Rạch Giá (White Wax Market) and Sa Đéc (Iron Market) suggest a long history of trade involvement in this riverine network. It was through this route that non-native plants and fruit trees were introduced into the delta. Durian and mangosteen are examples, as well as a certain type of bananas called Siamese bananas (chuối Xiêm), later domesticated as Mỹ Tho bananas (chuối Mỹ Tho). Part of this riverine route included trade with Cambodia, its favorite port being Cái Bè. The latter actually means the place where ghe bè[44] are gathered or anchored. Besides its location on the Tiền Giang branch of the Mekong—therefore close to Saigon—it was situated next to Mỹ Tho, the main producer of betel nuts, one major item loved by the Cambodians.

Another item traded was the special "red" salt from Sốc Trăng, whose purity and mild flavor were greatly appreciated. It was used to process salted fish and to make fish sauce. Trade of this salt was highly profitable in Cambodia. On their way back, traders would buy deerskins and canoes, which were abundantly available and cheap in that country.[45]

One network fed into and was dependent upon the other for business. Although these two networks appeared to function independently, they depended on each other for survival and growth. Chinese junks returning from trading business with Thailand or Malaysia could also stop by Vietnam to pick up or trade goods. This third network overlapped the previous ones and boosted exchanges between the countries involved.[46] A look at trade records gives us a glimpse of how the system, which was initially not regulated by any single government but by supply and demands, worked.

Canton (China) junk trade in the 18th century exclusively focused on the Mekong Delta, Cancao (Hà Tiên), and Cambodia. Of the 37 Canton junks sailing between Canton and Southeast Asia, 85 to 90 percent traded with Cochinchina, Can Cao, and Sóc Trăng.

In 1761, 2,539 piculs of sappanwood[47] were exported from Cochinchina—an area producing no sappanwood—while only 563 piculs left Siam, the main producer of sappanwood[48] in the region. Similarly, in 1768, Siam, a tin exporter, shipped only 200 piculs of tin compared to 2,700 piculs by Cancao, a purely importing area.[49]

Minor ports thus adjusted their shipping loads based on supply and demand. They also thrived by "smuggling" out goods: "smuggling" meaning selling to passing traders or bringing goods to other regional ports without paying taxes. Goods changed hands many times before arriving in China, the major stop of a string of terminals of this lucrative trade.

Other goods were traded or smuggled in. In the late 19th century, Cà Mau smuggled tobacco from Cambodia rather than buying from Gò Vắp, the state's tobacco producer. Rice smuggled from Siam to Hà Tiên was cheaper than that of the Mekong Delta. Combat elephants were bought in Phnom Penh and Battambang. In 1797, Nguyễn Ánh ordered all junks from Siam to bring between 10,000 and 30,000 can of pig iron[50] and some saltpeter to exchange for silk or cotton fabrics.[51] Rice of course was an important commodity, especially after China dropped its importing ban on rice. The beneficiaries of this policy were Siam, Luzon, and then Saigon. Nguyễn Ánh exported rice to South China and bought arms in exchange.[52]

The number of Chinese junks visiting Cochinchina (South Vietnam) increased fourfold between 1750 and 1820.[53] When John Crawfurd visited the region in 1820, he noticed that "by far the most considerable branch of [Singapore's] traffic [was] with Siam, and next ... with the port of Saigun [sic]."[54] The Saigon-Bangkok-Singapore trade triangle highlighted the heavy regional trade between these countries.

The size and importance of this trade can be estimated from the yearly arrival of 300 Chinese junks, great or small, varying in size from 100 to 600 tons in the ports of Cochinchina.[55] This did not include boats from other countries (Southeast Asian and European).

The trade, which ran free from government interference in the 16th and

17th centuries, came under the control of Saigon once Nguyễn Ánh consolidated his power. In the late 18th century, Saigon became the dominant player in the trade business by marginalizing the secondary ports.

The South was known to have been a fine source of shipbuilding timber back in the 17th century. The logging areas included some regions of the present-day Tây Ninh and Sông Bé provinces. "The ship-timber, and planks, excelled anything I had ever seen.... It was sawed out of the trunk of a teak tree, and I believe there is no part of the world where these gigantic sires of the forest arrive at such magnitude as in Cochinchina."[56] Tree trunks were then rafted down the East Vàm Co River or Saigon River to the Saigon's shipyard, where they were processed.[57] Certain villages along the Cái Bè River in Định Tường even specialized in building large capacity boats for trading with Cambodia. The shipbuilding business began in the mid–18th century when the Chinese began settling in the Mekong Delta. The Chams also built ghe bầu (Cham-Malay prahu type of galleys) under the Nguyễn Ánh era. The other Asian shipbuilding place at the time was Siam.

Shipbuilding, however, peaked only under the leadership of Nguyễn Ánh, who needed a large amount of ships for trade as well as for war. He first provided ships to Siam in the 1780s in exchange for military help and armament. The remaining ships were either used for transporting rice or sold to other Asian countries. The Chinese not only bought the rice but they also brought Vietnamese ships because shipbuilding cost half as much in Southeast Asia as in China. As the trade of rice and other products grew, it also boosted the production and sale of ships. This was exemplified by the case of a Portuguese ship, which arrived in Cochinchina in 1798 to purchase several thousand piculs of betel nuts. The main ship was loaded with merchandise, which forced the owner to buy a smaller local ship to carry the several hundred piculs left over.[58]

Shipbuilding played an important role in Nguyễn Ánh's quest to reclaim his throne. It was under him that Vietnam became an important maritime state in Southeast Asia, a role envied by other Asian nations at the time. Between 1778 and 1818, he had 1,482 ships of various sorts built. They included "235 *ghe bầu* (Cham-Malay type prahu), 460 *sai thuyền* (bigger galleys), 490 *chiến thuyền* (war boats), 77 *đại chiến thuyền* (large war junks), 60 schooners, 100 *ô thuyền* (black junks), and 60 *lẽ thuyền* (carved and decorated vessels)."[59] Mast's design was different from that of Chinese boats: they were made with joints rather than of one piece and the sails were made of cotton fabric.[60]

It was Nguyễn Ánh's strong navy that helped him defeat the Tây Sơn who also had a large maritime fleet. His main 1,500-meter-long shipyard was located in Saigon between the Saigon River and Thị Nghè arroyo. The other stood at Biên Hòa, 30 miles away: Destroyed by the Tây Sơn, it was later abandoned. The third one was set up in Mỹ Tho. The shipbuilding industry began in the late 18th century and lasted until 1830, when shipbuilders fled to Chantaburi, Siam, to avoid persecution by Minh Mạng.[61] In 1835, five or six thousand people lived in Chantaburi; the majority were newly arrived Cochinchinese. The latter were skilled carpenters or blacksmiths.[62]

Nguyễn Ánh undertook agrarian reforms in present-day South Vietnam. Devastated by the constant wars with the Tây Sơn, the region became under-exploited agriculturally, causing local owners and farmers to suffer econom-ically. He decided to open new đồn điền. Large amounts of lands were thus brought into cultivation and soon resulted in surplus of grains. This allowed Nguyễn Ánh to raise and feed an army of 100,000 people and to service a navy of 1,200 vessels in 1800. The surplus of rice was sold to European and Asian traders and allowed the purchase of iron, bronze and sulfur needed for the conduct of war. Everywhere his army went, he had new granaries build to sup-ply food to his soldiers and the conquered population.[63]

By 1800, revenue from overseas Saigon trade alone was 489,790 quan compared to the total state revenue of 380,700 quan for đàng trong between 1746 and 1752. By that time, Saigon and Bangkok had become the two promi-nent economic and political centers in Southeast Asia.[64]

Expanded revenues led to the purchase of firearms and gun powder from surrounding cities like Penang, Goa, Melaka, Macao, and Singapore. Trading profits from the Mekong Delta allowed Bishop Pigneau in 1787 to buy "several cargoes of arms and ammunitions" from Pondichery for Nguyễn Ánh at a time when the French King Louis XVI refused to give him support. In 1791 Nguyễn Ánh was able to purchase 10,000 muskets, 2,000 cannons, and 2,000 shells. The court of Huế also bought a steam warship for $50,000 Spanish in 1844 and 200 guns, mortar and iron.[65] Nguyễn Ánh was also able to build himself a citadel, which was topped with Chinese-style pavilions.

*   *   *

Nguyễn Ánh took a quarter of a century to recover the throne of his ances-tors. His early battle losses from 1778 to 1788 may have rendered him extremely careful and risk-averse. His strategy was relentless and methodical. He reor-ganized his army, expanded his navy, and introduced western technology into the art of war-making in Indochina. He had a huge citadel built in Saigon, which could make any Asian country proud. Other citadels were also built around the country, as were bridges and roads. He promoted shipbuilding and transformed the town into one of the best shipyards in Southeast Asia. Had he pursued this route, Vietnam would have had the best naval fleet in Southeast Asia and, perhaps, would have improved its commerce, technology, and the well-being of its citizens and would be too strong and modern a country to be defeated by any western invasion. Saigon was a melting pot of various minori-ties, which energized the country economically. His stay in the Mekong Delta allowed him to learn and to understand the political, religious, social forces that played out in the region. Open-minded, he knew how to use and channel the best entrepreneurial, hard-working, and free-spirited qualities of these minorities. Any other leader would not have been able to deal with the unique and complex social problems of the region.

Under Nguyễn Ánh, the economy took off with unexpected vigor. He centralized the administration in the Mekong Delta, a region previously run by warlords, and gave stability to a world divided by wars. He promoted large-scale rice culture, controlled and expanded commerce (especially in the water world), and made Saigon one of the two new economic and political powers in Southeast Asia—the other was Bangkok—in the late 18th century. The rise of Saigon marginalized smaller trade centers (Biên Hòa, Hà Tiên, Mỹ Tho). Thanks to that economic dynamism, Nguyễn Ánh was able to build a formidable army, which allowed him to defeat the Tây Sơn. The economic rise in turn attracted more Vietnamese to the South who soon displaced or neutralized other ethnic minorities like Chams, Khmers, Chinese, and Lao.[66]

Although Nguyễn Ánh had crushed a social movement, he did nothing to relieve the grievances of the peasants and the poor who had flocked to support the Tây Sơn. He then embarked on a building spree in Huế, imposed corvée requirements on the peasantry, and reestablished a Confucian bureaucracy, which perpetuated the social ills of the past. This resulted in further political instability, uprisings that soon weakened the dynasty.[67]

From the frontier land that had brought him fortune and fame, Nguyễn Ánh longed to return to his ancestral land, Huế, and its surroundings, where his forebears had reigned for generations. He was a man of tradition who was attached to the past. He was far from being a futurist like his forebear Nguyễn Hoàng. The latter chose to build a new empire from nothing: he ventured through darkness to create something that had not existed before. He dared to break with tradition and his ancestors and to be called a "rebel."[68] In the end, Nguyễn Hoàng created South Vietnam which was carved out of the lands of the Chams and the Khmers and more than doubled the size of the country.

Nguyễn Ánh, on the other hand, ventured into the land of the future where trade, technology, freedom reigned, and then decided to turn his back on it and to retreat to the past. He chose to follow tradition instead of modernization, and in so doing, led his nation and successors to a downhill course. He closed his eyes to the future, which was right there in front of him. Maybe he did not like what he saw. Maybe he was scared of what modernity could bring to his reign and his successors. Maybe he yearned for stability within an autocratic regime, after two decades of daily fighting, instead of political instability and challenge. One cannot blame him for returning to his roots, the crown, and the land of his forebears which he had spent decades to recover, even though it was a poor region with a gilded past. Saigon, the siren with all its economic power, the new land with all its mirages, did not entice him.

In the end, he chose conservatism, family tradition, and old rules over the call for openness and modernity. He made the choice that only an old and tired warrior would have taken. Keith Taylor commented that the decision to return to Huế "deprived [his] successors of the perspective that had enabled his success and left Nam Bộ [South Vietnam] vulnerable to other powers."[69]

3

Saigon Under the Warlords (1802–1835)

Having reunified the country under his leadership, Nguyễn Ánh was enthroned under the name of Gia Long.[1] He began building the Nguyễn dynasty in Huế. From 1802 to 1820, Saigon, although downgraded to a regional city, still wielded considerable power because its southern army had supported Nguyễn Anh during the war. Its Tổng Trấn Quân (governor general), representing the central government, controlled the whole South from Biên Hòa to Hà Tiên including Cambodia, as the latter became Vietnam's tributary in 1812.

General Lê Văn Duyệt

Born in 1763 in Quảng Ngãi (central Vietnam) from poor parents, General Lê Văn Duyệt tended buffaloes during his childhood. Attracted by the possibilities of the "New South," his family moved to Gia Định. Most likely an intersex person,[2] Duyệt was drafted as a eunuch at the age of 18 to take charge of the royal household before being able to display his military ability. He served in the Tả Quân (left division) of the southern army from 1787 onward before becoming the commander of the Tả Quân in 1802. And it was that division under his command that captured Thăng Long the same year.[3] A stern and eccentric man, he used to keep 100 chickens and dogs with him. Whenever he returned home, he had one tiger and 50 dogs follow him. However, he had great military and administrative talents and was well liked by his men and people because of his fairness. He dressed up very simply and once appeared at a court audience late because he was busy watching cockfighting. He then proceeded to explain in detail to the king about the funny aspect of the game. He was governor general of Saigon from 1812 to 1813 and from 1820 to 1832. To all southerners, he was the local hero who would eventually have his own shrine in Saigon.

The problem of succession was raised when crown Prince Cảnh died in 1801. Gia Long eventually chose his fourth son, Chi Đàm (future Minh Mạng), as his heir, bypassing Prince Cảnh's son, Mỹ Đàm. In the beginning, Duyệt sided with Mỹ Đàm.[4] When he realized that some officials plotted to support Mỹ Đàm so that they could control him in the future, Duyệt switched sides and began supporting Chi Đàm.[5] Minh Mạng, however, never forgot Duyệt's opposition to his selection and did everything in his power to undermine the general.

Minh Mạng and Lê Van Duyệt could not be more different—due to their very different upbringings. Duyệt was a soldier trained in the South among Southerners: he was as straight and blunt as he could be, and didn't worry about hurting anyone.[6] He earned his rank and title through hard and often dangerous work. He had minimal education and was considered to be "coarse and ignorant" by the court people. Despite all his titles, he was a commoner who was more at ease in front of his soldiers than in the corridors of a palace. When Duyệt and Lê Chất visited Huế in 1804, Duyệt mentioned that both of them had risen from a military background. They therefore were unaware of princely manners and official rules. He suggested that both tendered their resignations to avoid mistakes.[7]

Minh Mạng on the other hand was trained and educated by Huế court officials. Being a fine product of eastern civilization, he was knowledgeable in Confucian dialectics and rarely said what he thought.[8] As the protector of Confucianism, which his regime embodied, he was cunning, resourceful, dangerous and was used to the manipulations of palace politics.

Lê Văn Duyệt from Minh Mạng's perspective was a political nemesis who not only opposed his ascension to the throne, but also maintained an autonomous power base in Gia Định that resisted the Huế government. On one hand, he did not want to offend a close friend of his father, a savior of the crown, and a one-time tutor. His classic upbringing would not allow him to do that. On the other hand, he definitely wanted to get rid of him. Therefore, he posted Duyệt to Gia Định away from the court as soon as he was crowned emperor in 1820.[9] Gia Định, however, was Duyệt's second home and it was where he felt at ease and was popular. Duyệt did not want to stay at the court to begin with: he only relented after Gia Long's multiple requests. Minh Mạng thus had to tolerate him for the next 12 years.

Both men, therefore, differed on many issues, especially religion. Duyệt, who had been in frequent contact with bishop de Behaine and Frenchmen during the war years, saw foreigners as people who could help the Vietnamese build a better society. He had witnessed foreigners help Nguyễn Ánh build citadels, a naval fleet, and wage war against the Tây Sơn. He did not feel threatened by foreigners. Taberd, a French priest reported that Duyệt told him, "The king [Minh Mạng] does not remember the services performed by missionaries. They gave us rice when we were hungry, they gave us cloth when we were cold ... the king is repaying charity with ingratitude."[10]

The report should be considered cautiously because the opinion expressed was spoken in a private dialogue between Duyệt and Taberd—not communicated in form of a letter. In general, Duyệt treated foreigners deferentially and allowed them to practice their religion openly and to build a church right in the center of Chợ Lớn.[11] A seminary was actively training students in Biên Hòa during that period. When father Regereau was ordered to report to Huế, Lê Văn Duyệt allowed him to safely remain in Saigon[12] to avoid a possible arrest since he had been sought by the Huế court. No western missionary had been persecuted under Lê Văn Duyệt's regime despite central government orders to clamp down on priests.

Minh Mạng, on the other hand, brought up in the court under stern Confucian teachers who were nationalistic and suspicious about foreigners' motives, had a different perspective on Christianity and priests. He did not like the religion on the grounds that it did not protect ancestor worship. He always remembered how his eldest brother, Prince Cảnh, refused to bow to Gia Long, as a good Confucian son would, after his return from France. He linked Christianity to sedition when he became aware that a western missionary, Father Marchand, fought on the side of Lê Văn Khôi against the Huế court. Worse, the rebels had even asked the Siamese for help. When the rebellion was controlled, Marchand was captured and executed.[13] Minh Mạng also knew of stories of the Old Testament—like those of Noah's ark and the Tower of Babel—which he considered implausible and irrational. For him, the implausibility of the stories reflected the lack of reason of westerners.[14]

Even Gia Long was weary of foreigners. Aware of the British expansion in China,[15] he refused a British request to open a factory in Trà Sơn in 1803. He wanted to trade with the Europeans only if he could control the terms of the trade. Although he treated missionaries with great respect and tolerance, he viewed them as nothing more than the means to achieve his goal of reunification. Although he did not persecute Catholics, he considered Catholicism a "heterodox" religion that was threatening people's morality.[16]

The second disagreement between Minh Mạng and Lê Văn Duyệt related to the handling of convicts. In 19th-century Vietnam, undesirable elements of society were punished by exile. Northern convicts were sent to the South and vice versa. In the underpopulated Gia Định, convicts remained an important part of society because they could be used as soldiers or officials—a normal practice handed down by Nguyễn Ánh. Thanh Thuận and An Thuận were troops made of northern insurgents who had sworn obedience to the government. Hồi Lương and Bắc Thuận were composed of soldier-lawbreaker-northerners. Duyệt even used them as bodyguards.

Convicts sent to Gia Định, however, were given the chance to redeem themselves by working on land they were given until they completed their sentences. Sentences were sometimes commuted. Their wives and children could join them in their workplaces. Once pardoned, they could enroll in the army where they were known as hồi lương. They could be used as low-level officials. Minh Mạng, on the other hand, believed that convicts should serve their sentences and that enrolling them into administrative work was akin to breaking rules of law.[17]

The third disagreement centered on the Chinese, who were suspected of smuggling rice and opium. Rice harvest, although produced in large quantities in the Mekong Delta, was on occasion not large enough to supply the demands of central Vietnam as well as the demand for export. Factors affecting rice production were numerous. Gia Định area was so under-populated in the 18th and early 19th centuries that convicts were enrolled in military settlements to keep peace as well as to farm lands. Since half of the able villagers had to report for military duty, there were not enough people to cultivate the land. Wars and insurrections caused additional disruption in the production and distribution of rice. The many wars against the Siamese and Tây Sơn had scarred the countryside. Revolts from different minorities—Chams, Khmers, Chinese, as well as peasants—caused unrest in the region. There was no stable government in the South to protect the investments of rice producers and this was coupled with an increased worldwide requirement for rice in the early 19th century. All these factors contributed to the shortage of rice—especially when weather and natural disasters were factored in. Prices of rice rose between 50 to 100 percent in the North as well as the South between 1825 and 1830.[18]

The court, however, did not believe that there were production problems. On the contrary, it suspected that people smuggled out Gia Định's rice because it was half the price it was on the world market. Rice was a bulky substance which was heavily regulated, and anyone caught smuggling rice faced decapitation.[19] Therefore, smugglers were very discreet, if not careful, in their acts. On the other hand, the Mekong Delta, with its many estuaries, was a porous frontier that favored smuggling. In addition, what merchants brought back from their trips (linen, flannel, muskets, teapots, knives, swords and so on) was worth more than smuggled rice. Each boat trip between Saigon and Singapore could bring its owner 200 to 400 percent profit over costs.[20] Profits were higher when opium was brought back. British opium, which was reserved for China, was diverted to Gia Định on occasions. With its free trade the town was the open door for opium's entry into Vietnam.

The Huế government blamed the Chinese for rice smuggling because of their stranglehold on river transportation. Lê Văn Duyệt, however, offered three reasons for the rice shortage. The Mekong Delta was an excellent destination for Chinese immigrants (3,000 new families arrived in Gia Định in 1826), who not only increased the state's rice consumption but possibly smuggled opium during these trips. Second, there were always cunning merchants (gian thương) who stored up rice to sell it at a higher price later on. Third, local Vietnamese, besides the Chinese, were also involved in the lucrative rice business. While the Chinese focused on regional overseas trade, the Vietnamese, with their lighter boats, dealt with local business. When they ferried rice from Gia Định to Huế, they could divert some of this rice to Chinese traders waiting at prearranged areas at high sea. Some transport junks had been seen out of course and as far as Guangdong or Hainan.[21] The gian thương, therefore, could either be Chinese or Vietnamese.

Duyệt, however, did not deny his responsibility. In 1832, prior to his death, he complained that rice smuggling was a "serious problem" in Gia Định because his government failed to patrol the seas.[22] As a result, the "cunning merchants" were able to smuggle out rice and bring in opium. Whether the problem was related to lack of manpower or lack of a good navy fleet or a combination of both is not known. The fact that the French could sail up the Saigon River unharmed and take over the town in 1859 suggested, among other things, that the country's naval fleet had been slowly deteriorating since Minh Mạng took power in 1820. That deterioration accelerated after 1832 when boat-builders and Catholics fled to Chantaburi following Lê Văn Khôi's rebellion. This had not always been the case, for in the late 18th century, as their maritime expertise increased, the Vietnamese had navigated to the island regions of Southeast Asia by themselves. John White observed, "It is perhaps, of all the powers in Asia, the best adapted to maritime adventure ... the Vietnamese rivaling even the Chinese as sailors."[23]

There were important Chinese in the Gia Định government: Trịnh Hoài Đức, acting governor, was a minh hương. Ngô Nhân Tĩnh and Nguyễn Hữu Nghị played important roles in the Gia Định government. Lưu Tín was a thanh nhân born in Hội An, central Vietnam. He was a successful businessman who kept his Chinese identity. His business prospered thanks to his relationship with Duyệt. The latter adopted him as a son and appointed him to the Gia Định trade department. The influence of the Chinese in the South inclined the Gia Định government to protect them from the court's regulations. While the central government specifically forbade the Chinese to get involved in maritime rice trade, Gia Định gave them free rein. The Chinese later evaded Huế's maritime ban by using Vietnamese people as front men: boats were registered under concubines belonging to Vietnamese or Chinese.[24] They sometimes used fake documentation, a fact that exasperated Minh Mạng. By 1837, the latter banned all Chinese (minh hương or thanh nhân) from making or purchasing ships for sea travel. He basically did not trust Chinese settlers.[25]

New Chinese immigrants often avoided paying any taxes at all. They claimed upon arrival to be too poor to pay taxes. But once they became financially successful, they did not upgrade their status as taxpayers. Minh Mạng, therefore, suggested to fully tax all newcomers while poor immigrants would pay only half of the taxes the first three years. When he realized that his suggestions had been ignored, he sent his men to take over the Gia Định's department of revenue in 1830.[26]

Between 1802 and 1832, Gia Định Thành was a semi-autonomous area with its own powers. Lê Văn Duyệt was the most powerful of the three governors during that period as he enjoyed the longest tenure and held the position twice: 1812 to 1813 and 1820 to 1832. Although he supported the central government, Duyệt remained faithful to the Gia Định's particular needs of catering to Chinese and Christian special interests.

As the king's representative, he personally presided over two major celebrations: the longevity-wishing ceremony (lễ triều kiến vua) and the military review ceremony (lễ hành binh). Each year, besides sending gifts of allegiance, the Khmer king, as the vassal, had to participate in the well-wishing ceremony for the Vietnamese king on the occasion of the Chinese New Year. Therefore, on the 30th December of the lunar calendar, the Khmer king would arrive in Saigon to be ready for the ceremony the following morning. One year, he was delayed because he had stayed in Chợ Lớn instead of close to the citadel. The governor did not want to wait for him and proceeded with the ceremony. When the Khmer king finally showed up, he was fined 3,000 taels of silver and was not released until the fine was paid.

Likewise, on the sixth day of the first lunar month, a military review and parade of all the forces of the six southern provinces took place in Saigon. The goals of this were to impress Vietnam's neighbors with its military superiority and to allay people's fears about spirits. If the review and parade went well, locals, believing that the majesty of the governor would overwhelm the spirits, would feel safer living under his protection. On the day of the ceremony, he would wash himself carefully, don the ceremonial robes and be transported on a palanquin to the king's pagoda where he offered his well wishes to the king. He then headed to the Plain of Tombs where the military review took place. Following completion of the ceremony, he made a tour of the Quy citadel and the Ba Sơn shipyard before heading back home.[27]

Duyệt was the personification of Saigon, the South and its free spirit. A man of humble origin and minimal education, he rose to the rank of governor of the South and confidante of King Gia Long. This would have been an unlikely scenario had he been born in the đàng ngoài, simply because he lacked a Confucian education. He was a self-made man—a frontier man who climbed the ladders of the society through his "street smartness" and military prowess. A formidable warrior and keen administrator, he allowed the town to expand and grow into a strong commercial and political center.

The Lê Văn Khôi Revolt

In Minh Mạng's eyes, Gia Định/Saigon was a semi-autonomous town where Catholics were able to practice without fear of repression, Chinese sold and traded rice and opium, and convicts led lives of normal citizens. Unable to tolerate these violations of state rules, he looked for ways to dismantle Gia Định's power. Since Lê Văn Duyệt's authority and prestige were substantial, steps had to be taken with care. The king would go after Duyệt's men first, his power over Cambodia, then his military forces.

In 1823, he had someone accuse Trần Nhất Vĩnh, one of Lê Văn Duyệt's influential deputies, of illegal rice trading and running a brothel. Although Lê Văn Duyệt was able to vindicate him, Vĩnh was forced to transfer to the North in 1828, outside Duyệt's jurisdiction, where the Huế government ordered him jailed. Although Duyệt tried to help him out, he was powerless against Minh Mạng's manipulation. Minh Mạng then named one of his men, Nguyễn Khoa Minh, to take Trần Nhất Vĩnh's place in Gia Định.

When Nguyễn Văn Thoại, the protector of Cambodia who worked under Duyệt's command, died in 1829, Minh Mạng rejected Duyệt's replacement. He instead named one of his men to directly supervise the office—causing Duyệt to lose direct control over Cambodia.

In 1831, Minh Mạng dispatched officials to begin the incorporation of the South into the central Huế's administration. General Nguyễn Văn Quê was sent to oversee Gia Định: All of Duyệt's orders had to be approved by Quê before being sent to the Huế government for review. Quê dismantled Duyệt's military forces and sent them to central Vietnam. Weakened militarily, the South would no longer be able to resist either Huế or any foreign invasion.

Lê Văn Duyệt's death in 1832 gave Minh Mạng the momentum to act. In 1833, he decreed a prohibition of Christianity throughout the country. Priests who had been well tolerated under Lê Văn Duyệt were hunted down. Churches were destroyed and Christians were ordered to step on the cross to prove they had renounced their religion.[28] Those who did not were jailed and sentenced to death. Many either escaped abroad or suffered from martyrdom. Hồi lương convicts were removed from each province and transferred to the outermost frontier where they were mixed with other convicts. The government also looked at the commercial practices of Chinese.

The government turned its attention to Lê Văn Duyệt himself. Bạch Xuân Nguyên was assigned to unearth and manipulate any "crime" suggestive of resistance against the Huế government.[29] He found "evidence" of widespread corruption and abuse of power by the governor and his associates. He called for a posthumous humiliation of Lê Văn Duyệt,[30] the execution of 16 of his family members spread over three generations, and the arrest of many of his subordinates. Whether the charges were true or fabricated remains unknown.

Saigon under Lê Văn Khôi (Duyệt's adopted son) rose to rebel against Minh Mạng in the fifth lunar month of 1833. The rebels killed Bạch Xuân Nguyên and Nguyễn Văn Quê, the Huế-installed governor general. Surprise attacks were launched against imperial troops stationed in the South. Within three days, the six southernmost provinces fell into the rebels' hands.[31] Thousands of people who joined the revolt were inspired to avenge their benefactor,

Lê Văn Duyệt, and to secede from the Nguyễn regime. The same people who fought so hard to put the Nguyễn on the throne were at the core of taking the regime down. Christians, Chinese settlers, and former convicts who lost their rights under the Nguyễn's new edicts were at the root of this rebellion. Among them was the Chinese thanh nhân Lưu Tín, adopted son of Duyệt, who had spearheaded the revolt since its beginning. Khôi asked the Siamese to assist him in future battles against the Huế army. Siam sent an invasion force that was beaten back only in 1834.

The royal army recovered five provinces by the end of 1833. Over 1,000 Chinese were killed or captured before the rebels retreated into the Saigon citadel. Khôi died either from illness or poisoning in December 1834. The citadel fell to an assault in September 1835 after two years of resistance. Of the 499 persons who surrendered, only 66 were native Catholics. Following the surrender, thousands were killed by the royal army, and according to court records, 1,200 men and women, regardless of age, were buried alive in a mass grave close to the area where the 10,000 Chinese killed by the Tây Sơn were buried: "the Plain of Tombs." This was the second mass killing—senseless and tragic, albeit not as bad as the first one—of the Saigon citizenry. The six principal leaders were sent to Huế to be executed. Among them were the French missionary Marchand, accused of being the leader of the Catholic-rebel group; Nguyễn Văn Trầm, the leader of the hồi lương who took the command of the revolt after Lê Văn Khôi's death in 1834; and Lưu Tín, the Chinese leader.[32]

In the end, many Christians and Chinese were either killed, captured, or relocated to another region. More than 2,000 Gia Định Christians and Chinese fled to Siam. Any Chinese suspected of being a participant in the rebellion had four fingers of his right hand cut off before being exiled, and his property confiscated even after he surrendered.[33] Groups of ex-convict hồi lương were disbanded and their members were sent to new frontier lands. Intimidation by government forces through searches, arrests, and stationing of military forces outside Gia Định persisted until 1837. Gia Định people lost top ruling positions in their own land to strangers who came from northern or central regions of the country. The town felt like a colony of Huế after 1835. The resentment at the repression would lead to future insurrections with the thanh nhân Chinese as participants.

Lê Văn Duyệt's tomb was flogged because he was accused of planting the seeds of the revolt. Emperor Tự Đức resurrected his memory in 1848[34] and had his tomb rebuilt.

This was the first spontaneous rebellion against a Confucian state, a popular uprising that included all elements of the Southern society: Christians, Chinese, convicts, officials, and common people. The response was a violent repression, which killed all initiative and goodwill. Southerners were subdued to the point of not wanting to resist and/or help Huế in any endeavor.

Southern Identity

Lê Văn Khôi's rebellion suddenly exposed the huge rift between the central Huế government and southerners. What the latter saw as the right to do commerce and to practice religion was viewed differently by Minh Mạng. About southerners, he wrote,

> The vicious Huỳnh Công Lý (vice-governor-general) and the arrogant Lê Văn Duyệt
> ... led people to be contaminated by improper manners.... You became accustomed
> to ignoring higher authority.... Sĩ (literati) have fallen into laziness ... and you have
> become addicted to extravagance. Your way of entertainment is lecherous, you are
> attracted by opium, despise the value of rice, and are luxurious with clothes.... You
> did not know the existence of the central court.[35]

In the above edict, written after the rebellion was quelled, Minh Mạng suggested that: (1) southerners had acquired improper manners, (2) they were more interested in commerce than rice culture, and (3) the work of southern Confucian scholars was to be desired. Although these characteristics somewhat defined southerners, they were not entirely correct. They simply reflected the heterogeneous and multicultural aspects of a frontier country that had grown apart from the central government for many centuries. As the Huế-Thanh Hoá region was culturally different from the Thăng Long-Hanoi region, the Saigon-Gia Định area was even more different than the Huế-Thanh Hoá region. As they migrated southward, the Vietnamese had shed some of their original culture in order to embrace and accommodate native civilizations and cultures. And the further south they went, the more open and the less original they became. Gone were the strict Confucian rules, the original traditions, the classic wardrobe, and even the tonality of the voice. This was what Minh Mạng had witnessed at that time: a Saigon-Gia Định that was different than his traditional Huế-Thanh Hoá.

Southerners were thought to be "contaminated" because they did not follow traditional Confucian rules, which meant obedience to the king, practicing ancestor worship, and getting involved in rice culture instead of commerce.[36] Although Minh Mạng failed or forgot to acknowledge it, Confucianism had been replaced by Buddhism in the South by the Nguyễn to allow a better integration of the multi-ethnic groups into the new society. Besides, Gia Định was a peripheral region that was only incorporated into the rest of Vietnam until 1802 and was then run as a semi-autonomous state. It was, therefore, no wonder that southerners had for centuries possessed these "improper manners" that Minh Mạng—a strict Confucian—despised.

The fact that Gia Định markets were bustling with activity suggested a vibrant and developing trade, but not that Southerners were more involved in commerce than rice agriculture. Villages at that time still registered one merchant for every nine peasants: a number that showed that labor-intensive riziculture required a lot of manpower. Contrary to what Minh Mạng had suggested, the practice of smoking opium and wearing luxurious clothes was not a manifestation of depravation, but of the prosperity of the South compared to other regions in the country. As foreign and local junks brought in various foreign goods, habits of luxury began spreading even to the conforming literati.[37]

Minh Mạng was also not impressed about the work of Southern Confucian scholars. He called them lazy, for Confucian teaching was barely visible in the South and the number of Southerners passing state examinations was low. This may be related to many factors. Proportionally, the Southern population was much smaller than that of the North, as suggested by the number of registered male adults in the 1841 census: 122,410 and 970,516 respectively. Northern students had a longer and richer tradition of preparing for the state examination. Economic opportunities, which were plentiful in the South, led to a better and more comfortable life conducting business rather than serving as government officials. Even after graduation, none of the eight cử nhân graduates in 1813 became officials. This data suggests Southerners' indifference toward state examination and governmental position.[38]

It is interesting to note that while they adopted Confucian theories from the Chinese, the Nguyễn practiced them differently. While the Chinese did not see anything wrong with doing commerce, the Nguyễn shunned it and stuck to the rule that peasants were more valuable than merchants. The latter were the least desirable people within the society at the time: first came the sĩ (literati), then nông (peasant), công (artisan), and finally thương (merchant). Minh Mạng and the Nguyễn failed to see the age of commerce coming to Asia and to accept the fact that commerce not only symbolized modernity, but also brought riches to the nation. What the Vietnamese shunned was turned over to the Chinese, who, from that time onward, took control over all the trade in Vietnam until today. While the Chinese increased their stranglehold on the economy, the Vietnamese did not fare well by limiting themselves to farming, soldiering, artisanry, and officialdom.

Faced with unruly Southerners, Minh Mạng decided to "cultivate" (giáo hóa) them by building schools at the prefecture and district levels and to assimilate non–Vietnamese southerners. Roughly 30 percent of the southern population belonged to the latter group (Chinese, Khmers, Chams, and others). They were forced to assimilate into the Vietnamese culture through incorporation of ethnic villages into Vietnamese villages, interracial marriages, and sending their children to Vietnamese schools. Resistance to assimilation resulted in a series of insurrections that tore apart the South from 1841 to 1847.[39] Southern Vietnamese who did not like the Huế government from the beginning were forced to take a stand and to side with the central regime while non–Vietnamese southerners would take the opposite side. The southern society, which under Lê Văn Duyệt formed a common block against the Huế government, became radically divided. When the French came in 1859, southern Vietnamese Confucian scholars and landlords would support Huế and resist French invasion while Catholics, Chinese settlers, and some landowners—who had suffered under the Nguyễn—would side with the French.[40]

Weakened by this internal division, the South did not put up a strong fight against the invasion.

Saigon Before the Arrival of the French

The most impressive building viewed from the river was the Saigon citadel, also named Bát Quái citadel. For soldiers who fought with spears, lances, halberds, and muzzleloaders, the citadel, located high on a plateau, was an impressive structure to take down. Built under Nguyễn Ánh in 1790, it was a grandiose Vauban-type fort, the largest in the South. Although Bát Quái denotes its physical structure (eight diagrams), it was also known as Quy or Turtle citadel, whose thick walls would hold off any frontal assault.

It was comprised of two walls separated by a ditch of 75.5 m in width and 6.8 m in depth. The outer and inner circumferences were 3,820 m and 2,592 m respectively. The wall was 6.3 m high. Nguyễn Ánh's palace was located in the middle of the citadel. In 1830, Lê Văn Duyệt had the citadel reinforced to increase its resistance against foreign attacks. Lê Văn Khôi only needed a few hundred troops to hold thousands of royal troops at bay for a couple of years. The real problem lay in the royal cannons, which were unable to blast through the walls of the citadel because of their weak fires.[41]

Following the rebels' surrender, Minh Mạng decreed that all citadels in Vietnam must be smaller than his Huế citadel "to be in line with hierarchy." Placing his prestige before the country's security, he ordered the Bát Quái dismantled in 1835: The latter had lasted only 45 years (1790–1835).

A year later, he ordered the Phụng citadel built. Ten thousand people were requisitioned for the project, which did not last long. Walls were built with materials removed from the previous citadel. The Phụng citadel was roughly half the size of the Bát Quái, with an outer circumference of 1,960 m, a ditch of 52 m wide and 3 m deep and a 4.7 m high wall. It was located in the northeast corner of the old Bát Quái. Minh Mạng thought that a small citadel, even if taken by rebels, would be easier to repossess than a large one like the Bát Quái. The next rebels would not be locals, but foreign invaders who would easily breach the earthen walls.

If citadels were almost impregnable in the 16th or 17th century, they were obsolete in the face of modern cannons. While Huế soldiers took two years to take down the Bát Quái citadel, on February 17, 1859, the French needed only two days to capture the Phụng citadel. They blew it up weeks later with the help of 32 well-placed mines.[42] The Phụng citadel lasted 23 years (1836–1859).

	Bát Quái (Quy)	Phụng
Circumference (outer)	3,820 m	1,960 m
Each side	955 m	490 m
Wall height	6.34 m	4.70 m
Width of ditch	72.52 m	52.07 m
Depth of ditch	6.82 m	3.19 m
Date built	1790	1836
Date destroyed	1835	1859

Table III. Characteristics of the two citadels

The map of Saigon drawn by Trần Văn Học in 1815 clearly showed two distinct communities. Bén Nghé (the administrative and Vietnamese center with the *Bát Quái* citadel) in the east, bordered by the arroyos of Thị Nghè and Bén Nghé and the bend of the Saigon River. Heavy human concentration was noted on the eastern and southern sides of the citadel while the northern and western sides were sparsely populated. Two large roads connected Bén Nghé with Chợ Lớn, the Chinese and commercial western center where "some streets are paved with flags; and the quays of stone and brick stone work extend nearly a mile along the river."[43]

From Bén Nghé, rice was shipped all the way to Manila, Batavia (Indonesia) or Malacca (Malaysia) on board Chinese boats and foreign junks. The trade surplus was used to open up canals and improve riverine transportation.

Surrounding hamlets and villages had their own specialized commercial and trade shops consistent with the tradition of the time. Some sold stones, others iron and so on: Chợ Sỏi (Stone market), Chợ Quán, Chợ Lò Rèn (Iron market), Chợ Bình An, etc.

The Naval shipyard of Ba Sơn—where Nguyễn Ánh had his ships built—was located on the eastern side of the citadel: "There were one hundred and fifty gallies [*sic*] of most beautiful construction, hauled up under sheds; they were from forty to one hundred feet long, some of them mounting sixteen guns of three pounds caliber.... There were besides forty other gallies afloat."[44]

Close to the riverbank lay a long row of nice buildings that served as storage areas for rice, a royal monopoly and the exportation of which was prohibited and punishable by decapitation. "A large Siamese junk was lying hauled up in a creek, the captain and officers of which had been executed, a short time previous to our arrival, and the crew was then in prison, for a violation of this edict."[45]

Of the monuments built prior to the French arrival, only a few pagodas remained (Giác Lâm, Giác Viên, Thiên Hậu) and Lăng Ông or Lê Văn Duyệt Mausoleum. When Duyệt died in 1832, only a tomb and a small mausoleum were built for him. In his ire in 1835, Minh Mạng had everything torn down and the tomb "chained" for a thousand generations.[46] Luckily for him, King Tự Đức raised his memory and had a new mausoleum built in 1841. It was enlarged in 1847 and upgraded on many occasions, the last time by Indian architect Hamin in 1973.[47] Following the fall of Saigon, the communist government attempted to diminish the influence of *Lăng Ông* by banning any maintenance and encouraging thieves and addicts to hang around the mausoleum, creating an unsafe area for worshipers. People, however, came to pray at the mausoleum because Duyệt was considered a responsive deity. Later, after recognizing the immense role of the mausoleum on the psyche of the people, the authorities allowed its restoration. The mausoleum became one of the most popular places of worship in Vietnam.[48]

*   *   *

If the feud between the royalists and the Tây Sơn led to the destruction of Saigon in 1782, the feud between Minh Mạng and Lê Văn Duyệt caused the second military and economic destruction of the town in 1835.

The Southern frontier, or Nam Kỳ Lục Tỉnh,[49] was a melting pot of free spirits and Duyệt diehards, who looked for ways to survive, thrive, and build a new nation. Not having lived among these people, Minh Mạng failed to acknowledge their particularities. He not only did not know how to woo them, but he also tried to suppress their independent spirit, which was at the core of southern economic growth and expansion. By antagonizing them, Minh Mạng became a "foreigner" in his own land. When the French came, some of these factions did not want to fight for a king they did not trust and many sided with the invaders instead.

To consolidate his central power around Huế, the political capital, Minh Mạng tore apart and downgraded Saigon by destroying its economic center and shutting down its vision of modernity and riches. The result was a revolt and an outflow of people—businessmen, traders, and craftsmen—to Cambodia, Thailand, Malaysia and the Philippines.[50] The economic center and the shipbuilding business moved from Saigon to Bangkok. While the Huế regime got stronger with time, it also became more conservative, repressive, and less open to modernity and commerce. Its assimilation policy worsened the political instability and caused widespread insurrections. Huế's regressive attitude weakened the state socially, economically and militarily, and facilitated France's conquest of Vietnam.

4

Colonial Saigon
(1858–1920)

Twenty-seven years after being erased on Minh Mạng's orders as a southern center of power, with its best troops and generals dispatched far away to central and North Vietnam, its citizens demoralized, Catholics and Chinese uneasy and unwilling to support the Huế regime, the Saigon/Gia Định region could only offer a weak resistance to western invaders.

The Capture of Saigon

The first missionaries (Spanish, Italian, Portuguese) arrived in Vietnam in the mid–16th century while the French came later: the renowned Alexandres de Rhodes in 1624 and Pigneau de Behaine in Hà Tiên in 1767.[1] It was only in the 19th century that Europeans and some Americans who had been circling the South China Sea plotted ways to establish commercial enclaves in Southeast Asia. They were just looking for the right excuse or the right time to jump in. That desire only increased when Britain easily seized Hong Kong in 1842.[2]

In March 1843, the *Heroine* arrived in Đà Nẵng harbor, asking for the release of five imprisoned missionaries. King Thiệu Trị complied. In June 1845, the *Alimene* arrived in Đà Nẵng, requesting the release of French missionary Lefebre. The latter was released and transported to Singapore. Lefebre, who illegally re-entered Vietnam in 1846, was captured and released this time into British custody. The headstrong bishop, however, re-entered Vietnam illegally the following year.[3]

Under pressure from French Catholics, Napoleon III wrote a decree from Paris requesting that Vietnam release all imprisoned missionaries, give them the freedom to teach religion, and open its ports for commerce with Europeans. The decree precipitated a diplomatic deadlock that ended with the French Navy shelling Vietnamese ships and defenses in the port of Đà Nẵng on April 15, 1847.[4] Although the French left empty-handed, five bronze-plate Vietnamese vessels were sunk and many Vietnamese died as a result. King Thiệu Trị became enraged when he learned about the unprovoked shelling and its casualties; he immediately ordered missionaries banned from his kingdom.

The Đà Nẵng incident set the tone for future French policy: whatever could not be obtained through negotiations would be taken by force.[5] "Gunboat diplomacy," which had been initiated in Asia by Great Britain against China during the Opium Wars, was later duplicated in Vietnam by the French.

In 1852, Napoleon III again felt pressured by various factions in his government to take firm action in Vietnam. The most vocal proponents of intervention were the missionaries from the Societe des Missions Étrangères who, arriving in Asia after the Spanish, Portuguese, and English, desired to have their own sphere of influence. The Ministry of Navy and the naval officers stationed in the Far East also proposed a conquest of Vietnam to offset other European powers. Then, there were the merchants and the masses who were always ready to jump in whenever the costs of these adventures were not too prohibitive. A commission finally recommended that France obtain a protectorate over Vietnam. Cited in this decision were France's opposition to "persecution" of Catholic missionaries in Vietnam, "imperial ambition and commercial opportunity" as well as the prestige of having colonies.[6]

In 1857, Napoleon III, using the decapitation of Spanish Dominican Monsignor Diaz in Tonkin as the reason, ordered Vice Admiral Rigault de Genouilly, commander of the French Far East fleet, to land in Đà Nẵng. He was one of the two officers responsible for the bombing of Đà Nẵng a decade earlier. A combined Franco-Spanish force was assembled in front of the port on August 31, 1858. The French had 2,500 troops and 13 warships and the Spanish one warship and 450 troops. The plan was to attack Đà Nẵng, followed by an overland assault on Huế, the Vietnamese capital, located 40 miles away.

The attack on September 1, 1858, was checked by an elaborate system of trenches and walls designed by General Nguyễn Tri Phương. The invaders were repulsed and they settled in for a siege on Đà Nẵng beach which they thought would be short. Five months of fierce combat ended in a stalemate that shook the confidence of the French. The lack of fresh food and water and the poor hygiene of the soldiers who were pinned on the beach led to a disabling cholera. As the disease spread around, the morale of the French troops sunk. The rain that steadily fell on the region dampened their spirits. Genouilly accused the missionaries of having misled the French about the simplicity of the enterprise, the help of local Christians that never materialized, and the harsh climate.[7]

Unable to take over Đà Nẵng, Genouilly set his sight on Saigon, which he expected would offer less resistance than the former. Once captured, Saigon would serve as bargaining chip against the Huế government. He asked for and received permission from the Navy Ministry to go ahead with the operation.

He took two thirds of his troops, along with two ships and three gunboats, and left the rest in Đà Nẵng. Upon his arrival on February 10, 1859, he bombarded Vũng Tàu—at the mouth of the Saigon River—and easily overran its local fort. For five days, he blasted his way on the river and destroyed three river barriers and 12 wooden fortresses. No Vietnamese boat was encountered. Saigon's commander, General Võ Duy Ninh, who had noticed that his troops were not well trained in modern warfare, had them undergo military training right at the time of the French arrival in Saigon. Therefore, only a small number of troops were left to guard the citadel.

On the right side of the Saigon River stood many houses built of wood and covered with palm leaves. There were a few a brick houses here and there with red tiles that brightened the view. One could also see a pagoda with curved roofs. A couple of small arroyos served as parking places for local junks. On the second row grew palm trees along with lush local vegetation. Hundreds of junks that pressed against the riverbank gave an image of a small floating village. Vietnamese, Chinese, and Hindus walked along the streets. On the Chinese arroyo stood nicer houses, some very old, that had withstood the rebellion of 1833. Close by was a farm hidden behind palm trees.[8]

The citadel was visible from the river. It was located high on the plateau about 800 meters (half a mile) from the river (just to the southwest of present-day National Zoo) on the south side of the Thị Nghè arroyo, and it occupied an area of about 2.5 acres. That was the Saigon the French saw in 1859: a busy trading and commercial town with a mixed population.

On February 16, Genouilly had the citadel shot pointblank. Following a short exchange of fire between Genouilly's ships and the fort's cannons, French and Spanish troops went ashore. They moved in two columns and attacked the northeast wall under the command of General des Pallires. By 10:00, they had scaled the walls. Surprised and unable to resist, its defenders fled. The fort fell on February 17, 1859—after less than two days of fighting.[9] Although the Vietnamese counterattacked, they were easily pushed back.

The local navy was blocked for three months in one of the river channels. Cornered and unable to get outside assistance, the mandarin commander, instead of surrendering, had all the vessels burned and released his soldiers from duty. He then killed himself in front of his staff by slicing his belly open.[10]

The French landed in the town and found its citadel deserted. There were "85,000 kilograms of powder, saltpeter, sulfur, lead, military equipment, rice to feed 8,000 men and 130,000 francs in local money."[11] In Saigon, they found a deep water river port with many local products: white ground sugar, abundant dyeing wood, splendid wax and cinnamon, and the exotic merchandise they were looking for.

Genouilly then received word that the contingent in Đà Nẵng had come under attack and was in danger of being overrun. No reinforcements would be forthcoming because Napoleon III was preparing to declare war to Austria. Not having enough soldiers to control the town, Genouilly decided to blow up the citadel to prevent the Vietnamese from retaking it and waging another attack. He also ordered the rice depot burned. When they came back two years later in 1861, the fire was still smoldering. White dust was seen on the ground. In certain spots it appeared that rice grains had kept their shapes, but it was just ash; wind or light pressure could disperse it into dust.[12] In 1859, the French left the river posts under the control of a small contingent of French soldiers. Genouilly sailed north and upon his arrival pushed the Vietnamese back into Đà Nẵng. He tried to negotiate a settlement with the Huế court but was unsuccessful. Taking ill suddenly, he was replaced by Admiral Page.

The French troops pulled out of Đà Nẵng in February 1860 to assist in a multi-nation attack against China (second Opium War). Surprised by the withdrawal, the Huế court sent reinforcements to Saigon under the command of Generals Nguyễn Tri Phương and Phạm Thế Hiển. With 20,000 men in hand, they reinforced the defensive complex of Kỳ Hòa, west of Saigon. The complex was the gateway to the southern provinces and their riches.

The Battle of Kỳ Hòa (1861)

When Genouilly left Saigon in February 1859, the small Franco-Spanish contingent in Saigon remained under the command of Jaureguiberry, the second in command. The French repaired the Phùng citadel and used it as a stronghold. They also upgraded a former Vietnamese post at Cây Mai into a fort. In April 1959, Jaureguiberry, wanting to expand his control of the town, launched an attack against the Kỳ Hòa fort, which resulted in 14 casualties and 31 wounded out of the 800 participating soldiers. Finding the losses too high for the small foreign garrison to bear, he wisely decided against any new attack.[13]

Admiral Page arrived in December 1859 to replace Genouilly. He delineated lines of defense, had a hospital, lodging, and storage areas built, and opened the port of Saigon for trade on February 22, 1860. Sixty-six ships and 100 junks loaded 60,000 tons of rice in just four months and made plenty of money in Hong Kong and Singapore. Nearby villagers came to participate in the trade.[14]

The Vietnamese army in the meantime settled in the Kỳ Hòa fort three miles away. In March 1860, about 10,000 Vietnamese soldiers began to lay siege on the French garrison. In June 1860, they dug a trench from Kỳ Hòa toward Cây Mai with the intention of cutting the latter off from Chợ Lớn where all the storage areas were located. The French reacted by occupying two nearby pagodas, which they named des Mares (due to the presence of two ponds) and Clochetons. The latter, which was only a half-mile away from a Kỳ Hòa outpost, was reinforced with sand removed from the tombs of the Plain of Tombs. In the middle of the night of July 3 and 4, 1860, Vietnamese soldiers launched a surprise attack on the pagoda of Clochetons, which was held by 100 Spanish and 60 French troops. The attack lasted one hour until reinforcements came from the citadel. There would be no more attack, although the Vietnamese continued to dig the trench, which, instead of aiming straight toward the French positions, then took a course parallel to them. The French just held the partly destroyed citadel, the Cây Mai fort, a few pagodas, and the riverbank. The Vietnamese controlled the outskirts of Saigon, Kỳ Hòa fort, and had access to Chợ Lớn.[15] The stalemate lasted until 1861 as neither side was strong enough to dislodge the other.

The Plain of Kỳ Hòa was a flat and lightly wooded area with scattered ravines and gullies. It stood on the western edge of Chợ Lớn and the Plain of Tombs. The French had to cross that terrain should they decide to frontally attack the Vietnamese defensive works, which had been strengthened for about a year. Trenches had been dug and lengthened, walls heightened and thickened, and outposts and obstacles built. The main earthen complex consisted of five connected, walled enclosures that sat astride the main road to Cambodia. It measured one kilometer wide with wooden watchtowers outside the walls. The complex stretched over 2.5 kilometers along a northwest-southeast axis. Extending west and south ran a network of trenches, outposts, and obstacles more than 12 kilometers long.

The Vietnamese had superiority in their numbers and defensive network. Troops, however, were poorly trained and armed only with halberds, lances, pikes and antiquated muzzleloaders. The artillery was old and not precise.

In January 1861, after completing the Chinese expedition, 3,500 French troops under Vice Admiral Leonard Charner were dispatched back to Saigon to complete their conquest of Cochinchina.[16]

Instead of a frontal attack, which would have met stiff resistance and thus could have been very bloody, Charner decided to attack from the southern edge of the Kỳ Hòa Plain, starting from the pagodas. From the westernmost pagoda, the Cây Mai pagoda, a dirt road led to the southern defensive outpost of the Kỳ Hòa complex less than two miles away. The French called the outpost the "Redoubt," which ironically had been built under the direction of a French engineer. Once the Redoubt was taken, troops would move along the road north north-west to attack the main Kỳ Hòa fortification from the rear. They could intercept Vietnamese reinforcements and at the same time avoid the formidable frontal defenses.

The French thus moved troops and cannons to the Cây Mai pagoda and began attacking on February 24, 1861, at 5 A.M. under the command of General de Vassoigne. The ship cannons opened fire on Kỳ Hoa. Heavy guns set on the pagoda's ground also fired at the Vietnamese fortifications while troops moved toward the objective in three columns. First came the infantry, then the sappers with their ladders, the marines and navy infantry with their ladders, the artillery, the ambulance service, 600 Chinese coolies and 100 beasts of burden. The Vietnamese signaled the alert by banging on their gongs and firing back. Since the range of their guns was shorter than that of the French, they redoubled their firing effort; as a result, white smoke was seen surrounding the ramparts of the Redoubt.[17]

French artillery, consisting of 4- and 12-pound cannons and howitzers, was pulled by horses toward a position about 0.8 miles from the Vietnamese defenses, lined up and pounded the Reboubt. Counter-fire from artillery and small arms was heavy. Infantrymen took a break while cannons were firing. Orders were given to move to a distance of 0.4 miles from enemy lines. Guns were lined up again and pounded the fort. At close distance, the gun forts were precise and caused casualties, among them General de Vassoigne and Spanish Colonel Gutierrez. Firing was heavy from both sides. Charner took over the command and gave the attack order. Infantry moved ahead in two columns. They struggled through a row of obstacles while the enemy fired at them. Ladders were applied against the walls and grappling hooks were thrown over the ramparts. Once French troops were able to climb over the wall, Vietnamese resistance ceased and defenders retreated. The attack lasted two hours. The French moved forward but encountered only sporadic resistance. They took a break at 3 P.M., sustained a mild attack at 4 P.M., and moved again at 6 P.M. At dusk, they camped in a village about one mile from the main Kỳ Hòa complex.

On February 25, the attack on the Kỳ Hòa fort proceeded like the one on the Redoubt. Attackers moved to 0.8 miles from the fort, positioned their cannons and shot at the fort. They moved to 0.4 then 0.2 miles and repeated the same procedure. Counter-fire was intense, causing high casualties since troops were on the open. Obstacles were plentiful in front of the fort walls. There were six rows of trous-de-loup (wolf-pit) hidden under a layer of grass and separated by palisades; seven rows of spikes; two large ditches with bamboo stakes and filled with three feet of muddy water; a sharp five-foot slope studded with sturdy cheveaux-de-frise.[18] Attackers used their ladders to cross over the trous-de-loup. They climbed the walls on ladders or on their friends' shoulders. Defenders on the ramparts were waiting for them, shooting them pointblank or pushing them down with their spears and halberds. Attackers threw grenades and grappling hooks. They climbed over the outer wall of the fort and met stiff resistance. Defenders pulled back into the fort and fired back at the invaders.

Resistance was so intense that Charner almost pulled out his troops. Captain Laregnere and Lieutenant Colonel Testard were severely wounded and died during the night. A company of native troops working for the French scaled the back wall of the fort while French engineers managed to breach the main gate. Caught between the two forces, the defenders withdrew. The bitterness of the fighting enraged the attackers who slaughtered any Vietnamese who could not escape. By late morning, the French took complete control of the Kỳ Hòa complex and with it the key to the South. The French and Spanish forces suffered 225 casualties. At least 300 defenders were dead. An unknown number of fallen local soldiers had been retrieved by the defenders. They left behind 150 cannons of all sizes, spears, halberds, and stone-guns.[19]

The French proceeded to conquer the three neighboring provinces of Gia Định, Định Tường, and Biên Hòa. Other southern citadels fell one by one: Tân Bình on February 28, 1861, Định Tường on April 12, 1861, and Vĩnh Long on February 23, 1862. With the dismantling of the imperial army, rebel forces switched to guerrilla tactics. They harassed French forces in the countryside but were ineffective against citadels.

The French were not alone in the fight: They were helped by Catholics who began to join them in September 1858. One group of northern Catholics reached Đà Nẵng and was trained by the French at the Tiên Cha camp. While one detachment fought with the French in Đà Nẵng, the other was sent to Saigon to assist with the Kỳ Hòa assault. After the battle, they remained with the French as soldiers, interpreters, guides, or coolies. Because of this association, the Huế court ordered the imprisonment of Catholics who assisted the foreigners as well as the close monitoring of Catholics. Edicts were, however, not uniformly applied. Even in Nghệ An during that period, Nguyễn Trường Tộ, a great scholar, was invited to teach at a northern Catholic seminary. Two high-level province officials were downgraded in rank for allowing Vietnamese Catholics to travel freely in exchange for French medications.[20]

Charner was replaced in November 1861 by Admiral Bonnard, who increased the number of attacks and expanded the territory under French control. By April 1862, having overextended himself, he sought to negotiate a treaty with the Huế court, but his efforts were to no avail.[21]

The success of the French invasion was due to two main factors: the superiority of French armament and the rebellion of a Catholic Lê pretender. Lê Duy Phụng was raised from a young age by missionaries who sent him to Penang for further schooling. In 1855, after his return to Vietnam, he requested French support for an anti–Nguyễn rebellion in return for various concessions but was not taken seriously. In 1861, he reappeared in Tonkin at the head of a rebellious group comprised of northern Catholics, Lê dynasty partisans, and Chinese and Vietnamese pirates. He again asked for French assistance in order to establish a "theocratic kingdom" under the protection of France. Although Bonnard dismissed Phụng as an illegitimate pretender and an unreliable potential ally, he was, however, glad that Phụng's army attacked Hà Nội in 1862, tying down the imperial forces on the northern front. He was well informed of Phụng's moves by the missionaries. The Huế court, of course, was not happy to have to deal at the same time with the French army in Saigon and Phụng's army in Hà Nội, and could only offer minimal opposition to the French demands.[22]

The French, in general, were impressed by the martial abilities of their opponents, especially in Đà Nẵng where the latter resisted the invaders for three and a half years without faltering. The main problem was related to the military situation in the South. In order to subdue that region, Minh Mạng from 1833 onward had sent the South's best generals and troops to serve elsewhere, leaving Saigon weakened and almost unprotected. On the technical level, the Vietnamese had only 5,000 rifles for 32,000 troops; the rest were equipped with spears and sharpened staves. Their rifles were muzzle-loaders with a firing range of 300 meters. Loading and firing were technically difficult and training was limited. Each soldier was allowed to fire one shot a year for practice. The Europeans used breech loaders that fired with ease and accuracy. Vietnamese canons were cumbersome and inaccurate while European artillery pieces were light and precise. The French's superiority in armament easily offset the number of Vietnamese ground troops. With a few thousand troops, they were able to defeat the overwhelming Vietnamese forces at Kỳ Hòa. While Vietnam had only seven steamships that were only used for river patrolling, the Europeans had at their disposal 70 warships after the mission in China.[23]

Overall, the French had complete control of the sea lanes and proceeded with the blockade of central Vietnam. By that time, they had realized the importance of Saigon's rice supply to Huế—especially at a time when drought played a role in that area. French vessels attacked fishing, transport, and commercial boats along the coastline. They also terrorized peasants and razed the villages of Khánh Hòa and Quảng Nam. They not only interfered with the commercial traffic from Saigon to Huế, but also with traffic in the north. Their goal was to "reduce those who remained under Huế's authority to misery or famine." That policy of piracy and terror exacted its toll on the country's economy. The price of rice in Huế skyrocketed as a result. People went hungry and the state suffered a financial and moral crisis. Attempts to bring rice in through other routes were also unsuccessful.[24]

The 1862 Saigon Treaty

The Huế court deliberated lengthily about how to deal with the French and it fell on Phan Thanh Giản, a southern mandarin, to negotiate the return of the three eastern provinces.

The court in 1860 was divided between the chủ chiến (war advocates) and chủ hòa (peace advocates). The chủ chiến, represented by Nguyễn Tri Phương, Hoàng Diệu, Hoàng Tả Viêm, and Tôn Thất Thuyết, were the same people who advocated a tough stance against missionaries and Vietnamese Catholics. As righteous people, they wanted to keep on fighting against the invaders although they did not have any strategy with which to confront the French's armament superiority. They also failed to rally the masses—especially northerners and southerners whom the central government had antagonized in the past—against the invaders. They were also aware of the French's territorial ambitions. However, they lacked confidence and a resolute will to victory. All they could do was sacrifice themselves in order to preserve moral purity. Such was the case of Võ Duy Ninh, the commander of the citadel, who killed himself rather than surrender after the fall of Saigon.

The chủ hòa were represented by Phan Thanh Giản, Nguyễn Bá Nghi, Trương Đăng Quê, and Lâm Duy Hiệp. Aware of the French's armament superiority, they felt that people would only suffer more in the case of a protracted war against the French. Nguyễn Bá Nghi had personally witnessed that superiority when he saw the French navy sink five Vietnamese bronze-plated ships in the wink of an eye in Đà Nẵng in 1847. However, they misunderstood the French intentions and did not understand the depth of the French territorial ambitions.[25] Had they been aware of the dark motives of the French, they would have been more careful.

After the chủ hòa won Tự Đức's approval, Phan Thanh Giản and Lâm Duy Hiệp were dispatched to Saigon, then occupied by the French, to negotiate peace. The "unequal treaty"—also known as the Hòa Ước Nhâm Tuất or the Treaty of the Year Nhâm Tuất—was signed on June 6, 1862:

> Granting the three eastern provinces (Gia Định, Mỹ Tho, Định Tường) and the island of Poulo Condore to France,
> Opening three ports to trade with the west,
> Granting missionaries freedom of action.
> Paying four million piasters in indemnity over ten years.

Tự Đức became upset once he was made aware of the details of the treaty. Although he had explicitly told his negotiators not to cede any land, they obviously did not listen to him. He severely criticized them in front of the court. But when other court officials suggested that the offenders be punished, he argued that they were "talented and virtuous." He also kept them in their former positions, which allowed them to continue negotiations with the French in Gia Định.[26] The court ratified the treaty in April 1863.

By 1863, Giản, who was 67, had submitted his retirement twice. Both requests were denied by emperor Tự Đức. He was re-assigned to the post of finance minister, which he completed so successfully that his titles were returned to him as a reward. He was then posted as governor of the three western provinces despite his continued request for retirement. Having traveled abroad to negotiate the return of the eastern provinces and having witnessed France's modernity and power, he realized his country's weaknesses and foresaw the future loss of the three western provinces. Aware of France's territorial ambitions, he warned the Huế court about western military might and even requested troops and armaments to beef up the defenses of the south, but his efforts were to no avail.

True to his Confucian education, Tự Đức reassured Giản that everything would fall into place if a person was confident and righteous—fierce tigers would even run away, crocodiles swim away for "everyone listens to *nghĩa*."[27]

The French did not see it that way. Sensing minimal resistance to their conquest and using the excuse that the Huế government had encouraged local resistance, they moved their frigates along the Mekong River on a foggy summer night in 1867 and dropped anchor in front of the town of Vĩnh Long. Threatening the fort with their cannons, they forced the viceroy, Giản, to cede the remaining provinces: Vĩnh Long, Hà Tiên, and An Giang. Caught off-guard by the attack, the old Giản surrendered.

Having failed his emperor, he decided to commit suicide. He gathered all his seals and 23 of the royal awards he had acquired in a lifetime of distinguished service and returned them to Huế. He mentioned that the French were well armed with powerful cannons that could penetrate any wall. "Therefore, I have written to all the mandarins and all the officers to break their lances and hand over the forts without fighting.... In sparing the people great misfortune, I have become a traitor to our King in handing over without resistance the provinces that are his.... I deserve only to die."[28] In his straw-hut, he tried to starve himself to death, but was still alive two weeks later. He took an extra dose of poison, which killed him at the age of 71.

After Phan Thanh Giản's suicide and Lâm Duy Hiệp's death from natural causes, the chủ chiến group set out to take revenge on the two negotiators who were found guilty of negligence in ceding the provinces. However, in view of Giản's suicide, they suggested he be spared posthumous decapitation (trăm hầu). Tự Đức was not happy with the recommendation. He decreed that Giản and Hiệp's titles and positions be revoked, their names chiseled off from the stele of degree-holders, and their bodies exhumed for decapitation. He stated that the severe treatment would serve as a warning for those who were still living. The message, however, was ambiguous at best since the court had not done anything since 1862 to promote resistance or to wage war against the French.

Phan Phú Thu, in his funeral oration for Phan Thanh Giản, said: "You have accepted the role of the culprit in order to bring some repose during a difficult period.... The surrender of the territory must ... be decided by the king. Everyone considers you to have been in error, but how many people know the true situation in our country?"[29]

When the 1862 Saigon treaty was signed, resistance flared up throughout the South. Local patriots led uprisings and rallied people to their chính nghĩa (just cause). These fighters were called nghĩa quân (righteous soldiers). Since the court did not support them, they pilloried king and mandarins in verse and song: "Phan and Lâm sell out the country; the court does not care about the people."[30]

Resistance groups rallied under the banners: "Pacify the South, Wipe Out Heresy," "Royalist National Salvation," and "People Self Defense." Although they showed heroism in abundance, they did not have the economic or technological means to oppose the French. Protest literature appeared overnight.

The blind poet Nguyễn Đình Chiểu (1822–1888) chastised those who collaborated with or did not fight against the foreigners. He refused to use or touch anything of western origin, even soap powder. He wrote many poems encouraging resistance and non-cooperation in order to preserve moral integrity. "Why ape those creatures garbed in wool?" he once wrote.[31] In another poem, he clearly defined conformity and betrayal of traditional values, urging people to rally to family and country.[32]

Many volunteers turned out to fight against the French. The best known guerrilla fighter was Trương Định or Trương Công Định. Born in central Vietnam in 1820 or 1821, he moved to Gia Định with his father, a colonel in the royal army, who was transferred there. At a young age, he was known for his martial skills. Instead of returning home after his father unexpectedly died, he married the daughter of a wealthy Định Tường landowner and used her dowry to establish a đồn điền (military colony). After Saigon fell and the commander Võ Duy Ninh committed suicide, royal troops fled in disarray. Trương Định rallied the troops and added his đồn điền men to form a new army.

Starting with only 600 men (200 đồn điền colons, 200 disbanded royal troops, and 200 local militia), his forces gradually grew to 1,000 men. Despite the small size of this army, he was able to cause a lot of trouble to the French forces because of his knowledge of the terrain and his guerrilla tactics. The court elevated him to deputy regimental commander (phó lãnh binh). He also treated his tenants better than other đồn điền owners. Other armed groups soon arrived under the direction of Trần Thiện Chánh and Nguyễn Hữu Huấn, better known as Thủ Khoa Huấn, to provide help.[33]

By 1861, he had retaken Qui Sơn and his troops numbered 6,000. Because he had instilled discipline and organization in his troops, the king was happy with his work and promoted him to commander of all southern nghĩa quân. Truong attacked the French in the province of Gò Công. The skillful attack caught the French by surprise. Pallu de la Barrière commented that the Vietnamese, instead of being cowed by French armament superiority, were driven by a "spirit of national independence."[34]

Although after the fact the Huế court encouraged resistance to the French by giving rewards to individuals and villages, it slowly distanced itself from these activities for fear of provoking retribution from the invaders, which could mean more territorial loss for Vietnam. After the signing of the 1862 treaty, the king ordered the rebels to disband and provincial heads to capture any rebel working in their provinces. The goal was to prevent any rebel from giving the French any reason to expand their invasion.

Phan Thanh Giản wrote a letter to Định asking him to lay down his arms: "Since the Court has signed the peace treaty, the duty of officials is to call off their struggle. There is no reason for any exception to this rule. Loyalty and filial piety deserve equal praise, but both have limits not to be exceeded." Knowing obedience had its limits too, Định replied that since southerners would not accept the partition, he was convinced he had acted according to people's will and that of heaven. He continued: "We are therefore determined to give our lives to our struggle.... As long as you speak of peace and surrender, we are determined not to obey the Court's order."[35]

For ten long months, the partisans waited for a change of heart from the Court, but it did not come. It was like expecting rain in the dry season. As Trương Định refused to submit, he was stripped of his titles and honors. Although he asked the king for forgiveness for having disobeyed him, he felt that as a man of honor, he should continue to fight against the French. He told his partisans, "The Emperor calls us rebels but in the depth of his heart, he cannot help but praise our loyalty. When the day of victory comes, not only the Emperor will forgive us, he will furthermore grant us all kinds of awards."[36]

Định waged a furious guerrilla war without support from the king and court for a few years,[37] hoping to bleed the French slowly and letting his ally, malaria, compensate for his inferiority in armaments. He and his soldiers would launch attacks on isolated French positions whenever they felt they could over-power them. Otherwise, they would disappear, leaving the French frustrated. He, however, had no backup gathering intelligence about his enemy and was almost fighting in the dark.

In February 1863, with sufficient reinforcements, Admiral Bonnard was able to dislodge him from his hideout. Forced to flee, he lost many soldiers and a large amount of weaponry. On August 19, 1863, betrayed by a former rebel who revealed his hideout to the French, he was ambushed and wounded. Facing imminent capture, he killed himself instead of surrendering.[38] His son, Trương Quyền, then 20 years of age, carried on his struggle for a while longer, but, again, had minimal success.

Resistance slowly tapered off following Trương Định's death. Some nghĩa quân continued to fight and others, seeing the futility of resistance, decided to cooperate with the French. Others just moved out of the French-controlled South and others still, like Nguyễn Đình Chiểu and the intellectual elite, with-drew to themselves and abstained from doing any work for the French to pre-serve their moral purity.

Politico-religious sects, however, picked up the resistance where the Pop-ular Self Defense Movement had left off. On one hand, they stressed a familial type of Buddhism (tu tại gia) without ritual ostentation: daily prayers and pros-trations in front of home-based altars, observance of Buddhist fasts and absti-nence, but also use of Taoist-influenced magic and amulets. The key was simplicity, flexibility, and frugality. Popular Taoism flourished in the frontier South in the absence of monastic Buddhism and Confucian scholarship. These were brave, passionate, but illiterate peasants who went into battles armed with spears and amulets that were supposed to protect them and give them invincibility. Led by charismatic leaders (who were healers or had mastered geomancy, or divination, but were no more literate than their followers), they lacked strategy and armaments and could not coordinate their plans of action nor pool their resources. They were no match for French guns. Their resistance was also short-lived and sporadic for the loss of a charismatic leader would doom the movement until another charismatic leader rose to lead them anew.

These groups represented the essence of the southern delta's frontier men who rose to fight for their freedom and religion/sect. The weakness of these sects lay in their inability to create institutions capable of dealing with the changes that were occurring (strategy, armament, intelligence...). Their strength lay in giving voice to popular discontent thanks to charismatic leaders who could enroll tens of thousands of converts. They were pre-modern forms of political participation.[39] They existed before the communist revolution was born and were native and spontaneous in origin while the communist revolution was based on Soviet or Chinese ideology. They were the only hope for these disenfranchised poor peasants and pioneers who lived at the fringes of the new and poorly-integrated society.

The Đạo Lành (Religion of Good) group referred to its leaders' slogan: Làm lành, tránh dữ (Do good, avoid evil). It turned out to be the greatest source of continuous resistance against the French after the death of Định. In the summer of 1867, led by Nguyễn Văn Thanh (who was chief regimental officer at the time the French invaded Gia Định), it launched raids on the French military position in Châu Đốc. Thanh was also involved in a revolt in Vũng Liêm in the province of Vĩnh Long. The French forced him to retreat into the marshes of Bảy Thừa in Châu Đốc, where he established his new headquarters. Surrounding villagers protected him and provided him with material support. He was eventually killed by the French army in 1873, and they exposed his body for three days to prove to the population that he was really dead. The Đạo Lành's apostles spread the rumor that he was merely retreating from the world of the living and would reincarnate.[40]

Năm Thiếp (a healer and master of hypnotic trances), the new leader, rallied the dispirited group around him. He passed off his decisions as orders from the other world during his trances. In 1878, 600 men armed with spears, led by Ông and Kha, converged toward Mỹ Tho to attack French military positions. The French, alerted by a spy, waited for them and easily dispersed the group with their rifles. From that time onward, constructions of new religious buildings were strictly regulated and sects and secret societies were hunted down. Năm Thiếp settled down and built the village of An Định where followers continued to flock. Another insurrection was launched from 1882 to 1883, but it also fizzled due to armament mismatch. The French finally raided An Định and put an end to the insurrection.[41]

The French policy of confiscating lands belonging to the military settlements and the rebels caused untold hardships to the Mekong Delta peasants, especially those close to the Cambodian border. It robbed many peasants of the fruits of their labor and was at the root of further unrest. The upgrade of provincial roads, which as a consequence forced peasants to provide money and labor, further polarized the issue. In Sốc Trăng, because of a labor shortage right in the middle of harvest season, authorities just surrounded the market and neighborhood and hauled away peasants to worksites. The low wages and the fact that they were not released during harvest time contributed to the labor shortage.

In March 1913, 600 peasants dressed in white, wearing amulets, carrying spears and swords and led by Phan Xích Long, converged on Saigon, angry about injustice. They were easily routed by the French after a brief battle. Long was tried and sentenced for deportation to Guyana. But the boat on which he was due to sail could not leave port because of the outbreak of the war. He was therefore locked in the Saigon Central Jail. In 1916, more than 100 peasants marched toward the Central Jail, chanting, "Let's free Big Brother (Long)!" The second contingent of armed peasants did not show up because of failure of communication. Sixty-five people were arrested and 38 men were condemned and publicly executed. The Central Jail attack was part of a coordinated attack throughout South Vietnam. Riots occurred in 13 out of 20 southern provinces. The Phan Xích Long rebellion demonstrated for the first time that sectarian unrest was not linked to any natural catastrophe, but to resentment against French injustice.[42] Unrest got worse with the advent of the Cao Đài and Hòa Hảo sects, which will be discussed in the next chapter.

From 1863 onward, Napoleon III's interest in Vietnam declined as he got involved in the French-Prussian war. The Vietnamese soon got some respite because France was defeated by the Prussians in 1870. Napoleon III himself was taken prisoner. This humiliation badly shook the spirit of the French who no longer had any interest in pursuing colonial expansion. However, Tự Đức failed to capitalize on this political break because he did not have a foreign ministry—embassies or consulates—that could analyze and evaluate the ramifications of the event.[43]

Emperor Tự Đức (r. 1847–1883), who had never left his gilded palace in Huế except for rare trips to the surrounding provinces, lived in a utopian world where he was the ultimate power holder, the Son of Heaven. Without a foreign ministry to serve him, he had not grasped the overwhelming technical advances and economic changes happening in the western world. He only knew the world through the eyes of his mandarins. The mandarins, who either resisted changes—which could relieve them from their positions and powers—or did not want to upset their monarch, kept him in the dark or fed him only information he would like to hear. The major party at court was openly supported by Tự Đức's ultraconservative and domineering mother.

Tự Đức was himself not without fault. At times, he seemed upbeat and quickly agreed on suggested changes submitted to him by various reformers, only to let them fall by the wayside because of lack of follow-up. He was a smart and intelligent scholar who fired off many questions to many people. He well understood the precarious political nature he was facing and the importance of reforms, but failed to act.[44] He asked a mandarinal candidate in 1874 to explain to him why the French took the six southern provinces but returned Annam and Tonkin. "Do not let yourself be hindered by fear. Express your opinion very freely," he advised him. He was indecisive at best, seeking various opinions but postponing decision in the end. He acted as someone "who merely accepts fate" and justified his inactivity by comparing Vietnam to China, which, although much stronger than Vietnam, was still defeated by western powers.[45]

Beset by various physical ailments, he was quiet by nature, a man of letters, a poet. He appeared depressed on occasion and might have suffered from bipolar depression. He dwelled morosely on his weak health and named the mausoleum he had had erected "Humility." It sat where "the hills are not so high and the site is remote. The choice of this place marks Our self-imposed humiliation. Our person is too weak to accomplish great accomplishments. That is why Our territory has been occupied."[46]

The court mandarins' narrowness of views, arrogant pride, aversion to change, and paralytic inaction—even when the ship was sinking—were at the root of Vietnam's downfall. Overcommitted to a strict neo–Confucian orthodoxy that saw change as both ephemeral and undesirable, Tự Đức and his mandarins failed to adapt and take action in due course.[47] The result was disastrous.

In a Confucian world where every role had been scripted and everyone knew his place within society, Tự Đức believed that everything should fall in its place. He saw a world that moved according to a certain order and followed a scripted role. Raised within that system (which had lasted for two millennia) before becoming its high priest, he did not see that change was necessary. He could not understand that the French did not abide by these Confucian rules, but only valued economic interests, territorial control and domination.

French conquest, however, at that time was not a *fait accompli*, only a hazard of history. Siam and Japan, which also shared a similar feudal and rudimentary political system had managed to preserve their independence and the integrity of their countries in the face of western attacks. The king of Siam, who was forced to give certain privileges to England in 1855, turned around and signed similar treaties with France, Portugal, Denmark, Holland, Prussia, and the United States. By playing one superpower against the other, he kept his country independent.[48]

A few mandarins who had traveled abroad at that time, had suggested political and military reforms to make the country more competitive against western powers. Besides Phan Thanh Giản, Phạm Phú Tu, Trần Đình Tục, and Nguyễn Huy Tế, the other well-known person was Nguyễn Trường Tộ. His fame rested less on his originality—his proposals were not different from oth-

ers'—than on his relentless pursuit of change.[49] Born in 1930 in central Vietnam
to a Catholic family, Tộ received a traditional education and was a good Confucian scholar, but was not allowed to sit for the imperial civil service examination because of his religion. He earned his living teaching Chinese at home,
then at a seminary. When the French attacked Đà Nẵng in 1858, government
restrictions on Catholics forced him to seek the protection of the French.
Bishop Gauthier of the Society des Missions Étrangères sent him to Penang
and Hong Kong for further studies. After his return to Vietnam in 1861, he
helped translate Chinese and Vietnamese documents for the French. He warned
the court of the French plans to take over the three western provinces and to
use Lê Duy Phụng to harass royal troops in Tonkin.

He sent to the court more than 15 petitions urging changes in almost all
government functions. In foreign affairs, he urged cooperation with foreign
powers and also suggested playing one against the other; internally, he urged
separation of judiciary and administrative powers as well as a decrease in the
number of officials and control of corruption; in education, he advocated the
teaching of exact sciences and replacement of Chinese by nôm, translation of
foreign books, as well as sending students abroad. He urged the modernization
of agriculture, development of industries, commerce, the re-organization of
the army, fabrication of arms and ammunitions, the implementation of fair
taxation, and so on.

Tự Đức was so impressed by the comments that he called him in for consultation on various occasions and sent him to France in 1866 to buy modern
machinery, books, and to hire experts to serve as instructors in Vietnam. When
the French seized the three western provinces in 1867, Tộ was recalled from
Paris and the project was aborted. He was well treated after his return but was
not given any work. He helped Gauthier build a church in Saigon and continued
to send his petitions. In 1871, he suggested to the court to launch an offensive
against the French in Vietnam while the Paris government was in disarray following France's defeat by Prussia. He even volunteered to lead Vietnamese
troops to war, but the indecisive Tự Đức in the end refused to lift a finger.[50]
Despite all these reformers' good will, the court mandarins managed to torpedo
all their suggestions and keep the status quo, which, in the end, helped the
invaders.

Left on their own, French military personnel in Vietnam took personal
initiatives in the face of Paris' inaction. They conducted actions in a haphazard
and uncoordinated fashion that somehow led to the capitulation of Vietnam.
Under French bombardment, the imperial court at Huế decided to capitulate.
On August 25, 1883, the court signed the Treaty of Huế, which accepted that
the country would be a French protectorate. Vietnam had ceased to exist after
900 years of independence. By the end of 1883, there were more than 20,000
French troops in North Vietnam waging war against Vietnamese and Chinese
fighters.[51]

Saigon Under the French

By 1861, "peace" had settled on Saigon-Gia Định area—this time under French administration. The colonials, under the direction of Admiral Bonnard, began their plans to transform the oriental Saigon into a French town, a home away from home.[52] Their temporary military camp was surrounded by swamps, shanties and wooden huts. The moats were filled in, riverbanks raised, docks extended. Between 1861 and 1865, plans for a hospital, governor's palace, barracks for troops and officers, a church, schools, and a 12-hectare botanic garden were laid out.

The 1815 map of Saigon reveals the towns of Saigon (Bến Nghé) and Chợ Lớn separated by a large sparsely populated plain. Bến Nghé, with its citadel, was crowded on its eastern and southern sides. The French who first landed in Saigon found a town sitting amidst a flat countryside intersected by the various branches of the Saigon River. Vegetation was lush: "ficus, teak, palm and banana trees interlock their branches and leaves in all imaginable ways."[53] Under this thick vegetation were huts made of "osier and bamboo" that sheltered people along with their buffaloes and pigs. The town was surrounded by immense rice fields.

Vietnamese men and women wore trousers with long tunics falling to their ankles and open from the waist down. The sleeves ended at the wrists. Although silk was exclusively reserved for the emperor and the mandarins, southern civilians took it upon themselves to wear silk. Mandarins wore a cap with wide metal badge bearing the name and coat of arms of his majesty the king, along with two side appendages "in black gauze, nine inch-long and not so badly imitating the wings of a night butterfly." They were mostly barefoot, except for mandarins, who wore sandals. Most men and women chewed betel. They ate little—mostly rice, yams and peas. Once a year during the New Year festival, they sliced pigs and ducks and devoured "in one or two meals their annual savings."[54] This "Tết" festival was, therefore, celebrated in Saigon as far back as the 19th century.

The French then requisitioned most of the land in Bến Nghé and subdivided it into plots, which they put on auction as early as Feb 20, 1862. Bonnard assigned Coffyn the task of supervising the building of the new town. Coffyn decided to subdivide it into four separate sections—administrative, commercial, industrial and residential—then into plots.

The cheapest plots, located in the lower section of Saigon, at a cost of one hundredth of a piaster per unit, would be offered to local merchants. The most expensive ones, just right on the pier, were valued at six hundredths of a piaster per unit. They would be reserved for major store owners, maritime companies, and later banks. Larger lots, valued at three hundredths of a piaster and located on the plateau overlooking the river, would be the site for a new European town.

The idea of indemnifying Vietnamese families who had lost their lands to the project was rapidly cancelled. Bonnard conceded to them instead a section of the right side of the Bến Nghé arroyo on the southern end of the town. The purpose was two-fold: first, not to antagonize the local populace or provoke a rebellion; and second, not to get rid of all the Vietnamese, but to keep those who were wealthy enough to pay taxes in the future. On the other hand, Catholic families that were thought to be more westernized than the locals and likely to be supporters of the new regime, were given lands at the periphery of the town (Dakao and Tân Định) upon which to build churches and schools.

With these plans, Bonnard introduced to the Saigonese the concept of land speculation, which has not stopped since. The plan, which was slow to start in the beginning because of a lack of investors picked up pace in 1890 when people decided to gamble on the piaster. Authorities fueled land speculation further by increasing auctions to finance infrastructure development and building constructions.[55]

The French began their building process in 1865 after having conquered the rest of Cochinchina (South Vietnam). The governor's palace, a massive and grandiose building, was completed in 1875 after a seven-year construction. The style turned out to be purely western without any Vietnamese trait at all.

The architectural design at that time was to contrast the upper administrative European section and the lower town, which was commercially oriented and reserved for locals. On one side, planners wanted to stress the "space of image and representation" (espace de spectacle and representation) where buildings, like the Saigon Cathedral or the governor's palace, were huge, impressive, and removed from the streets to give them a grandiose look. On the other end, the straw huts, houses, buildings, pagodas in the Vietnamese and Chinese sections were small, crowded, and close together and conveyed a space of "contact" (espace de contact). Many families lived in their junks—which also served as transport carriers of merchandise—on the arroyos. The contrast between the two sections of the town would represent one of the characteristics of Saigon: the segregation between rulers and ruled.

Urban design also tended to reflect the military concerns of the conquering French admirals of the time. Coffyn, a military engineer, in the 1880s drew up the first plans for the redevelopment of Saigon. He stressed the need for wide streets, which would allow military surveillance, and rejected the notion of large open spaces to prevent unauthorized indigenous gatherings. He placed a few ostentatious buildings to attract European investors and to give the town a French flavor and a symbol of French greatness. Thus, by design, the Saigonese, who were not given any downtown place to congregate, had to block off large sections of streets and boulevards to promote major gatherings like the one during the Tết festival.

Because of military concerns, the indigenous city of Saigon was razed and rebuilt with western architecture. The destruction of the native town stemmed from the intense dislike of mixing motifs native to French architecture to avoid a potential eyesore. The rebuilding was intended to convey a "domineering and inviolable image of the imperial nation." Buildings were formalist and grandiose. They were to exude an air of western concepts and beauty with baroque and classic motifs. Saigon, the "Paris of the Extreme Orient," was an embodiment of French cultural superiority and a symbol of French prestige and cultural hegemony.[56]

The first meeting, on June 17 and 18, 1867, of the Saigon municipal commission—purely advisory in design—was convened by and in the presence of Admiral de La Grandiere, governor of the colony. Present were 12 councilors and a president. However, it would be only two years later, in 1869, that the municipal council was created with half of the members being nominated by the governor and the rest elected proportionally to the number of French citizens residing in the town. The duration of each mandate was two years. The council was, therefore, overwhelmingly white. The natives, despite being more numerous than the foreigners, were only represented by the rare few people who had recently been naturalized. The erudite Petrus Trương Vĩnh Ký became the first Vietnamese council member directly nominated by the governor. Since the latter assumed broad powers and could veto any decision of the council, councilors realized their powerlessness. They argued their case with the governor, but to no avail; in despair, they disbanded themselves in October 1870 and were replaced by a new council the following month.[57]

In August 1882, the council voted to change the composition of its members to eight French and four Vietnamese members, besides the mayor and his two assistants. The mandate was increased to three years.[58] Because of the constant dispute between council members and governor, many important decisions had been left dragging for a long time. Most of the major decisions were "suggested" by the governor and acted on by the municipality. The governor, for example, suggested the building of a museum inside the botanic garden to attract visitors and to preserve cultural heritage. The council argued for a long time, citing a lack of funds, before finally agreeing to it.[59] With the population rapidly expanding, the governor decided to annex surrounding villages (including Tân Định, Hòa Mỹ, and Xuân Hòa) to the town in 1894. On April 14, 1906, the municipal council voted to subdivide Saigon into six districts:

District of Phú Thanh, including the former village of Phú Thanh;
District of Tân Hòa, including the former village of Tân Hòa;
District of Tân Định, including the former villages of Tân Định, Phú Hòa, and Nam Chon;
District of Hòa Mỹ, including the former village of Hòa Mỹ and limited by the Chasseloup-Laubat and Mac Mahon Streets;
District of Saigon from the Cầu Ông Lãnh to Chasseloup-Laubat; and
District of Khánh Hội, including the former village of Khánh Hội and part of Tâm Hợi.[60]

The vision of a town sparked by the folly of grandeur pushed city planners to envision and create grandiose buildings instead of working hard on the city's infrastructure. As a result, needs for water supply and sewage were pushed back.

Lack of drinking water, especially during the annual dry season, had been a problem since 1868. One council member talked about the "urgent" need of bringing water to the city.[61] People used rain or well water, although most of the water in and around Saigon was polluted. Studies revealed that wells drilled close to the Grand Canal, in Chợ Quán and Chợ Lớn had good water while well water from the plateau and the Plain of Tombs was polluted.[62] A decision was made to build water cisterns as well as filtrating tanks. The Thủ Đức tank, completed in 1881 at a cost of more than one million francs, was expected to produce 4,000 cubic meters of water daily for a population of 16,000 people or 250 liters per person. Because of technical problems with the Thủ Đức tank, wells close to the cathedral were drilled deeper and were expected to produce 2,400 cubic meters daily. In 1886 and 1888, the production at both the Thủ Đức tank and the cathedral wells lagged behind urban needs creating shortages of water.[63] A decision was taken to drill more wells in 1889 and discussions about capturing water from the Đồng Nai River at Trị An, 75 km from Saigon, were entertained. Demands for water, however, were rarely satisfied in view of the insufficiency of proposed solutions. By 1907, the total amount of water produced was 6,500 versus 9,000 cubic meters promised.[64] Forty water wells were built between 1888 and 1908 compared to only 12 in the 1920s.

Public hygiene could not be guaranteed because of the proximity of the waste dump's location close to the town. Therefore, one could feel proud of living in Saigon amidst grandiose buildings but fearful of fetching water from public fountains located near piles of rotten garbage.[65] An insufficient sewage system would later result in backup and street flooding following heavy tropical downpours. U.S. city planner Gwendolyn Wright labeled the vision of the town-planning "superficial."[66]

Part of the local central market, which was an agglomeration of straw huts, burned down in late 1869, displacing merchants and customers. In one of its meetings in 1870 the municipal council earmarked 70,000 francs for the building of a sturdier brick and steel marketplace, which would offer more resistance to weather and fires.[67] Members then realized that materials had to be ordered from France and would not arrive until 18 months later. A temporary wooden structure—similar to a large hangar—covered by flat tiles was therefore built in its place with five sections dedicated to the sale of meat, fish, goods/food, clothing, and restaurants. The floor was paved with granite blocks. Due to a lack of funds, the permanent project was shelved until 1893, when a second round of discussions took place. They centered on budget availability, location, size of the market, and need to buy out adjacent buildings to give it more space. By 1909, the 39-year-old wooden structure, which had been decaying for many years and was in danger of falling apart, forced another round of discussions. City members, realizing the emergency of the situation, rushed to solve the problem.[68] Work finally began in January 1914 and the new central market was inaugurated by the end of March, 44 years after the first deliberation took place.[69]

Since Saigon sat on marshy land connected by arroyos, the sanitation of the canals became an important feature in the development of the town. Besides the dark waters that sometimes regurgitated debris and the carcasses of dead animals during tidal changes,[70] the stench was horrible even for natives. The Grand Canal or Canal Charner, the largest in town, ended close to the present-day municipal building. Merchants used this waterway to bring their products to the central market that was located less than a mile away. Due to health problems and business interests of citizens, the council began discussing the management of the canal in August 1867.[71] Temporizing measures included building a bridge over the canal, and partial obliteration and recurrent cleaning of the canal until the council voted to completely obliterate it, which was done in 1887—20 years after the first deliberation.[72] The result was the nice and wide Charner Boulevard (Nguyễn Huệ) that led all the way to the Saigon River. Other canals were also obliterated or cleaned. The whole process of sanitizing the canals and arroyos took more than three decades.

City council members who tried to preserve their personal interests were legendary for their procrastination. It took them 27 years of deliberations and many consecutive administrations just to make up their mind in 1898 about the site and architecture of the City Hall, even though the site had been chosen by the Saigon Public Work board back in 1871.[73] Work began in 1898 but was halted the following year by order of the lieutenant-governor who requested a few changes in the floor plans. The painter and sculptor Ruffier, who was charged with providing four mural paintings and a number of outside sculptures and ornaments, demanded an advance on his payment and indemnity for the delay. Work restarted in September 1901 and Ruffier was asked to return to work in May 1902. In the meantime, the change in floor plans required a modification of the size of the paintings, which required the drawing of an additional contract for Ruffier. When the project was completed in 1908—37 years after the first deliberation—the total cost of the building was estimated at 469,822 piasters.[74] Although Ruffier did not complete the paintings, he requested additional payments due to other changes requested by the city. The city disagreed and fired Ruffier. Bonnet was assigned to take over and complete the painting work. The case went for arbitration with the ruling in favor of the city in 1914: the artwork and sculptures belonged to the city and Ruffier had to reimburse 60,000 piasters for cost and interests. Ruffier by that time had returned to France without leaving a forwarding address.[75]

The management of Saigon's public services contrasted with that of Chợ Lớn: The failure of urban services and rarity of public equipment were more frequently seen in Saigon than in Chợ Lớn. The Chinese in Saigon also received more goodwill from the city council than did the Vietnamese. These discriminatory politics was used to exploit the tensions between locals in order to better control them. In 1911, it took Đỗ Hữu Phương three years to receive permission to buy a parcel of land in order to build a Vietnamese school for girls while a French-Chinese school was already in service in 1908. By 1918, Chợ Lớn could boast of having 31 schools teaching in Chinese, as well as three Catholic and three secular schools, while Saigon had only three kindergartens, two primary schools and the one built by Đỗ Hữu Phương. By 1914, Chợ Lớn had seven medical establishments compared to two for Saigon (Chợ Quán Hospital and the Polyclinic, which was opened in 1914).[76]

It is interesting to note that people died of different diseases than today—mostly from infectious diseases. From January 1 to August 30, 1907, the following cases were noted in Saigon:

Typhoid fever	3
Varicella	11
Cholera	10
Plague	355
Measles	8

During the great epidemic of cholera of 1895, 111 of the 158 deceased prisoners and vagrants had died of cholera.[77]

In the 1920s, France invested heavily in Vietnam (417 million Francs from 1924 to 1929). This resulted in an explosion of buildings: from 100 in 1925 to 214 in Saigon and 143 in Chợ Lớn in 1929. During the same period, four clinics were built, along with five markets (two in Saigon and three in Chợ Lớn).[78]

In July 1872, the French steamer *La Creuse* dropped anchor in the port of Saigon and was surrounded by local sampans that reminded European passengers of Venitian gondolas.[79] These sampans had shaded seats in the middle for customers and were manned by oarsmen. Saigon had been under French control for a little more than a decade and newcomers were pouring into town. The right bank of the Saigon River remained underdeveloped and was clustered with small straw huts. The three-story Cosmopolitan hotel stood across from the pier. Tamarind trees lined up on both sides of Catinat Avenue, the main axis, which led to downtown. Its name was given by Admiral-Governor de La Grandiere on February 1, 1865, in honor of the boat *Catinat*, which had participated in attacks of Đà Nẵng in 1858 and Saigon in 1859. Red dusty earth was still visible under the colonials' feet as the district was still underdeveloped.

The real center was the place of the Municipal Theater, an ornate 800-seat theater dotted with harp players that had been inaugurated in 1900 with great pomp in the presence of prince Waldemar of Denmark. Close by was the Continental Hotel—spacious with an inner garden.

Chinese merchants set up shop along the low-lying sections of the city and sold, among other things, the famous salaco or pith helmet of the tropics to the newly arrived who could not tolerate the hot tropical sun. There were many Hindus, Chinese, and Saigonese in the streets. Two Chinese men, naked to the waist and wearing broad, bell-shaped straw hats (nón lá) attempted to sell their wares to the visitors. They walked one in front of the other, each holding on his shoulder one end of a pole, the center of which was attached a large bag containing all their parcels. Vietnamese men and women had the habit of chewing a leaf of the betel tree, a piece of areca nut along with shell lime. The combination produced an intense red saliva that was spit out onto the ground.

Downtown boasted the Hotel de l'Univers, with its own restaurant frequented by Europeans. Ventilation was manually provided by a person sitting in another room who, through a system of pulleys and ropes, rhythmically pulled up and dropped a punkah, a ceiling fan made of cloth reinforced by a wooden frame. The stream of air provided a break to the oppressing heat and dispersed mosquitoes and other insects. The newly arrived passenger had to spend the night under a muslin mosquito net to ward off mosquitoes—likely his first experience with these tropical insects.

The town had multiple European houses as well as the palace of the director of interior, the palace of government and the building of the engineers. Vegetation was still lush and deer could occasionally be seen near downtown. The botanical garden was built around 1870 and provided the Saigonese and Europeans a place to breathe the fresh evening breeze.

The tomb of the bishop of Adran, which was built with earth and brick, covered with concrete, and more richly decorated than other tombs, was located on the road to Gò Vấp, a suburb of Saigon. It was surrounded by an enclosure, and cared for and watched by a guard. Locally painted frescoes adorned the walls of the monument, including a huge tiger with a bright yellow body and black stripes.[80] That tomb was carefully preserved for almost two centuries until February 1983, when the communist regime, in an effort to erase all vestiges of the southern government and colonialism, decided to tear it down. The 6 by 3 meter sarcophagus was opened. "A two-century old smell filled the air and the coffin revealed its intact beauty of precious wood lacquered with gold and red.... It was opened. The bishop of Adran appeared in his mandarin robe with golden buttons, the last gift of the king (Gia Long) ... a well preserved skeleton; the head still coiffed by a bonnet adorned with laces." On March 2, 1983, the Saigon department of Health presented to the French consul five urns containing the remains of the bishop of Adran, two other French bishops, along with those of Francis Garnier and another sailor.[81]

The hospital of Chợ Quán was opened for business early on and treated patients afflicted with leprosy, a common tropical disease at the time. Since no one knew then that the disease was caused by a bacterium, it was labeled as incurable and left patients with the loss of digits, and deformities, swollen limbs, open sores and severe facial deformities.

By 1872, Chợ Lớn was a town of 80,000 people—the second largest in Indochina after Saigon. It was located five miles west of Saigon. Chinese junks and Vietnamese sampans filled the arroyo, bringing in and out merchandise from all the provinces south of the Mekong River. The town also boasted crocodile parks that housed 100 to 200 animals. Crocodile meat was offered for sale and was well-received by Saigonese customers.

Saigon was located on the northern bend of the Đồng Nai River (or Saigon River), about 60 miles upstream from its mouth. Boats had to steam up the river through its meandering curves amid lush forests of mangroves and trees. The port could not compete with Singapore, Hong Kong or Batavia because of the transit time on the meandering river and high pilot cost. There were talks about moving the port facilities to Vũng Tàu at the mouth of the river where access and docking would be easier. But Saigon, with its infrastructure, factories, road access, commercial and administrative sites, and consumers won over the debate. The deep riverbed, which allowed large ships to easily dock at its pier, tipped the scale in favor of Saigon. Besides, the 80-mile road trip between Saigon and Vũng Tàu under tropical heat presented a challenge for European passengers who had just gone through a rough four-week boat trip from the south of France to Saigon.

The port was constructed with a refitting basin to repair damaged vessels. By 1909, Saigon had only one dry dock belonging to the French navy. Finally, traffic forced modernization. By 1931, Saigon had storehouses with a capacity of 30,000 square feet and large cranes lifting up to 50 tons. By 1936, port activity was measured at 2,607,998 tons.

Rice accounted for 97 percent of the exports in 1861 and 54 percent in 1928. Rice export increased to 1,400,000 tons by 1935. Exported items included rubber, maize, fish products, pepper, cane sugar, fruits and skins. Textiles (cottons, calicoes, silks), flour, wheat, tobacco, and opium were the most frequently imported items.

Rice husking was centered in Chợ Lớn. Before 1870, there were two European husking plants. The Chinese opened their first plant in 1877. By 1911, of the ten plants eight were Chinese. The number then increased to 60 by 1931.[82]

Many banks opened their doors in Saigon. In 1875, La Banque de l'Indochine monopolized the trade until 1927 when the first Vietnamese bank opened for competition.

The first ever newspaper published in Vietnam was the *Gia Định Journal*, which appeared in Saigon in April 1865. The brainchild of Huỳnh Tịnh (Paulus) Của (1834–1907) who was its editor for many years, it was originally designed to spread the quốc ngữ to the general population. Up to this date, all documents were written either in Chinese or nôm, the Vietnamese or southern script using Chinese characters. Although nôm was designed in the tenth century A.D., it was used in literature only in the 13th century under the Trần.[83] Official documents under the 19th-century Nguyễn were still transcribed in Chinese. Therefore, only mandarins were knowledgeable enough to read and write Chinese and possibly nôm.

On arrival in Vietnam, western missionaries realized that the Chinese script was the major barrier that prevented the spread of religion among the almost illiterate populace. Alexandre de Rhodes and other missionaries in the 17th century, therefore, went to work and developed the quốc ngữ, a new Vietnamese script based on the Roman alphabet. Although it proved to be easier to use than the nôm or Chinese, it never caught on because mandarins did not want to change the system that kept them in power and quốc ngữ was thought to be a tool for foreign invasion.

It was Huỳnh Tịnh Của and Trương Vĩnh (Petrus) Ký (1837–1898), Catholic Southerners who, through the *Gia Định Journal* and the French administration's support, attempted to resuscitate and popularize the quốc ngữ in 1865. Despite their innovative and valiant efforts, it was only until 1918 that quốc ngữ was frequently used, although French remained the official language until 1954, when Ngô Đình Diệm promoted quốc ngữ as the Vietnamese national language.

The governor of Cochinchina, M. Roze, wrote in 1865 that the *Gia Định Journal* was intended to disseminate all the news worthy of the indigenous population's attention and to provide them with some knowledge of cultural matters and developments in agriculture.[84] The four-page journal appeared monthly and contained official announcements and decrees as well as national news. Historical essays, poems, legends, and cultural materials were later added to the contents. In 1869, it was published twice a month and then three times a week.

Petrus Ký eventually achieved better recognition than his colleague Của due to the depth and width of his cultural work, his involvement in politics, and his ability to work with the Huế government and the French. Ký became orphan when he lost his father at the age of eight. A Catholic priest who was protected from persecution by Ký's father took him under his wing and sent him to study in Catholic schools in Vietnam and Cambodia, then in a seminary in Penang, Malaysia. Living and working among students who came from many Asian countries and were gifted in languages, he became fluent in 14 of them and acquired basic knowledge in western and Asian civilizations. He returned to Vietnam at the age of 21, a few months before the French stormed ashore at Đà Nẵng in 1858.

In 1863, he became the official translator for Phan Thanh Giản and his delegation at the negotiation table with the French in Paris. Following the completion of his assignment, he visited France, Spain, Italy, and many middle eastern countries. On his return, he became director from 1866 to 1868 of the newly opened School for Interpreters and was named editor in chief of the *Gia Định Journal* in 1868. Over the next three decades, Ký and Của standardized the quốc ngữ, developed Vietnamese literature, and promoted understanding between the French and Vietnamese. Ký wrote many textbooks on French and Vietnamese language and produced Vietnamese-French and French-Vietnamese dictionaries. Của wrote the first dictionary in quốc ngữ. Both these men also wrote many articles on Vietnamese history, geography, and culture.

Although Ký owed a huge moral debt to his benefactors, the French priests who fed and educated him, he chose to remain a Vietnamese when French citizenship was offered to him. He felt that he could serve France better because the Vietnamese king, the court and the people would trust him more as a Vietnamese than a naturalized Frenchman. That decision, of course, cost him a lot materially because of wage differences between a Vietnamese and a French. Some low-level officials discriminated against him because they could not understand how a Vietnamese could be loyal to France.[85]

In the 1870s and for many years afterwards, he became the first and only Vietnamese member of the Saigon city council.[86] Although they did not see their effort bear fruit in their lifetimes because of competition with the French, Ký and Của laid the foundation on which others, especially Nguyễn Văn Vĩnh, would build.

By 1892, only military gunboats, torpedoes, and navy boats docked in the naval section of the port while commercial ships were moored further upstream in a newly built public facility. The Messageries Maritimes, the French commercial shipping industry that dealt with passengers and cargo loads, had its headquarters there. From the pier, the steeple of the Saigon cathedral was visible. Among the gardens and lush vegetation, the admiral's mansion, the arsenal and the navy's supply warehouses were seen. A new hotel was also built to accommodate foreign travelers, although the majority headed downtown a few miles away.

The French, eager to spread their culture to Cochinchina, decided to transplant French culture into Saigon. A cathedral was built, and the Rue Catinat in downtown Saigon was an exact copy of the Rue de la Paix in Paris with its balustrades and shops. Roads were widened, cobblestoned, and lined with trees. They were frequented by open or enclosed horse carriages drawn by small but valiant horses. After a long three- to four-week sea trip, travelers were dreaming about a warm bed and fresh food. Some dove into the pubs for a cold drink or beer while others looked for a cozy environment. Colonists wore a white jacket and a pair of trousers equally white. By 5 P.M. each day when the sun was less hot, they dropped off their hard colonial hats and started their daily walkabouts. Carriages crowded the streets and people frequented shops and stores. By then, no naked torsos or bare legs of Asian nationals could be found, as they could be in other cities. Downtown Saigon was strictly European: it exuded a Parisian atmosphere, causing the French to call it the Paris of the East.

After finding a house or an apartment to their liking, the newly arrived colonists went to "auction houses" to look for furniture. Since their stays in

Saigon were likely to be transient, those returning to France sent their furniture to these auction houses, which, for a small fee, would dispose them to people who had just arrived in the city. Everything could be found at these houses: horses, carriages, chests with inlaid mother-of-pearl and ivory, porcelains, pottery, and silkware.[87]

Since bachelors rarely had family-type dinners, they would organize cook-out parties where each of them in turn became "chief of the kitchen." They threw dinners at one of the houses and asked local cooks to prepare the feast. They all ate very well, for the cooks were "artists and prepared the dishes with pleasure." The dishes were varied and could be European as well as local. And cooks excelled in pastries, which delighted the guests. Since lamb was a luxury in Cochinchina, cooks also learned to prepare lamb "à la bretonne" to satisfy their masters' palates.[88] Besides providing the luxury of intimate gatherings, hostesses threw balls or dance parties enlivened by the music of navy bands. Colonials sipped champagne while pleasant oriental nights filled with "balmy scents and phosphorescent fireflies."

Every day after 5 P.M., they enjoyed the "inspection tour." Sitting in their carriages, they took a tour of the city that led them to Gia Định, which at that time was a suburb about five miles from downtown Saigon. The road ran through rice fields shaded by high trees or bordered with luxuriant flowery hedges. Steam could be seen seeping up from the ground following a rainy monsoon day and many felt the air was fresher than in the city itself. The scenery was pleasant and bucolic. The road led either to the "acacia avenue" or to the "lake tower." The return road went by the botanical and zoological gardens where they could stop and watch representatives of the local fauna or flora. There was also a daily walking tour around downtown if one was not interested in the inspection tour.

Buildings and monuments rose rapidly during the first three decades of colonization. The first Catholic church was renovated from an abandoned Vietnamese pagoda. When the latter proved to be too small for the congregation, it was moved to a wooden building, which was soon destroyed by termites. Construction of the cathedral began in 1877 and was completed in 1880 with original materials coming from France. Two bell towers were added in 1895 and were topped with crosses, each measuring 3.5 m high and 2 m wide with a weight of 600 kg. The height of the church is 60.5 m. The cathedral, which was built in the best Roman style high up in the city, could be seen from the river many miles away because there were no tall buildings to obscure the view. It was during the construction of the cathedral that an underground lake was found, following which a water tower was built close by to provide the Saigonese with fresh potable water. The sandy ground on which the cathedral stood caused many problems: the requirement for deep foundations, and the sinking of one of the towers. The Saigon cathedral, like the French Notre Dame, had towers of unequal height which did not affect their performance or beauty.

In the flowerbed in front of the church was erected a bronze statue of de Behaine, bishop of Adran, holding the hand of Prince Cảnh. The statue was removed in 1945 although the pedestal was left intact. In 1959, Bishop Phạm Văn Thiện ordered a peaceful Notre Dame statue made of granite in Rome to replace the statue of de Behaine. It was installed on the pedestal and the cathedral became known as the Notre Dame Cathedral. In 1962, the Vatican conferred to the cathedral the title of basilica; therefore, it is now known as the basilica of Notre Dame of Saigon.

On the square was built the main postal office, which took the shape of a palace. On the back of the cathedral ran a north-south boulevard that was named after Norodom, the king of Cambodia. Norodom Sihanouk once studied at the Saigon lycee Chasseloup Laubat. Having witnessed French culture, he decided to ask the French to assume a protectorate over his country. In return for his largess, France placed his name on one of Saigon's thoroughfares. The name stuck to the boulevard for more than half a century. The remaining city streets were adorned with names of famous French or Vietnamese people. On one end of the boulevard stood the zoological garden and on the other end, the palace of the government. This palace was later replaced by the presidential palace. Nearby was erected a bronze statue of Gambetta, the French politician who strove to throw out a foreign invasion from France's soil ironically stood as an invader on Vietnamese soil. The statue was removed in the late 1950s.

One ship arrived in Saigon each week, bringing visitors, mail and magazines from France. Once it had signaled its arrival at the pier by blowing its horn, people started lining up at the post office to get their mail and news from families and friends from France. Colonists were thus three weeks behind in news from their capital. Merchant junks busily traveled up and down the river bringing merchandise back and forth between Chợ Lớn and the countryside.

To entertain themselves, colonials built a theater, as well as many dancehalls. There was also a racetrack at Phú Thọ where horse races and buffalo cart races took place. They could hunt deer, monkey, palm rat and peacock in Thủ Dầu Một, a few hours north of Saigon by boat. They could go bathing at the seaside resort of Vũng Tàu or enjoy the country life at Mỹ Tho. There were thus many recreations for the colonials.

The road from Saigon to Chợ Lớn went through the "plain of tombs," a deserted non-descript area strewn with mausoleums and tombs. There was no fence or border, neither greenery nor trees. It had been the site of important battles between the Nguyễn and Tây Sơn a century earlier, the Huế soldiers and the Lê Văn Khôi rebels, and then the French and Vietnamese.

On the other side of the road ran the tramway on narrow tracts that connected Saigon to Chợ Lớn. The service was frequented mostly by Chinese who took pleasure riding the tram. Chợ Lớn, Saigon's Chinatown, was run by the Đốc Phủ Sứ, or district chief, who was under the supervision of the French administrator. The mayor gave lavish banquets to all visitors, although women were not allowed to sit at the table. Exceptions were made on occasion to Europeans of higher ranks. He had one wife and 14 children.

Industry belonged to the Europeans, while trade and banking rested in the hands of the Chinese. The latter used usurious tactics to profit from the labor of poor farmers. Saigon remained the main trading center with entry of 481 ships and 521,884 tons hauled. It ran a surplus of 91 million French francs by 1892.[89]

By moving his capital from Saigon to Huế in 1802, Gia Long reduced Hà Nội to the status of provincial administrative center. Soon Hà Nội was eclipsed politically and culturally by Huế and economically by Saigon. To counter the power of the colonial traders in Saigon, the French in 1900 made Hà Nội the capital of Indochina and returned the power to the bureaucrats sent in by Paris.[90]

Saigon's population grew in three phases:

From 1860 to 1923, Saigon grew from 6,000 to 100,000 due mostly to improved hygiene and medicine but also to the dynamism of colonization.[91] Once the marshes were drained, arroyos obliterated, and vaccinations against measles and smallpox begun, life in Saigon became sustainable and resulted in an exponential population growth. The village in the insalubrious marshes, which through many centuries had failed to thrive, began to expand.

From 1921 to 1946, its population grew to 500,000 at a modest rate of 1.7 percent, because of World War I and the 1930 depression. During that period, Saigon, handicapped by a lack of good port installations, remained a regional port because of its location, but also because of French frugal colonial policy. From 1946 to 1954, it grew to 1.7 million people and remained a haven of peace during war time.

From 1954 to 1974, it grew from 1.7 to 4 million due to the rapid influx of people from the countryside seeking refuge from the war.[92]

* * *

Resistance to the French invasion was minimal at best because of: (1) the superiority of French armaments and military capability; (2) Huế's attempt to abide by the 1862 treaty; and (3) the disconnection between Huế and the South following the 1832 violent repression of Saigon's revolt. With improved hygiene and medicine, Saigon's population grew rapidly and the economy also expanded, making the town one of the new emerging Asian political and economic centers.

5

Saigon Through
World War II
(1920–1945)

Between the two world wars, Saigon was politically affected by unrest from new sects in the provinces (Hòa Hảo and Cao Đài) and from northern revolutionaries. Saigon was also a busy town brimming with underground and open resistance to the colonial administration. Without the trials and errors of the burgeoning militant Saigonese middle class, changes would not have succeeded elsewhere in Vietnam.

This was also a period of modernity and inward soul-searching, which resulted in Buddhist revival and a redefinition of nationalism,[1] the place of women in society, the nature of "tradition," and even history. It was the time southerners and Saigonese "engaged the past, faced the present, and wondered about the future."[2]

Cao Đài and Hòa Hảo Sects

Founded by people who had served in the French colonial administration and unlike previous sects, these newer movements were organized with religious and administrative hierarchies and their leaders did not pretend to possess supernatural powers.

The official founder of the Cao Đài sect was Ngô Văn Chiêu (1878–1932), a French civil servant who had the vision of the Cao Đài Tiên Ông spirit in 1919 in Cần Thơ in the Mekong Delta. He adopted the great Eye as the symbol of the Cao Đài spirit in 1921. Once back in Saigon, he and his friends built a temple to continue their spiritist sessions. It was only in 1925 that Cao Đài became a formal religious organization, and a center was built at Tây Ninh. Chiêu handed over his leadership to Lê Văn Trung in 1926.[3] By 1935, the sect had split into at least four different and rival centers: Tây Ninh, Mỹ Tho, Bạc Liêu, and Bến Tre.

The Cao Đài sect is a syncretic religion that brings together eastern (Taoism, Buddhism) and western (Christian) philosophies, although Taoism is the most prominent of the three. Caodaist séances were based on Taoist beliefs about the nature of spirits. Although the spirit-belief was Chinese in origin, the spirits channeled were often European, like the poet Victor Hugo and the French heroine Jeanne d' Arc. Others included Cao Đài Tiên Ông, who turned out to be no other than Ngọc Hoàng Thượng Đế or the Jade Emperor, a Taoist deity. The full name of the religion, however, Đại Độ Tam Kỳ Phổ Độ or the Great Way of the Third Era of Salvation, suggests a Buddhist idea.[4] The Cao Đài believe in salvation and in the imminent end of the world.

Caodaism, with its roots deep in Chinese history, was transplanted to South Vietnam and the Mekong Delta. It was not the product of nam tiến, but the result of transmission by Chinese migrants in the 17th century onward. If it is present today in central or northern Vietnam, it was the result of propagation from the South. The "Vietnamization" of the cult eventually produced the actual structure and terminology of Caodaism.[5]

Huỳnh Phú Sổ, the Hòa Hảo founder, was born in 1919 to a well-to-do peasant family. Contracting malaria at the age of 15 gave him a sickly look. His illness put him in close contact with many healers who were the keepers of the Bửu Sơn Kỳ Hương lore[6] and legends and from whom he learned the basics of his trade. In 1939, he went through a religious crisis during a ceremony and told his father he was a messenger of the Jade Buddha. His emaciated face, coupled with a burning gaze due to his ill-health, gave him the look of a visionary. Although he had only received a French primary education, his easy expression allowed him to sustain long monologues. He had unshakable faith in his divine powers and his healing abilities. Prone to fainting spells, he put them to good use; these spells, he told his followers, allowed him to communicate with the other world. They were similar to Năm Thiếp's hypnotic trances,[7] a characteristic that placed him above the rest of humans. He held open sessions, which allowed him to proselytize and enroll new converts. He composed obscure litanies and poems, which were combinations of exhortations to do good, prophecies, lamentations, and descriptions of injustice or evil.

The French, alarmed by Sổ's rapidly growing popularity and strange prophecies, did not know how to deal with him. Was he a potential troublemaker or a psychiatric case? They decided to send him to a psychiatrist in Cần Thơ for evaluation. He was referred to Chợ Quán Hospital in Saigon for psychiatric observation. After examination the new Vietnamese doctor, Nguyễn Văn Tâm, labeled him "mentally weak with a dysharmony of the intellectual activities." Despite his "weakness," Sổ was able to convert a few wardens at the hospital as well as Dr. Tâm. In 1941, after ten months of hospital confinement, he was sent to Bạc Liêu under house arrest. Hearing the news, his followers flocked to the town and turned it into a center of pilgrimage. The French decided to send him to Laos to put a distance between him and his followers, but the Japanese freed him and gave him protection against future arrest.

The Cao Đài and Hòa Hảo sects became militarized during the war for their own protection and armed bands were deployed as self-defense groups. They also competed against communists (Việt Minh) for followers and influence.[8] By 1944, Sổ, who was only 25 and had had no formal religious education, had corralled one million followers. He decided to use Cần Thơ— the capital of the Mekong Delta—as his headquarters, but he was challenged by the communists who had had the same thought.

When the Japanese deposed the French on March 9, 1945, a power vacuum was created at every level of the colony's administration, giving sects and political parties the freedom to jockey for power. As the Japanese forced farmers to produce more rice to feed their war machinery, Sổ told farmers to cut down on the production so that the harvest did not fall into Japanese hands. The communists, on the other hand, desperately needed southern rice to supply the North, which was suffering from famine. They wanted rice production to increase while trying to prevent it from falling into Japanese hands. Relations between Hòa Hảo and communists soured as a result.

When the Japanese surrendered on August 9, 1945, the sects (Cao Đài, Hòa Hảo, and other minor ones), caught by surprise, formed a United National Front to oppose the return of the French. They organized an impressive demonstration in Saigon on August 22. Four days later, the Việt Minh staged a coup and took over Saigon. In Cần Thơ, their Mekong Delta headquarters, they outmaneuvered the Hòa Hảo and jailed 30 Hòa Hảo leaders. Thirty thousand sectaries marched toward Cần Thơ and other towns a few days later to challenge the communists. A war between Hòa Hảo and communists broke out with one side taking revenge on the other and vice versa. The communists put down the revolt and Sổ and his associates barely escaped from capture. Sổ's brother and Trần Văn Soái's son were not lucky and got caught.

The French returning to Saigon on September 23 forced the communists to retreat to Rạch Giá then Cà Mau with the Hòa Hảo blocking their retreat. The communists, caught between the French and Hòa Hảo, called for a truce, but Sổ turned them down. On October 7, they took their revenge by executing Sổ's brother and Trần Văn Soái's son, dimming any hope for reconciliation. By continuing to reoccupy the delta, the French put the communists in disarray. The French soon signed an agreement with the Hòa Hảo to combat the Việt Minh.

Hùynh Phú Sổ was tried in absentia by the Việt Minh on April 25, 1945. He was caught while sailing through Long Xuyên on the Dốc Vàng Hạ River. The Việt Minh executive committee issued a communiqué stating Sổ had been executed on May 20. His body was cut into pieces and buried in different secret places. The Việt Minh wanted to convince Sổ's followers that he would never lead them again.[9] The war between Hòa Hảo and Việt Minh continued unabated despite Sổ's disappearance.

Phan Bôi Châu and Phan Chu Trinh

By the turn of the century when the "soldiers of *nghĩa*" had disappeared from the scene, the Vietnamese, stung by their growing feeling of inferiority vis-à-vis France's achievements in building railroads, highways, and bridges in their own country, realized they needed to master western culture and its secrets before they could make any progress, let alone regain independence. The French, by breaking new ground, tearing down mountains, filling the marshes, and basically rebuilding a new society, opened the eyes of the natives.

Nothing was more striking in the north than to witness Governor General Paul Doumer making up his mind to build a bridge over the Red River, which flowed through Hà Nội. Local people believed the river could not be mastered and that the mythic dragon that lived in the river would be upset if the French attempted to work on it. Dire warnings were present on many lips and well-meaning people even attempted to dissuade the governor, but to no avail. The French went ahead, driving pilings and pouring concrete into the riverbed and raising up a fancy steel bridge right into the heart of the dragon. When the two-mile-long Doumer bridge was completed—the longest in Asia at that time—many people were impressed, though some became resentful.[10] Overall, that feat struck a blow deep into the psyche of the Vietnamese. How could the French do it while they, the Vietnamese asked themselves, were still afraid of waking up the mighty dragon? Who gave the French the right to impose themselves on Vietnamese soil?

All of these economic developments, which went far and beyond the country's needs and capabilities, forced tax hikes and continuing demand for corvée labor, which in turn weighted heavily on the poor. Everything was taxed, including salt, which was commonly used by everyone. In 1907, the price of salt was five times its price in 1897. A salt worker had to sell every grain of salt to the government and then repurchase it for household use at six to eight times his previous sale price. Alcohol became the colonial government's monopoly. Each province had to buy a quota of liquor each month—whether they needed or not—based on "normal usage," lest it be charged for illicit distilling. The government then gave itself the right to enter, search homes, and look for illegal distilling of rice whiskey, which was used by the poor during local festivities. The poor, who could barely afford it, had no choice but to buy the government's expensive alcohol. Opium, which was illegal in France, was purchased raw in India, processed in Saigon and sold at official outlets at a profit of 400 to 500 percent. Thus, besides imposing taxes on alcohol and opium, France encouraged their use and addiction. Crushing taxes, forced labor, oppressive law enforcement, combined with three consecutive years of poor crops (1903, 1904, and 1905) eventually caused widespread rebellions.[11]

Gone were claims from the natives of a proud "four-thousand-year old culture" and the empty feelings of moral superiority. The latter were replaced by the wailings of despair and self-doubt. While the king and his mandarins, twice a year in spring and fall, gave a ritual offering to Heaven, Confucius, their ancestors, and the god of agriculture and sat back, afraid to change the status quo, the Europeans moved ahead by changing their environment and experimenting with one method after another. From there sprang the idea of modernizing the society to make it more competitive.

The new leaders of this generation of activists were the two Phan: Phan Bội Châu and Phan Chu Trinh, who were not related. As a matter of fact, they could have been more different as they espoused opposite philosophies and strategies.[12]

Châu, a neo–Confucian scholar, traveled to Japan where he was struck by the remarkable technological advances of this country and its naval victory over a western country, Russia. The realization hit him like a thunderbolt. On his return to Yokohama in 1906, he wrote in his *Hải Ngoại Huyết Thư* (Overseas Book inscribed in Blood), that the country was lost to the French because the monarch knew nothing about popular affairs, the mandarins did not care about the people, and the people only cared about themselves.[13]

Châu was a man of action, an activist, although he remained a firm believer in traditional Confucian values and the people. Ideas for him were only tools to more concrete ends. He symbolized the continuity of resistance, a stubborn unwillingness to be cowed. When the Japanese and later the Chinese turned down his request for armaments, he took students out of Vietnam, sent them for training in Japan or wrote propaganda in preparation for an eventual rebellion. He was the role model for future anti-colonialists, including the communists.

For him, the failure of the king and court to serve their people lay at the root of the problem. He was particularly unhappy with mandarins, each of whom could "suck the blood of many thousands of common people." Enlightened by these findings, he called for a continuing struggle, unity of all societal classes, and advocated modernization of the country and education of its people. To achieve these goals, he became a fundraiser, recruiter, and inspirational leader who would send hundreds of young Vietnamese students to study in Japan through the Đông Du (travel east) movement with the hope of bringing change to the society upon their return. He also advocated violence to get rid of the French but believed in the monarchy as a regime although he had previously blamed the king for the loss of the country. He even enrolled Prince Cường Đề, a direct descendant of Gia Long, in a Japanese military school.

In May 1907, Châu made connections with the Saigon middle class, especially Trần Chánh Chiêu or Gilbert Chiêu, editor of the Saigon quốc ngữ newspaper *Lục Tinh Tân Văn* (News of the Six Provinces—that is, South Vietnam) and the most influential bourgeois intellectual at the time. The contact led to a Chiêu-Châu meeting in Hong Kong, following which Chiêu sent funds to support the Đông Du movement. By October 1907, there were more than 100 students in Japan—more than half from the South—compared to only 20 in 1906. By mid–1908, southern students became the majority, with 100 from the South, 50 from the center, and 40 from the North. The French Sûreté reported "about three hundred students" by 1908.[14]

Funding support from Cochinchina stemmed from the work of the 27-year-old Nguyễn Quang Diệu. He and others founded the Khuyên Du Học Hội (Society for Encouragement of Learning) for the purpose of moving southern students to Tokyo through Hong Kong by raising money from wealthy landowners throughout the South. Gilbert Chiêu separately founded the Nam Trung hotel in Saigon and the Minh Tân hotel in Cần Thơ to provide financial help to students going abroad. These hotels also served as storage and distributing centers for documents smuggled in from abroad.

The Sûreté, however, was able to infiltrate the movement and document the transactions between Cường Để and donors from Vietnam. This led to police raids on the hotels, which yielded piles of smuggled items from Japan. Gilbert Chiêu, although a French naturalized citizen, was placed under arrest and France, through the Franco-Japanese Treaty, forced Japan to expel Cường Để, Phan Bội Châu, and most of the students, putting an end to the Đông Du movement. Having nowhere to go, the distraught Châu and Cường Để, expelled from Japan in 1909, moved to Hong Kong, then settled in Thailand for a year before returning to China in 1912.[15]

As his relations with Chinese supporters soured, Châu landed in a Chinese jail from 1915 to 1917. The French handed him an olive branch and offered him a position in the Huế court if he disavowed his "revolutionary doctrines." Châu refused. While traveling to Peking in 1920, he stumbled on a Japanese study of Russian communism. Curios, he asked representatives of the Soviet Union if it would accept Vietnamese students for training. Whether he followed through on this lead is not known. In 1924, he wrote about a revolution involving workers and peasants but under the control of the Vietnamese elite.[16]

A plot had developed in 1925 to "sacrifice" Châu to the French to replenish revolutionary finances. Apparently Comintern agent Hồ Chí Minh sent Châu a message asking him for a discussion-meeting in Shanghai on June 30, 1925. When Châu walked out of the Shanghai train station to catch the boat for Canton, two Sûreté men grabbed him and placed him on a boat for Hải Phòng, Vietnam. Hồ justified the betrayal on the grounds that Châu was a nationalist, not a communist. Besides, the reward would be used to build up the communist movement and the execution of Châu would create an atmosphere of resentment and unrest inside Vietnam conducive to a full-fledged rebellion. Châu was tried on November 23, 1925, and condemned to death. He was no longer a rival to Hồ Chí Minh.[17]

Phan Chu Trinh, a Confucian scholar, witnessing the same Japanese miracle as Châu had, advocated educational changes through non-violent reform and gradual progress toward independence as a democratic republic with the help of the French. He represented the reformist group. A loner and a proud, sensitive dealer of ideas, he was not a leader of organizations. He was averse to violence after having witnessed his father's killing by scholar-gentry associates. From then onward, he irrevocably broke with the monarchy, which he considered aloof, and the mandarinate system, which he loathed and found corrupt. These assessments were unusual and remarkable, especially coming from someone who was trained and grew up under the Confucian system. But knowing the system from the inside, he could be trusted for his opinions. He was not alone in his thinking, for Trần Quý Cấp and Huỳnh Thúc Kháng, respectively second and fourth graduates from the 1905 court exams, shared his opinion. The three walked through many towns in central Vietnam advising mandarins to throw off their caps. The walk ended after Trinh got sick during the trip.[18]

Trinh's most memorable venture was the opening of the Đông Kinh Nghĩa Thục or Eastern Capital Non-tuition School, where mathematics, science, geography, hygiene, political history, economics, French, and Chinese were taught. Designed to educate 400 to 500 students, it emphasized the romanized alphabet of the Vietnamese, quốc ngữ, formerly popularized by Alexandre de Rhodes in 1650. In fact, it was the first school that taught quốc ngữ in Vietnam. Providing a free education, it was opened to students of both sexes and had a male and female volunteer faculty staff. The idea of opening a school was unprecedented, for never before had Vietnam had a public educational system. The other revolutionary idea was to include women, not previously allowed to receive any education, on the teaching staff. Traditional education at the time was provided by private teachers with the state organizing the final examination; it was uneven, without scientific curriculum,[19] and reserved only for those who could afford it. The majority of people, therefore, were illiterate.

Stunned by the decision, the French administration gave the school a temporary permit in March 1907. Eight levels of instruction were available, primary through high school, with special classes in quốc ngữ, Chinese and French. Science was a new course for teachers and students alike. For the first time, students were introduced to mathematics and geometry, as well as social science and hygiene. History and geography were also discussed. Overall, students young and old, male and female, were exposed to courses that they never imagined had existed. Their Confucian world, which was limited to their parents, villages, mandarins, and king, was widened in scope and depth. One could just imagine a peasant's son or daughter walking to school for the first time in his or her life to learn sciences, mathematics, and history, without having to pay anything. The experience must have been as exhilarating as it was mind boggling.

As months went by, there was a mood of incipient nationalism at the school. Students were encouraged to buy local products instead of French imports. School songs referred to the French as exploiters. Besides teaching, the school was also involved in fundraising, proselytizing campaigns, and publishing. Among the teachers, Trinh was the school's most popular speaker, with his folksy humor.[20]

Trinh was a reasoned debater and a master of the symbolic gesture, although not a profound thinker.[21] He was in love with words and ideas, but did not question whether they fit together or conflicted with each other. Since he did not learn French until he was jailed in Poulo Condor in 1908, his knowledge came from inexact Chinese translations and interpretations of the works of Montesquieu and Rousseau. He was deeply connected to Mencius and his *Analects*. He was opposed to a violent overthrow of the colonial regime because it would only lead to a massacre of young Vietnamese since the country was technologically inferior. He stated that he would rather live under an "enlightened" colonial regime that would help modernize Vietnam than under the traditional Confucian regime. He, however, did not ask himself whether the French would help modernize the country or give it back to the Vietnamese for self-determination. On the other hand, Trinh's idea was good because it would acclimate the Vietnamese to modernity, free them from the traditional culture, and serve as a stepping-stone toward independence. Trinh was, therefore, regarded as a reformist, the godfather of an "evolutionary," slow albeit gentle, approach to independence.[22]

In their different ways, Châu and Trinh managed to convince the country, especially the youth, to change their way of thinking. They emphasized modernization instead of armed rebellion. Everyone had to sacrifice for the good of the country: students were subsidized to study abroad by rich landowners of the South who would donate the funds.

In a passionate speech at the Đông Kinh Nghĩa Thục School, Trinh stated that two millennia earlier, the Vietnamese had been forced by the Chinese to wear their hair in a bun. He told them to go out and get rid of their buns to prevent parasites to colonize the top of their heads, and suck their blood.[23]

The audience broke into wild laughter and applauded. In one sentence, he had linked the Chinese and French as parasites (lice) that fed on the blood of the people. That allusion spearheaded a movement of haircutting. Students were seen at street corners giving haircuts to whomever wanted while chanting: "Comb in the left hand. Scissors in the right. Snip. Snip. We cut. Off with stupidity."[24]

The haircutting movement began in Hà Nội in 1907 and rapidly spread to other cities in the country. Although benign in nature and scope, it marked a significant change in the thinking and mood of young people at the time. For a long time, they were dispirited, disillusioned, and did not know how to react to the French presence. No longer did they have to go into hiding in order to wage guerrilla warfare against the French—modernizing their country would be a better idea. And it started with getting rid of simple things, like hair in buns. In reality, the move was a quantum leap for these youngsters, for hair in a Confucian culture represented a precious "gift" bestowed by their parents. Getting rid of hair was akin to breaching filial piety and failing to acknowledge a moral debt to one's parents. In one sentence and with one symbol, Trinh advised them to cut themselves off from the Confucian culture and to turn toward modernity.[25]

The political implication of the haircutting movement was clear, as suggested by the poem that extolled the virtue of "shaving their hair, to become monks, to pray for independence and prosperity for the country."[26] This was followed by getting rid of the tunic mandarin men used to wear in public and adopting western clothes. The tunic was a loose, long-sleeved piece of clothing that was split on both sides at the hips.

Facing a demand for modern education and suspecting dark political motives behind the creation of the Đông Kinh Nghĩa Thục and the sending of students abroad, the French reacted by creating the University of Hà Nội and a government-sponsored school to compete with the Đông Kinh Nghĩa Thục.

Demonstrations multiplied in 1908 as demands for modern education, tax cuts and reduced corvée labor increased. They began in Quảng Nam, central Vietnam, where peasants complained about heavy corvée labor at the Nồng Sơn coal mines. They spread to neighboring provinces where others complained about high taxes. Tax collectors were chased, beaten, and threatened with death. Prefectural headquarters were occupied. Demonstrators were met harshly by the police and colonial troops. Some were killed, others were jailed and received long-term jail sentences at the Poulo Condore island jail, about 80 miles offshore.

Alarmed by the demonstrations during which many leaders were either imprisoned or killed—especially after the attempted poison plot of a French garrison in Hà Nội—the French reacted by closing the Đông Kinh Nghĩa Thục in January 1908 and rounding up all the reformists. Phan Bội Châu, still in Japan, was sentenced to death in absentia. Trinh was also sentenced to death with commutation to life imprisonment after which he was sent to Poulo Condore in 1908.[27]

On the island, Trinh was assigned the duties reserved for inmates: breaking up rocks to build roads and a jetty or transporting wood for use in the furnaces. Life was repetitive and boring with minimal outside news filtering to the island and mail only every three months. He used his spare time to write poems about his life at the Con Lon Island. As a prisoner, all he did day in and day out was to shatter rocks into pieces—all his strength going into producing hundreds of hundreds of stones.[28]

He was pardoned in 1911 after intervention by the French League for the Rights of Man and sentenced to house arrest in Mỹ Tho, where he protested the restrictions on his activities. In the end, he was allowed to leave for exile in Paris.

The Đông Kinh Nghĩa Thục movement was an anticolonial, antitraditionalist phenomenon. In its short existence (ten months), it failed to offer any solution to the problem of colonialism; however, it did allow people to realize how backward the country was and that battling colonialism would imply modernization. In a country that did not even have a simple common language, let alone a common goal, quốc ngữ became the tool that would allow them to reach their goal. By providing the same writing for all the Vietnamese, it brought them together and allowed simple and effective communication, mass education, and indoctrination, which would be critical for the organization of a coordinated rebellion.[29]

Châu and Trinh were two nationalist leaders who had introduced the Vietnamese to two ways of fighting the French: the activist method spearheaded by Châu would be followed by northerners while the moderate southerners would adopt Trinh's reformist way. Activism would lead to communism in the North while reformism was more compatible with the capitalistic, business-oriented South.

Bùi Quang Chiêu and the Constitutionalists

Six decades after the French landed in Saigon, changes were noted everywhere, although there were small in nature. The population of Vietnam was estimated at 19 million in 1937; there were also 217,000 Chinese, 326,000 Khmers and 39,000 French. A small bourgeoisie with voting rights had emerged: about 7,000 Vietnamese families of big landlords, 750,000 middle-level farmers and 500,000 petit bourgeois (shopkeepers, small traders, clerks, managers, technicians, artisans, interpreters, school teachers, journalists).[30] Although Saigon had grown to 132,000 inhabitants and Cholon to 184,000 in 1931, the Vietnamese electoral section counted only 4,332 out of the tens of thousands of eligible electors.

Despite strict regulations—there was a license needed requiring French citizenship and prior authorization before publication—dozens of journals were published by the locals. They included daily newspapers like *La Dépêche d'Indochine* by the métis politician La Chevrotrière, nationalist newspapers like *La Tribune Indigène* (1917), *l'Echo Annamite* (1919), *La Cloche Fêlée* (1923) and the *Đuốc Nhà Vietnam* (Vietnamese Torch). The average circulation of these papers was about 1,200. There were also leftist French newspapers like le *Bulletin Socialiste de la Cochinchine*, which became more active politically by the end of 1930s. Only one quốc ngữ newspaper, *Trung Lập Báo* (Neutral News), regularly issued 15,000 copies a day.[31] All these newspapers brought fresh air into the socio-economic environment in Saigon. Discussions centered on the best way to educate youth and women, to obtain progress and to maintain health.

People slowly realized that national independence would not be possible without individual freedom and without deep changes within the society. This implied a rejection of the Confucian tradition and its iconoclastic rules like filial piety, the absolute authority of parents and teachers, and oppressive familial pressure. Although education was important, it was one of the limiting factors to progress, as the French seemed to discourage serious learning. For a population of close to 20 million people, only 130,000 Vietnamese experienced primary schooling and 20,000 had upper primary education (grades 7 to 10) between 1920 and 1939. A mere 465 were enrolled in secondary schools (grades 11 to 13) in 1939.[32]

The youth turned inward by thinking about themselves rather than their families or country. They also delved into occidental novels, or even Vietnamese novels, that expressed new ways of thinking. The *Phụ Nữ Tân Văn* (Women's News), which discussed various ideas pertaining to women, was one of the most influential papers in the 1930s. Later the tone switched to forthright discussions on prostitution, religious escapism, attacks on fascism, and critiques of bourgeois feminism. There were also sensitive treatments of birth control, female psychological disorders, and suicides among young Vietnamese women. Western customs like ballroom dancing, fingernail painting, and beauty contests were deemed unsuitable for the country. The journal on the other hand played a major role in popularizing the áo dài—the national Vietnamese dress.[33]

In Cochinchina in 1917, some wealthy local landowners and Vietnamese capitalists (Bùi Quang Chiêu and Nguyễn Phú Khải) formed the Constitutionalist Party and published a French-language newspaper, *La Tribune Indigene*, to address economic modernization and administrative changes within the colonial system. Chiêu (1873–1945), born in Mỏ Cầy, Bến Tre, went to France to study before returning to Saigon in 1897. He did agricultural engineering work for the government general of Indochina and was posted at various regions of Indochina. He might have met Phan Bội Châu (1867–1940) and Phan Chu Trinh (1872–1926), the founders of the Duy Tân Party, in Hà Nội, although a large gulf separated these men who were born a few years apart: Chiêu was trained abroad while the Phan were brought up under the traditional mandarin system. Chiêu thought that if modernization of the country was the goal, the Vietnamese might as well learn from the French, who were already in Vietnam, rather than secondarily from the Japanese. While Phan Chu Trinh asked that the governor general treat the Vietnamese favorably if he wished for their support, Chiêu and the Constitutionalists requested specific reforms laid out in *La Tribune Indigene*.

Diệp Văn Cương (1876–1918), who might have been more prominent in the movement had he not died in January 1918, made the following requests:

Transformation of the traditional xã (commune) into municipalities with elected councils;

Abolition of the mandarin system, which would be replaced by a modern
   administrative hierarchy;
Reduction of minor Vietnamese officials and increase in salary for the rest;
Establishment of a justice of peace in every province;
Reform of the naturalization law to make it easier for Vietnamese to become
   French citizens; and
Increased representation of the Vietnamese in the Conseil Colonial, the rep-
   resentative body of the people.[34]

The governor general, Albert Sarrault, however, was more interested in
educational changes rather than administrative and political changes. Therefore, none of the Constitutionalists' requests were approved.

In 1920, the Constitutionalists—the only organized political group in
Cochinchina between 1917 and 1924—organized a boycott against Chinese
commercial firms, but failed badly because of the firm Chinese grip on the
economy. Nevertheless, the Vietnamese elite of Cochinchina were able to show
they could organize themselves politically.

In 1922, they were successful in helping elect several of their members
to the colonial council but they faced strong opposition from French colonialists. The new governor general, Maurice Long, increased native representation
in the Conseil Colonial from six to ten and expanded the Vietnamese electorate
from 1,500 to 20,000. The French, however, still held the majority in the conseil
as their number increased to 14.[35] Young radicals (Nguyễn An Ninh and Trần
Huy Liệu) later joined the Constitutionalists, although the association proved
to be temporary as they became more militant and took their case directly to
the proletariat and peasants.[36] The thrust of the Constitutionalists was to gain
for the middleclass, through non-violent means, economic and political privileges similar to those of the colonials.

Alarmed by the demands of the Constitutionalists, the French neutralized
Chiêu by transferring him to Cambodia in January 1925. *La Tribune Indigène*
was closed the next month.

By 1925, however, other concerns (new travel and mail restrictions
imposed by the colonial administration) caused the debate to turn political and
violent. The year 1925 also marked the passing of the torch between old (Phan
Bội Châu, Phan Chu Trinh) and young (Nguyễn An Ninh, Bùi Quang Chiêu,
Trần Huy Liệu) generations of revolutionaries. While Châu and Trinh, trained
at home under the Confucian system, talked about Jean Jacques Rousseau,
Montesquieu, Confucius and Mencius, the younger ones who were schooled
abroad debated about Nietzsche, Kant, Marx, and the revolutions in Russia
and China. The society had changed too. By 1929, a small, politically-conscious
laboring class had emerged in Saigon and was led by Bùi Quang Chiêu and
Nguyễn Phan Long. There were 220,000 workers in Vietnam in 1929—roughly
two percent of the population.[37]

Chiêu was a moderate whose work was soon challenged by extremists and groups like Nguyễn An Ninh, the communists, then the politico-religious groups. The gulf between the moderation of the Constitutionalists and the extremism of other groups tended to coincide with the gulf between town and country. But in Vietnam, the country ruled and although the colonialists won seats in the *Conseil Colonial*, it was not enough to change the mentality of the secret groups. Chiêu then left Vietnam to become an Indochinese representative of the Conseil Superior de la France d' Outremer from 1932 to 1941. By the time he returned to Saigon, the extremist groups had taken over the political fight. Chiêu was taken from his house in Phú Nhuận, a suburb of Saigon and executed by the Communists in 1945. With him died the Constitutionalist movement.[38]

In the North, Phan Bội Châu, after being caught in Hong Kong, was brought back to Hà Nội for trial. Found guilty of sedition against the colonial empire, he was sentenced to life in prison. The decision drew widespread demonstrations. The new socialist governor general, Varenne, to show his goodwill and to the despair of the colonists, commuted his sentence to confinement at home, which the tired Châu, who had been traveling from one country to another for the last two decades, gladly obliged. He retired from politics and spent the rest of his life in a small house in Huế by the Hương River. Phan Chu Trinh, a towering nationalist who had been critical of the French colonialist system, after more than a decade of exile in France returned to Vietnam to deal with the end-stages of tuberculosis. Too weak to travel to Huế, he settled in Saigon. He finally passed away on March 24, 1926.

On that same day, the Constitutionalist Party leader, Bùi Quang Chiêu, returned from a speaking trip from France. A small crowd of local people greeted him at dockside and asked him to intercede for Nguyễn An Ninh's release. The latter had been jailed for having participated in recent demonstrations against the government. The news of Trinh's death spurred the formation of a funeral committee, week-long funeral observances, followed by a long procession through the city.

On April 4, 1926, 60,000 mourners in ranks of four followed the procession in spite of police bans from downtown Saigon to the present-day Tân Sơn Nhứt airport. First came ten groups of students, workers, and women's associations, each holding identification banners. Six prominent individuals escorted the horse-drawn hearse, followed by row upon row of mourners. Tea, lemonade, and mint gelatin were offered free to the mourners by supporters along the route. Two hundred laudatory banners in Chinese, nôm (demotic characters) and quốc ngữ dominated the gravesite. Bùi Quang Chiêu and Hùynh Thúc Kháng gave orations.

The funeral was followed by a strike at a rice mill in Cholon. Aroused by Trinh's death, students felt the need to challenge the government. Requests for authorization to attend the funeral were denied at all schools while students wearing armbands were punished. Strikes became more organized and politicized. Ninety students went on strike at the private Catholic institution Taberd. Students at the School for Native Ladies also went on strike after a girl was punished for being loud during class. Things escalated when the supervisor and then the principal sided with the teacher. Strikes were organized and then spread to all provinces, and then to the North for the next two years.[39]

The death of the patriot Phan Chu Trinh galvanized Saigon and the nation. Although Phan Chu Trinh and Phan Bồi Châu had not been able to take down the colonial government, they succeeded in creating symbols of resistance and ideals for future generations. Without them, there would have been no continuity and historical purpose for action.[40]

Nguyễn An Ninh

Ninh (1900–1943) represented the modern southern version of the two Phan. Born in Quán Tre village, Hóc Môn district, Gia Định, he studied at the Saigon French lycée Chasseloup Laubat, which he completed in 1917. His father was a scholar who translated Chinese works into quốc ngữ, a landowner who supported the reform movement and was an important fundraiser for Phan Bồi Châu in the South.[41] Ninh went to Hanoi—the only university in Indochina—to study medicine. He changed his mind and switched to law shortly thereafter before deciding to go to France for further studies in 1920. His father took him to Lê Văn Duyệt's shrine and asked him to pledge never to forget his duty to his country. He got a bachelor's degree in law from Paris in 1923. He loved to travel and was a romantic philosopher and an intellectual loner rather than an organization man.

Upon his return to Saigon, as he made speeches to promote his anti–French ideas, he was called to the governor's office to explain his position. The governor of Cochinchina, Cognacq warned him: "There must be no intellectuals in this country. The country is too simple. If you want intellectuals, go to Moscow. Be assured that the seeds you are trying to sow will never bear fruits."

Ninh then founded *La Cloche Fêlée* (Cracked Bell), with Dejean de la Batie as manager, to express his own views and to advance his ideas. The son of a Vietnamese woman and a Frenchman, de la Batie was anti–French and was willing to lend his name to many Vietnamese journalistic ventures. Unlike his elders who suggested moderation and compromise with the French system, Ninh emphasized the need for a new moral order. On December 10, 1923, he blasted the Francophiles and wrote, "The notion of European prestige is based neither on moral nor on intellectual superiority but on skin color."[42]

He urged youths to break with the past in order to free themselves from both the tyranny of old Confucian ideas and French collaboration. He contrasted French ideals against France's humanitarian record in colonial Vietnam. He was able to publish only 19 issues from December 1923 until July 14, 1924, when the newspaper had to close because of lack of paying readership. The Vietnamese were too scared of the French Sûreté's tactics to accept being acknowledged as one of the paper's readers.

Ninh viewed national independence as an extension of personal freedom. For him, true nationalism, far from creating discord or hate among various nations, would instead help them to respect and live harmoniously with each other. He thus had an idealistic view of humanity and the world, based on French ideas of solidarity and fraternity. Liberty was for him more than a political status: it was a spiritual quest. Although in the beginning he rejected the idea of violence, he later saw revolutionary violence as inevitable. On November 30, 1925, he wrote:[43] "Liberty is to be taken, it is not to be granted. To wrest it away from an organized power, we need to oppose to that power an organized force."

He was, however, more of a thinker than a man of action. Since he was not concerned with issues of organization, he had few followers.

Trương Cao Đồng, who wrote about the ill treatment of workers sent to work in the rubber plantations of the South, was subjected to deportation. This treatment had been used by the colonialists to silence native Vietnamese who were vocal opponents of the colonialist government. On March 21, 1926, Ninh wrote on a tract opposing the deportation of Đồng, "We have been slaves for seventy years. During this time, a tyrannical government has oppressed us.... We should march from North to South." If government officials wanted to expel them, they would answer—to Moscow.[44]

A large crowd came to the meeting that, besides opposing Đồng's deportation, asked that the rights of man and citizen be respected in Indochina. The government had Ninh arrested after the meeting and sentenced him to two years in jail.

Ninh was a bridge between the tradition of peasant rebellion and the secular political culture. After returning from a trip to France in 1927, he settled in his village of Mỹ Hòa in the district of Hóc Môn, Gia Định. He shaved his head and placed an altar in a prominent position in his house. He and Phan Văn Hùm gave public lectures while others recruited people in secrecy. The Nguyễn An Ninh society was born. Through minor indiscretions, the existence of the society was revealed. What frightened the officials was the revelation that for the first time, this sect of poor peasants was led by a western-trained intellectual, one of popularity and stature.[45]

He would be imprisoned four more times before dying on August 14, 1943, in the Côn Sơn jail after four years of incarceration. He once wrote, "In jail, the heart either breaks or hardens."[46]

This was another significant loss for the nationalists who were decimated both by the communists and the French.

Society and Women

Saigon became the publishing center during the two wars because it was the most politically open city in Indochina. According to French sources, the Vietnamese published 13,381 different books and tracts between 1922 and 1940. At least 163 Vietnamese language periodicals appeared in Saigon between 1918 and 1939. Hanoi overtook Saigon in publications by June 1938.[47]

This did not mean that freedom of press was respected. On the contrary, the press was rigidly controlled by the colonial government because of the fear of printing subversive materials. Restrictions were numerous. The owner of the paper had to be a French citizen and Vietnamese articles had to go through censure prior to being allowed to go to press. Vietnamese printing shops were only allowed to buy second-hand machines, which put them on a less competitive level than French or Chinese newspapers. Many newspapers failed within the first year. Most of the publications dealt with moral and religious topics (religious books or tracts).[48]

Introduced in Vietnam in the third century A.D., Buddhism flourished under the Lý kings (10th century) who spent part of their lives in monasteries. It was pushed aside by a resurgence of neo–Confucianism in 1428, especially under king Lê Thánh Tông. In the 17th to 18th centuries, the Nguyễn made Buddhism the state religion in đàng trong and built hundreds of new pagodas.

By the late 18th century, Vietnamese Buddhism had declined because most of the temples had been destroyed by the Tây Sơn. In addition, Buddhism had become an oral tradition that did not rely on classic Buddhist texts. Because of lack of centralization, monks were poorly educated: they lacked book sutras and books to study, and therefore could not lead commoners. Women learned by repeating by heart the words they would narrate, although they did not understand the meaning of the religion.[49] Taoism, Buddhism, Confucianism were intertwined and simplified and associated with animistic beliefs in order to become a Vietnamese folk religion.

By 1920, monks decided to launch a movement to revive the religion. Texts were printed and distributed to people. Because of lack of direction, some people simply turned to variants of Buddhism like Cao Đài and Hòa Hảo religions, which had charismatic leaders.

Life has always been easier and more secure in the southern third of Vietnam. Southern villages have always been more open, less corporate, and more tolerant of individual initiative and cultural heterodoxy.[50]

There was tremendous economic growth and relative prosperity in the 1920s. French investment increased 600 percent between 1918 and 1930. The acreage used for rubber plantations tripled in the South. Rice exports increased while its local consumption decreased. Imports into Vietnam from France also increased from prewar levels while local industries were discouraged.[51] Most of the benefits, however, went to two banks and a few dozen businesses with interlocking interests. A handful of men controlled the financial and economic structure of Vietnam.

Two new classes slowly emerged within this economic system: a working class and an urban middle class. They were not large nor cohesive enough to have major political or social input, although they had some influence on the transformation of the society and culture.

The working class was small, made up of less than two percent of the population. These workers were transient and moved rapidly from one job to another. They worked in mines, plantations, and industries. The majority were peasants who left their lands for a job in the cities. The countryside was changed. People owned bicycles, flashlights, thermoses. They were used to trains, automobiles, and ships. Despite having access to modern conveniences, they experienced a deep malaise with low self-esteem and self-worth. They felt like second-class citizens in their own land as their highest earners (professor with a doctorate degree from Paris) made less money than the lowest-ranked French representative in Indochina.[52]

There was an explosion of new literature, especially novels. Although they wrote for money, writers also wanted to express the feelings, anguish or problems they faced within their "outmoded" Confucian society. With its strict rules and regulations, Confucian society imposed heavy moral burdens to the point of choking the people. They wanted to get out of its constraints, although its power remained pervasive and strong. Unable to escape the reality, they wrote to transform the society and to remake it at least in writing.

The first successful modern novel, *Tố Tâm*, was written in 1925 by Hoàng Ngọc Phách. Tố Tâm, a young and beautiful girl who had graduated from a French high school a few years earlier met and fell in love with a man through an acquaintance. The two youngsters pledged to each other and she even proclaimed she would not marry anyone she did not love. When her dying mother implored her to marry another man through a prearranged marriage, she was stunned but finally agreed because of hiếu (moral duty toward her mother). After getting married, she became depressed and ill and passed away. She left a diary asking her husband to engrave on her tomb: "Here lies one ill-fated person who died because of love."

This story, which does not seem of note today, was in itself a revolution in the making in 1925. For more than a millennium, a woman had to follow the tam tồng (three rules), which included obeying her father when single, her husband when married, and her elder son if widowed. She would not be a perfect woman if she did not abide by those rules.[53] She had to please her parents by going through a prearranged marriage, whether she liked it or not. Only by making it work had she fulfilled her duty.

The story, therefore, depicted the dilemma she faced between duty (hiếu, nghĩa) and romantic love (tình). Torn between contrasting feelings—hiếu and tình—she had to make a critical choice. Duty often prevailed, although she was not happy with it. To be truthful to herself, she would not consume her marriage and chose death.

The most common conflict depicted by these first-generation writers was the clash between eastern and western cultures. Westerners were taught to be individualists who thought and acted for themselves. Children learned to break away from the family to build their own nests. Easterners saw life differently. They lived for their families as they were the extension of their parents. Honor bestowed by parents flowed downstream to children. The latter, in turn, married for their parents to make them happy.[54] They cared for the elders at home when they became old. Two or three generations would thus live under the same roof, one depending on the other through a living symbiosis. They formed a cohesive unit, from which they did not want to dissociate. Individualism was not part of their thinking. They could love poetry and novels, but not detective stories. "The emotional basis for such individualism was underdeveloped in the personalities of most Vietnamese," remarked Jamieson.[55] In the same vein, they would never be solo adventurers, discoverers of new lands. They tended to be ultraconservative—making them less likely to reject communism (see, for example, Vietnam, China, North Korea), even though that doctrine had been discarded everywhere else.

In March 1933, Khái Hưng (Trần Khánh Giư) released *In the Midst of Spring* (Nửa Chừng Xuân). As both her parents had passed away, Mai, a young woman, tried to survive by selling her family's modest holdings while raising her younger brother Huy. Lộc, an old friend and college student, bumped into her one day and decided to help her out. Lộc and Mai fell in love. He one day told his mother, Mrs. Judge, about his plan to marry Mai.[56] Mrs. Judge reminded him about hiếu and about not defying her. As a future clerk and the son of a judge, he should think about marrying someone of his class, she told him, not a country girl. Disappointed, Lộc moved in with Mai without Mrs. Judge's knowledge.

One day, Mai advised Lộc she was pregnant. Lộc notified his mother about Mai's condition. Mrs. Judge got mad and told Lộc to get rid of Mai and return home to live with his parents. When Lộc refused, she decided to sow doubts in her son's mind, and she suggested that the fetus was not his.

Mrs. Judge went to see Mai and begged her to let her son go free. Mai thought Mrs. Judge spoke for her son, who did not have the nerve to tell her directly. Deeply hurt, she moved out of the house with Huy. She went through difficult times, living in the slums, subjected to scorn and sustained by charity. Eventually, her life stabilized. Huy graduated from high school and she took a teaching job while raising her son. Lộc in the meantime married a province chief's daughter although he still loved Mai. Many years passed. One day, Lộc met Mai again and asked her to come back and live with him. Mai refused despite still loving him. As Lộc insisted they could run away and rebuild a family life, she told him that at that moment two people were unhappy, Lộc and her. Running away would not solve the problem, but would spread unhappiness to a lot more people. She asked him to sacrifice themselves for the good of others: him to his wife and children, her to her child and younger brother.[57]

In the Midst of Spring was one of the best-written and most widely read Vietnamese novels of the 20th century. It tackled the theme of duty and love that faced many youngsters during that period. Lộc chose duty over love, following his mother's advice. He lived in a traditional world where he was at ease, although he remained unhappy as years passed by and torn between the call of love and duty. He did not know how to extricate himself from this world now that he was bound into it. Mai, on the other hand, was forced to choose between freedom and self-reliance. She went through rough times, trying to survive while being pregnant and raising her younger brother.

Khái Hưng seemed to tell his readers that there are two ways of dealing with situations: the traditional way and a new, independent, responsible, although difficult one. The hero of the story was not the traditional male person, but Mai, a young lady who managed to rise to the occasion despite being besieged by many social problems. The story was a departure from the Confucian textbook, a break with the past as the author attempted to show that women could be successful and survive on their own.

In 1935, Nguyễn Tường Tam wrote *Breaking the Ties*, where he presented a more militant version of individualism. Loan, the protagonist, fell in love with one man but had to marry another one because of hiếu. She gave birth to a boy, who later got ill. Mrs. Clerk, her mother-in-law, took the boy to a traditional healer who gave him a drink of incense ash in water and a mulberry switch to drive away evil spirits.

As the child worsened, Loan was incensed to learn about the healer's treatment. She took her son to a western physician, although it was too late to save him. Mrs. Clerk ordered her son Thân, Loan's husband, to bring the child home so that she could take care of him: "He's your child, but he's my grandchild."

Things got worse. Thân had an affair and got a girl pregnant. Mrs. Clerk wanted him to take her as a concubine. During the wedding ceremony, the girl had to prostrate herself before Mr. and Mrs. Clerk and then before Loan. The latter was upset by the ritual and the fact that another person was brought home to be a "baby-making machine ... a little servant without any wages."

As time passed by, Loan became more estranged from her husband. During one of these arguments, Mrs. Clerk jumped in and slapped Loan, labeling her behavior disrespectful. Loan argued back and Thân hit her, causing her to fall. "Beat her to death for me. If she dies, I'll be responsible," Mrs. Clerk shouted. As Loan responded, Thân hurled a vase in her direction. She ducked, backed away and grasped a paper cutter to defend herself. As Thân ran toward her, he tripped and fell on the knife, killing himself instantaneously.

In court, Mrs. Clerk, testifying as the witness, accused Loan of having premeditated the killing. The prosecutor argued that Loan had forgotten her heaven-mandated role of being a "devoted daughter-in-law and gentle wife, of being a pillar of the family." If the family were destroyed, society too will be destroyed. Loan, therefore, should be punished for her bad behavior. The defense lawyer argued that the whole family had ganged up against Loan, a nice young woman who just wanted to live in peace with them. She was only guilty of having been educated and returning to live with an old-fashioned family. She should be free, he argued, because she had been unjustly accused. The French court found her not guilty.[58]

Breaking the Ties was widely read in Saigon and the South in the late 1930s and was required reading for high school students before 1975. It presented many arguments against elements of the traditional culture: healing practices, wedding rituals (concubine, prostration), and values (filial piety), which needed to be reevaluated and set aside. It is interesting to note that in many of these novels, the protagonist was a young woman with some education who wanted to move ahead and change society. On the other side were women like Mrs. Clerk and Mrs. Judge, who wanted to preserve the status quo as well as their roles within the society. As long as they remained Mrs. Clerk or Mrs. Judge, they were respected and had power. Males, the representatives of the Confucian culture, also stood for the status quo and clung on to the old culture in which they felt at ease. They appeared to be lost in the new world where they were no longer propped up on pedestals, and felt socially diminished.

Although there are many more novels that offered a vision of the new society, the above three are representative of the novels published at the time. They all urged the young to change and to work for the modernization of the society, which the latter gladly followed. Each of these factors: modern education, novels, haircutting, made its small impact on their minds and slowly moved them on the road to modernity. The move, however, was gradual because the imprint of the two-millennia-old Confucian culture still bore heavily on the society. While some people became westernized rapidly, others hung on to their traditional culture, afraid to make the jump.

The clash between the yearning for modernity and the old culture or the colonial oppression, however, led to revolts, rebellions, and strikes because differences between new and old were striking. Among the old things to target were monarchy, Confucian culture, and the education of women. Then, there was the problem of colonialism and the French. The problem was twofold: internal and external. The internal problem related to the political, social and educational structure of the country, while the external had to do with the French. Youth and adults—middleclass, urban, Western-educated, and male— looked at the problems and shook their heads in despair. They asked themselves where to begin, which thing to change first, and how to proceed. Faced with this mountain of problems, many were subject to feelings of ambivalence, guilt, and frustration, and in some cases to a painful sense of impotence and inferiority.[59]

Some leaders looked at the monarchy with respect and wished to keep it
(Phan Bội Châu); others wanted to establish a republic right away (Phan Chu
Trinh). Some liked Confucianism and the orderly way with which the society
functioned, others wanted to discard it. As for the education of women, many
would like to keep them in the kitchen and give them a modicum of education;
others would offer them the same education as their male counterparts. As for
the question of independence and colonialism, some would cooperate with the
French (Phan Chu Trinh, Phạm Quỳnh), others would get rid of them by force
(Phan Bội Châu, Nguyễn Tường Tam).[60] The permutations and options were
plentiful, and so too were the cacophony of voices and the multiplicity of
political organizations that offered solutions to these problems.

Saigon Strikes

The year 1930 began with a revolt in Saigon. On 4 February, 3,000 workers
at the Phú Riêng rubber plantation north of Saigon went on strike. This was
followed by strikes at other factories and workplaces. Overall, there were 125
worker strikes in 13 of 21 southern provinces, which tapered off by October
but continued in February 1931. During one of these incidents, a French police-
man was gunned down by a 14-year-old worker who was sent to the guillotine.
Thousands of people were sent to jail in the summer of 1930. The criminal
court in Saigon doled out a total of 900 years of hard labor and jail to 101 condemned prisoners.[61]

Faced with the vengeful action of the Saigon police, radical nationalist
intellectuals who had studied in France became Trotskyites.[62] They included
Tạ Thu Thâu, Huỳnh Văn Phương (1906–1945), Hồ Hữu Tường (1910–1980),
Trần Văn Thạch, Nguyễn Văn Tạo and so on. On their return to Saigon in
1933, they—known as the fighters—founded La Lutte (the Fight) to promote
a continuing campaign against repression and to alert their readers about the
deplorable conditions suffered by 4 to 5,000 internees at the Poulo Condor
Island jail. They then published reports on the miserable conditions of the poor
who lived in the stilted-huts of the Thị-Nghè area and on the abysmal working
conditions of the plantations, warehouses, and factories. Seven hundred million
francs were invested in the cultivation of rubber trees between 1925 and 1929.
About 100,000 to 200,000 workers were deceived into working for the "red
earth" rubber growing plantations of Cochinchina under horrible conditions,
including endemic malaria, contaminated or insufficient food and water, long
working hours, the docking of wages, and vicious punishments. The turnover
rate due to escape or death was very high.[63] Sustained by public support generated by these reports, workers continued their demands and prisoners
unleashed their hunger strikes.

Workers' strikes recurred in 1936 as a reaction to an increase in the cost of living. From June 1936 to August 1937, a total of 347 strikes caused 100,000 workday losses. No violence or incidents with the police were noted as these legal and well-coordinated strikes demanded wage increases, payment of salary loss, cessation of reprisals, and social legislation. The reelection of the "fighters" Tạ Thu Thâu, Nguyễn Văn Tạo, and Dương Bạch Mai to the municipal city council increased their political standing among the workers and the colons.

The Trotskyites and communists fought against each other for the leadership of the strike movement. Tạ Thu Thâu was killed by the communists in Quảng Ngãi on September 1945. His friends Phạm Văn Hùm and Trần Văn Thạch had suffered the same fate a month earlier.[64]

Two main prisons were built during that period in the South: the Khám Lớn (Big Jail) in Saigon, later known as the Chí Hòa jail, and the jail at the Island of Poulo Condore in the middle of the shark-infested Pacific Ocean about 80 miles southeast of Saigon. Besides these jails, where political prisoners and hardcore criminals were housed, scores of local and regional jails were erected all over the country. Huỳnh Thúc Kháng, before leaving home for the Poulo Condore penitentiary, bid farewell to his friends and family by writing that although things could change, "our hearts of stone and iron shall stay true."[65]

Only in 1939 did he relate the story of his stay in Poulo Condore between 1908 and 1921 in *Thi Thư Tùng Thoại* (Prison Verse). Phạm Văn Hùm described his incarceration at the Khám Lớn Jail in his memoir *Ngồi Tù Khám Lớn* (Sitting in the Big Jail), following his release in 1929.[66]

The fact that these jail terms were mostly known through communist literature was because the Hà Nội government, after their takeover of North Vietnam in 1954, encouraged people to write memoirs about their imprisonment with the goal of celebrating the early heroic struggles of the Communist Party. Secondly, many non-communist southern patriots who ended up in the same jails failed to jot down their "heroic" memoirs. Thirdly, most, if not all, of the prisoners in the 1920s through the 1940s were nationalist because the Communist Party was in its infantile stage at that time.

During the first four decades of the 20th century, the Vietnamese slowly awakened from their long dream under the monarchy only to, literally speaking, face the French sitting at their dining tables in their own country. Stunned, they tried to cope as best as they could with the situation only to come face-to-face with the competing forces of modernity and traditional culture. The fight between old and new forces led them into a collision course with history.

6

Saigon Under Bảo Đại
(1945–1954)

Vietnam's political landscape became dysfunctional in the mid–16th century when the weak Lê kings served as figureheads with the real power resting on the powerful Mạc, Trịnh, and Nguyễn lords. From 1600 onward, the country was divided into two different and separate political systems: đàng ngoài (present-day North Vietnam) and đàng trong (present-day central Vietnam). South Vietnam was still in the hands of the Chams and Khmers.[1]

When Nguyễn Ánh reunified the country in 1802, he directly controlled central Vietnam and let his governor generals run North and South Vietnam to ease the trauma of reintegration. By 1835, Minh Mạng got rid of them when he completed the integration process. When the French took over South Vietnam in 1861, the short two-and-a-half decades of "unification" did not allow the Nguyễn to blend the country into a cohesive political force. The Vietnamese still thought and acted regionally instead of as a united nation.

The French officially redivided the country into two regions. The South (Cochinchina) was run by the French under French laws as a colony. The center (Annam) and north (Tonkin) became protectorates and remained under the nominal control of the Huế court. By 1900, the center of power moved from Huế to Hà Nội where the French governor of Indochina resided and controlled the five regions that formed Indochina: Laos, Cambodia, and the three Vietnamese regions.

A divided political landscape and segregated administrative powers controlled by different armies made the situation in Vietnam extremely complex, volatile, and difficult to resolve.

By 1940, two main political forces competed for the leadership in North Vietnam. On one side, the nationalists were fractured into many groups: the Nguyễn Tường Tam-led Vietnamese Nationalist Party (VNQDD), Đại Việt, and other smaller groups. On the other side were the communists who hid behind various fronts and names in order to not alarm the general population. All these political parties fought against each other, had their bases in China and were partly supported by Chinese warlords and later by Chinese communists.

Saigon during World War II

Cooperation between the French Vichy government and the Japanese in 1941 allowed the French to continue their control over Indochina while giving the Japanese access to airfields and freedom to move their troops around. Indochina also had to supply the Japanese with rice and other strategic materials.

In the South, the absence of major political parties was filled by politico-religious sects (Cao Đài, Hòa Hảo), which were strong enough to raise their own armies and to protect the lands they controlled.

The Cao Đài, uniquely southern in origin, was founded in 1925 by four civil servants: Ngô Văn Chiêu, Cao Quỳnh Cư, Phạm Công Tắc, and Cao Hoài Sâm. Facing a Buddhist meltdown, they formed their own religious sect, which attracted many followers, especially peasants, within its first year. In 1927, it moved its headquarters from Saigon to Tây Ninh to accommodate the large number of followers and the Holy See with its garish eclectic architecture. The sect is monotheistic with the Creator God depicted by one eye, usually the left one. It venerates a pantheon of saints and spirit advisers like Buddha, Confucius, Jesus Christ, Lao Tsu, French poet Victor Hugo, and Sun Yat Sen. With its blend of Confucianism, Buddhism, Catholicism, romanticism, and non-violence, the sect appealed immensely to southern peasants, who converted in droves. It controlled swaths of lands that were patrolled by its own militia and kept the Việt Minh at bay. It had its own schools and courts and its own social welfare programs. It even planned to transform Tây Ninh into a metropolis with boulevards and parks.

In the Mekong Delta around Long Xuyên (after failing to claim Cần Thơ as their headquarters), lived the Hòa Hảo, under the leadership of Huỳnh Phú Sổ. They were more provincial and less grandiose than the other sects, although no less zealous or devout. Their militia wielded machetes and rifles to protect their lands.

On August 24, 1940, the French moved against the Cao Đài. They raided 328 Cao Đài temples and closed 284 of them. A total of 5,000 converts were arrested, of which 1,983 were members of the clergy. They remained jailed for the duration of the war until their liberation by the Japanese on March 9, 1945. "Pope" Tắc was first placed under house arrest in Gò Công and then exiled to the Comoros Islands.[2]

Southern jails were soon filled with people who were accused of sedition. Insurrections occurred in Cholon, Tây Ninh, Mỹ Tho, and Cần Thơ. Government buildings were burned, ferries and bridges were destroyed. Insurrections were, however, brutally crushed by the French army. Fifty people were guillotined and 400 to 500 others were jailed.

While the French reigned over some politico-religious organizations, the Japanese closely watched other personalities: Prince Cường Đề in Tokyo, Trần

Trọng Kim and Đặng Trung Chu in Bangkok, Trần Văn An and Nguyễn Văn Sâm in Singapore. Because they were tightly controlled by the authorities, Southerners lost their chance to rally around a person and to "have their own Sukarno."

War finally came to Saigon as the Allies closed in on the Japanese. American B-24 bombers raided the Saigon docks on May 5, 1944, killing 200 Vietnamese civilians and wounding 350 others from the neighboring Khánh Hội area. Planes from the U.S. Third Fleet bombed the oil tanks of Nhà Bè by the Saigon River and the hangars at Tân Sơn Nhứt and Biên Hòa airports. A B-29 raid on January 27, 1945, killed 130 civilians and wounded a similar number of people. Another raid on February 7 mistakenly hit a hospital, killing 150 Vietnamese without causing any damage to the Japanese.[3]

On March 9, 1945, the Japanese in Saigon caught the French by surprise by giving them an ultimatum to surrender. The Americans, having broken the Japanese code, had advance notice of the Japanese move. They passed the news to the French who did not take them seriously. Caught by surprise, French commanders reacted as best as they could. There was sporadic resistance and French officers who resisted were executed after surrender.

On March 11, Masayuki Yokoyama, the supreme adviser of the Japanese forces, went to see Emperor Bảo Đại at his palace in Huế and asked him to declare independence from the French. Bảo Đại convened his Cơ Mật (council of ministers), in front of which he declared: "The Government of Vietnam publicly proclaims that from today [March 11, 1945] the protectorate treaty with France is abrogated and that the country resumes its rights to independence." The proclamation, although abrogating the 1884 Treaty of Patenotre, did not mention anything about the reunification of Vietnam.

Bảo Đại was studying in France in 1930 when he was 18 years of age and ready to ascend to the throne. The French decided to keep him there for a two-year "maturation period." From France, he arrived in Tourane (Nha Trang) on September 8, 1932, bypassing Saigon, which he never knew. He proceeded to Huế where he was met by Governor General Pasquier. One of his first decisions after the coronation was to abolish the lại, the ritual prostration that was a sign of deference to imperial authority. Under the colonial system, he had only a ritual power that barely extended beyond central Vietnam.

Five months after his return on May 8, 1933, he abolished his cabinet of old ministers and replaced it with a group of younger ones, including Ngô Đình Diệm. In 1934, he married Marie-Therese Nguyễn Hữu Hảo, the daughter of a wealthy Cochinchinese who became empress Nam Phương. Disenchanted with the French refusal to grant him more power, his enthusiasm gradually waned. He let the resident superieur and the governor general make the final decisions in all matters.[4]

On March 17, 1945, the six members of the Cơ Mật resigned, clearing the way for Bảo Đại to set up a new government. The leading candidate at the time was Ngô Đình Diệm. The Japanese, after discarding Prince Cường Đê, who had been their primary choice, favored Trần Trọng Kim, a respected scholar, educator, and historian who had been in exile in Bangkok for some time. The Japanese flew Kim back to Huế to meet with Bảo Đại while keeping Diệm waiting in Saigon. Kim got the job.[5] Educated in Hà Nội and France, he was the author of many works on Buddhism and Confucianism as well as a history of Vietnam up to 1893, which was published in 1920. He was made a chevalier of the Legion of Honor. In hindsight, his overwhelming educational qualities were not the ones that were called for during that brutal period. He was not strong but was flexible enough when needed to deal with the fluidity of the situation.

The new cabinet, formed on April 16 under the 62-year-old Kim, was composed of young (from 33 to 49) western-oriented professionals. It adopted the yellow banner with three horizontal stripes as the national flag and "The King Mounts His Throne" as the national anthem. Although he had a foreign minister, Kim did not have a defense minister or an army since security had been taken over by the Japanese who also controlled the Bank of Indochina, post office and telegraphic communications, railways, and radio stations. This turned out to be Kim's Achilles heel.

Right in the beginning, he faced enormous economic challenges. First, a series of floods destroyed all the harvests in North and central Vietnam in 1944. Then the unusual winter cold caused serious damage to secondary crops. These shortages were worsened by continuing Japanese requests for rice and other crops to support their army. Famine thus ensued. While the Kim government worked hard to supply rice to the North, its transportation was interrupted by continuous Allied bombing on land as well as on sea. American aircraft, by sowing mines around the Hải Phòng area, prevented the distribution of rice. Allied troops contributed to the worsening of the famine. Economic inflation grew worse because the Japanese who controlled the Bank of Indochina continued to print more currency. Between March and August 1945, they printed 770 million piasters, more than the French government had used during the previous 53 months. In the North, the Việt Minh prevented the distribution of rice in the regions they controlled. They also stole government rice for their personal needs. Desperate, the Kim government did all it could to ship rice to the north to the point of using oxcarts and small junks that could evade American aircrafts. Overall, the great famine of 1945 claimed between one to two million people in the North. Hà Nội residents reported having to daily discard emaciated bodies sitting or leaning against fences or people's doors.

The Kim government only controlled Huế and central Vietnam while the North still remained a separate entity. Việt Minh and non–Việt Minh nationalists met in Hà Nội to stir up opposition against the Huế government. To decrease the political tension, Kim decided to appoint Toại as its resident superieur in Tonkin. When Toại met with the Japanese, they told him that the prime minister governed not under the direction of Bảo Đại, but under the Japanese governor general Tsuchihashi. Toại explained that his instructions from Huế were different and that the common people wished to see Tonkin reunited to Annam. He offered his resignation the following day. Kim explained to the Japanese that if Toại resigned, the whole cabinet would do the same. The Japanese gradually transferred Tonkin's powers to Toại.

Tsuchihashi still refused to grant autonomy to Cochinchina. He argued that he had to clear territorial claims that Cambodia had on the Mekong Delta. After lengthy negotiations, Kim was able to negotiate the return of Cochinchina with the reunification ceremonies set for August 8. In the mean time, Bảo Đại was discussing with Tsuchihashi for the return of the cities of Hanoi, Hải Phòng and Nha Trang. While discussions were progressing, youth minister Phan Anh organized a large rally in Hanoi in support for the reunification of the country. One more time Kim jumped into the negotiations and wrestled the three cities back from the Japanese with the turnover scheduled for July 20.

Trần Trọng Kim, therefore, scored his biggest political success by completing the reunification of the country for the first time in eight decades. He proved to be a "capable custodian of Vietnam's sovereignty" during the short period he held power.[6]

While the Kim government labored in lengthy and contentious negotiations with the Japanese and dealt with the famine issue in Tonkin, the Việt Minh did their best to torpedo the government's programs. They organized village demonstrations, calling for suppression of taxes, and an end to the requisition of rice, which had been causing anarchy and unrest in the North. They then used the occasion to challenge the authority of local officials and to assault them for the purpose of disrupting services and taking over the administration. When Kim, who did not fully understand the seriousness of the disturbances, insisted on going to the ceremony turning back Cochinchina to the Vietnamese, his ministers resisted. Upset that discussions about the unrest were not entertained, they resigned, causing the government to collapse. On August 12, Bảo Đại asked the old cabinet to continue as caretaker while a new one was being formed.

On August 14, Kim declared Cochinchina reattached to Vietnam and abrogated all the treaties between France and the Huế court. On the same day, the United National Front (Mặt Trận Quốc Gia Thống Nhứt, UNF) was formed in Saigon. It included the Vanguard Youth, the Vietnam National Independence Party, the Cao Đài, the Hòa Hảo, the Phục Quốc, the Trotskyites and a number of smaller groups. All these parties pledged their support to the Kim government.

On August 15, the Japanese announced their surrender on Radio Saigon and Radio Hà Nội (Bạch Mai). They surrendered the radio, the police station and the National Guard in the North to Toại, the imperial representative in Hà Nội who was under heavy pressure by the Việt Minh. Toại later resigned—not to the emperor but to an armed political party. On August 17, in Hanoi, a large crowd gathered at the National Theater to support the Kim government. Armed Việt Minh arrived, took over the demonstration, and denounced the "puppet government of Kim." The following day more Việt Minh troops arrived in town. Without competition, their propaganda took a firm grip on the mood of the crowds. On street corners, they declared that the Kim government was full of collaborators and the Việt Minh were the only representatives of the state and the U.S. was supporting the Việt Minh. On August 19, Việt Minh troops staged a march on a circular route, passing by a same fixed point to give the impression that their army was a huge one. Villagers were also guided to march to the opera house and to shout the slogan "Down with the Kim government."

When news of events in Hà Nội reached him, Kim felt ambivalent. He was embarrassed by the turn of events and by the way the Việt Minh coup had put him in. As a scholar and a righteous man, he was not about to compete with a force that he believed had the support of the United States. He had no idea about the Việt Minh plans for a revolution. His ignorance was shared by the common people in the streets. He was relieved to find someone who would want to lead the nation toward the future. He, therefore, put in his resignation that August 19, 1945. Kim's government was made up of honest and capable men, but they were not born to be heroes. And the summer of 1945 was the time for heroes.[7]

Leaderless, the government collapsed, opening the door for the Việt Minh to take over the country. Had Kim checked with the U.S. government, he would have known that the U.S. did not care much about the Việt Minh and had he put up some resistance, the revolution could have been controlled by that time. In the ensuing months, the Việt Minh plowed ahead with the purging of all non-communist political rivals: Huỳnh Phú Sổ, Tạ Thu Thâu, Ngô Đình Khôi, Phạm Quỳnh, Quan Trọng Ưng and Đặng Vũ Chu from the medical school faculty; Đặng Văn Bút and Đặng Văn Nghiên, two law school students; and Trương Tử Anh, the Đại Việt leader, and a number of other party members.[8]

On August 21, members of the United National Front marched through Saigon streets chanting: "Long Live Vietnamese Independence" and "Down with French Imperialism." The following day, the Vanguard Youth withdrew from the UNF to join the Việt Minh. It was later revealed that the Vanguard had all along been a Việt Minh creation. Without the Vanguard troops, the remaining political parties were doomed to watch on the sidelines. Following the same blueprint used in Hà Nội, the Việt Minh under Trần Văn Giàu took the central government's representative in Saigon prisoner, forcing him to resign, and then proceeded to take over the Norodom Palace, the post office, the port, the airport, and the Bank of Indochina. They also organized a demonstration on August 25.

Bảo Đại in the meantime was not sitting idle. On August 18 in response to de Gaulle's decision to name a new military commander and high commissioner for Indochina, he sent a message to France and de Gaulle advising them not to try to reconquer Vietnam by force but to respect the country's independence.[9]

The message was also sent to President Truman, Britain, China and the Soviet Union. De Gaulle never answered the message. While the message was being broadcast on the radio, the Việt Minh made their way into Huế and began forming revolutionary committees to take over government offices. Without military support, officials did not know how to react to these armed gangs: some resisted, others simply surrendered. A provisional revolutionary committee even sent Bảo Đại a message asking the emperor to abdicate. To avoid any bloodshed, Bảo Đại made his decision to step down. The abdication paper was dated August 25.

On the 30th, during a public ceremony, Bảo Đại, or, simply, citizen Vĩnh Thụy, surrendered the symbols of empire—a golden seal and a golden sword with ruby-encrusted handle—to a representative of the Việt Minh. As such, the August 19 events in Hà Nội represented not a revolution, but a coup d'état. The well-organized Việt Minh had taken over the control of a country that was defenseless before an armed political party. The shrewd Bảo Đại had shown during the August 30 ceremony that as a private citizen he no longer had any power to transfer to the new government.[10]

Nationalist revolutionaries from north to south were particularly unprepared and unlucky during this period. While Hồ was able to remain in China to bid his time, nationalists had no place to hide: They were either killed by the Việt Minh in the North, or arrested by the French or controlled by the Japanese from Tokyo to Bangkok. The law-abiding and unarmed Kim government was equally unable to compete against the armed Việt Minh. The absence of an armed non-communist political leadership nationwide allowed the Việt Minh to expand and take over the country.[11]

The State of Vietnam

Being a colony, the South marched to its own drum while communists and nationalists fought each other to take over the North and the royal government collapsed in Huế. Religious groups and communists competed to carve out their political influence in the South. Nowhere had political breakdown and confusion been more complete than in Vietnam during and after World War II. Although linked together by a common heritage, politically the three regions appeared like three separate countries. Vietnamese intellectuals and students were stunned if not confused by such an array of conflicting political options, none appearing better than the other. Their mood was, therefore, amorphous, unfocused, and uncommitted to any party or program. They simply wanted to regain independence for their country and their own dignity.[12]

The Việt Minh Trần Văn Giàu organized a demonstration in Saigon on September 2, 1945, to coincide with Hồ's declaration of independence.[13] Without warning, shots were fired and the demonstration turned into a riot. A French Catholic priest was found dead in front of the Saigon Cathedral. The murder led to reprisals by the French as well as further killings: In the end five Frenchmen were killed. Although Giàu denied any responsibility, he was accused by the Cao Đài and Trotskyites of collaborating with the Japanese. Anti-French feeling continued to rise and the city was in turmoil. The Cao Đài had strong paramilitary forces in the shipyards. The Hòa Hảo and the Việt Minh also had their own forces.

According to Allied plans, British troops under General Douglas Gracey arrived on September 12 to disarm the Japanese and to await the arrival of the French. They gradually took over the post office, the police stations, and the city hall and turned them over to the French. Gracey, on the advice of the French Cedille, freed and then rearmed the 11th R.I.C., the French unit that had been imprisoned by the Japanese since March 9. The undisciplined soldiers of the 11th R.I.C. and the French living in Saigon exploded in a brutish expression of pent-up anger and resentment, causing a rash of rioting on September 23. Soldiers shot at empty buildings. They roughed up men and even imprisoned women. The Bình Xuyên recruited by the Việt Minh retaliated the following day and killed 150 French citizens. Others were taken hostage and later killed. Pandemonium reigned over Saigon. Arson, sabotage, and killings continued on the 26th when an OSS mission arrived in town. OSS Major Albert Dewey was ambushed and killed by unknown assailants while he was on his way to the airport.

Trần Văn Giàu called for a general strike and told the Saigonese to evacuate Saigon and to leave nothing but burning rubble behind them. A truce was negotiated but it lasted only a week. Violence flared up again but was controlled by arriving French troops. Saigon became a beleaguered French city; the Mekong Delta, a battlefield.[14]

In the meantime, De Gaulle sent Vice-Admiral Georges d'Argenlieu to reestablish French sovereignty all over Indochina. The latter landed in Saigon on October 30 and fired thousands of dedicated and knowledgeable French civil servants from the previous administration. On March 6, 1946, he signed, with Hồ of the DRV (Democratic Republic of Vietnam), a shared sovereignty agreement in the North, allowing the French to return to Hanoi.

Having temporarily set aside the French problem, Hồ departed for France and left to Giáp the order to crush the remaining nationalist parties. Under Giáp's hands, the Đồng Minh Hội was finished as a force by the end of June. The Việt Minh surrounded many cities held by the VNQDD and engaged battles against them. They even got the assistance of the French to chase the remaining VNQDD members out of Hà Nội. They also wiped out the Đại Việt.[15] By the end of July, at least 15,000 nationalists had been massacred.[16] When Hồ returned from France months later, most of his rivals had been eliminated. The League of the Parties, an association of all the parties in Hà Nội, now consisted only of the Việt Minh. The guerrilla war between the French and the Việt Minh began.

After the communists wiped out his VNQDD in Hà Nội, Nguyễn Tường Tam moved to China where he tried to organize an anti–French and anti-communist organization. Few of his former colleagues were with him. Khái Hưng had been kidnapped and killed by the Việt Minh in 1947. Xuân Diệu and Huy Can had switched to the communist side. Hoàng Đạo was trying to form the Liên-Việt party.

After stepping down from his office, Bảo Đại became "supreme adviser" to the communist regime. Realizing he had minimal power, he used the excuse of traveling to China on March 18, 1946, to move to Hong Kong, where he followed political developments with a shrewd eye. He knew the non-communist nationalists would be looking for him because of his stature.

After speaking with Bảo Đại, Nguyễn Tường Tam formed the National Union Front, which was composed of former members of the Đồng Minh Hội, VNQDD, and Đại Việt. The front was dedicated to forming a government that would be led by Bảo Đại. As the popularity of Bảo Đại increased, Tam's influence withered, forcing him to retire in exile in China in October 1947. The Việt Minh launched a vigorous propaganda against Tam and Bảo Đại, sensing them as opponents, and staged rallies and burned them in effigy.[17]

As successive French governments failed to solve the Indochinese problem, in July 1947, Paris called on Bảo Đại, who then resided in Hong Kong, for help. On September 18, after meeting with 24 nationalist leaders from North to South, including Ngô Đình Diệm, he issued a proclamation expressing his pain on hearing about the people's suffering amidst the war and under the French government. He told them he was ready to talk to French authorities and to arbitrate the conflict between the different parties. Hồ quickly criticized the "puppet regime" that the French were about to set up and in a hypocritical manner declared, "I cannot stand by and see our own people divided in an internal fratricidal war."

Within 24 hours of each other, the Việt Minh death squads had liquidated Nguyễn Văn Sâm, the southern National Union Front leader, and Dr. Trương Đình Thi—two of the nationalists who had talked to Bảo Đại. Sâm had the courage to publicly comment that the Hồ regime was a communist government that pursued a partisan and totalitarian policy. Having stepped over the boundary, he was liquidated. Around the same time, Huỳnh Phú Sổ, the blind Hòa Hảo bonze-leader in the Mekong Delta, was also liquidated.[18]

Negotiations with the French continued at a snail's pace, with Bảo Đại even talking to French President Vincent Auriol. In June 1948, he and the

French signed the Hà Long Accord in which France for the first time agreed to "solemnly recognize the independence of Vietnam." Once Cochinchina was allowed to be reattached to the rest of the country, the French National Assembly approved the creation of a Free State of Vietnam. Bảo Đại returned home after three years of exile and moved into a villa in the southern resort town of Dalat.[19] On July 1, 1949, he signed and ratified the Elysée treaty. The yellow banner with three red horizontal stripes was then raised amidst a 21-gun salute. This was a rare moment of glory for Bảo Đại, who for many years had patiently wrestled with Vietnam's unity and independence from the French.[20]

The ecstatic Bảo Đại told the nationalists he had at least a framework for independence but they needed to be careful about the Việt Minh. The nationalists, however, were in a quandary. If they cooperated with Bảo Đại, they would be stigmatized as being associated with the French rather than the Americans. On the other hand, they could not remain idle while out there the communists were working on a solution on their own. It was a tragedy for which there was no good solution.

When Cao Đài Pope Tắc returned to Vietnam from exile, he declared his full confidence in the French to bring peace to the country. The declaration caused General Nguyễn Văn Thanh and his captains Trịnh Minh Thế and Dương Văn Đăng to break away from the Việt Minh. In retaliation, the Việt Minh attacked the Holy See, and rounded up and executed 800 Cao Đài faithful. The Cao Đài forces were comprised of 3,300 men grouped in brigades. They were mobile and effective and easily competed for territorial influence with the Việt Minh.

After Huỳnh Phú Sổ was assassinated by the Việt Minh on April 1, 1947, his lieutenant Soái took over as commander of the Hòa Hảo forces. The French used them as policing forces in the provinces of the Mekong Delta in exchange for arms, uniforms and trainers.

The Bình Xuyên switched allegiance and rallied to Bảo Đại, and their leader Bảy Viễn was made colonel. From common thieves and murderers they transformed themselves into respectable businessmen, protecting the wealthy Chinese in Chợ Lớn. They were given custody of the Grand Monde gambling den and operated gambling, opium and prostitution monopolies.

By arming these sects, the French expected to counterbalance the Việt Minh forces in the South. This action not only did little to build up a national army, it also caused immense problems for the Vietnamese national government in the future.

Although the State of Vietnam under Bảo Đại was recognized by many nations in the world, it failed to attract the service of men of competence. The latter stayed away, fearing their reputations would be tainted by association with a government that did not have a clear policy, ideology and purpose. Others feared a loss of integrity and identity.

Bảo Đại's prime minister from June 1953 to December 1954 was the hard-working but corrupt Nguyễn Văn Tâm. Although strongly anti-communist (his sons had been killed by communists), he was so conciliatory toward the French that most Vietnamese loathed him. He even had a Frenchman as his personal secretary, placing a foreigner between himself and his cabinet ministers.

After working hard to obtain a law degree, he became a provincial governor who was known for his courage in fighting the Việt Minh. He earned the nickname of "Tiger of Tân An." Although a competent administrator, he was not well liked as the leader of the nationalists. He lost the ability to mobilize and control large segments of the population because of his social insensibility and moral coarseness. He was the butt of many jokes, although he did not realize it. On one Tết occasion, notables presented him with a gold lamé scroll to wish him well during the lunar New Year Festival. The four Chinese characters read: "All the crimes in the world can be traced back to our own hearts." However, since "heart" was homophonous to the prime minister's name "Tâm," the words could be understood as, "All the crimes in the world can be traced back to Mr. Tâm." These experiences, which were mortifying for the prime minister once he realized them, revealed that the government's problem was moral—a spiritual shortcoming not an administrative, military, or economic defect.[21]

In September 1954, to put additional pressure on the French, Bảo Đại invited representatives from significant political parties for a three-day National Congress. After heated debates, they unanimously called for full independence from France. U.S. Ambassador Heath, however, explained that although the United States supported Vietnam's independence, he thought the resolution went too far. The relations between the United States and France were "multifaceted." The Vietnamese felt that issues that were important to them were just bargaining chips in the Americans' pursuit of global policy.[22]

Bảo Đại wanted the declaration of independence to be signed prior to the opening of the Geneva conference because as long as Vietnam was not independent, it was bound to play a subordinate role to France within the French Union.[23]

The French, since March 1954, had been fighting against the Việt Minh in Điện Biên Phủ on the western hills of Tonkin close to the Laotian border. General Navarre understood the importance of a base that would control road access to Laos. Later, the Americans would use the same concept to defend the outpost of Khe Sanh.[24] The idea was borne out of the successful operation at Nasan months earlier. Between October and December 1952, Colonel Gilles held off multiple Việt Minh attacks in a valley narrower than that of Điện Biên Phủ. By responding aggressively to attacks by artillery fire, air bombardment, and troop sorties, he prevented the enemy from putting pressure on an airfield his ground troops depended on.

However, Điện Biên Phủ was not like Nasan. The French commander Colonel Christian de Castries underestimated the tenacity of the enemy, which took down the artillery guns piece by piece and hauled them up the hills with great difficulty. Once the pieces were put back together, installed and wedged between cracks in the rocks, the fate of the outpost was sealed. The valley around the outpost was larger than that of Nasan, making it difficult for defenders to control the inward-facing slopes. Castries was not as aggressive as Gilles and did not respond immediately to enemy attacks. He failed to order troop sorties for fear of increasing casualties.[25] The lack of air support doomed the resistance of the French at Điện Biên Phủ. On May 7, unable to withstand any longer, the garrison finally surrendered.

Bảo Đại decided to look for someone who could appeal to the Americans (chercher les Americains). He found this in the person Ngô Đình Diệm, who was favored by the Americans. American diplomats in France talked to Bảo Đại about Diệm, who was cut from a different cloth than all the francophone people in Bảo Đại's entourage. Besides, he was a patriotic man who had been condemned to death in absentia by the Việt Minh in the late 1940s. They also attempted to kill him in Vĩnh Long but failed.[26]

When Diệm arrived at his residence, Bảo Đại[27] asked him whether he would like to return to a life of politics. Once Diệm agreed, he led him to an adjoining room where a crucifix was hung on the wall. He then told him: "There is your God. You will swear before Him to preserve the territory that is entrusted to you. You will defend it against the communists and if necessary against the French." After a moment of silence, Diệm said: "I swear."[28]

As the negotiations lingered, talks focused on an eventual partition. On June 10, between 10 P.M. and midnight, two French and two Việt Minh diplomats secretly met in a rented villa outside Geneva. Absent were the Saigon diplomats—especially Colonel Lê Văn Kim, who represented the State of Vietnam. France's ally had become inconvenient to the peace-talks. Mendes-France, who became French prime minister on June 17, stated he was not bound to his predecessor's commitments to Vietnam's independence. He was trying to keep Diệm, the prime minister designate, "quite in the dark" while informing Bảo Đại of the partition talks only on July 4. The State of Vietnam's foreign minister, Trần Văn Đỗ, only learned about the talks on July 12 (one month after they took place)—not from the French or the Americans, but from the Chinese.

By 1954, options were few for the South Vietnamese. They were wary of the Việt Minh and of their brutality. They did not feel comfortable with the Hòa Hảo and Cao Đài, these armed politico-religious groups in the Mekong Delta that did not seem very progressive or intellectual. The Bình Xuyên, a group of river pirates, were not trustworthy at all. The State of Vietnam was the only alternative, although up until then it did not inspire a lot of confidence because of its weak and uninspiring leadership. People, therefore, withheld their support and adopted a neutral wait and see attitude, which was frequently seen in the South.

Bảo Đại, realizing the dire situation, finally made the tough decision to call on the only person who was clean, untouched by past political turmoils, and strong enough to argue with the French and to rally around him the various political groups and the neutral and disenchanted populace. That person, Ngô Đình Diệm, had his work cut out for him, for his northern adversary, Hồ, already controlled the northern part of the country, and had clamped down on basic human rights and gotten rid of the French. The sparsely-populated South, which was culturally heterodox, ethnically diverse, open to the world, and easy-going but fractious, would be more difficult to handle than the North. That task was complicated by the fact that the country was still controlled by the French and Bảo Đại and was divided by many political groups that fought for their share of power.[29]

Saigon Buildings and Streets

Climate was France's worst enemy in Saigon. Extreme heat, high humidity, and torrential rains tended to affect colonial architecture. Buildings required wide overhanging roofs and verandas to keep room interiors from the sun and rains. Mosquito screens replaced glass in windows so that air could circulate freely. High ceilings were used to create a cushion of air that enhanced natural ventilation.

Buildings had to stand either perpendicular to the wind direction (with a southwest orientation) or in the direction that avoided the direction of the sun (main facade facing north or south). Concrete or bricks were used because they are low heat conductors. French architecture was about power and appearance. The ground floor was reserved for common areas with kitchens, laundry rooms, and servants' quarters, while other areas were pushed to the back. The facades were colorful and geometrically shaped to better exude an aura of benevolent confidence.[30]

Saigon's Notre Dame Cathedral, with its Gothic vaulting, had a ventilation system more suited to a temperate climate than to the tropical heat and humidity of Indochina. It was only in 1942 that the French conceded the need to pierce additional openings in the lateral chapels following the traditional Vietnamese practice for ventilating pagodas.[31]

By 1921, a decision was made to hire a professional urbanist to create an esthetic that reflected the new associationist spirit. Ernest Hebrard added a few indigenous buildings to "engage the sympathy of the natives" and used Indochinese technical mastery over the environment (stilts, verandas, thinner walls, etc.) in his building design. The new Indochinese design—a combination of French and Indochinese motifs—was different than the original one and marked a break with indigenous architectural continuity. By the 1930s, Saigon had become a potpourri of 19th-century French buildings, newer ones in an Indochinese style, and traditional indigenous villages and dwellings.[32]

Under French occupation, Saigon was embellished with palaces, churches, villas, and new streets that reflected architectural works in Paris. Notre Dame de Saigon Cathedral looked similar to Notre Dame de Paris. Begun in October 1877, it was completed on Easter day, April 11, 1880, with a ceremony presided over by the then-governor of Cochinchina, Charles LeMyre de Vilers. The total cost at the time was 2,500,000 French francs. The Saigon Municipal Theater was built by Olivier, Guichart and Ferret (1900) and the Saigon Post Office by Foulhoux and Vildieux (1891).

Almost all the streets bore French names of admirals and officers participating in the conquest of Vietnam, such as Bonard, de Lagrandière, Charner; or of French politicians advocating colonialism, like Chasseloup Laubat. The boys' high school was called lycée Chasseloup Laubat before being assigned a less conspicuous name: Jean Jacques Rousseau.

Streets also bore the names of World War I battlefields, such as Belgique, Verdun, La Marne, and La Somme. Chasseloup Laubat (Hồng Thập Tự after 1954, and Xô Viết Nghệ Tỉnh after 1975), Gallieni, and MacMahon were the longest streets in Saigon. Chasseloup Laubat wound from Thị Nghè to Cholon. Gallieni, linking Saigon and Cholon, became Trần Hưng Đạo after 1954. MacMahon, which linked Tân Sơn Nhứt airport to Saigon, became Công Lý (Justice) after 1954 and Nam Kỳ Khởi Nghĩa after 1975. The busiest and most fashionable street bore the name of the battleship *Catinat*, which had carried French soldiers who fired on the Saigon fort. Catinat Street was the main artery linking Notre Dame Cathedral to the Saigon River. In downtown, it was flanked on each side by the renowned Majestic and Continental hotels. It was renamed Tự Do (Freedom) Street in 1954 and Đồng Khởi (Uprising) after 1975, causing the Saigonese to joke that "they lost freedom after staging an uprising."

Norodom Sihanouk, the Cambodian king who once studied at the Saigon lycée Chasseloup Laubat, after listening to Monsignor Miche appealed for France to establish a protectorate over Cambodia. The French, appreciating his request, named after him the largest street in Saigon, linking the zoological garden and Saigon Museum on one end to the palace on the other. The presidential palace was also named Norodom Palace, later renamed Independence Palace.

Other streets were given Vietnamese names. Tổng Đốc Phương[33] was one of the early collaborators with France in the 19th century. His son Đỗ Hữu Vị, the first Vietnamese pilot, also had a street named after him. Tôn Thọ Tường, a discontented scholar who collaborated with the French, had his street. He had advised Trương Công Định and Nguyễn Trung Trực not to fight the French. Pétrus Trương Vĩnh Ký and Paulus Huỳnh Tịnh Của, who made precious contributions to journalism and the quốc ngữ literature, had their names on smaller streets.

Many streets were covered with shade trees, which gave the city beauty and charm. Taberd (Nguyễn Du), De Lagrandière (Gia Long) and others were edged with tamarind trees while Hui Bông Hoa street was bordered with silk trees. Hui Bông Hoa was a Chinese millionaire who had once cooperated with the French.[34]

*　*　*

The war ended in 1954 for the French Expeditionary Corps, who had lost 59,745 dead and missing in action. The Vietnamese national army lost 58,877 dead and missing in action. There were 400,000 civilian casualties, of which an estimated 100,000 to 150,000 had been assassinated by the Việt Minh.

The French had negotiated an armistice over the head of the Vietnamese delegation, which was a flagrant violation of the condition on which Bảo Đại had agreed to participate in the conference. The Vietnamese nationalists (Southern) not only missed the chance to get their independence, they also had to accept without their consent an armistice, which rewarded the rule of violence, not law. Therefore, July 20 was observed in Saigon as a day of shame.[35]

7

Saigon Under the Ngos (1954–1963)

[The war] was fought mainly by Vietnamese against other
Vietnamese—over the nature of the Vietnamese society.
—Jamieson, 1993, ix.[1]

If the July 20, 1954, armistice marked the end of the first Indochinese War, it ushered in a new one between two adversaries: nationalist South Vietnam against communist North Vietnam, Saigon against Hanoi and Ngô Đình Diệm against Hô Chí Minh: a fratricidal war with widespread and far-reaching international consequences. Saigon, all of a sudden, became a bastion against communism, the main front in the Cold War.

When Diệm took over the premiership, he only hoped to regain his country's independence and to rebuild it with American assistance. He did not realize that part of his job was to fight the hottest conflict in the Cold War. Neither did his compatriots. His failure to emphasize and deliver it eventually sealed his demise.

Ngô Đình Diệm

Southerners accepted with stoic resignation the news coming out of Geneva. Flags were flown at half-staff. There was no jubilation, only tears. North of the 17th parallel, the people in "non-liberated" areas—areas that were not communist yet—began their southward exodus while the Việt Minh consolidated their control over the rest of the northern territory.

Diệm was born in 1901 in Quảng Bình, central Vietnam, into one of the oldest Catholic families in Vietnam. He studied law and administration at the Hà Nội University,[2] served as governor of Phan Thiết in 1929 and became Bảo Đại's youngest minister in 1932. He quit a few months later after accusing the French of blocking reforms, and he would not hold any important position for many decades.

125

Through a combination of networking, hard work, and sheer luck, he built up enough effective power that Bảo Đại had no choice but to offer him the premiership. When Diệm landed in Saigon on June 25, 1954, he had no political constituency. A small, stocky, unimpressive 53-year-old man, he was greeted by a small crowd of 500 people. His dependence on American aid doomed his republic and prevented him from ever establishing a government of popular legitimacy—a cruel paradox for a man who must be counted among Vietnam's staunchest nationalists.[3]

Despite his excellent credentials—he was courageous, incorruptible, pious, ascetic, hardworking, and a dedicated nationalist[4]—no one was optimistic about this new leader. Bảo Đại, who offered him the job, even commented, "Diệm was not a natural statesman, not overtly intelligent." The French found him "too narrow, too rigid, too unworldly, and too pure to have any chance of creating an effective government." The American media gave the Diệm government only six months. He was more like a teacher than a leader, an old mandarin than a modern politician, a traditionalist than a modernist. Among past leaders, he was closer to Minh Mạng than to Phan Bội Châu or Phan Chu Trinh.[5] Besides, the outlook was grim when he took over the post. The country was in bad shape economically, the war against the communists was forthcoming, independence had yet to be won, soldiers from religious sects roamed freely in Saigon streets, and one million new mouths would need to be fed.[6]

But for the communists, Diệm was the only Vietnamese nationalist they were worried about because of his staunch anti-communism. Diệm was seized and jailed by the Việt Minh in 1945. Hồ then made advances in an attempt to bring him into his administration. Diệm told Hồ frankly that he was a criminal who had burned and destroyed the country and even killed his brother Ngô Đình Khôi, and Khôi's son. If Hồ was stunned, he did not let it show. In the end, Diệm probably owed his life to his bravery and determination.

> HO: Your mind is focused on the past. Think of the future—education, improved standards of living for the people.
> DIEM: You speak the language without conscience. I work for the good of the nation. I shall always be a free man. Look me in the face. Am I a man who fears oppression or death?
> HO: You are a free man.

With that, Diệm walked out.[7] He bravely remained in the North for months to organize anti-communist guerrilla bases. What made Hồ change his mind, no one knows. The communists, however, realizing Hồ's mistake, sentenced him to death in absentia. By the time Diệm returned to Saigon in 1946, he was a marked man.

Diệm returned to Cần Thơ where his brother Ngô Đình Thục was a bishop. He then traveled with Thục to Washington DC and then to Europe in mid–October 1950 to put some distance between the communists and him. For the next two years, Diệm shuttled between New York and Washington, DC, where he cultivated relationships with political activists, clergymen (Cardinal Spellman of New York), journalists, academicians, and politicians to advance the cause of an anti-communist, nationalist alternative to the Việt Minh and the Franco–Bảo Đại government.[8]

Having heard about Diệm, Supreme Court Justice William O. Douglas asked him to proofread the chapter about Vietnam from his book *North from Malaysia*. Calling him a "hero with considerable following in the South," he introduced him to Senator Mike Mansfield, a Democrat from Montana, in May 1953. Mansfield would later become Diệm's "godfather."

On May 16, 1954, Bảo Đại mentioned that Diệm, who was in Paris, was offering to return to Vietnam. He made Diệm and the Americans wait for almost one month before announcing on June 17 that he had charged Diệm with forming a new government.[9]

The Battle of Saigon

In 1954, the country's infrastructure was in ruins. Bridges had been demolished. Canals, roads, and railways were in a state of disrepair. A quarter of South Vietnamese troops had deserted the national army. Without a centralized government, the South Vietnamese were splintered into many factions.

Colonel Edward Lansdale was sent to Vietnam as the head of the CIA's Saigon Military Mission. He was told to duplicate his work in the Philippines, where he had helped the nationalists defeat the communists. When Lansdale showed up at the palace to offer his services, he found no guards or reception, just a "few harried-looking people" wandering around the hallway. Upstairs, he found a "middle-aged Vietnamese" in a small office and asked where he could find the premier. "I am Ngô Đình Diệm," the man answered. Diệm was, during his first year in office, a king without a kingdom. His authority did not extend beyond the walls of his office.[10]

Nineteen fifty-four Saigon was different from the imperial Huế that Diệm had served in 1933. It was a restless, confusing and chaotic place. No longer were the people ignorant of politics, as had been suggested by the repeated strikes of the 1930s. One million refugees from the North had landed in and around Saigon. They flew the Vatican's white and blue flag (an anomaly in a Buddhist country), were staunchly anti-communist, and highly vocal. They urgently needed food and shelter, and the Diệm government that had taken office a month earlier did not have the funds or infrastructure to solve this problem overnight.

There were the French who just turned over the reins of the government to the new administration but were still there. The French army was still there also with its Foreign Legion and a Senegalese component. Even before Diệm landed in Saigon, the French were already plotting against him. Since the question of South Vietnam's independence had not even been addressed yet, the ultimate political power rested on the French and the newly-arriving Americans.

The Việt Cộng, or VC, lay low to avoid being detected—a core of 50,000 soldiers were left behind waiting for an opportune time to act up. There were the Bình Xuyên, an overgrown gang of river pirates based in Cholon, 40,000-strong, that ran the police, prostitution, a gambling complex that occupied several city blocks (the Grand Monde Hotel), as well as an opium factory that refined a high grade product for distribution throughout Indochina. In return, Bảo Đại received about $1.25 million in bribes and kickbacks for the rights to run these vice mills without fear of reprisal.[11]

Two other religious sects—the Hòa Hảo and the Cao Đài (two million-strong in the northwestern Mekong Delta)—each with a private army of 30,000 soldiers, were also vying for power. The Hòa Hảo followers wielded machetes and rifles and flew a purple and yellow flag. Their leader, Sổ, was revered for prophetizing events in Vietnam. The murder of Sổ by the Việt Cộng made the Hòa Hảo into the most fanatical anticommunists.[12]

The newly-formed 30,000-man South Vietnamese army (SVA) was led by Lieutenant-General Nguyễn Văn Hinh, a naturalized French citizen and a Bảo Đại admirer. Hinh, son of former Prime Minister Nguyễn Văn Tâm, imbued with his power, threatened to unseat Prime Minister Diệm.[13]

Diệm also faced an absent head of state who, from Monaco, France, could at any time create problems; worse, he faced the commander of the Legionary Force, General Paul Ely, who linked up with the American envoy to Saigon (General J. Lawton "Lightning Joe" Collins) to try to unload Diem. Ely called Diệm "a losing game." Ely and Collins proposed a reorganization of the SVA without consulting Diệm.

The State of Vietnam was in disarray. "We have five separate armies; until recently an open clash between the (army) chief of Staff and the Premier; gambling houses and worse, all operated with the tacit, if not open, approval of the chief of state; two religious sects with their own private domains; a pope; an active underground Việt Minh; a Foreign Expeditionary Force; an absent emperor," wrote General Collins. He urged Washington to replace Diệm with another Vietnamese politician.[14]

The immediate threat came from the Bình Xuyên, which was led by Văn Viễn (Bẩy Viễn), whose deputies controlled the security and police force. To combat them, Diệm decided not to renew their gambling monopoly. Bẩy Viễn retaliated by arming his 5,000 soldiers and followers in the Saigon-Cholon area. Diệm brought three battalions of Nùng minority soldiers[15] as well as two battalions of paratroopers led by Colonel Đỗ Cao Trí. When the Bình Xuyên positioned mortars around the presidential palace, Collins called for a truce. The two sides met, but rapidly walked out of the conference room.

On March 27, Diệm ordered the paratroopers to occupy the police head-quarters, a heavily fortified building in a densely populated area. The Bình Xuyên retreated from the police headquarters before the paratroopers arrived. When Trí's forces attacked the Sûreté building the next day, General Ely talked to Diệm to call off the attack. Sporadic clashes on March 29 between Bình Xuyên and the paratroopers caused casualties on both sides.

A ceasefire went into effect. The sects told their representatives in the Diệm government to resign, which they did. Diệm was without a defense min-ister or a foreign minister. Collins advised Washington that Diệm should be replaced. State Secretary Dulles had to call Eisenhower after midnight to read the message to him. Dulles was told to not give up on Diệm yet. Senator Man-sfield, once consulted, conceded Diệm's failings but suggested that the alter-natives were "worse than keeping Diệm in office."

Saigon appeared like an armed camp as troops filled the streets. In some ways, it was similar to the confrontation there between Nguyễn's royal troops and the Tây Sơns in 1780. In some areas, SVA troops and Bình Xuyên thugs resided in fortified encampments on opposite sidewalks of boulevards and streets. Close by, on a newsstand, the 4 April issue of *Time* magazine featured Diệm on its cover as a determined man staring forward while a red scythe tore the South Vietnamese flag in half in the background. Diệm was described as a resilient, deeply religious nationalist who was "burdened with the terrible but challenging task of leading 10.5 million South Vietnamese from the brink of communism into their long sought state of sovereign independence."

While Collins returned to Washington for consultation, repeated gun fights between the SVA and the Bình Xuyên brought the city to the brink of a civil war. On April 23, Diệm went on the radio to explain that he had restrained himself in order to avoid bloodshed. He urged the sects to come out and talk with him, and he hinted that the French may be behind all the misunderstand-ing. The next day, he dismissed the director of the Sûreté, Lại Văn Sang, and replaced him with Colonel Nguyễn Ngọc Lê.

On April 28, a SVA truck was fired on as it passed in front of a building held by the Bình Xuyên on Gallieni Boulevard (Trần Hưng Đạo). The army dispatched four battalions to other Bình Xuyên strongholds. The Bình Xuyên forces then fired four mortar shells onto the palace grounds. Shelling trans-formed a square mile of the city into a free-fire zone, house-to-house combat drove thousands of residents into the streets and artillery and mortars obliter-ated the poor districts, killing 500 civilians. During the exchange of gunfire, the areas around the Bình Xuyên headquarters got set on fire, rendering 20,000 people homeless.[16] Dark smoke billowed up over the city.

In the face of the paratroopers' determination, the Bình Xuyên resistance collapsed and the last units left Cholon on April 30. They were counting on the support of the French forces which never showed up. On hearing the news, Ely expressed his displeasure with Diệm but did not react to the move. In the following days, the Bình Xuyên were again defeated by the SVA and driven into the marshes of the Rừng Sát south of Saigon. At the Bình Xuyên headquarters, the Vietnamese found evidence the French helped the Bình Xuyên during the fighting.

News of Diệm's victory galvanized his supporters in Washington. When Collins returned to Saigon on May 2, the SVA was mopping up the battlefield. Damages to the city and the civilians had been high. Diệm proclaimed to his troops:

> "Your courage has written a glorious page.
> Free Vietnam is immortal!
> Righteous nationalism will triumph!"

Collins wanted to return to his NATO assignment. France decided to withdraw from Vietnam. It was at the Paris Conference of 1955 that Vietnam became America's war.[17]

Diệm gradually terminated his association with France. The French High Command was eliminated in April 1956 and French troops were withdrawn between April and September, 1956. The tricolor was lowered in Vietnam for the last time on September 27.

On October 23, 1955, the South Vietnamese were allowed to vote for the first time in their lives. They got to choose between Diệm and Bảo Đại. The size of the turnout was impressive: Of the six million people who went to the pole, 5,721,735 voted for Diệm. The Republic of Vietnam was thus proclaimed according to constitutional and legal procedures contrary to the illegal and illegitimate takeover of the DRV.[18] Southerners went to vote again for delegates and representatives on March 4, 1956. Diplomatically, South Vietnam was formally recognized by 55 countries by August 1960.[19]

1954 Exodus

About a million northerners were resettled in the South through what the U.S. called "Operation Passage to Freedom." The Saigon government, however, labeled it, the 1954 Exodus. This was the largest movement of people from North to South in Vietnamese history until it was dwarfed by the 1975 Exodus, during which more than two million Vietnamese left their country forever.[20] If in 1954, the Vietnamese only lost their homes, in 1975, they lost their country.[21] These two exoduses were caused by communist takeovers of the North, and then South in 1954 and 1975, respectively.

Many peasant-refugees coming from inside North Vietnam had to pass through communist "liberated" areas before arriving in Hải Phòng and the coastal areas, where they could be picked up. They had little to eat and drink for days. The communists had spread propaganda that the Americans would beat them and throw them overboard. They forcibly detained many when their propaganda was not working.[22] They forced villagers back to their village in Phú Lý. They denied refugees access to ferries to prevent them from leaving. By the time the refugees arrived in Hải Phòng, the designated pick-up area, they were severely traumatized morally and physically. "Covered with open sores, they bore scars and disfigurements of mistreatment."[23] In their haste to escape, they did not carry any belongings. "Miserable, filthy, lame, blind, crippled, and war wounded come aboard.... Eighty percent are old men and women, and others are infants, all swollen with malnutrition and starvation."[24]

While more than 800,000 refugees were transported by a combination of U.S. Navy and western ships over a 300-day period (August 7, 1954–May 15, 1955), about 200,000 people were evacuated by planes. Six to seven thousand people escaped by land through Laos, the demilitarized zone, and some used their own boats.[25] Health risks were common within this large group of refugees. The USS *Bayfield* on one trip reported two cases of measles, two cases of typhoid, 31 cases of dysentery, 57 cases of conjunctivitis, six cases of pneumonia, five cases of impetigo, ten cases of tuberculosis, and 12 cases of influenza.[26]

Refugees were transported either to Saigon, Huế, or Nha Trang. The first U.S. Navy ship, *Menard*, carrying 1,925 refugees from Hải Phòng, landed in Saigon on August 19 after a 59-hour trip. During the trip, refugees refused to eat the first meal because the communists had told them the food was poisoned.[27] The first two reception centers in Saigon were located at Gò Vắp and at the Hippodrome, next to the race court. Other refugees landed in Vũng Tàu, 80 miles east of Saigon, after which they were dispersed throughout the country.

About 300,000 refugees, former government officials, and others not eligible or not wanting to wait for support, resettled themselves in the greater Saigon area. By December 1954, some 271,208 others had been moved to relocation areas, a number that increased to almost half a million by April 1955. Saigon's nearby Biên Hòa province received 130,000 refugees, of which Hố Nai was the most populous refugee village with 50,474 people. Gò Vắp, a partly urbanized area of the Gia Định province, accepted 30,600 refugees. The large influx of refugees created a logistical nightmare for the young government of Prime Minister Diệm, who took office a few months earlier. Had help from the U.S., other nations, and non-profit organizations not arrived in time, the Diệm government would probably have collapsed. The U.S. contributed $56 million in 1955 and $37 million in 1956. The Catholic Relief Service provided $35 million dollars by 1957.[28]

It was hard to find a house in Saigon because of the sudden influx of one million northerners. Nga's family lived at a friend's house before moving to a house in Chợ Lớn: two rooms and a kitchen for nine people. At night, the kitchen area was filled with wall-to-wall cots and people had to crawl from one cot to another to get up. Baby cries woke everyone at night. The outdoor public outhouse was a big, dirty can.[29]

The year was 1954. There were not many fancy apartments or houses with private indoor toilets. Nga was so shy she had to get up at five to go to the outhouse, otherwise she would have to wait in line. She soon would notice the differences between Southerners and Northerners. The South has only two seasons: dry and rainy, while the North has four. People eat sweeter food with more coconut sauce in the South. Working ethics are also different: while northerners worked hard and saved, southerners spent it all without thinking about the future.[30]

With the influx of one million new people (eight percent of the southern population), conflicts over jobs, housings, lands, and positions abounded. Although southerners were good hosts, they felt that northerners, favored by Catholic President Diệm, took jobs away from them. Some merchants reacted by raising their prices when they dealt with northerners, when they recognized by their skin, tone of voice, and clothing.

In December 1955, President Diệm announced the opening of the largest resettlement project (100,000 people), Cái Sắn, in the province of Kiên Giang near the Gulf of Siam. Each family was given three hectares (7.5 acres) of land in tenancy to be bought later in installments. Others were moved to the highlands—a sparsely-populated area occupied only by native highlanders. Overall, 319 refugee villages housing 605,000 people were built with 207 in the Mekong Delta, 50 in the central coastal highlands and 60 in the highlands. Two hundred eighty-eight of these were agricultural, 26 were fishing communities and five were devoted to artisanry.

By March 6, *Marine Adder* embarked the 500,000th refugee seeking a new life in the South. By May 15, the total number of people evacuated stood at 800,786. There were 184 recorded births and 66 deaths among the refugee population.[31] If Allied ships were designed to transport refugees to the South, the communists also used them to transport personnel, materiel, and intelligence from North to South Vietnam: this was known as Operation Trojan Horse in American circles. Communist cadres used Polish and Russian ships to make the ride from South to North Vietnam, and then used Allied ships to ride back to the South. Attempts to identify the communists had been difficult.[32]

The refugees, most of whom were Catholic, changed the religious balance of Vietnam. The number of Catholics in the North decreased from 1,113,000 to 457,000 while the number jumped in the South from 461,000 to 1,137,000. In 1956, the Diocese of Saigon had more practicing Catholics than Paris or Rome. With their sheer number and their association with and reliance on the Diệm government, they also changed the political landscape. They were more vocal politically and were staunchly anti-communist. The presence of refugees—an alien element throughout South Vietnam—and their use by Diệm, helped to polarize the South Vietnamese society and weaken the cohesiveness of the country.[33] One of Diệm's biggest achievements, however, was the resettlement of Northerners.

The exodus also caused a traumatic dislocation of the refugee population. Besides having to abandon their homes, villages, and lands, families were torn apart as many, for one reason or another, opted to remain in the North while the rest went South to serve in the new administration. Brothers and sisters, parents and children, would be separated for another two decades before another reunion would take place. Of course, no one knew at that time how long the separation would last.

Personalism

The U.S.–Vietnamese relationship was a difficult and rocky one, due mainly to a misunderstanding between the two sides. While the Americans wanted to offer an American solution, Diệm preferred a Vietnamese approach to Vietnam's problem. Therein lay the conflict. Although the relationship was neither a colonial one nor an alliance of equals, it more often approached the former than the latter.

Diệm disliked his reliance on foreign power and was acutely aware of the puppet image he projected. "If you order Vietnam around like a puppet on a string, how will you be different—except in degree—from the French?" he once asked Marguerite Higgins.[34]

Diệm and Hồ shared many similarities and differences. Both were bachelors and "personally lonely men." Both spent large portions of their adult life in obscure, self-imposed exile. Each tried to be the "father" of his own country. Both were strong authoritarian leaders and stern disciplinarians; neither was very nurturing or forgiving. But Hồ avoided the aloofness by calling himself "Uncle" and by letting the party discipline "family members." When the land reform got out of hand, he disavowed the "excesses" and removed Trường Chinh. His popularity suffered minimal damage as a result. He presided over a Marxist doctrine, with no room for competitive ideologies or individualism. Diệm, on the other hand, was a president. Like the father, he took personal responsibility for the nation as a corporate unit. He presided over a collection of fractious and unruly religious-political groups that vied for power as well as freedom. He bore the brunt of the constant attacks and demands of these individualistic and heterodoxical people and got killed for his mistakes.[35] Diệm would have made an excellent leader in the North where people were more conservative and disciplined than in the South. His attempts at banning dancing, divorce, the use of contraceptives, the wearing of "falsies," in Saigon, where morals and manners were more eclectic, pragmatic, and flexible than anywhere in Vietnam, put him unnecessarily at odds with many Southerners. Despite these drawbacks, he was immensely successful in his first three years in office. He got rid of Bảo Đại, the French, took control of the army, and sub-dued the religious sects. These achievements in the chaotic Saigon of the late 1950s were remarkable. He gave a new direction to the country, and respect to the office of the presidency, which had been lacking under Bảo Đại. He infused stability and trust in the fight against the communists.

Diệm was obsessed with the specter of collaboration, which the Americans did not understand. He expected them to treat the alliance as a partnership instead of a patron-client relationship. He justified the partnership on the basis that the South Vietnamese bore the brunt of communist attacks and made a major sacrifice by holding the line against the red tide and manning the ram-parts of the Free World.

What the Ngos wanted was aid without conditions, without strings attached. They considered ideas that Washington pushed on the regime as interference. The same could be said about the call to liberalize the regime. They argued that the communists would not be defeated because freedom of press and political freedom were established in South Vietnam. They also thought that people should play an active role in building the country. These ideas put the Ngos squarely at odds with the Americans who wanted the regime to emphasize what it could do for the people and not vice versa.[36]

The Americans, on the other hand, viewed Diệm as a man out of his time, a "power hungry autocrat" who was the heir to a dying tradition. Diệm was indeed a conservative person who felt intense pride in his country's history and its Confucian tradition. They "tried to tarnish me by calling me a man-darin.... But I am proud to be a mandarin," he once told Higgins.[37]

Yet Diệm was not a patriot without a program, nor was he an old-fash-ioned "Oriental" despot. He was more like a conservative modernizer. He knew his country needed to modernize, although capitalism would put individual freedom above collective discipline and usher in materialism with the predatory instincts of free market. On the other hand, communism turned people into cogs in a machine and ignored human dignity. Saigon saw salvation as a "third way" between capitalism and communism, a model that could achieve industrial revolution without the evil consequences of the first two.[38]

To achieve this goal, the Ngos drew upon a European doctrinal import called Cần Lao Nhân Vị, or personalism. Personalists advocated a kind of communitarian socialism—with worker control and ownership of industry. Active participation of the people in the political and economic life of the society was needed in a personalist democracy.

He suggested that people sacrifice and "tighten their belts" in order to achieve economic independence. He also tried to improve national education. From 1954 to 1960, he ordered almost 5,000 elementary and secondary schools built, raising the national total from 1,780 to 6,774. During the same period, school enrollment jumped from 443,865 to 1.5 million. He thought that for a country that had just emerged from colonialism, with an infantile political experience and an absent economy, certain rights should be curbed.

From 1957, the USIS (United States Information Service) tried to introduce American culture and society to the Vietnamese by extolling the virtues of U.S. democracy: high standards of living, personal freedom, and cultural progress. This strategy may have created positive attitudes about the U.S., but they did not improve Diệm's standing with his people.[39] American aid was not offered in such a way to promote sustained economic development in South Vietnam. From 1955 to 1963, the U.S. provided almost $2 billion in aid to South Vietnam. Eighty percent of the aid came in the form of consumer goods. From 1957 to 1960, American aid contributed to the building of 47,000 square meters of movie theaters, but only 6,500 square meters of hospitals and 3,500 square meters of rice mills.[40]

While Diệm called on all South Vietnamese to sacrifice for the cause of Vietnamese independence, the U.S. suggested that everyone in a capitalist society could be wealthy and happy. These contradictory messages undermined Diệm's nation-building policy and created unnecessary rifts and acrimony between U.S. and Vietnamese officials at a time when Diệm really needed his American "friends" the most.[41]

Southern and Northern Cultures

It is known that northern and southern societies are different geographically, socially, economically, and politically.[42] While northern culture was characterized by uniformity and orthodoxy, and where deviation was a rarity (read severely sanctioned), southern culture was diverse and heterodox, and deviation was tolerated and sometimes considered the norm. Besides the drumbeats of war, soft voices argued for nhân and diệu, of compassion and reason.[43] There was nothing absolute in the South, for everything could be negotiated and toned down. Even in the ugliest fights, one of the parties eventually disengaged from the encounter, leaving the remaining person a temporary winner. Despite the existence of censorship, diverse views about the war, economy, and social issues were expressed with more freedom than in the North.[44]

To put the cultural differences in perspective, one could fast forward five decades. A northern Vietnamese family who had migrated South in 1954, had been transplanted in the U.S. in the mid–1980s during the era of the boat people. In 2009, rites were rigidly followed by that family. The elder son and his wife—the daughter-in-law—had to come and visit the patriarch and matriarch, both in their 80s, a few days before New Year's eve. Then, on the first day of January 2010, they visited them again to wish them well. The sequence would be repeated on the occasion of the Chinese New Year, which fell on February 6, 2010. That would be four visits for each New Year celebration. As the elder matriarch had done it before in her youth, the daughter-in-law had to follow the same ancestral rites: bid farewell to the old year and offer wishes in person on New Year's day. This did not include all the other routine festivities the daughter-in-law had to participate in and lead. The perpetuation of these rites heavily impacted the daughter-in-law who had had the misfortune of marrying the elder son. As the elder matriarch had paid her dues, the younger daughter had to pay hers, and the rites would go on until the next generation. These rites were followed rather loosely by other southern Vietnamese families, who had also emigrated to America. Children were only expected to visit the elders on the occasion of the Chinese New Year and that would be more than enough.

While one main paper, *The People* (Nhân Dân), the official journal of the party, dominated in the North, 27 different Vietnamese-language newspapers were published in Saigon and vied for its audience. There were also several papers in English and French and half a dozen in Chinese. Nearly 700,000 copies of Vietnamese-language newspapers were printed daily in Saigon by the end of the 1960s, two thirds of which were distributed to the provinces.

There were 125,000 radio sets in 1960 and 2,200,000 by 1970. Television appeared in Saigon in 1966 with four hours of programming in 1969. There was one television set for every 40 families in South Vietnam by 1970. Besides the news, the cải lương shows (reformed theater) and traditional music attracted a lot of viewers to television sets and in some way blunted the traumas and tragedies of the war. There was also a U.S. Armed Forces channel broadcasting American programs.

Rapid urbanization was encountered. Saigon had half a million people in 1945. By 1954, it was two million and leapt to three million in 1965 with 20 percent of the population living in Saigon. With Americans landing in droves, the fabric of the society began to unravel. Construction workers, bartenders, busmen, hostesses, waiters—those who dealt with Americans hit the jackpot and earned considerable money. The middleclass—teachers, soldiers, university professors, doctors, dentists, lawyers—who worked for the government were paid with local money that devalued rapidly with inflation. The severe loss in economic well-being led to a decrease in social status and prestige. A bargirl or construction worker could earn more money than a tenured university professor. That economic turnaround threatened the stability of the traditional society.

Inflation worsened the overall situation. An egg cost 2.1 piasters in 1960, 8.8 piasters in 1967, and 21.9 piasters in 1970. A kilogram of rice cost 5 piasters in 1960, 13.4 piasters in 1966, and 53.2 piasters in 1970. The consumer price index by 1970 had risen 600 percent compared to 1963.

War losses became worse as time went by. From 1960 to 1965, Saigon suffered 11,000 dead and 23,000 seriously wounded. In 1966 and 1967, it encountered 24,000 dead and 50,000 seriously wounded. In 1968 alone, there were 63,000 dead and 144,000 seriously wounded. During these nine years, one of every five soldiers or one of every 20 adult males in South Vietnam had been killed or seriously wounded. By 1975, Saigon had lost more than 300,000 soldiers.[45] There were 50,000 widows and 700,000 orphans by 1969. The number of civilians killed or seriously wounded reached one million people by 1969 (300,000 dead). These numbers suggested that the South Vietnamese had fought very hard for their freedom and paid a hefty toll in personnel and material.

Could this song, "A Souvenir for You," by Phạm Duy—the most popular southern folk-singer and writer[46]—be played in Hanoi during the war? Probably not. In response to his lover who asked him when he would come back from the war, he answered, "Very soon," but most likely wrapped in a poncho (dead) or crippled. He will return on a pair of wooden crutches, one leg blown off, to go down the street on a fine spring afternoon to sip a cold drink with her. The refrain talks about returning and he and his lover looking at each other as strangers.[47]

This song was a hit in Saigon and the South in 1971. It was played and replayed thousands of times. Singers delivered it languorously in Saigon cafes and throughout the South before jam-packed youth audiences. What was poignant about it was that its writer died in combat after he wrote the song. Southerners empathized with the lyrics while soldiers went to war listening to them on their transistor radios. They realized the truth behind the lyrics and knew they would be maimed, injured, or might never come back alive. If they died, their young brides would mourn them; if they were disabled, their girlfriends, feeling sorry for them, would leave them. There was suffering everywhere. But many went to war anyway, for it was their war and because their country was damaged and torn apart by northern invaders.

A few other songwriters shared the same feeling. Trịnh Công Sơn in "Who's Left Who Is Vietnamese" advised combatants to open their eyes, for there were only Vietnamese fighters around and by that time one million of them had died during the war. Turn over the human corpses, the lyrics said, and one could only see Vietnamese faces. Indeed, this was a fratricidal war, a war of brothers against brothers. Hanoi had had it wrong all along. This was not a war against the Americans who were in Vietnam for just a short term. The fight was about the nature of Vietnamese society and the regime under which they lived—communism or capitalism. Soon there would be no Vietnamese left, Sơn mentioned, if the war kept going on.

In "It Is We Who Must Speak," Sơn told people to rise and demand the unification of the country—under whom, he did not say—as well as to refuse to kill brothers and to stack up their weapons. Many young Vietnamese considered Sơn the Bob Dylan or the Joan Baez of Vietnam. Sơn, in turn, was influenced by the shrill demands of American anti-war protesters, which had been brought to Vietnam by none other than young American soldiers. The latter, who were sent to help save South Vietnam, brought with them the dissatisfaction and the anger of mainland war resisters.

In another song called "I Must See the Sun," Sơn wished to see a day when the homeland was bathed with humanity and people would rise to demand peace.[48] From whom would they demand peace? Strangely enough, not from Hà Nội, the initiator of the war and the eventual benefactor of the collapse of the Saigon government. Although the demand was ludicrous, supported by the hippiness of the song, the brashness of the demand, the lack of responsibility, and the impudence of youth, thousands joined the call. "Rise to demand peace; stop killing; stack weapons" would certainly be unacceptable in Hà Nội, although tolerable in Saigon. Any government at war, under attack by the enemy, would call these songs "subversive" and sentence Sơn to jail. Saigon never did. It let youths sing and listen to the songs.

The communists, when they arrived in Saigon in 1975, labeled these songs "yellow music" and banned them.[49] As for Sơn, who had promoted defeatism in the Southern army and tried to help the communist cause, he was sentenced to a few years of reeducation by the communists after the war. It was ironic to see that Sơn was never jailed by the Saigon government, the fighting spirit of whose soldiers he had undermined, but by the very same Hà Nội government he had tried to help during the war.

Agroville System

Diệm pursued three major projects on an unprecedented scale: land reform, land development to increase people's material well-being, and strategic hamlets.

Although land reform was the most important project, it was pursued with the least vigor because of the difficulties Diệm faced consolidating his regime in 1954 to 1955. He still managed to introduce Ordinances 2 and 7, which ensured security of tenure, limited rent payment between 15 and 25 percent of the main crop and gave rights to tenants to farm abandoned and uncultivated lands. This was followed in 1956 by Ordinance 57, which aimed to expropriate land in the Mekong Delta. Diệm, however, did not want to openly antagonize landowners, who formed the base of his support group. Peasants who had not paid rent for a long time were not eager to see the return of rent collection. The inadequate number of land reform officials hampered the project.

Land development was designed to resettle people from the overcrowded central lowlands, and demobilized soldiers and refugees, to the highlands and the Mekong Delta. Each settlement could house 100 to 150 families. By 1959, there were 84 centers housing 125,000 people. Six centers with a population of 6,000 were reserved for Montagnards. By 1962, there were 171 settlements with a total population of 230,000 people.

As guerrilla activity increased from 1960 onward, fueled by an upsurge of infiltration of People's Liberation Armed Forces (PLAF) from the North, Diệm decided to build strategic hamlets, which focused on existing settlements.

Conceived in the corridors of the palace and implemented by Saigon in 1962, they reflected Vietnamese goals and methods. They aimed not only to defeat the NLF but also to build a new society. "The program was to create a true revolution," recalled Colonel Hoàng Văn Lạc, "not the sort of temporary and superficial reforms that were done in the past."[50] It was headed by Nhu himself, and therefore reflected Saigon's vision of a modern Vietnam.

The Ngos considered self-reliance to be both a virtue and a necessity. People would build defensive walls around their hamlets with the support of the Saigon government. A hamlet-based citizen militia would assume the defense with the regular army reduced to a supporting role. By electing their own management team, they would participate in the social and political transformation of the society.

The Ngos, however, set a blistering pace for building the hamlets, which sacrificed quality for quantity. They wanted to build all 16,000 hamlets within 12 months. The Herculean job was sabotaged by Colonel Phạm Ngọc Thảo, who turned out to be an undercover enemy agent.[51]

Local officials protested the lack of materiel and personnel. Many were forced to cut corners; some even reported non-existent hamlets complete. The peasants were unhappy about the new program, which brought with it significant costs. They were too poor to devote time and money to the program. Guerrilla activities increased the burden on the populace. They enlisted peasants to destroy during nighttime what they had built during daytime.

The Ngos' ideas were great and could have ushered in a new revolution if given more time and if adequate mobilization of the populace had been carefully accomplished. Without time and attention to details, their promises of a new life in strategic hamlets simply lacked substance.[52]

If 1961 was the "front year" in terms of territory and population gained, 1962, "the year of strategic hamlets," however, must be largely credited to Saigon. "This was perhaps the time of greatest hope," recalled William Bundy. Had the U.S. increased military support and Saigon consolidated its hamlets at that time, the current stalemate could end up with an eventual victory for the allies.[53] However, two events in 1963 changed the course of the war: the increased insurgency attacks and the Buddhist crisis.

The crisis diverted Saigon's military resources during which the NLF dismantled the III Corps' hamlet program. Continued insurgency attacks put the ARVN on the defensive forcing the U.S. to step in militarily.[54]

The Buddhist Rebellion

Diệm was not a man who liked to deal with intellectuals and city-dwellers: he was most at ease with the common people. He often toured remote villages and districts and had a genuine interest in discussing with villagers about their problems: agriculture, irrigation, water supply, roads and canals, housing, land rents, health care, and schools.

Schooled as a mandarin, he behaved like a father to these villagers. He felt he had to educate them and bring them up to par with the rest of the society. He was very informal and bowed à la Vietnamese instead of shaking hands to make them feel comfortable. Between July 1, 1958, and September 30, 1959, he made 45 trips to the provinces. During the last half of 1960, he made 17 trips to 14 provinces.[55]

In April 1960, a group of nationalist leaders led by Phan Huy Quát, Trần Văn Đỗ and Trần Văn Tuyên, gathered at the Caravelle Hotel in downtown Saigon and drafted a manifesto in which they advised Diệm to liberalize the regime, recognize opposition, and respect civil rights. Since the group never received any acknowledgement from the palace, it leaked it to the press. The signatories were rounded up and jailed.

The November 11, 1960, coup d'état broke out because mid-level officers were dissatisfied that deserving officers were passed over in favor of those who were associated with the government-sponsored Cần Lao party. The coup, however, fell apart as soon as it started because of lack of planning and forethought on the part of the plotters.

While Diệm struggled against local and foreign plotters, his enemies went into action. In a clearing in the Tây Ninh province about 80 miles west of Saigon, on December 19 to 20, 1960, Nguyễn Hữu Thọ, a Saigon lawyer, Trương Như Tảng, chief comptroller of a bank, Drs. Dương Quỳnh Hoa and Phùng Văn Cung, along with other dissidents, met with communists to form the National Liberation Front (NLF) with the goal of unseating Diệm.[56]

The NLF has the telltale marks of Hồ's organizing skill. The name Mặt Trận Giải Phóng (Liberation Front) indicated the techniques utilized to draw in the nationalists, to use and to discard them later. It also suggested the method of destabilizing the South in order to take over the country. Some southerners, with their naiveté and romanticism, thought that insurrection was a cool way to remake the society. It was only after 1975 that Lê Duẩn disbanded the NLF and talked about "the Party that organized, governed, and controlled the entire struggle" that people realized the true nature of the NLF. By that time, it was too late.[57] Their sacrifice was merely an exercise in futility.

Before leaving Saigon, Mendenhall wrote a damaging 1961 memo to the deputy of Harriman, in which he suggested the removal of the Ngos. It included the following points:

(1) the war is to be won *by* the U.S.;
(2) the need to get rid of Diệm and his family;
(3) Diệm will be succeeded by Vice President Thơ or General Minh;
(4) the need to keep American involvement *secret*;
(5) the willingness to see the Ngos killed.[58]

It was associated with a massive infusion of U.S. troops. To reduce this complex war to a toppling of a government and the execution of a military operation would lead to catastrophic results for millions of people.

This blueprint would in time be activated by Ball, Harriman, and Hilsman at the State department and Forrestal of the National Security Council staff. Opposed to the plan were: General Taylor, Robert Kennedy, Robert McNamara, and General Harkins. American correspondents in Saigon (Malcom Browne of the AP, David Halberstam of the *New York Times*, and Neil Sheehan of UPI) shared the same anti–Diệm feeling. How much they played into the hands of the communists is not known, for they were in close contact with the double agent Phạm Xuân Ẩn.

In 1962, Trần Kim Tuyến, the CIO director, tired of Mme. Nhu's interference, urged Diệm to remove her. Once her husband knew about it, he exiled him to Cairo. But before departing, Tuyến shared details of a coup with Ẩn. He also freed many incarcerated VC. Tuyến's assistant was Ba Quốc (the code name of North Vietnamese Intelligence Major General Đặng Trần Đức). Ba Quốc had access to all important documents in the South's intelligence network. His main role was counterinsurgency (infiltration of his own agents and disruption of the South Vietnamese agent network) while Ẩn dealt with strategic intelligence (information and disinformation). Phạm Ngọc Thảo, on the other hand, worked on destabilizing the government through a coup.[59]

The order to take down flying Buddhist flags on May 7 in preparation for the anniversary celebration of Buddha sparked unrest in Huế. Monk Thích Trí Quang used the occasion to make an anti–Diệm speech. In the evening, he told the crowd to march to the Huế radio station where he demanded the tape of the speech be broadcasted. The director called for help. Colonel Đặng sent for armored cars to disperse the unruly crowd that was hurling insults and throwing stones at police officers and firefighters. As the armored column under Major Đặng Sỹ reached the scene, a loud explosion was heard. The crowd ran away. Sỹ, fearing a VC attack, ordered concussion grenades thrown. Once order was reestablished, eight decapitated bodies with no wounds below the chest were found on the ground. At the trial of Sỹ in 1964, it was determined that the injury was caused by Semtex, a powerful plastic substance used by terrorists.

On June 11, a procession of monks proceeded to the intersection of Lê Văn Duyệt and Phan Đình Phùng in Saigon. Seventy-three-year-old Thích Quảng Đức stepped out of a car and took the lotus position. Another monk poured gasoline on him and Đức set fire to his robe. He burned for five or ten minutes before falling backward. Banners saying, "A Buddhist priest burns for Buddhist demands," were unfurled. Monks and nuns who formed a protective ring around Đức prevented policemen and firemen from extinguishing the flames. Browne, who had been informed of the incident beforehand, was ready to take pictures. A cable drafted by Wood and Hilsman and cleared by

Harriman was sent to Trueblood, who was substituting for Ambassador Nolting. The memo, which threatened to reassess the U.S.–Saigon relationship, was handed to Diệm the following day. The substance of the cable was leaked to the *New York Times* and printed on the front page of the June 14 issue.

Made aware of the June 11 memo, President Kennedy decreed that "no further threats [would be] made and no formal statement [would be] made without his own personal approval." This was transcribed into a memo for the record. The June 11 memo also underlined the divergence of views between the pro– and anti–Diệm factions in Washington.

At midnight on August 20, on the advice of his generals who were alarmed of the increasing activity at the Xá Lợi and other pagodas, Diệm declared martial law throughout the country. He ordered his own security force to evict the agitators from the pagodas. Although the military had sympathized with the Buddhists, more recently they had become tired of the prolonged agitation that had caused the government to pull military units from warzones to provide and maintain security in cities. Trí Quang had continued his verbal attacks against the government by asking for more suicide volunteers: There were four self-immolations by fire in August.[60]

The plotters at the state this time sent a signal authorizing Ambassador Lodge to overthrow Diệm. The story, which was again leaked to the *New York Times* by Harriman, suggested that the solution to the unrest was the forced removal of Diệm and Nhu by a military coup. The cable was dispatched that Saturday, August 24, as Deptel 143. They then made everything look like the entire government had approved Diệm's overthrow. Kennedy, however, recorded his disapproval for Deptel 143.

Lodge began isolating Diệm. Rumors of a coup finally reached Diệm.[61] Blinded by their zeal to demonize and discredit the Diệm government, the plotters did not think far ahead into the future. By encouraging the generals to depose their benefactor, they had destroyed the constitutionality of a country and transformed the generals into hired guns.

CIA Station Chief Richardson was the only one who had a good rapport with Nhu and sent impartial reports back to Washington, although his subordinate Conein worked closely with Lodge. Sensing that Richardson was not a team player, Lodge had him recalled.[62]

The Murder of Diệm

The first casualty of the coup was Captain Hồ Tấn Quyến, a navy commander who was lured at 1:30 A.M. on November 1, Saigon time, to attend a surprise party and was then murdered. Another early victim was Colonel Lê Quang Tùng, commander of the Special Forces. The official attack began around 4 or 5 A.M.

The Saigonese were awakened by the sounds of gunshots and artillery shells. It was like a repeat of the 1960 coup except that it lasted much longer. Military music had replaced the usual program. Curfew was announced and people were told to hole up in their houses. Shops and markets were closed. The price of rice and other commodities shot up instantaneously. Only rice and preserved products like salted duck eggs and cabbage were available.

At 4:30 P.M., Diệm telephoned Lodge wanting to know about the position of the U.S. government. Explaining he had not received any news yet, he also mentioned, "Those in charge of the current activity offer you and your brother safe conduct out of the country if you resign." Diệm knew by that time that Lodge was in contact with the generals.

At 8:30 P.M., Diệm and Nhu left the palace through a tunnel, walked to Lê Thánh Tôn Street and were driven away by Cao Xuân Vỹ to the home of Mã Tuyên, a Chinese trader in Cholon. They spent the night trying to get help but were not successful. At 8 A.M. on November 2, he called the palace guard to order a ceasefire.

At 7 A.M. Diệm, fearing for his life, called Lodge asking if he could help him out. Lodge enquired as to his whereabouts then excused himself after asking Dunn to keep the line open. When he returned, he told Diệm he could offer asylum to him and his brother. By offering the Ngos asylum and refusing to pick them up, Lodge had made himself an accomplice to the murders.[63]

General Minh asked General Xuân, Colonels Lắm and Quan, and others to arrange for a convoy to pick up the Ngos at the Seven Corners Church in Cholon near Mã Tuyên's house. Diệm, tired, eyes glazed from lack of sleep, asked Xuân to stop by the palace so they could get a few personal things. A group of soldiers tied their hands behind their backs and led them to an armored personnel carrier.

When the convoy stopped at a traffic light, Captain Nhung jumped out of his car, opened the door, entered the carrier and gunned them down. The bodies were then stabbed repeatedly with knives and bayonets. The convoy continued to the JGS headquarters where Xuân saluted Minh and told him, "Mission accomplished." The bloody bodies were dropped unceremoniously on the grass in front of the JGS where they lay for most of the day. They were buried in unmarked graves behind the JGS headquarters.

The cause of death was attributed to suicide. Pictures of the blood splattered, bullet ridden bodies were printed in the newspapers accompanied by stories about the "suicides." As the Saigonese could not understand how two Catholics with their hands tied behind their backs could have committed suicide, the report was later amended to "accidental suicide."

Kennedy declared about Diệm's death: "The way he was killed was particularly abhorrent." De Gaulle told his cabinet, "Messieurs, we at least did not have blood on our hands."[64]

The Ngos' remains were exhumed and reburied at Mạc Đỉnh Chi Cemetery in 1965. After 1975, the communists, with the goal of removing all the vestiges of the Saigon regime, ordered all the remains in the cemetery exhumed and relocated. Diệm and Nhu's remains were then transferred to a Lái Thiêu cemetery. This was the tale of two warriors. Hồ, the victor, was enshrined in a Hanoi mausoleum while Diệm, the vanquished, finally lay in a remote and low-key cemetery with a simple sign on his tombstone: Huỳnh (elder brother), his Christian name, and his date of death—without name or title. There was no birthdate either.

As the news of Diệm's death reached the streets, Saigon exploded in jubilation. People poured into the streets to celebrate the end of a regime. They smiled, shouted and screamed "Freedom" and "Long live the junta." They danced the twist, the tango and all the other dances Diệm had banned. In the Saigon harbor, they pulled down the statues of the Trung sisters for the simple reason that they had been molded after Mme. Nhu and her daughter. They ripped up all Diệm's portraits wherever they could find them. They ransacked buildings and offices owned by the Ngo families. All the pent-up frustrations built during the last nine years were suddenly decompressed in a few hours.

"By destroying the Diệm regime, the Buddhists produced a political vacuum filled by the United States."[65] Emboldened by its victory, the Buddhist group led by the radical and charismatic Trí Quang[66] for the next two years would engage in violent and brutal demonstrations that caused considerable damage to the government of Saigon, thereby helping the communist cause in the countryside.[67]

Fitzgerald commented, "After the crisis had passed, the people of Saigon rarely spoke of the Diệm regime again. There was nothing more to be said."[68] That statement could not be further from the truth. The political vacuum created by his death and the ineptitude of the generals who followed him rapidly rehabilitated him in the eyes of the Saigonese. By dying in martyrdom, which he had courted since he took over the country in the 1950s, Diệm had assured himself a permanent place in the heart and mind of the South Vietnamese.

8

American Saigon

The fall of the Ngo regime left a huge political void that neither the generals nor the various political and religious factions could fill. The result was a long period of political and military instability exacerbated by ever-changing Buddhist demands and an upsurge in insurgency. This soon led to massive U.S. military involvement. South Vietnam came close to becoming America's 51st state.

Trần Văn Hương and the Buddhists

The generals' popularity was quickly fading. They were so ineffectual that South Vietnam had a "power vacuum at the top." Killing Diệm and Nhu had disrupted the system they had set up. Diệm's experienced appointees were replaced by new ones who were not familiar with the system. And there were not enough qualified people to immediately take over these old positions. The junta replaced all the district and provincial chiefs—people charged with running the militia, the strategic hamlets, the police, and the political programs in the villages—and dissolved the organizations that made the strategic hamlet program a success—the Republican Youth and the hamlet committee. They gutted the leadership of the Civil Guards and the Self Defense Corps. Nine of the top 22 military commanders had been replaced.[1] The new government became rudderless despite the fresh air it brought. The end-result was a partial paralysis of the central administrative bureaucracy down to the province chiefs.

The Buddhist problem, on the other hand, did not disappear: three Buddhist suicides occurred during the regime's first month in office. The problem lay in the fact that the Trí Quang–led Buddhists believed that a coalition government with the NLF and communists "outweighed the destruction wrought by the U.S. military in Vietnam."[2] They pretended not to understand that the NLF was just an arm of the Hà Nội communist government.[3]

The VC, profiting from the political instability, launched waves of attacks in the countryside to test the new government. The pacification program drifted aimlessly as the new and inexperienced provincial chiefs did not know how

145

to handle the VC without input from above. Militiamen turned in their weapons and stopped fighting. Government weapon losses shot up and its operations plummeted. The VC made dramatic gains in many parts of the country. A communist assessment prepared in March 1965 revealed that "eighty per cent of the strategic hamlets had been destroyed" in the 16 months since Diem's killing. In the Long An province close to Saigon, nearly all the hamlets had been destroyed. All the military gains were lost after Diệm's downfall.[4]

The problem rested on the generals who had never claimed to be good administrators. General Lê Văn Kim was upset at the lethargy of the junta and especially the lack of direction of General Minh. The resentment led to another coup three months later.

On the early hours of January 30, 1964, Khánh's army surrounded the residences of Generals Đôn, Kim, Đính and Xuân, who were taken to custody in Dalat. Khánh appointed himself council chairman with three associates: Generals Khiêm, Thiệu, and Đỗ Mậu. He ordered the arrest and execution of Captain Nguyễn Văn Nhung, Diệm's murderer, fulfilling at least part of Diệm's last-minute request. Khánh rose faster than any other officer in the Vietnamese National Army. By enthusiastically supporting Diệm, he became general by the age of 30. His weak administrative skills and lack of political experience began to show and caused him to always turn to Ambassador Lodge for political advice, thereby decreasing his popular standing among the Saigonese.[5]

The Buddhists, sensing Khánh's weakness, went on the attack. They threatened to veto his cabinet. The Catholics, not to be outdone and fearing a backlash from a Buddhist-leaning cabinet, expressed their disagreements. Mobs of Catholics and Buddhists fought one another in the streets of Saigon and in the provinces.[6]

Khánh proposed a new charter from Vũng Tàu calling for a stronger presidential system. Students jumped in, arguing against what they called an attempt from the military to "consolidate power." The Buddhists demonstrated and demanded the revocation of the Vũng Tàu charter. Under pressure, Khánh gave in to Buddhists' demands. To appease the Buddhists, he had the army remove all its Catholic chaplains. Buddhist Trí Quang pressured Khánh to give Đặng Sỹ, the Catholic officer who had confronted the Buddhists in Huế, a life sentence. He demanded that Cẩn, Diệm's brother, be put to death, which Khánh did.[7]

Street demonstrations continued unabated in September and October, forcing markets, stores, and schools to close and disrupting civilian life. Streets were on many occasions filled with smoke gas used by the police to disperse the demonstrators. People began barricading inside their homes. Unnerved, Buddhists made one demand after another. Profiting from the instability, vigilante groups popped up. In August, mobs armed with clubs roamed through the city and attacked not only demonstrators but also the police. Thirteen people died in one day, four more on the next. Catholic houses and churches were set afire. Khánh not only failed to control these demonstrations, but also continued to dole out concessions that in turn incited more demands.

Washington viewed the chaos in Saigon with great anxiety. The CIA then labeled Trí Quang a "fanatic." Taylor, who had sheltered him in the past, described him as "the most effective and dangerous politician in Vietnam." General Westmoreland stated that the monk "wanted a dominant voice in the government," while Defense Secretary Robert McNamara referred to him as an "ambitious, dangerous, unpredictable, powerful, political force antagonistic to the Khánh government."[8]

Concerned by the persistent rioting and continuing political instability, the army decided to step back and formed a High National Council, which appointed Phan Khắc Sửu head of state. Sửu made Trần Văn Hương, a former schoolteacher and prefect of Saigon, the prime minister. The new civilian government took power on November 1, the first anniversary of the coup.

Both Sửu and Hương were respected southern nationalists. They had opposed the French, then Diệm. Sửu was born in 1905 in Cần Thơ, the son of wealthy landowners. He studied in Saigon and then France and graduated as an agricultural engineer. He served as the director of the Economic and Agricultural Service from 1930 to 1940. In 1941, he was sentenced to eight years of hard labor at Poulo Condore for having founded the Unified Revolution of Annamese people under the Decoux government. Released in 1945, he continued his nonviolent nationalist activities.

Hương was born in 1903 in Vĩnh Long to a landless day-laborer father. Educated in Vĩnh Long, he lost his scholarship for protesting against an overbearing French official. Undaunted, he worked his way through high school by making extra money as a coolie. He studied at the Lycée Chasseloup Laubat and got a scholarship at the School of Pedagogy in Hà Nội. After graduation, he became a teacher of French and Vietnamese for the next 19 years. He joined the Vanguard group in March 1945 and fought for the resistance against the French. He quit the Việt Minh group in December 1945 and became a member of the Red Cross and then prefect of Saigon from 1954 to 1955. He then worked as secretary general of the Vietnamese Red Cross from 1955 to 1960.

But Hương's biggest problem was dealing with the enigmatic Trí Quang. The latter even intimidated the American Embassy by holding it responsible for the government's repression of the people. He then disappeared for weeks from Saigon on mysterious missions without giving one single explanation. But no one dared pin him down. He was divisive in his leadership role: a good orator, he knew how to inflame passions and turn people against the Saigon government. Thirty years later, in 1994, Malcolm Browne found him swabbing the latrine floor of the Xá Lợi palace where he had once reigned as king. He was reduced to the lowest echelon of society for having played too many tricks on the communists, as he had on the Americans and the nationalists.[9]

As demonstrations continued, Hương declared a state of siege and vowed to get rid of the hooligans. He closed schools, prohibited public meetings, and gave wide powers to the military commander of Saigon-Cholon to search and arrest without warrant. Order was soon reestablished. The Saigonese, tired of the chaos, applauded the draconian measures. For the first time since the fall of the Ngos, they felt someone had better control of the situation than the soft generals.

The fall of 1964 saw the emergence of a group of young military men known as the Young Turks. Among them were Nguyễn Cao Kỳ, the 35-year-old commander of the air force, and General Nguyễn Văn Thiệu, who seemed to be more mature than Kỳ. They requested that the old guard, generals Kim, Đôn, and Big Minh, be pushed aside. Head of State Sửu, however, refused to sign the order. On the night of December 19–20, the army quietly arrested 22 people, including some members of the High National Council. The coup was spearheaded by Khánh and the young Turks who went to see Hương at 2 A.M. on December 20 and asked him to remain prime minister. Hương answered that he would remain in his post only if the army did not behave as a "state within a state."

The new U.S. ambassador, Taylor, was furious and demanded to see the army representatives. Huong, accompanied by Thiệu, Kỳ, Thi and Cang, went to see him in the morning. Taylor chewed them out, making the group feel bad.[10] Deputy A. Johnson told them that the coup basically destroyed the legality and the good order of the government. Taylor wanted Khánh to report to the embassy about the takeover. Khánh retorted that if Taylor wanted to see him, he could meet him at his headquarters.

On December 21, Taylor met with the representatives of the Armed Forces Council at the Saigon JGS headquarters. When asked who gave the order for the coup, Khánh answered it was the common decision of the Armed Forces Council, including himself. He added that the High National Council, having exceeded its powers, deserved to be removed.

The differences between Khánh and Taylor widened, causing the latter to look for ways to withhold aid. Khanh even wrote a report to Washington on how Taylor treated him and his four generals. His standing rose among the members of the Armed Forces Council. He declared, "We will not carry out the policy of any country," and, "Better live poor and proud as free citizens of an independent country rather than in ease and shame as slaves of the foreigners and communists." He started sounding like Diệm. The Buddhists suddenly became quiet.[11]

Under pressure from the Buddhists, Hương was forced to reshuffle his cabinet. Yet in spite of the reshuffling, street disorders still broke out again. Rioters ransacked the American library in Huế, burning 8,000 books. In Saigon, small crowds dressed as monks shouted in front of the embassy: "Taylor is killing Buddhists." Hương mentioned that more than 100 people were arrested during the incident, although none of them turned out to be a monk. Trí Quang and followers announced they would start a hunger strike until Hương stepped down. Thiện Minh, Trí Quang's associate, added that if Huong was not removed, the Buddhists would "call for peace," with the communists suggesting a collaboration with communists and Buddhist leaders.[12] Khánh negotiated a truce with the Buddhists in exchange for Hương stepping down.

For the second time in 14 months, the Buddhists had taken down the Saigon civilian government. But as soon as the announcement was made, they asked Khánh to return the agreement they had signed with him. The Buddhists' duplicity infuriated some of the generals.[13]

Phan Huy Quát, the new prime minister, turned out to be a weak one.[14] The Quát government set free everyone who had been previously detained during anti–Hương demonstrations. It carried another round of purges within the military to satisfy Trí Quang: Many fervent anti-communist officers who opposed the Buddhists were let go. This resulted in a weakening of the officer corps and the armed forces. Monk Quang Liên and other Buddhist officials espoused a peace plan that called for withdrawal of all foreign troops from the country. Trí Quang in May displayed violent anti–American and anti–Catholic feelings in his speeches.[15]

On February 19, 1965, another military coup took place. Khánh was deposed but managed to escape to Vũng Tàu.

Americanization of the War

The communists continued their southern infiltration: 4,500 in 1960, 5,400 in 1961, and 13,000 in 1962. The newcomers wore DRV uniforms and in 1964 carried AK-47 machine guns—top-of-the-line Soviet armament. The South Vietnamese received the American M-16 only four years later after the 1968 Tet attack.

They increased their attacks against Vietnamese and U.S. targets: they mortared the Biên Hòa Airbase on November 1, 1964, killing four and wounding 30 Americans. They exploded a car bomb under the Brink Hotel in Saigon on Christmas Eve, killing two and wounding 38 American military officers. On February 7, 1965, they shelled the Pleiku Airbase, killing nine Americans, wounding 126 and destroying or damaging 20 American aircrafts.[16] Khánh flew to Pleiku and met with Bundy and Westmoreland. The U.S. finally decided to react.

American advisers had been working with the ARVN since 1954. Between 1961 and 1964, their number had grown from 900 to 23,000. The switch from an advisory to active participation came around February 1965. The process, which lacked clarity in long-term goals and purposes, hinged on the "absence of understanding and communication between the two allies, the arrogance of Washington, and the impotence of the government of Vietnam."

Without warning, two battalions of Marines landed on Đà Nẵng on March 8, 1965. The Americans asked Quat to issue a communiqué announcing the landing. Although he had discussed the event with Taylor a few days earlier, Quát had not requested the troops. Although opposed to the deployment, Taylor wanted to put a Vietnamese face with the fact. Bùi Diễm wrote how, on the morning of March 8, he was called to come immediately to Quát's house to draft the document: "Be as brief as possible. Just describe the facts and affirm our concurrence." The abruptness of the decision and the lack of preparation caught Bùi Diễm by surprise. As he tried to argue, Quát told him, "They are landing on the beach right now. They are already ashore. Please, just draft the communiqué and we can talk about the situation later."[17]

Quát could have delayed or rejected the American move. But the newly-minted prime minister (he took the job three weeks earlier) did not have the aura or power to make such an important decision. He did not have the full back-up and support of civilians and military. He would need time to make consultations, which he did not have. He would have looked incompetent had he faced the Americans and his own generals—who did not object to the decision—head-on and been told to get lost. Besides, Taylor had argued that the Marines would only play a defensive and limited role. Quát, therefore, brushed his doubts aside and reacted mildly to the landing. Besides, he had no means to oppose it.[18]

Whether Quát realized the seriousness and importance of his decision or lack of it, he did not let anyone know about it. It was, however, a crucial one, for the landing of a few thousand Marines portended the introduction of more than a half-million foreign troops. In his wildest dream, Quát had not anticipated that the mighty U.S. would move a full army from the other side of the world to Vietnam. Military assistance would become a full invasion. What seemed to be a tolerable misty rain would turn into a violent tornado with far-reaching implications. Quát was probably as stunned and surprised in 1965 as the Saigonese 1859 who witnessed the arrival of the French in Saigon and their takeover of South Vietnam less than a decade later. Neither had foreseen the future. Neither had understood the American mentality, so well summed up by Wesley Fishel: "There is an American obsession that if 100 Americans can do a job well, 10,000 can do it better."[19]

Two weeks after the 3,500 Marines landed in Đà Nẵng, General Harold Johnson asked for the deployment of three more divisions. When Taylor and Quát objected, the White House compromised and sent only two battalions, which made Westmoreland very unhappy. The joint chiefs forced Taylor to accept a substantial troop size increase: up to 82,000 U.S. and 7,250 "third country" in Honolulu on April 19. The forces, however, would be confined to the coastal areas per Taylor's request. Quát began feeling more and more nervous about the situation. Following another government crisis linked to the rice supply to Saigon, Quát stepped down.

Kỳ was named prime minister with Thiệu as president of the National Directory Council and chief of state. By naming Kỳ instead of Thi—Trí Quang's ally—the military leadership had broken Trí Quang's stranglehold on the government.[20] Kỳ's first action was to break diplomatic relations with France. For years this country had been plotting in the backroom in favor of the DRV.

The arrival of the Americans rapidly changed the face of Saigon and the countryside—militarily as well as socially. During the last days of June, the 173rd Airborne Brigade began attacking warzone D, a forested area northwest of Saigon. This was the first U.S. ground force attack in Vietnam that was of course preceded by loud B-52 bombing which shook the ground and shattered the rare glass windows in the city. The Saigonese even wondered whether the tremors were earthquakes. The sonic booms of U.S. jets rattled the air and made people jittery. They felt that the war would be waged in a different way: it would be a massive, noisy, and destructive one. There was, however, minimal enemy contact—probably because they had burrowed themselves inside their underground complex.

The Americans arrived like a tornado. By the end of July 1965, 193,000 troops had been scheduled to land in Vietnam. The war, which became an American enterprise, reduced the Saigon government to complete passivity. The Vietnamese were awed by the massive display of manpower and hardware in the cities as well as in the countryside. Military camps rose out of nowhere. In place of lush forests stood camps with soldiers, trucks, runways and asphalted roads. The change was dizzying and no longer controllable.

Westmoreland formulated the three-pronged policy: "search and destroy," "clear and hold," and "securing operations"—in which the ARVN would establish authority over pacified villages. General Cao Văn Viên, chief of the South Vietnamese JGS who wanted to cut off the Hồ Chí Minh trail—the bloodlife of the Việt Cộng—confided after the war, "We did not have the strength to wipe out the sanctuaries ourselves and we had no say at all in the deployment of American forces." Successes were, however, only partial because the enemy avoided combat and slipped away to their sanctuaries in Cambodia or Laos. While the whole Indochinese peninsula was the battlefield, U.S. ground forces restricted themselves to South Vietnam.

Buddhist Insurrection

After their return from Honolulu, Thiệu and Kỳ faced another Buddhist revolt in March 1966—this time led by General Thi, the I Corps commander. Thi had headed the failed coup against Ngô Đình Diệm in 1960. He lent his support to another group that brought down Minh, Đôn, and Đính in 1964. By switching his allegiance to the Young Turks, he helped to bring down Khánh in 1965. As a warlord in the northern part of South Vietnam, he felt as qualified to rule as Thiệu and Kỳ.

In early March, Kỳ's visit to Hue ignited the crisis. The resentful Thi snubbed Kỳ and said, "What is this little man doing here anyway?" Kỳ took the remark as a challenge to the government. Once back in Saigon, he obtained from the military leadership the order to dismiss Thi. General Nguyễn Văn Chuẩn, commander of the ARVN First Division, was named temporary chief of the I Corps. The Buddhists used the occasion to launch the Struggle movement and to ask for the resignation of the military government. Trí Quang asserted that Kỳ had become more despised due to his slavish adherence to American goals.[21] Chuẩn switched to the Buddhist side. Kỳ sent his negotiator to Huế but the latter was held prisoner. He defused the rebellion by promising a constitutional assembly by the end of the year. Since Ambassador Lodge supported Kỳ, Buddhist anger was also directed at the United States.

Kỳ appointed General Tôn Thất Đính to replace Chuẩn. Đính's appointment, however, represented a considerable risk because of his reputation for cunning and intrigue. The communists benefited tremendously from the Buddhist-inspired disorder, which forced ARVN forces to pull back to the cities to enforce order. The VC were free to move troops and ammunition around and to attack the minimally protected countryside.

The Catholics looked with fear at the growing violence and disorder in the country as well as the ascendancy of the militant Buddhist group. The Vietnam Quốc Dân Đảng (VNQDD)—a rightwing nationalist group—also disapproved of Buddhist political interference. The Vietnamese people, although weary of the war and its economic cost, greatly feared the prospect of a communist victory in South Vietnam. They were tired of the continuing political turmoil and the outright revolt in the I Corps. All these groups coalesced in support of the government. They were especially concerned about the breakdown of discipline of the I Corps, especially of Buddhist chaplains who urged soldiers to join the Struggle movement.

Buddhist protests in central Vietnam during 1966 laid bare a simmering debate between Marine Lieutenant General Lewis Walt, commander of the Third Marine Amphibious Force (IIIMAF), and the army-dominated Military Assistance Command, Vietnam (MACV), in Saigon, led by General William Westmoreland, the overall U.S. commander in South Vietnam. A raging controversy over war tactics arose in 1966 between MACV and IIIMAF. Marines, who were used to jungle warfare, insisted that the war could only be won in the villages. They developed the Combined Action Platoon (CAP) whereby small units of Marines and ARVN lived and worked beside villagers in the hope of forming bonds with them and denying the insurgents access to the local populace.

Westmoreland, on the other hand, demanded that the Marines engage in search-and-destroy missions. Marine commanders believed this tactic would allow the guerrillas to lure the Marines into small bloody engagements and to overextend U.S. forces. The feud between Walt and Westmoreland betrayed the concerns of many commanders over Westmoreland's leadership, flawed attrition strategy, and the U.S. role in Vietnam.

In May, Kỳ sent his crack troops to Đà Nẵng—this time without warning—to control the situation and within days Buddhists and dissident soldiers were routed. The revolt of the Buddhists in Huế ended on May 21 and left 150 dead and 700 wounded.[22]

The situation in Huế did not calm down immediately. Buddhist crowds burned the U.S. Information Service Library on May 26 and the U.S. Consulate on May 30. Everything calmed down in mid–June and General Thi left for exile in the United States. The three-year-long Buddhist rebellion finally ended and marked the beginning of political stability. As the radical Buddhists faltered, Trí Quang tried to have his rival, moderate Thích Tâm Châu, removed as the titular head of the Unified Buddhist Church (UBC). Tâm Châu called on members of the UBC to cease demonstrations against the government. The moderates who continued to gain ascendancy in the UBC persuaded followers to return to pagodas for prayer rather participate in demonstrations. Tâm Châu soon regained his title and led the movement toward cooperation with the government.[23]

The Elections

Lodge's discussions with the Polish ICC commissioner in Saigon resulted in a ten-point communiqué that was relayed to Đồng in Hanoi. Point two was the most important: "The present status quo in South Vietnam must be changed *in order to take into account the interests of the parties presently opposing* the policies of the United States in South Vietnam." The parties involved were none other than the DRV and NLF. A meeting between the DRV and the U.S. was scheduled for December 6, 1965. The "peace" initiative known as "Marigold" by the U.S. fell through because the American representative waiting in the Polish embassy failed to call the DRV embassy. Thus, as of December 1965, the U.S. had "cared" more for its opponents than its ally. Saigon somehow became aware of the secret talks and began to enquire about them. It was only after the Polish commissioner leaked news about the talks that Lodge began to fill Kỳ in. Kỳ dropped a hint that Catholic leaders were alarmed about the "peace" talk. From then onward, Washington kept all the Marigold negotiations secret from Saigon.[24]

On September 11, 1966, 80.8 percent of the 5,288,512 registered voters went to the polls to vote for the 117 seats of the Constituent Assembly. The new members were diverse in their religions: 34 Buddhists, 30 Catholics, 10 Hòa Hảo, five Cao Đài, and seven Confucians. Presidential and Senate elections took place on September 3, 1967, with Thiệu-Kỳ (34.8 percent), Trương Đình Dzu (17.2 percent), Sửu-Đán (10.8 percent) and Hương-Truyền (10.0 percent). The people elected 60 senators. The Lower House elections held on October 22 yielded 137 new representatives. Thiệu took office on November 1, 1967.

Born on November 24, 1924, in a hamlet near Phan Rang in central Vietnam, Thiệu was the youngest of seven children. His father taught him the basic Confucian virtues: righteousness, loyalty, courage, respect, and magnanimity. He excelled at school and learned French and English. After the war he was a Việt Minh youth leader and later district chief. He questioned communist doctrine and was warned that he was on a list for assassination. He fled to Saigon and enrolled in the first officer class of the military academy of the State of Vietnam. He was a bright, skilled, and ambitious officer. As a colonel commanding the 5th Division, he was instrumental in the attack on Diệm's palace on November 1, 1963.

In his inauguration speech, he talked about peace and negotiations. Hubert Humphrey told him Saigon needed to make significant changes in order to continue receiving American aid. Thiệu began to answer when Humphrey interrupted him: "Perhaps, I haven't made myself clear." The remark reminded him of Taylor's question to him, Kỳ, Thi, and Cang at the embassy on December 20, 1964, "Do you understand English?"[25]

State Building

South Vietnam's infrastructure, which had been primitive under the French, was further damaged by decay, neglect, and decades of war and unrest. To bring in troops and armaments, the U.S. had to rebuild it from scratch. By 1966, the Builders—a consortium of all contractors—had paved 1,260 acres in airfields alone, imported 1,628 miles of water pipe, and poured enough cement monthly to pave 35 miles of four-lane highway.[26] Construction materials competed with an increasing flow of military aid, commodity aid, imports for limited dock space, and airfields.

A decision was made to build or upgrade the Long Bình camp, the Saigon Newport, the Tân Sơn Nhứt airbase, the Cam Ranh Bay, and the Đà Nẵng air-sea terminal. These five facilities stood out for their scope and scale.

To fight the growing problem of inflation brought on by the war and exacerbated by the presence of Americans in and around Saigon, a decision was made to build an "instant city" at Long Bình, 15 miles northeast of Saigon. This new base, at a cost of over $60 million, served as an army headquarters consisting of 475,000 square feet of barracks, 20,000 square feet of commercial structures, 15,000 square feet of mess facilities, and 420,000 square feet of administrative buildings. It required the removal of 1,200 acres of heavy first-growth jungle, the building of 180 miles of roadways and streets, the erection of 3,500 buildings, two dozen helicopter pads, and barracks for 40 to 50,000 troops.[27]

The port facilities of Saigon, although expanded in 1965, could not accommodate the growing flow of goods. Designed to handle 1.5 million tons of cargo per year, it soon saw its load triple to 5 million tons per year. Ships had to wait for weeks and sometimes months to unload their wares. The latter had to be off-loaded directly to a myriad of barges, junks, and sampans, which clogged the Saigon River estuaries.

Expansion included the construction of new deep draft berthing and docking facilities equivalent to several city blocks in length. It also involved the creation of a new facility two miles upstream from the Saigon docks. Named Newport, this new facility was connected to Long Bình base and the air terminal at Tân Sơn Nhứt. At completion in July 1967, it provided 2,400 feet of deep draft berthing space, and hundreds of thousands of square feet of warehouse/storage space, along with maintenance and repair facilities. It involved the transformation of 60 acres of marshland into a major harbor facility.[28]

The Tân Sơn Nhứt airport, built in 1954, also underwent transformation to keep up with the demands of air traffic. It became a modern airport and a main army headquarters base. Expansion included 9,000 feet of new taxiways, a new 10,000-foot runway parallel to the old one and capable of handling jet aircraft, a new communication center, new hangars, an ammunition depot, barracks and dormitories.[29] As an airfield re-dedicated in June 1967, Tân Sơn Nhứt became one the world's busiest commercial airports. Although handling mostly military traffic, it was also the hub for major commercial liners.

All these constructions and others at various centers across South Vietnam improved the military infrastructure and the movement of troops and armaments, but did not aid in the development of an economically independent southern state. Most of the spending channeled into the military system lay bare the economic needs of the civilians.

Escalation of the war on both sides[30] worsened the inflation rate and forced refugees to escape to cities like Saigon for their own protection. Healthcare needs soared although they remained mostly unmet. Saigon spent only less than one percent of its budget on health services. It was estimated in 1967 that one third of the Vietnamese had tuberculosis and 30,000 to 50,000 amputees would likely have to wait many years for artificial limbs.[31]

Saigon as Seen by an American

Wendy Wilder Larsen accompanied her war correspondent husband to Vietnam. While he followed troops in battles, she taught literature at the faculty of pedagogy in Saigon. She saw her students arriving on Honda motorbikes and "wearing áo dài, the pastel panels floating out behind them like dragonfly wings."[32]

As the well-known ca dao[33] "The Lotus" was discussed, she pointed out to her students that it speaks of appearance and reality.

> There is nothing more beautiful than the lotus in the pond.
> Green leaves, white petals, yellow anthers,
> Yellow anthers, white petals, green leaves.
> Growing out of mud, yet not giving off the mud smell.

One student immediately replied that since the Vietnamese lived in their own country, they knew that lotuses grew in stinky waters. For them, the ca dao thus reflected reality. For the Americans who were foreigners, it was about appearances.[34] As they were prepared to modernize and build up the backward ARVN and Saigon, they wanted the former to become an American army and Saigon an American city. They did not want to realize that the ARVN and Saigon did not have the infrastructure, knowledge, or organization to become Americanized overnight. A few years might not do it—a few decades would be necessary.

While wives of American journalists talked about baby showers indoors, a peasant woman driven into the city by the bombing slept in the street, a child pulling at her breast.[35] Larsen probably did not realize that the woman's husband was fighting somewhere in the countryside or perhaps had been killed by communist insurgents. She had no family to support her. Her parents were either dead or held in captivity in a "liberated communist area" and prevented from moving to town.

At night, geckos crawled out of their hideouts and settled along the walls or ceilings. They patiently stalked their prey and in due time, one would uncurl his thin tongue and swallow a moth whole. The game was repeated every day and Larsen would look forward to the geckos coming out.[36]

While natives went about their business with their devalued piasters and worsening inflation, the city's bars provided entertainment for the GIs. One bargirl told a GI in her broken English: "You give me baby, I give you VD."[37]

Americans in Saigon had maids to iron their clothes and clean their houses, chauffeurs to drive them around, and cooks to prepare their dinners. Larsen did not know anything about her maid who daily cleaned her house and ironed her clothes because of language problems until the maid became sick one day. She was 27 and pregnant for the eighth time. Larsen found her at home with her deserter husband hiding behind a wardrobe. She took her to the hospital and when they laid her on the gurney cart, she saw the maid in her missing silk underpants.[38]

Saigon was crowded with Honda and Suzuki (Japanese) motorcycles. They served as cheap mode of transportation for teenagers or families alike. Built to carry two people, one motorbike was seen carrying up to seven people, including a grandmother and presents. Teenagers used their bikes to drive their girlfriends around town. Sitting on their bikes, lovers kissed each other under a banyan tree or in a park. The woman who guarded the bikes took a nap across the seats, a conical hat over her head.[39]

Once, Larsen was invited to the presidential press dinner. The menu was printed out so that reporters knew what they were eating. One menu read:

Hedgehog
Duckfeet
Crisp baby sparrows on the nest.

She gagged down the first duck's foot with Scotch. When the host saw it, he ordered her another.[40] Although these menus were unusual for western palates, baby sparrows were known to be an expensive delicacy in Asia. Chicken feet were also highly valued by Asians, especially Chinese. In 2009, the Chinese bought $853 million worth of U.S. chicken feet and wings.[41] The world is strange: the Americans ate the meat, the Asians the feet of chicken.

* * *

The murder of Diệm cost South Vietnam four years of horror, major economic and human losses and the loss of the countryside to the insurgency, which in turn led to the Americanization of the war.

It is regrettable that the Struggle movement, another political group in disguise, inspired by the radical Trí Quang, was allowed to topple the Diệm and subsequent nationalist regimes. Had Lodge not shielded Trí Quang in the U.S. Embassy in 1963, would the four-year-peace—instead of the four-year-Buddhist insurrection—give the Saigon government enough strength to vanquish the insurgency and prevent an Americanization of the war? It could have meant the difference between success and defeat in the war effort.

During a February 28, 1968, cabinet meeting, President Johnson warned cabinet members: "Hồ Chí Minh never got elected to anything.... He is like Hitler in many ways.... But we the President and the Cabinet are called murderers and they never say anything about Mr. Hồ.... They all say 'Stop the war,' but you never see any of them over there [Hanoi]."[42]

The majority of South Vietnamese wanted peace, but not peace under a communist regime. As a matter of fact, they were deeply afraid of the communists.[43] That was why they ran away from the communists: "The exodus constitutes the severest judgement the Vietnamese people have ever expressed against those who govern them."[44]

They were mad at the war, the cost of the war, and at themselves for not having found a solution to the problem. The war, which had been going on for a decade, never seemed to end. And it would not end. All the pent-up rage blew up, tore down the Saigon's administration and, in turn, caused serious damage to the war effort.

9

Saigon and the Generals
(1967–1975)

Thiệu, who presided over the remaining ten years of the republic, fought the most challenging battles of his life: the Tết Offensive, the 1972 Eastern Offensive Tide and the Final 1975 Offensive. This did not include boardroom battles like the Paris Talks.

The Tết Offensive

The rest of 1967 seemed, on the surface, to be quiet. Buoyed by the success of the elections, the generals wanted to "march North" to strike at the source of their ills. The U.S. retorted that since they could not even put their own house in order, why would they want to invade North Vietnam? The U.S. forces were confined to a "limited war." Although the Vietnamese wanted to do more, they were always elbowed aside at every turn. They resented American attitudes that were based on ignorance of Vietnamese customs and values. There was never a productive cooperation between the two allies.[1]

As the air assault on North Vietnam stepped up, so did U.S. opposition to the war. *Life* magazine, which had always supported the president's policies, condemned the war in an editorial.

Faced with a stiff military resistance in the South, the DRV decided to weed out those officials who favored concessions. In the fall of 1967, over 200 party members were arrested, including Hoàng Chính Minh, the superintendent of the party's school of political studies, Colonel Lê Trung Nghĩa, director of the intelligence agency, and other high officials. A secret decree was enacted to eliminate all domestic opposition to its war policies.

From mid–1967, the VC had stockpiled 81,000 tons of supplies along with brand new AK-47 machineguns and rocket launchers. Their two new weapons were PT-76 tanks and 122-mm rockets. They had built up 200,000 troops with seven complete infantry divisions and 20 independent battalions. They infiltrated arms into Saigon and other cities which they hid under merchandise, in cars, boxes and even in coffins. They made surveys of all the blocks, wards, and precincts of all major cities, including Saigon. Names of officials and other opponents to the VC were located. The survey was so precise that when they took over Huế, they went to the right locations to round up over 3,000 officials and opponents. They either killed them on the spot or marched them out of the city and massacred them. No one knew what would happen if they had taken over Saigon at that time. At the same time they launched diplomatic offensives with the objective of opening negotiations with the U.S.

There were plenty of warnings about the attack. The most important included the fact that a B-3 Front Command directive was captured by both the United States and the ARVN in Dak To and Kontum respectively, calling for "many large scale, well coordinated combat operations" to destroy the puppet (ARVN) army and "to annihilate a major U.S. element."

A U.S. Airborne Infantry company captured in Quảng Tín Province a document from Vũ Sinh Viên containing notes about Resolution 13 adopted by the Lao Động Party. It was titled: "Hồ Chí Minh's Order for Implementation of General Counteroffensive and General Uprising during 1967 Winter and 1968 Spring and Summer." The document was translated and circulated to the Defense Intelligence Agency and the U.S. Embassy.

An ARVN company found another document on January 18, 1968, ordering the launching of heavy attacks in order to destroy the enemy and material resources.

On January 28, the South Vietnamese military security service captured 11 cadres at two different meeting places in Qui Nhơn. The cadres revealed they would attack Huế, Đà Nẵng, Saigon and Qui Nhơn on Tết day.[2]

National Security Adviser Walt Rostow had cited a November CIA Saigon report. Washington, therefore, knew about the possibility of the attack, although few believed it. Westmoreland and MACV took chances: They focused upon the evidence, which supported their strategic preferences, and ignored the rest. MACV was caught, and disaster followed: An intelligence failure had occurred.[3] Only General Frederick Weyand insisted on repositioning his units closer to Saigon. The attacks, therefore, caught most of the people in charge by surprise.

Fifteen VC battalions were involved in the Saigon attack. Starting at 9:45 A.M. on January 30, 1968, Radio Saigon announced the cancellation of the Tết truce, which the VC had agreed to weeks earlier. Since many soldiers had gone home for the holidays, many units were only at half strength. Most of the attacks had been repelled except in Saigon and Huế where the battles raged on for many days.

In Saigon the principal targets were the Joint General Staff (JGS) headquarters, the Independence Palace, the Radio Station, the American Embassy, the Navy headquarters and Tân Sơn Nhứt Airbase. The C-10 City Sapper Battalion, with a strength of 250 men, swooped in first to gain control of the objectives.

At the JGS headquarters, the goal of the attackers was to take the generals or their families hostages. The first platoon, arriving by bus at gate 5, was distracted by the presence of a U.S. Military Police jeep and got involved in an exchange of fire that led to the failure of the mission. The second platoon, despite arriving late at gate 4, penetrated inside the complex and dug in at the Language School, believing it was the headquarters. An airborne unit took care of them later on.

A 34-man platoon of the C-10 Sapper battalion crashed through the front gate of the Independence Palace. The attack was repelled by the police and the palace guard. Attackers pulled back to the building across the street, and over the next two days all of them except two were killed. Down the road at the U.S. embassy, another group of sappers charged through the gates at 2:45 A.M. The first two were killed by the Marines. The rest blew a hole in the concrete wall and penetrated the compound, but not all the way into the building itself. By 9:15 A.M., 17 of 19 attackers were killed, with the U.S. suffering five deaths.

The VC also attacked the Saigon radio station. Disguised as police troopers, they penetrated the station. The chief of the transmitter station switched the program to standby recording, preventing program interruption. By 7 A.M., the paratroopers had retaken the station.

The attack of the navy headquarters at the Bạch Đằng pier was immediately foiled at a checking gate. Ten of the 12 men were killed in an exchange of fire and the remaining two were taken prisoner. At the Tân Sơn Nhứt Airbase, the attack was repelled by a group of paratroopers who were waiting to be airlifted to Huế. The three battalions were driven back, leaving behind 300 dead.

The VC, however, were able to occupy the Phú Thọ racetrack and planned to take the Chí Hòa jail, but failed after they lost their guides. They put up a fierce resistance and caused severe destruction. They broke down into small units and took shelter in people's homes. They liquidated government officials and anti-communist figures as well as one of General Nguyễn Ngọc Loan's subordinates along with his whole family. Upset, Loan tracked them down and shot one of their leaders at pointblank in the head. The picture, caught by Associated Press member Adams, was sent worldwide. Without captions, the U.S. viewed the picture as an example of summary justice meted out by the corrupt and unpopular government of Saigon. After he read the news, Loan said, "I had the feeling that the Americans did not understand the reality of the war." Loan held no grudge against Adams. Years later, he came to the U.S. as a refugee and opened a pizzeria in Dale City, VA. When local people realized who was the owner, they boycotted the place. When Loan died, Adams went to his funeral, expressing regret that the photograph had caused difficulties for Loan.[4]

In Huế, the VC attacked one day after Tết. After a barrage of 122mm rockets and 84mm mortars, they threw two infantry regiments, two sapper battalions, and one artillery battalion at the city. Their targets were the 1st ARVN Division headquarters, the police headquarters, and the MACV compound. The battle was protracted and bloody. The VC settled in, freed 2,000 inmates from the Huế jail, and used them as porters and combat replacements. The communist-installed mayor turned out to be a former Huế police chief who had been involved in the Buddhist uprising a few years earlier.

The VC infrastructure was ruthlessly efficient. The VC occupied city headquarters, forced citizens to register and surrender arms and ammunitions, and to dig trenches and then line up along their edge. They were then shot in the back of the head.[5] North Vietnamese soldiers came to a house off Võ Thanh Street and asked its owners if there were any young men there. When the couple answered in the negative, the leader ordered a search. A captain, two lieutenants, and two sergeants came out of their hiding places and surrendered. They were taken away for a "meeting." The old woman found them dead under the fruit trees in the playground of the Gia Hoi high school. Their hands were tied and two of them had wires twisted around their necks.[6]

Trịnh Cong Sơn, a songwriter who lived in Huế at that time, wrote about bodies in the river, in fields, on roofs, and in the streets.[7] This was carnage. After attackers were driven out, mass graves were found within the city limits near the campuses of Gia Long and Gia Hội high schools. Hundreds of bodies were exhumed by friends, relatives and government officials and many of the victims had rags stuffed in their mouths and their arms bound behind their backs with wire.

A year later, VC defectors helped to locate other mass graves in the forests around the graves of emperors Tự Đức and Minh Mạng. Without their help, it would have been difficult if not impossible to locate all the graves that littered the path of the retreating VC. In a ravine, the skeletons of some 400 bodies were washed clean by the running brook. In all, about 2,800 bodies were recovered from concealed graves around Huế. Many of them were bludgeoned to death or buried alive.[8] Skulls showed evidence of fractures, deformities, and holes consistent with clubbing. The enormity and the brutality of the massacre continues to stun the Huế community. The Hà Nội government put the blame on the Buddhists and even denied the massacre had happened.[9]

The ARVN fought gallantly. They had shown they were capable of quick retaliation and effective fighting.[10]

This was the VC's biggest attack so far. They had used 80,000 soldiers and hit 36 of 44 provincial capitals, five of six autonomous cities, 72 of 245 district towns and the national capital. They left 45,000 casualties while the Allies had 4,324 killed and 16,063 wounded. In phase 3, the VC suffered 10,000 more casualties. Overall, 14,300 civilians were killed and 24,000 wounded. The offensive created 630,000 refugees on top of the 800,000 already displaced. There were 70,000 homes destroyed and 30,000 heavily damaged. Thiệu had to establish a National Recovery Committee to provide food to the refugees, work on the resettlement of the displaced, and build new housing.[11]

It was a big psychological shock for the Americans, who, for the first time, saw from their own living rooms pictures of dead people, destroyed houses and buildings, and hungry refugees. They were struck by the contrast between the enthusiasm of President Johnson's public relations campaign and the realities of enemy capabilities. Westmoreland and Bunker's optimistic statements had been blatantly mistaken or intentionally deceptive. The offensive undermined the Johnson administration's credibility. Big questions had been raised: How did the U.S. not know of the presence of so many enemy battalions around Saigon? Was there any collusion between the U.S. and the VC since U.S. forces were not attacked?

There was no uprising during this offensive. People had briefly seen these skinny VC and had not followed them. They felt that the ARVN could easily defeat the insurgents, especially with the Americans around. Displaced by the ongoing fight, refugees found temporary shelter at their friends' or relatives' houses. People opened their doors to the unfortunates, even if it was for a few days. Instead of rebelling against the government, they closed the ranks to fight against the invaders. In one area, they even attacked suspected VC with sticks and captured six of them.

The war had finally hit home—right in the Vietnamese cities and living rooms in the middle of a truce and the holiest day of the year: the Tết. Even the Buddhists had to condemn the communists. Saigon was invigorated and enthusiastic. The attack sparked patriotic moves: mobilization, anti-corruption drives, demonstrations of political unity, and administrative reforms. Several battalions were thus activated overnight: colonels and majors were carrying rifles acting as platoon leaders. A mobilization bill recalled 65,000 people who had less than 12 years of service. By September, 240,000 draftees reported for service ahead of schedule.

There were three different phases in the Tết attack: January 31, May 5, and August 11. This was a brutal war even by communist standards. Saigon was attacked again on May 5, 6, 7, and 8. Fighting erupted in Chợ Lớn near the racetrack and at the Tân Sơn Nhứt airport. Units fought house-to-house, supported on the government side by helicopter gunships and personnel carriers. Communists countered with mortars and B-40 rockets. While street fights ended in mid–May, VC launched Soviet-made 122mm rockets with 11-kilometer range. At least 379 rounds of rockets and mortar struck Saigon between May 5 and June 8, 1968. Thirty thousand homes were destroyed and 87,000 people were left homeless.[12] On May 19, 1968, communists launched the "fiercest rocket attacks" into Saigon. In June, rockets fell for 12 consecutive days on the city, killing more than 100 civilians and wounding several hundreds more. Enemy propaganda threatened 100 missiles a day for 100 days.[13]

Hà Nội's General Giáp was hard and uncompromising. "Every minute, hundreds of thousands of people die on this earth. The life or death of a hundred, a thousand, tens of thousands of human beings, even our compatriots, means little," said Giáp in 1969. "You can kill ten of my men for every one I kill of yours. But even at those odds, you will lose and I will win," Giáp said to the Americans.[14]

Paris Talks

Some cynical critics in Washington argued that the "Saigon regime's raison d'être was the war itself, and that for this reason alone Saigon systematically opposed any peace talks." The reality, was that the South Vietnamese people were fighting for their lives and to defend their country against North Vietnamese invaders.

In 1965, the United States took over the fighting and fought a "limited warfare" against a committed enemy waging total war. It has been said that the American war and peace initiatives were designed to serve American purposes, without much regard for the desires and needs of South Vietnam.[15]

Johnson ordered a halt to the bombing in the North on March 31 and Hà Nội responded by agreeing to talk. At the same time, the VC launched the second phase of the Tết offensive on May 5, 1968. Unable to prevent the United States from participating in the talks, Thiệu suggested a partial stop to bombing as a goodwill gesture. The talks opened at the International Conference Center on Kebler Avenue on May 13 between the Harriman-led-U.S. delegation and the Xuân Thũy-led DVR.

Saigon's National Assembly was concerned that the GVN was not a participant in the talks. The deputies suggested that the GVN (1) legally represented the people of South Vietnam and (2) would not accept any imposed solution to the war. U.S. Ambassador Bunker also questioned the restrictions imposed on him regarding briefing Thiệu about the talks. Withholding exchanges could only invite suspicions, he said. The State Department from then onward would pass only what it deemed "necessary" and would withhold the rest.

The size of the DRV delegation grew from 35 to 72 in July and Hà Nội asked that the NLF be considered a participant in the talks while launching the third phase of the Tết offensive on August 17. They counted on the help of the French and especially Manac'h, the director for Asia and Oceania. Manac'h treated the GVN like a pariah but helped the DRV to introduce the NLF into diplomatic corridors. Visas were granted to two NLF officials waiting in Prague. The Australian ambassador tried to delay the arrival of the delegates but to no avail. When Manac'h allowed Hà Nội to sponsor a war crimes tribunal in Paris during which the U.S. would be denounced as aggressors in Vietnam, the U.S. lodged a complaint.

On October 3, Hà Nội declared that Saigon should recognize the NLF, accept a policy of peace and neutrality, and show its goodwill. On October 13, it announced that if the U.S. stopped the bombing, talks could begin between the four parties. On October 15, Harriman read a five-point message indicating the U.S.'s willingness to negotiate with Saigon present, although he never said, "We would have to talk to the GVN before giving you an answer." Over lunch, Hà Nội apparently accepted the American proposition: this became known as the October 16 understanding, and it remained unwritten.

President Thiệu, with annoying logic, argued that the question was not bombing cessation but the end of the war. He was worried about letting the U.S. negotiate alone with the DRV and rightly so. Thirty-nine of 42 Saigonese senators opposed unconditional bombing cessation. So did the House of Representatives. On October 31, the VC shelled Saigon, again hitting a Catholic church and killing 19 worshippers.[16]

Johnson thus went ahead on October 31 to announce that the U.S. would stop bombing as of November 6. The GVN was "free to participate" in the talks that day. The DRV responded that the NLF would also participate in the talks. It was obvious the U.S. did not care about Saigon's point of view. Three and a half years earlier, it began bombing North Vietnam without asking Saigon's opinion, and now it had decided to stop bombing without Saigon's agreement. Logically speaking, by deciding to involve itself in the Communist War, the U.S. should accept the full responsibility of the outcome of the war. The rest was just for decorum. It is understandable that due to the cost of lives and treasure, the U.S. had decided to change its mind. But it seemed unimaginable that it had betrayed Saigon as early as 1968.

On November 2, accompanied by Vice President Kỳ and Prime Minister Hương, President Thiệu went before the National Assembly to state his government's position. Thiệu told the assembly that serious talks did not exist between Saigon and Hà Nội; therefore, the government of Vietnam would not participate in the October 6 session in Paris. His speech was interrupted 17 times by the audience, who stood up on their feet on several occasions.

Following the speech, both houses approved a communiqué condemning "the egotistical and arbitrary action of President Johnson." Some senators went to see President Thiệu at the palace to express their support. The Saigon press also reacted violently against the bombing halt while Senator Trần Ngọc Nhuận called it a "betrayal."

The American delegate refused to begin discussions with only three parties present. President Thiệu made sure the first meeting between the four parties in Paris would not take place until January 25, the date of Nixon's inauguration. The new U.S. delegation chief was none other than Lodge, the one who took down Diệm. Thiệu and Kỳ were suspicious of him because of the role he played in the Marigold affair.

The year 1969 proved to be a good one for Saigon. Depleted of soldiers from the Tết slaughter, the VC decided to lay low. Defections from their ranks ran high. This lull gave Saigon the chance to reopen roads and canals that soon filled up with traffic. The economy picked up. In the III Corps, 3.2 million rural people lived in government protected hamlets, 41,000 in VC controlled hamlets and 50,000 in contested areas. On February 20, the VC launched the fourth and final phase of the offensive. This consisted mostly of rocket shelling against more than 100 targets on Saigon, Huế and Đà Nẵng. Many rockets landed in the Khánh Hội area near the Saigon docks, causing many fatalities. Doubts about the commitment of the U.S. in winning the war—which had been raised since the unilateral bombing halt—resurfaced anew this time.

Unable to mount field attacks, the VC stepped up their terrorist attacks. On March 5, Prime Minister Trần Văn Hương escaped an assassination attempt two blocks from the American embassy.[17]

As Vance had suggested, the U.S. were in Paris to reach a compromise. Therefore, Kissinger, Lodge and Vance would bend backward to please the DRV. The South Vietnamese, who needed an advocate who could negotiate in a skilled and fair manner, never found it in the American team. While Kissinger called President Thiệu a "loyal ally," he, on the other hand, was not as loyal to Thiệu as he could have been. Kissinger's attitude caused him to be "distrusted and even hated" by the South Vietnamese.[18]

As Nixon had decided to pull his troops out, Thiệu suggested at the June 8 meeting with Nixon at Midway a "redeployment" of U.S. forces in order not to get into an argument with him. Nixon then proposed that the U.S. and DRV would meet at the presidential level to speed up the talks. Thiệu agreed on the condition that Saigon was informed of all discussions. He was not aware that the U.S. would use these talks to negotiate a settlement on American terms.[19]

In his May speech, Nixon mentioned that abandoning Vietnam would damage "other nations' confidence in our ability."[20] Neither Nixon nor Kissinger told him of future Kissinger-Xuân Thủy secret talks.

On August 4, 1969, Kissinger, Anthony Lake and General Walters made their way to Sainteny's apartment at 204 Rue de Rivoli to meet with Xuân Thủy. Kissinger told him the U.S. was willing to consider unilateral withdrawal without reciprocal concession from the DRV. By December, Lodge resigned as leader of the U.S. delegation. Week after week, he was sitting next to the Saigon delegation without being able to tell its members that Kissinger had been negotiating the most sensitive matters behind their backs with the North Vietnamese.

Kissinger met with Lê Đức Thọ on February 21, 1970, and backed down again: He was willing to recognize that DRV troops in South Vietnam were not foreign troops and that Hà Nội did not have any troops in the South.[21]

At Kent State University in Ohio, on May 4, four students were killed by the National Guard. Antiwar groups scheduled demonstrations in Washington on May 9 along with demonstrations around the country.[22]

On May 31, 1971, Kissinger proposed to Xuân Thủy to specifically separate American and allied troop withdrawal from that of the DRV. Under this proposal, the DRV could do anything they wanted with South Vietnam, Laos and Cambodia. Whether Kissinger did not explain the proposal well enough to Bunker or the latter misunderstood the explanations, Bunker believed that American troop withdrawal was linked to that of the DRV. He therefore briefed Thiệu as such on May 25 and June 3. Since Kissinger did not correct Bunker's misinterpretation, Thiệu all along was under the impression that there would be a DRV withdrawal coupled with the U.S. withdrawal.

When Thiệu learned about the proposal for unilateral American withdrawal on January 10, 1972 (the text was submitted to the DRV on October 11, 1971), he was understandably furious at the underhanded way he and his government had been treated. Nixon and Kissinger would frequently inform Thiệu on broad terms without telling him the specifics of the proposals to be made. Therefore, Kissinger's statement in his memoirs that "he [Thiệu] was kept fully informed of my talks with Lê Đức Thọ, approving every proposal," is a lie as many writers have shown.[23]

Suspecting Kissinger's duplicity, Thiệu complained about not being notified of the proposal; Kissinger dismissed it as "an oversight." Kissinger then argued, "We could have reached agreement over the summer by agreeing to overthrow him [Thiệu]." The idea of overthrowing Thiệu was suggested to Kissinger by Lê Đức Thọ. By approving that idea, Kissinger had sided with the enemy and therefore could not morally represent South Vietnam. Thiệu revealed the proposal half-an-hour after Nixon delivered the news on January 26 (25 in the U.S.).

The proposal also suggested a new election with NLF participation. With that suggestion, Kissinger implied the scraping and rewriting of the current South Vietnamese Constitution, for it did not recognize the NLF or allow its participation in politics. Upon hearing the details of the proposal, the Saigonese asked themselves how Kissinger could give himself the right to amend the constitution without talking to the elected representatives. Many groups in the senate called the proposal "beyond the limits of the Republic of Vietnam's Constitution."[24]

Thiệu's main accomplishment was in the area of land reform. Rents were frozen and 50,000 families received government-owned land in 1968. Two years later, he pushed through the Assembly the "land to the tiller" program, designed to make tenants land owners. By 1972, tenancy was down 60 percent and 400,000 farmers had received a total of 1.5 million acres of land.

However, at the moment of his greatest popularity, he proved to be a man without a plan, a man of indecisiveness. A self-made man of humble origins, he rose to the top position through his will and political astuteness. He had never been a corps commander before becoming commander in chief. Having once led the troops that stormed the palace in 1963, he knew he too could become a victim of another coup. Hoàng Đức Nhã, Thiệu's cousin who had studied in the United States, warned Thiệu one day: "The Americans are businessmen. They sell you out if you can no longer assure them of a profit."[25]

Thiệu's power depended on the Americans as well as his ability to divide his generals and to fight the war. He therefore surrounded himself with a number of yes-men. He often delayed making decisions that could undercut his own power.[26] He did not trust anyone—not even his comrades in arms—because American money could change people in a short time. Close by stood Minh and Kỳ, ready to plot an overthrow of the government. And the CIA was monitoring all his actions and deeds: He could not even go to the toilet without the Americans knowing about it. General Bình (chief of the national police) and General Quang had both been recruited by the CIA.[27] Watched by the CIA, pressed by Washington, surrounded by spies and potential opponents, he led a lonely war against the VC, the DRV and the Americans who tried to isolate and control him. Although he fought a valiant fight, he could not rely on a competent and supportive circle of friends. Had the Americans left him some breathing room and assisted him like a good advisor, they might have won the war.

By nature a cautious man, Thiệu sank into periods of inaction. Confronted by the magnitude of the problems and their consequences, he just froze. And when he tried to play catch-up, he ended up not making good decisions. When his ambassador in Washington, Bùi Diễm, advised him when the Nixon administration's policy had not been defined, to develop a set of concrete proposals on military, political and economic matters, he received no answer. When Bùi Diễm suggested that Saigon's policies might diverge from those of the U.S., Thiệu did not think so: He believed the U.S. would continue to support him.[28]

Thiệu's power depended on the army and the Americans. The American withdrawal escalated rapidly: 65,000 in 1969, 50,000 in 1970, and 250,000 in 1971—leaving only 139,000 U.S. troops in South Vietnam by January 1972. But Thiệu naively continued to trust the Americans. That failure to separate himself from the Americans caused him to lose support among Southerners. In fact, he did not have any choice. With the Americans leaving the country en masse, he felt diminished and vulnerable to the VC's attacks. The shift of power was dizzying: if the American and South Vietnamese forces had a tough time winning the war against the NLF and DRV forces, how could the South Vietnamese by themselves handle the attacks? Arms only would not fill up the military gap. Back in the 1950s the South Koreans at least could rely on the strength of 50,000 American GIs left behind, but the South Vietnamese would have none. Vietnam, devastated by a protracted and ongoing war, had one million refugees to feed. Without American aid and without the money the GIs spent ($100 minimum per month per GI times 500,000), the South Vietnamese economy went into recession. Thiệu did not know how to handle it. Hà Nội did not either: after it took over South Vietnam in 1975, the whole country went bankrupt.

The spring offensive was intended to break the back of the ARVN and to force the U.S. to accept Hà Nội's demands. It was a three-pronged attack on the I, II and III Corps.[29] Over 30,000 men from the 304th and 308th divisions, two T-54 tank regiments armed with SA-2 surface-to-air missiles, and five artillery regiments with 130 mm long-range drove across the DMZ at noon on March 30, 1972, into Quảng Trị province.

In his eagerness to negotiate a settlement, Kissinger in August 1972 decided to recognize the existence of two administrations and two armies in the South, one of which consisted mostly of northern troops. He thus "legalized" the presence of these foreign troops in the South and the aggression of Hà Nội. The DRV, which could not win on the battlefield, won in Paris its share of power in South Vietnam. When Thiệu was given the transcribed discussions, he saw the enormity of the concessions Kissinger had made. He immediately objected to Hà Nội representing both zones, North and South, through the NLF and PLAF. He argued against linking the release of POWs to the withdrawal of American troops. Kissinger ignored all these objections and proceeded with his plan.

Thiệu, in order to defend the constitutionality of his government, sent to Kissinger two memoranda on September 13, which the latter again ignored. A week later, during a ceremony celebrating the recapture of Quảng Trị, he stated: "No one has the right to negotiate, bargain or accept any solution in defiance of the South." While Kissinger was negotiating to get the POW back first then to provide for a ceasefire, Thiệu had in mind "a peace that can safeguard the ideals and interests for which the two countries had been fighting."

Exasperated by Thiệu's recriminations, Kissinger and Haig wrote a memo over Nixon's signature: "I would urge you to take every measure to avoid the development of an atmosphere which *could lead to events* similar to those which we abhorred on 1963 and which I personally opposed so vehemently in 1968." The final agreement was signed on October 12.[30]

On October 17, 1972, Thiệu saw for himself for the first time the draft peace agreement from a 10-page document captured from the VC in Quảng Tín close to the DMZ. Entitled "Instructions for a Cease Fire," it detailed the concessions made by Kissinger to Lê Đức Thọ in Paris. There would be a complete American withdrawal with no residual forces. The VC would be allowed to re-supply their forces through the DMZ. The formation of a National Council of Reconciliation and Concord was a coalition government in disguise. Thiệu was stunned: he had not been shown the draft agreement, nor had he been advised about it in detail by Kissinger. He said, "I knew for the first time what was being negotiated over my head. The Americans told me the negotiations were still going on and that nothing was fixed, but the other side had all the information."

Although the draft agreement had not been implemented, the VC had already drawn up a three-phase plan in order to violate the letter and spirit of the agreement.[31]

Through the sellout Paris Accord, Beech from the *Chicago Daily News* wrote: "We [the U.S.] legitimized the North Vietnamese presence in South Vietnam and arranged it so they could defeat the South Vietnamese at their leisure.... Thiệu was doing about as well as he could in the circumstances. But I thought it was a pretty shabby way to treat him."[32]

Thiệu felt betrayed by Kissinger and Washington. After many years of war effort and a loss of a million people, soldiers and civilians (five percent of the population) the South Vietnamese forces had assumed the initiative and had been fighting well. Now Kissinger was coming with a proposal that made fatal concessions to the enemy. He called a meeting with Vice President Hương, Prime Minister Khiêm, JCS Chairman Viên, and Hoàng Đức Nhã to prepare for Kissinger's visit. When Kissinger came on October 19, he handed Nixon's letter to Thiệu. The letter stated that an agreement had been reached. There was, however, "no alternative but to accept the agreement," Kissinger said. Thiệu was not asked to comment on the proposed agreement, just to accept it. He read the letter and invited Kissinger to meet with his National Security Staff. Kissinger then explained the details of the agreement. The session was tense and emotional. He handed an English version to Thiệu, who requested a Vietnamese version. Once it was available, the Vietnamese worked late into the night analyzing it. They found many differences between the two versions and wanted 23 points changed, clarified or deleted to preserve Thiệu's constitutional authority. While Thiệu wanted some more time to study the changes, Nixon suggested that failure to accept the proposal would negatively affect support for his regime.[33] Thiệu's rejection of the agreement attested to his stature as an independent leader. Nationalism, anticommunism, and personal pique were equally possible reasons for the rejection.[34]

Upon his failure to convince Thiệu, Kissinger returned directly to Washington. He was never again welcomed to South Vietnam. Thiệu gave a television address on October 24 explaining his position and preparing the Vietnamese for a ceasefire sooner or later. The Lower House in Saigon on October 27 passed a resolution overwhelmingly supporting Thiệu's stand.

After Thiệu had succeeded in delaying the signing of the agreement until after the elections, he allowed himself to be misled by Nixon's promises. What he did not know was that once the election was out of the way, Nixon and Kissinger would aggressively go ahead with the agreement in order to save the POWs. And the Americans would blame Thiệu for any delay in the negotiation process. This was where Dommen thought the sovereignty of South Vietnam passed to the U.S. First, the French invited the PRG to set up an office in Paris, and then to join the four-sided talks. The South Vietnamese accepted the arrangement in exchange for "direct talks" with Hà Nội. Once the talks began, the U.S. took over and talked to the DRV (Hà Nội) leaving the South Vietnamese sitting like wooden statues. Then the PRG was invited to share the power with the South Vietnamese. In the end, the latter were not allowed to talk to the PRG until after the agreement was signed.[35]

Thiệu mentioned that accepting the agreement was agreeing to the fact that the U.S. were the aggressors. It also meant sacrificing the justness of the cause of South Vietnam. To get Thiệu on board, Nixon sent Vice President Agnew to Saigon with the assurance of massive retaliation in case of violation of the agreement. Thiệu faced a dilemma: not to sign the agreement and risk a aid cutoff or sign and risk adverse political reaction and deterioration of the situation in South Vietnam. In the end, he "intended" to accept the agreement without signing it. On January 19, Thiệu asked his national security advisers whether he should sign the agreement. Hương stated that people would blame Thiệu if he signed, but he would do it anyway.

On a cold rainy day, January 23, 1973, in Paris, Lê Đức Thọ and Kissinger signed the agreement, which let the Americans out of the war but directly led to the demise of the South Vietnamese nation. The DRV had outmaneuvered Thiệu and the nationalists by negotiating only with the Americans.

During the 19-year (1954 to 1973) war between Saigon and Hà Nội, the latter had never won a victory on the battlefield that would determine the outcome of the war. The ARVN had held all along. The 1973 agreement that the Americans forced on Thiệu gave major concessions to the DRV, which left the ARVN demoralized and dispirited. From that time onward, the ARVN had lost its fighting spirit.[36]

The cease fire took effect at 3 A.M. Saigon time on January 28, 1973. Deprived by a clear mandate of sovereignty, Saigon was unable to do anything. Both sides were allowed to replace destroyed, damaged or worn out equipment on a one-for-one basis. The U.S. had given South Vietnam $750 million worth of military equipment between 1972 and 1973. Much of this equipment was badly worn out or lacking in tools and spare parts, so that its maintenance became an added burden for the ARVN. Corps commanders were frustrated when they were told not to actively engage the VC until the American POW release was completed.

Thiệu had poor public relations in the United States: He did not know how to win over votes from key American figures. Nixon no longer invoked the legal obligation to continue funding aid to Vietnam to the Congress once the POWs were out of harm.

As a result, Thiệu became more pessimistic as time went by. While U.S. military aid to Saigon dwindled, Hà Nội continued to send supplies to the South: 140,000 tons in 1973 or four times as much as in 1972. In addition, 10,000 tons of weapons were brought in and stored in the highland mountains. More than 100,000 cadres and soldiers, including two infantry divisions, two artillery regiments, one anti-aircraft division, one armored division and one engineer regiment headed to the South in 1973. The acquisition of anti-aircraft capability had been the biggest improvement for the DRV forces. Southern military hospitals lacked medicines, antibiotics and plasma. To conserve gasoline, a 2½ ton truck had to tow four ambulances in a row. Wounded soldiers had to wait for two or more injured comrades to be worth an evacuation by ambulance, causing many to die unnecessarily.[37]

Things did not look good in Washington for Nixon in 1973. Bob Haldeman and John Ehrlichman had resigned in April. It was the turn of Vice President Spiro Agnew in October. A week later, Attorney General Elliot Richardson and his deputy quit over the firing of special prosecutor Archibald Cox. Nixon's administration was in a debacle and the city seemed to be paralyzed. There was no one to talk to about Vietnam's lifeline. In November, Congress overrode a Nixon veto and passed the War Powers Act, limiting the president's power to use armed force. He was no longer able to fulfill his obligations to Vietnam under the Paris Agreements. In August 1974, Nixon's resignation shook Thiệu deeply. With Nixon's support gone, Thiệu could not expect much.

Thiệu was involved in a crisis of his own. For a variety of reasons—some sincere, some political—Father Trần Hữu Thanh launched the People's Anti-corruption Movement. He attacked President Thiệu, Thiệu's wife and many generals at a time of economic collapse and galloping inflation. People who were deprived flocked to him.

Corruption, as bad as it was, did not constitute the whole story. Corruption, which was more blatant and offensive elsewhere in Asia, did not bring any government down. It did not cause any campaign like Father Thanh's. In short, the campaign was just an outlet for the long suppressed anger of Thiệu's political opponents. Leftists, neutralists, Buddhists, and Catholics who had been denied a voice in the government transformed the corruption campaign into a crusade.

Thiệu did go on television to placate his enemies. Years later, Hà Nội acknowledged that it had planted many activists and moles inside father Thanh's group. And the fight drained the government's energies. The government did not look for compromise, while the opposition was too blind to see the approaching danger.[38]

The news of Nixon's resignation put Thiệu into a depressed mood. Without Nixon, he would lose his biggest supporter. What kept Thiệu's hope alive was the letter Gerald R. Ford sent to him, in which Ford stated that existing commitments "are still valid and will be fully honored in my administration."

ARVN had to hold fixed positions all over Vietnam. The DRV forces moved around them and concentrated overwhelming forces on any target they wanted to overrun. The DRV forces were very economical compared to the ARVN, which followed the U.S. lead. The ARVN did not have reserve units and intelligence resources. When the DRV attacked Ban Mê Thuột on March 10, it had 25,000 soldiers, compared to 1,200 defenders, in the city.

The Paris Peace Agreements were contingent upon the promises of aid and threats of retaliatory actions against the North—the linchpins of the agreement. Without implementation of these promises, peace "never had a chance in Vietnam."[39]

The Armed Forces of the Republic of Vietnam (ARVN)

Born in 1950 as the Vietnamese National Army (VNA) to serve an emperor who was seen as a French stooge, the VNA and its successor the ARVN always lacked national support. Vietnamese officers were rarely promoted beyond the rank of junior officer under the French system or given the chance to direct their own soldiers. They were embedded in the French army and had no chance to function as a unit. By 1954, the VNA had only a rudimentary general staff, no artillery, no heavy armor, and no logistic capability. Although it numbered about 150,000, it had been weakened due to desertion following the French withdrawal.

In 1955, the Americans decided to build from scratch a large, new, conventional force to face a North Vietnamese invasion instead of a small, maneuverable one designed to fight a war of insurgency.[40] The small force would be more motivated to protect local villages and would be more consistent with Vietnam's past. MAAG officials, however, insisted there would be no aid if Saigon did not follow their advice. Diệm reasoned that without military aid he would receive no economic aid either, and therefore could not develop his country economically. He accepted the American decision. "It was a bargain with the devil." His gamble not only cost him his life, it also rendered the ARVN inadequate to fulfill its counterinsurgency role and disconnected it from the peasant masses.[41] With a population of barely 20 million, five percent of its citizens were under arms.

If in the beginning it was a volunteer army, it later became one of the most conscripted armies in history (65 percent). From 1960 to 1963, troops were increased from 150,000 to 250,000, and then every year thereafter under U.S. request. Families looked at their sons going to war and not coming back without any significant change in the war effort. After the Tết attack, ARVN troops grew from 685,000 to 779,154 in 1969 and 801,000 in 1970. With changes in conscription rules, the length of service was extended to seven years and many would serve the duration of the war. By 1968, one in six adult males had fought in the ARVN. To ignore the important role of the ARVN and the unselfish contribution of these men is akin to stating that the fratricidal war did not occur. Without them, the war would have lasted a much shorter time and the red tide would have marched all the way to the straights of Malacca.

Saigon did not do enough to prepare the peasants for a lengthy sacrifice.[42]

It had not always articulated a political vision of South Vietnam's future that made sense to the average soldier.[43] Under Thiệu/Kỳ, there was no sustained promotion of chính nghĩa. Diệm at least tried to advance his personalism movement, although it was derailed by USIS.[44] Simple anti-communism was not enough to sustain the endless sacrifice of a long war.

ARVN soldiers did complain about food shortages. They never got paid adequately because of the inflation rate. From 1964 to 1972, the private saw his salary drop from $77USD per month to about $30USD per month.[45] Wives worked on the side to feed their families. Medical resources were so limited that disposable supplies (bandages, syringes, needles, surgical gloves, intravenous sets) were washed and reused. Lack of running water and proper sanitation were constant problems. There were not enough doctors and hospital beds.

ARVN's military shortcomings were the result of flawed doctrines.[46] It was trained for the wrong mission: a full-scale war instead of a war against insurgency. It also lacked political training. After 1965, it was pushed aside and taken over by the U.S. ARVN successes in the field in the 1970s came from operations in which the number of U.S. advisers had been purportedly reduced.[47]

The soldiers turned inward when they saw that Saigon officials allowed the Americans to dictate the conditions of the war. They found safety and comfort in their families. ARVN wives set up shantytowns all over Vietnam around military bases. They took great pleasure in serving their husbands as cooks, nurses, laundresses. They boosted the soldiers' morale and kept the family together. Some Americans suggested this practice was another evidence that the ARVN did not have "the fighting spirit." Although most Vietnamese were committed anticommunists, few found an outlet for their nationalism.[48]

By 1965, the U.S. decided to win the war by military means by themselves. Maxwell Taylor suggested: "We really never paid attention to the ARVN. We didn't give a damn about them."[49] Sixty percent of the ARVN was shunted into providing local security. The remaining 40 percent who remained in combat operations were exposed to an American type of war—massive firepower and logistic support—their country could ill afford.

Some young American officers and troops did not consider the Vietnamese as people because they did not have American houses or televisions, and their clothes were different. One GI truck driver sideswiped a little Vietnamese minibus, scattering all its ten passengers and their stuff all over the road. He never slowed down.[50]

By 1965, the North Vietnamese infantry had already used the infamous automatic AK-47, which surpassed the Garands and single-shot Carbines M-1 used by the ARVN.[51] The disparity in firepower left the ARVN outgunned and created unfavorable battlefield performance and low morale. It would be only three years later after the Tết offensive that the ARVN received their M-16s.[52] Three years in the battlefields of Vietnam meant an eternity.

The Americans created an ARVN that was unable to stand alone. Soldiers and officers were overly dependent on U.S. firepower to win victories and on the advisers to direct that firepower. Immediately after the Tết victory, the Americans decided to "Vietnamize" the war, forcing the ARVN to assume the burden before they even had the chance to grow up.[53]

The U.S. had 3,500 helicopters in Vietnam but supplied only 100 to the Vietnamese. An officer explained that the ARVN did not have the same needs as the Americans because they walked on foot and did not need hot meals like the American troops.[54]

The rapid U.S. pullout left gaping holes in territorial defenses. The 5th ARVN division covered an area along with two other U.S. divisions. With U.S. withdrawal, the 5th division suddenly had to assume the whole area coverage by itself.[55] Similarly, the new and untested 3rd division was assigned to defend the area along the DMZ and the highland approaches from Laos. The latter was previously covered by two U.S. divisions, the reinforced 3rd Marine division and the 1/5 brigade (mechanized). During the 1972 Eastern Offensive, the 3rd was rapidly blown apart by the NVA.[56]

Compared to their American counterparts, ARVN operations were simple and had a more rustic flair. Each morning, the units gathered for a hot tea session where the tea was boiled to ward off waterborne diseases. They patrolled until 10:30 and then broke for lunch, which usually consisted of rice balls. Patrolling resumed before they settled for night defensive positions. The cooks would prepare the evening meal by slaughtering the chickens the men carried tied to their rucksacks. In certain missions, helicopters would deliver a fresh load of unhappy squawking or oinking live cargo along with ammunition and water.[57]

Keith Nolan's *Battle for Hue* rarely mentions the ARVN at all, except for when he refers to them as "mopping up behind the Marines." The Marines had performed admirably, losing 147 killed in action. The ARVN, however, did the majority of the fighting in Huế, besting the NVA and VC without the aid of heavy fire weaponry. They lost 357 killed in action and inflicted 2,642 enemy deaths. The battle of Huế turned out to be ARVN's greatest victory ever.[58]

Phạm Văn Đính graduated as an aspirant from the Thủ Đức Reserve Officers School in 1961 and was assigned as a mortar platoon leader before studying at the South Vietnamese Ranger School and the Jungle Warfare School in Malaya. He was later assigned the command of the 200-man-*Hắc Báo* (Black Panther) Company—a rapid deployment company designed to assist regular forces in case of need. Trần Ngọc Huệ, also born in Huế, graduated from the prestigious Dalat National Military Academy as a second lieutenant in 1963. He was assigned as a platoon leader and assistant commander of the 3rd Company in the Ashau Valley.

After the Buddhist crisis, General Trưởng offered Định the command of the 2nd battalion, 3rd regiment of the 1st division (2/3) while Huệ became assistant commander of the Hắc Báo for two months before being promoted to commander. The Hắc Báo was at the heart of the ARVN war of attrition. The unit was constantly involved in combat from the Laotian border to the coastline. An Australian adviser suggested the U.S. would have "done a much better job if we had given the Vietnamese more respect and authority."[59]

During the Tết Offensive, the Hắc Báo had only 50 men to defend the Citadel proper. The rest of the unit was dispersed on the perimeter as reconnaissance teams. It defended the 1st ARVN Division HQ and prevented the enemy from taking it. The Hắc Báo and the 2/3 were assigned to retake the city from the enemy with the help of the Marines. Progress was slow. On 23 February, Định was assigned to take over the towers of the Citadel—still in enemy's hands. In the predawn hours of 24 February, his troops launched a rapid raid, with one company dedicated to the towers seizure while the remainder surrounded the structure. At 0500 hours, the VC flag was lowered and at sunrise the South Vietnamese flag was unfurled. The Hắc Báo Company in the meantime liberated the imperial palace.[60]

The Tết offensive had dramatic consequences for Trưởng, Định and Huệ. General Trưởng, commander of the 1st ARVN division, solidified his reputation as ARVN's best combat general and received the U.S. Presidential Unit Citation. Huệ, commander of the Hắc Báo brigade and popularly known as the Savior of Huế, was promoted captain and awarded the coveted U.S. Silver Star for his role in the battle. Định received a U.S. Bronze Star for valor. Định and his 2/3 ARVN men became famous for having raised the South Vietnamese flag above the battered citadel. For his feat, Định earned the sobriquet of "the Young Lion of Hue." Although Huệ was held in high esteem by the U.S. Marines, Định's case is different. The 2/3 ARVN role in Tết was little known outside Vietnamese circles and Định had been criticized for his "cautious" approach, although some U.S. advisors ranked him as one of the best battalion commanders in the ARVN.

In early 1969, both Huệ and Định were respectively promoted to major and lieutenant colonel. In May, during the fight for Hamburger Hill (Đông Áp Bia), although the U.S. 3/187 did most of the fighting, it was Định's 2/3 ARVN which was the first to control the summit of Hamburger Hill.[61] As 3/187 was pinned down, the 2/3 assaulted, and in the cover of darkness began its reconnaissance. The triple canopy forest was now a charred lunar landscape. In the half light, Định's men went on the attack and quickly reached the top, catching the defenders by surprise. The 2/3 alerted friendly troops of its presence and moved to aid 3/187. They were then ordered to withdraw from the top of the hill—otherwise they would be shelled by U.S. forces. Incredulous, Định and his advisers did what they had been told. Shortly thereafter, 3/187 moved to the summit and took their place in history. An hour and a half later, Định's men came back but missed making history.[62] A MACV command meeting on 21 May 1969, however, admitted that "the first people to the crest were the ARVN."[63]

On 5 March, Huệ and his 2/2 landed in Tchepone, Laos, to destroy and cut off the flow of arms and supplies going down the trail. He was promoted lieutenant colonel on the spot and continued his search for supply dumps. NVA troops counterattacked and fought against the 2/2, 3/2 and 4/2 troops. Huệ continued to fight on Hill 660 while air support was called in. Running low on supplies, men drank their own urine to survive and 2/2 neared the end of its ability to resist. Huệ requested extraction but a mortar explosion knocked him unconscious. When he recovered, he requested to be left behind because carrying him away would hinder his men's escape. Captain Chuốc led 60 men to safety while Huệ was taken hostage by the enemy. The NVA, having no medicine to give him, sent him north on the Hồ Chí Minh trail. His comrades in arms carried him all the way. Because of massive blood loss, he thought he would die, but somehow he survived the trip and his wounds. Huệ finally received care for his wounds but lost many fingers. They moved him and his men to the Hỏa Lò prison, the infamous Hà Nội Hilton. At age 29, he faced the prospect of 13 long years in jail. Of his 2/2, only 26 soldiers made it back to Khe Sanh. The unit's American advisers went numb: The unit was there one day and the next day ceased to exist. The ARVN suffered 8,000 casualties and the NVA 13,000 battle deaths. The U.S. lost more than 100 helicopters and seven fixed-wing aircraft.[64] The bravery of so many ARVN men went unreported because without the presence of American soldiers no western reporters would cover the operation.

To offset the U.S. withdrawal, the ARVN expanded from 650,000 to 1.1 million in five years. The rapid expansion caused a rise in inexperienced new troops as well as a lack of qualified company and battalion-level leaders. Military aid decreased from $403 million in 1971 to $213 million in 1972, causing an increase in inflation. The newly-minted 3rd ARVN division lacked equipment and logistic structure. Underequipped and undermanned, it was unable to function adequately.

In the 1972 Eastern Offensive, Hà Nội sent three divisions through the DMZ to test the untested 3rd ARVN division. Định and his 1/56 gathered at Camp Carroll. The battalion was outnumbered and outgunned by the enemy. Two thousand rounds fell on the camp on the first day. Four fire-base supports fell in quick succession, leaving Camp Carroll defenseless. When General Giai, 3rd ARVN commander, moved his HQ from Ái Tử to Quảng Trị and when General Lãm, Corps I commander, told him to hold onto his position until the last man, Định and his men felt abandoned. After investing 11 years in toil and blood for his country, Định had a change of heart and decided the war was no longer worth fighting. He felt he needed to save the soldiers under his command. On 2 April, General Giai rushed to the battlefield to rally his men. B-52s struck the NVA positions around Camp Carroll, while Định's men repulsed two human wave assaults. The enemy told him to surrender. At 1500, he gathered his staff, and upon a unanimous decision (except for one vote), he agreed to surrender. Định and his men were trucked to Sơn Tây prison where he defected with equivalent rank in service of NVA.[65]

When offered the choice of defecting, Huệ declined, claiming he was "not worthy of such an honor." Huệ and 70 other ARVN officers later shaved their heads and staged hunger strikes, sparking a brutal response from the NVA. When the war ended a few years later, five ARVN generals (Nguyễn Khoa Nam, Lê Văn Hưng, Lê Nguyên Vỹ, Trần Văn Hai, and Phạm Văn Phú) and scores of colonels took their own lives instead of surrendering. Huệ was asked whether the generals had been brainwashed during their training. He replied that devotion to Vietnam and a strong connection to the nation's martial past had driven these officers to accept death over dishonor.[66]

The ARVN, which wasted crucial "learning" time while being marginalized, was unprepared and not ready to assume its role when Vietnamization began. It had never been previously coalesced into a cohesive military force. The ARVN, by American design, was dependent on the U.S. for almost everything, including firepower. When left alone, it just crumbled due to lack of leadership, cohesion, and maturity.

The lives of Định and Huệ, although in no way representative of the ARVN, exemplified its tragic history—of courage and betrayal, of sacrifice and letdown, of unimaginable suffering and self-abuse, of victories and defeats all suffered in silence. It is the story of untold heroes who fought valiantly for more than two decades only to be marginalized in their own country, to suffer defeat and to be sent to concentration camps. It is the story of a dysfunctional state and army which had emerged from the holds of colonialism only to have to fight against another scourge: communism.

The ARVN was one of the most maligned forces in the world. If it showed heroism and sacrifice, it also exhibited betrayal and disloyalty. It stood under the worst artillery barrage for three months in An Lộc and then in Xuân Lộc, but it collapsed in 55 days—the most dramatic collapse of any armed force in history. It stood and fought with resilience and stoicism for two decades, but disappeared in the tick of a clock. If five of its generals and scores of other officers had decided to take their own lives at the end of the war—no country had ever done that before—it was also known for not fighting aggressively. And yet, it fought with courage and dignity for as long as it could. No one could argue to the contrary. It lost 300,000 men—a nation of at most 20 million people. That number, if extrapolated to the size of the States, would be equivalent to 3.75 million.

What the ARVN lacked was leadership at the highest level, which could galvanize the whole country into fighting the invaders. The raw material for success was there: stalwart warriors and leaders within the ARVN and the U.S.

military, firepower supremacy, and talented advisers. If a more cooperative military and better political structure could have changed the country's fate,[67] a different tactical military strategy along with a more gradual withdrawal might have saved South Vietnam.

The 7B Road of Sorrow

Right after the agreement was signed, Thiệu thought about giving up the highlands in order to reinforce the coastal areas. A successful retrenchment strategy would have taken six months to carry out. On 13 March, he met with Prime Minister Khiêm and General Viên, the JGS chief, and made the decision to pull out of Ban Mê Thuột, the II Corps HQ. General Phú, the II Corps commander, had only one full division in the highlands, the 23rd, which was already overextended.

The same afternoon, he met with General Trưởng, the I Corps commander, and told him to send back the airborne division to Saigon. Trưởng, who had only five divisions to protect the I Corps, including Huế and Đà Nẵng, could ill afford to lose the airborne division. Although very upset with the order, Trưởng, as a good soldier, tried to comply.[68]

Thiệu flew to Cam Ranh Bay with generals Viên, Khiêm, and Quang on March 14 to confer with General Phú. He and Phú were comrades-in-arms during the French days. Phú was more comfortable with day-to-day tactical planning than with the ambiguities of grand strategy. A plan was laid down to him: (1) the regular forces (23rd division, the Rangers and the Armor brigade) were to be moved to the coast from Pleiku and Kontum with the goal of retaking Ban Mê Thuột later on; (2) the regional and popular forces would remain in place; (3) the redeployment was to be implemented secretly; and (4) Route 7B would be used for the redeployment.

Routes 19, 14, and 21 had been blocked off by the communists. Route 7B branched off from Route 14 south of Pleiku and went through forested hills before emerging on the coastal plain at Tuy Hòa. It was a narrow logging track with a destroyed major bridge. Part of the track had been mined by the Koreans before they left the area. Withdrawing through that route was like setting up a 160-mile-long ambush.

Phú claimed that he could defend Pleiku, although Thiệu overruled him. The cutoff of American aid (thus B-52) would not allow the defending forces to resist for a long time. Retreating on a hilly road was not a good option either. Phú asked the reason for a retreat before an attack. He insisted that the morale would plummet if the retreat were ordered. Thiệu stood fast and told him to carry out the order or be dismissed and jailed. Phú accepted the order[69] although he did not have room to maneuver.[70]

When Phú conveyed the message to his staff, they were incredulous. He brushed off all discussions and told them the decision had been made by the president. He told General Phạm Duy Tất, the ranger commander, to take care of the redeployment, but he confused the issue when he ordered General Cam to "supervise" the withdrawal. Col. Lý asked Phú about the regional and popular forces, dependents, and all the people in the city. Phú told him he did not have to take care of them. Alerting them would cause a general panic. The next morning, Phú flew to Nha Trang with his staff. General Cam flew to Tuy Hòa and told Lý to take care of everything. Therefore, General Tất took care of his rangers and Lý had to inform the unit commanders. Phú did not tell Lý to inform the Americans in Pleiku, but he did it anyway. It was now every man for himself. When the Americans in Saigon called the JGS headquarters to find out what was going on, no one answered the phone.

When Lý informed the unit commanders about the plan, panic broke out. Discipline broke down also among regular forces when soldiers realized their families were not included in the withdrawal. At that time, the runway was shelled, putting a stop to flight operations. Lý sent engineer units to prepare the road. As the convoy entered Route 7B by March 17, soldiers and their families were shelled by the enemy. "The blood flowed on the road in tiny streams. The sound of roaring artillery and small arms, the scream of seriously wounded people at death's door, and children created a voice out of hell."[71]

Troops and civilians became intermingled, as everyone bullied their way to the front of the column. The 2,000 cars, jeeps, and trucks became mired in a river of mud as the road broke down under the heavy weight of the armored cars and tanks. West of Chèo Reo city, the 23rd ARVN Ranger group was attacked by enemy troops and suffered heavy casualties. They called for air support. A-37 planes launched a bombing run but hit their own troops, causing more damage to the ranger group. The latter was again attacked by communist troops, splitting the column in half: A few troops escaped to Chèo Reo, while 30,000 people were stranded on 7B.

On the 19th, the 200,000 troops and civilians were backed up behind the Tu Na pass and a river crossing, about 20 miles west of Tuy Hòa. Phú ordered Tất to abandon all heavy weapon material and move on. The following day, the enemy attacked again, causing heavy casualties to the column. Only 20,000 out of the 60,000 troops got down to Tuy Hòa. They were no longer fit for combat. And only 100,000 of the 400,000 civilians who had left Kontum got through.

Nguyễn Phú Đức, the ambassador in Brussels, appealed to NATO for help but was turned down. Kissinger asked: "Why don't these people die fast? The worst thing that could happen to them would be for them to linger on."[72]

As he had to send the first airborne troops back to Saigon, Trưởng had to reposition his troops for the second time in two weeks. The center of gravity shifted to Đà Nẵng as he did not have enough troops to protect Huế and Đà Nẵng equally. As the troops moved, the population did the same thing. The

150,000 Quảng Trị inhabitants moved to Huế following the militia and army stragglers. As they arrived in Huế, the citizens of this city were also getting ready to move south to Đà Nẵng. The result was a monstrous wave of honking cars, motorcycle riders and overloaded buses rolling on Route 1 toward Đà Nẵng.

The flood of fleeing civilians clogged the highways. Soldiers seeing civilians running away decided to take their families and move with the flow of people. Panic became infectious. Troops fell victim to the "family syndrome," moving away from the trenches to look for their next of kin. Only the Marines and the airborne who had their families in Saigon would remain at their posts.

Only a few days earlier, Thiệu had assured Trưởng that Huế was less important than Đà Nẵng, causing Trưởng to pull back all the troops to protect Đà Nẵng. Then Thiệu reversed his decision and wanted Huế to be defended at all cost. Trưởng lost his cool: he could not wage the war with fits and starts, he thundered. His forward lines were being dismantled and the artillery had been shipped out for the last few days. The marines were already dispirited because of the shifts in strategy.

On the 20th, the enemy severed Highway 1 south of Huế, cutting the escape route of the 1st ARVN. The shelling of the city caused panic to erupt among the civilians. With Highway 1 cut off, they moved east toward the beaches, making it difficult for the troops to get away by sea. Only the 147th Marine brigade was at its post. Trưởng asked for the abandonment of Huế to prevent further bloodshed.[73]

As the North Vietnamese raced south via Highway 1 after they took Huế, Đà Nẵng, and Nha Trang, they hit a roadblock at Xuân Lộc. On April 9, the NVA troops rained 2,000 shells on the town to soften the target. The town was protected by a 2,500-man regiment of the 18th division. Once known as the 10th division (the worst in the ARVN), it was redesignated the 18th. Something strange happened when General Lê Minh Đảo took over the division in 1972. Đảo was a fighter: He had earned his star and all his medals by ability, not by politics. The 18th suddenly woke up and did more fighting than any other division in the army.

Đảo ordered another regiment into battle to secure the flanks of the town. While the town was shelled, the communists endured an airstrike. Firepower was brutal as the two sides stood and fought each other. The communists moved into town, but by evening they had to pull back to fight another day. The fight went on day after day. The communists threw in another division, but the 18th held steady. They then moved along Highway 1 and cut it off, preventing entry and exit into and out of town. The nearby village of Trảng Bờm was also engulfed in the attack, causing villagers to run away to Vũng Tàu through Highway 15. ARVN troops fought hard, although they were unable to reopen Highway 1. As ARVN troops held Xuân Lộc, there was renewed optimism that Saigon would hold on.

Thiệu sent in one brigade of paratroopers considered to be the best of ARVN forces. They were trucked to Long Bình and airlifted to the rubber plantation about five miles east of Xuân Lộc. The lead company walked in without encountering resistance. Then suddenly, the communists went on the attack, cutting the force in two. This was a well-executed ambush. The paratroopers were outgunned three-to-one and did not have a chance. Some headed to Xuân Lộc, others to other directions. The airborne brigade was wiped out as a fighting force. The ambush meant another North Vietnamese division had joined the fight and the town was attacked from the north, northwest and east.

Đào's troops, however, hung on under the combination of attacks and the barrage of artillery shells. The town crumbled around them. Corpses littered the streets. The church was destroyed but the steeple stood. The attack on April 12 was softer and Đào smelled a possible victory. Facing four NVA divisions, he ordered his third and last regiment into the battle, down Highway 1 toward the west of Xuân Lộc.[74] The NVA division broke off Xuân Lộc and went to meet the relief force.

NVA General Dũng decided to leapfrog Xuân Lộc and to send some of his divisions south to Saigon. On 21 April, the communists went in for the kill. The paratroop brigade was bogged down in the rubber plantation while his reserve regiment could not punch through the siege on the west side. There were enough men to hold on to Xuân Lộc. Yet, while the much-honored airborne, marine and 1st division soldiers had to cut and run, the 18th was fighting on. Đào finally ordered the pullout. Four of the six battalions pulled out successfully while two battalions under Col. Lê Xuân Hiếu covered the retreat. For the 600 men remaining in Xuân Lộc, there were only two choices: surrender or fight on. What could the 600 men do against an army of 10,000 NVA soldiers?[75]

On April 11 while the war raged on, Saigon had the chance to talk to Hà Nội directly for the first time in 21 years. During a visit to Hà Nội by the Joint Military Team to discuss military matters between the GVN and DRV, South Vietnamese interpreter Đào Trọng Ngô encountered Mr. Quang, an escort officer of the DRV foreign ministry. Quang ridiculed the ARVN: "We scared the hell out of your soldiers so that all they did was run, run, and run."

Ngô responded immediately: "That they ran fast proves how they feared your 'liberation.' ... So, fear gave them wings, not the fear of being killed in combat, but the fear of not being quick enough and having to live under your regime."

Ngô's impudence drew an immediate response from the principal escort officer, Major Huyền. "Mr. Ngô, I don't think you know what the words 'communism' or 'socialism' mean."

Ngô replied: "I admit that many of us who are anti-communists don't understand what communism is, but I can see clearly that you who are against us don't understand one bit what freedom is either. Posterity may judge that we were both foolish."

"History will be on our side," Major Huyên replied. "Hasn't history shown you that more and more people representing the progressive majority of mankind are embracing socialism as the best political system? You cannot go against the force of history."

"You claim that the force of history is on your side," Ngô replied, "and I claim it is on our side.... Let's wait for a few hundred more years to see who is right, and let no one assert now that he is completely right if he really wants national reconciliation and concord."[76]

Thiệu resigned on April 21. Trần Văn Hương was sworn in the same night. Thiệu left with Khiêm on the 25th, aboard an American plane for Taiwan. Hương resigned on the 27th and Congress voted Minh to become the president.

Saigon's fall, although expected, came rather rapidly because of general letdown and strategic mistakes. After Kissinger embraced the Chinese, the Vietnamese realized they were being let go. Kissinger might have thought about fooling world opinion, but he did not fool the southerners who had become expendable. Colonel Lê Khắc Lý asked himself "why the Americans did this. This is my question—Why did you do that to a friend?"[77] This was echoed by Dr. Bruce Branson, the chief of surgery at the Saigon Adventist Hospital: "If we were going to have to fight a war ... then we should have gotten in there and done the job right.... By fighting a half baked sort of war, with limits, we made it impossible to win."[78]

General Lý Tồng Bá, who in 1975 was the commander of the 25th ARVN Division at Cu Chi, told his men to fight until the end. They fought hard against the 9th NVA Division. Soon they faced a total of three divisions with armor. He talked about his soldiers having a "mental sickness." The soldiers knew they had been lied to: The U.S. and their own government were not helping them. What were they fighting for? The 25th Division soon disintegrated and general Bá was captured. He was sent to a northern reeducation camp and was released only in December 1987.[79]

The Last Days

On March 22, while Bùi Diễm arrived in Washington trying to negotiate the release of $700 million in emergency funds that would bring additional ammunitions to the ARVN, Huế, the imperial city, was cut off. Hundreds of thousands of haggard refugees pushed southwards down the coastal highway to Đà Nẵng. In Washington, Congress was in recess for one week, Kissinger was in the Middle East and Ford was vacationing in Vail, Colorado.

On March 30, Đà Nẵng, 100 miles south of Huế and the second largest city in South Vietnam, was overwhelmed by 35,000 North Vietnamese troops. Pictures of women and children being trampled by mobs of escaping civilians and soldiers were shown on TV. One million refugees clogged Highway l lead-ing out of town.

Army Chief of Staff Frederick Weyand was sent to Saigon to reassess the situation. On his return on April 9, although pessimistic, he still thought that a reenergized South Vietnamese army could still fight back and hold if the emergency aid bill was passed. But it was a Congress that was sick to death of war and tired to supporting a weak ally that would make the ultimate deci-sion. The odds, therefore, were slim.

In the end, it had nothing to do with American credibility or the unfitness of Saigon's leaders. It was about the kind of lives 20 million South Vietnamese would have to endure once Congress made its decision. For the Vietnamese, the important issue was their lives and the lives of their children and grand-children. Two days later, the glimmer of hope brought by Weyand's mission died. The emergency aid bill was defeated. The defeat closed the chapter of American involvement on Vietnam. Unknown to the Vietnamese troops who were still fighting in Xuân Lộc, a death sentence had been pronounced on Capitol Hill on April 11.[80]

By early April there was still optimism in the air. People were lulled into that idea of a last minute deal. South Vietnam would be divided but Saigon and the South would remain. The Americans would come back and bomb the enemy. The hope of a deal was carefully supported by Hà Nội. On the Saigon side, people thought that if Minh, the neutralist candidate, could be president, he could negotiate with the enemy. No one really understood that Hà Nội forces were at the doors of Saigon and did not have to negotiate with anyone.

General Minh declined to be sworn in on 27 April because the stars were not right. To celebrate his inauguration the following day, the North Vietnamese shelled and bombed Tân Sơn Nhứt airport, causing the whole city to shake. Soldiers reacted by firing their arms into the air in the hope of shooting down airplanes.

Air evacuation called for: First priority, use commercial airlift as long as possible; and second, use military fixed wing aircraft (C-130) as long as pos-sible. Only the last option, Operation Frequent Wind, involved the use of hel-icopters. There was a lull on 25 and 26 April, Friday and Saturday, during which C-130s flights continued. The airport was bombed around 1800 on 27 April, causing flights to be halted.[81] At 0400 on 29 April, the NVA shelled the airport, disabling it and preventing any fixed wing aircraft from lifting off. Saigon was in a state of panic.

Frequent Wind began at 1108. Helicopters flew in and out over the city, dropping over the rooftops of various buildings, especially a house on 22 Gia Long Street, to pick up evacuees. The famous picture of the evacuees climbing up the stairs to the roof where a helicopter was waiting has become well-known to everyone. People remaining at the Defense Attaché Office (DAO) were also picked up before the operation shifted to the embassy.

Riots and lootings occurred. The American PX was looted, with people carrying away anything they could take. People were running all over the city looking for ways to get out of town. The central power seemed to have evaporated and government offices had only part of their staff. No day went by that someone didn't call in sick or didn't show up for one reason or another. The Saigonese were left to fend for themselves. And the main business was to find a way out of the city. Buses carrying Americans, third country nationals (TCN) and Vietnamese employees were seen heading either to the airport or the U.S. Embassy. The sight of the Americans leaving town caused other people to get nervous. They therefore mobbed the embassy and American offices looking for a way out.

Many had tried to get out but had not been successful because either they had no connection or their connection was gone. They calmly sat at home accepting their fate as it came to them. Although deeply anxious, they regained serenity in the most critical moment. The French had left them, then the Americans. They were left alone with their fiercest enemy and simply hoped that northerners would not harm them.

At the American radio station in Saigon, most non-essential personnel had left from Tân Sơn Nhứt airport on the 24th or 25th. The few remaining Americans were assisted by Vietnamese employees. The Vietnamese, afraid to be left behind, had brought their families to live right in the radio station. The families were not small. There was usually a mother, a grandmother, aunts and uncles and their friends. About 200 people crowded the small station that started to stink. At 11:30 on 29 April, the order to evacuate was given by a DAO colonel. The assistant notified his friends and popped into the big Gates Automatic Programmer the cartridge containing "105 Degrees and Rising" and "I'm Dreaming of a White Christmas." Only two or three Vietnamese engineers were told to go out by the side door and get into the van. Not to alarm the 200 remaining people, they assured them that they would be picked up later. The Americans drove out of the station and slowly made their way to the embassy.[82]

Even Americans had a hard time finding a way to get out of the besieged city. The ABC crewmen went from one predetermined area to another before being picked up by one of the embassy buses. Some Saigonese, after spotting the Americans, began gathering around them. They even fought to get on the buses with the Americans. The bus driver got lost and drove around and around. At the airport, Vietnamese soldiers prevented him from driving in. The driver turned around and drove to the wharf, where he dropped his passengers. Thousands of people crowded the area fighting to get on the few boats still anchored there. The Americans returned to the bus and decided to look for another departing area. As they drove away, one man handed them his baby: "Please take my baby. Take my baby," he said. He somehow stumbled and fell. The baby fell on the ground and was crushed by the rear tires of the bus. The bus driver kept going while people inside the bus shouted that the bus had run over a baby.

After a seven-hour trip around town, the driver finally delivered them to the embassy, which was also surrounded by thousands of Vietnamese trying to get in. The crewmen called in and were told the guards could not open the front gates because they would be immediately mobbed by the crowd. They were instead advised to go to the back of the embassy and climb over the wall. People trying to climb over the walls were pushed back by the Marines standing guard on top of the walls. The ABC crewmen moved through the crowd, climbed over the wall and were let in.[83]

Another drama was about to happen at the navy compound in Saigon. On 25 April, Captain Kiêm Đỗ, deputy chief of staff operations, sat down at the Saigon navy compound with Rich Armitage, former U.S. naval intelligence officer, to discuss the logistics of taking the Navy out of the country. Kiêm in turn had to inform the one-month-old chief of naval operations (CNO), Admiral Chung Tấn Cang, about the operation code, named E plan. Cang luckily saw that it was the navy's only honorable choice.

For the next three days, he made preparations while trying not to attract attention. Pulling the Sea Force into the Saigon River too early could set off a mass panic. Thirty of the Navy's 45 big ships had a chance to get out and carry tens of thousands people. On the 27th, Fleet Commander Sơn had let one of his skippers move their families onboard two well-fueled and well-stocked ships. Crew members had threatened to mutiny if their families were not allowed onboard. To disavow Sơn, Admiral Cang had to relieve him of his duty. Following discussion with Armitage, the E plan would be activated at 1800 hours on 29 April with the rendezvous located at Côn Sơn Island, 130 miles south of Vũng Tàu.[84]

On the eve of the 28th, while Minh was inaugurated, rockets rained down on Saigon throughout the night. Flares and explosions lit the horizon. Armitage came back to pick Kiêm up on his helicopter, but the latter decided to stay with his shipmen.

The weather was hot, sticky, and hazy on E-day. Stranded soldiers banged on the gates asking for the means to get out. Kiêm then met with ship captains to advise them about the plan. Around noon, he talked to staff members and told them to get their families onboard within the next two hours. Everyone wailed before rushing out. A short while later, power went out. Thousands of civilians surged against the compound fence. By dusk, a mutiny had occurred at one of the piers. Three ships were lined up abreast with the outer one, preventing the two fully-loaded inner ships from getting out. Kiêm had to bribe the sailors of the outer ship—using donations from the passengers—before they cut the rope to free the ships.[85]

By midnight, while the last ships were still loading, a Jeep came barreling down the pier. Out came Captain Bình, the "new" deputy chief of staff operations, who announced himself on the radio and ordered all ships to return to Saigon. Kiêm yelled at Bình, calling him an impostor and told the ships to go out. Captain Tân, the "new" CNO ordered all units to report back to their stations. Kiêm told him that if he did not want to leave, he should let the rest go. He then ordered the lines cast off and the engine on. His ship was the third to last to leave. Luckily, no one shot at them. On their way they picked up occupants of small boats who were chasing after them.[86]

At Côn Sơn, the convoy of 29 Vietnamese Navy big ships, a high endurance cutter, a Vũng Tàu ship, and three units from Phú Quốc, regrouped before heading to Manilla. Other Vietnamese ships had turned back after dropping off their passengers. It would take a full week before the convoy and its 30,000 passengers reached the Filipino territorial waters—only to find out that warships were not welcome in Manilla. Besides, the new revolutionary government in Saigon had wired President Marcos claiming title to the ships. However, the ships had reverted to the U.S. because they were no longer used by the VNN. The guns had to be dismantled, the ammo unloaded, the names painted over, and the flag changed. The scenario made them losers, causing the shame to be unbearable. Kiêm asked for proper changing-of-colors to soften the blow of seeing their flag yanked down like a flag. They then tossed their caps and insignia into the sea, becoming civilians who could help bring another country's warships into the bay without shame.[87]

Off the coast, U.S. Navy Task Force 76, with the carriers *Hancock, Okinawa,* and *Midway,* waited with 81 helicopters. Aircraft from Task Force 77 were to fly air cover. Operation Frequent Wind began at 1108 on 29 April with roof top evacuations ending at 1830 the same day. Evacuation at the U.S. Embassy ended at 0430 on 30 April. During these 18 hours, a total of 1,373 Americans, 5,595 Vietnamese, and 85 TCN were evacuated. The last flight carrying the flag and last Marines left at 0753.[88]

On 29 April, sailors aboard the USS *Midway* noticed on the horizon a swarm of black dots heading toward the ship. The dots grew bigger at every minute, revealing an armada of Hueys, helicopters used by the South Vietnamese Air Force. They came unannounced because there was no radio communication from them to the ship.

People on the deck tried to wave them off, but they landed anyway and anywhere they could as if to say, "To hell with what you say, we're coming in right now." There was mass confusion because everything happened almost at the same time: directing the landing, trying to prevent mishaps between helicopters, guiding passengers to safety, providing security, and freeing the deck by getting rid of incoming helicopters. Each aircraft disgorged many times more than its maximum load of 14 people—one of them carried 53 passengers, mostly women and children. The Marines locked the rotors of the helicopters and disarmed the passengers before leading them to the procession area. It was "constant activity, and excitement, hurrying, the roar of the engines, the feel of the prop wash, and the sounds of the rotors of the helicopters coming in and going out." It was also about saving these people who had just lost their homeland. The torment in their faces showed it all; there was a lot of crying among the refugees.[89]

All of a sudden, a lone aircraft showed up. No one knew what it wanted because there was no radio contact. This was a Cessna O-1 "Bird Dog"—a two-seater. Each time it passed over the ship, it dropped something, although it missed the deck three times. On the fourth trial, it dropped a wrench with a message wrapped around it. Onboard was Major Bương with a wife and five kids, and he wanted to land on the deck. In 30 minutes, helicopters and aircraft were moved to the bow so that he had the full deck to land on. Everyone expected him to crash, but he just came floating in like a bird, made two bounces then rolled to a stop. Everyone cheered him and surrounded the small plane. As he helped his family get out, someone asked, "Where in the hell did you learn to fly anyway?" He turned around and said, "Texas." And people cheered some more.[90]

On the USS *Blue Ridge*, helicopters came in and ditched at sea because of the lack of a place to land on the deck. They swarmed around the ship like bees because they were so many of them. The pilot would lift the plane's nose up and then jump out of the door. The maneuver was tricky because the plane could land on them. Besides the refugees, the embassy people were also on the ship.[91]

On the USS *Maddox* and other ships, once the helicopter landed on the deck, it was secured, rolled on the side and tipped overboard. Vietnamese pilots looked with horror at the waste but mostly with disgust and sorrow—they knew they would not be allowed to fight again. The war was over for them.

A civilian ship loaded with 3,000 people left the wharf on April 30. There was no food or water on board. As it sailed down the river, everyone was crying. As people saw Vung Tau for the last time, pain and anguish struck many of them. One soldier took his own gun, put it under his chin and shot himself to death. A few others jumped overboard and drowned in the sea. The rest sailed into the South China Sea for three days without food and water. A Danish boat found them and took the women and children off the Vietnamese boat and sailed to Hong Kong. The Danes gave the men food and water and showed them the way to Hong Kong.[92]

One family moved from Nha Trang to Saigon in early April 1975 then went to Phú Quốc Island. On the afternoon of 29 April, they were evacuated by the *Pioneer Contender*, which brought them to the island.[93] On 30 April, many islanders took to the sea and were also picked up by the *Contender*. Military helicopters from southern airfields, loaded with airmen and their families, in the meantime circled over the tiny airport trying to negotiate their descent. They looked like a swarm of hungry locusts descending on a field. The airport was crowded with abandoned airplanes, some of them parked right on the beach.[94] The *Contender* departed on the night of 30 April and reached the Seventh Fleet vessels offshore from Vũng Tàu the next morning.

The *American Challenger*, a civilian steamer, had picked up 7,500 refugees, though its capacity was only 1,080. A Catholic priest came onboard with a Honda, although they would not let him bring it onboard. The same thing happened to a dentist who came with a dentist's chair. On the night of 30 April, the ship picked up some more people offshore from Vũng Tàu. Once everyone was off the Vietnamese boat, they set it on fire and pushed it away. The South China Sea was ablaze with these eerie, burning and drifting fires of boats.[95]

In the embassy compound, evacuees were confined to the recreation area to wait for their turn to get on the choppers. Everyone decided to go to the mess to look for food. The manager just opened the refrigerators to let them help themselves. They grilled steaks and ate everything. Since the liquor locker was open, they uncorked the bottles and consumed all the contents. A few hours later, they became thirsty but the water was shut off from the outside. One American found a full bottle of Vichy water. As he was about to drink it, a 14-year-old girl asked him for a drink. She took a sip from the bottle and handed it over to her brother who handed over to another one. It was then the turn of their grandmother and friends, and by the time the bottle came back, it was empty.[96]

In the CIA operating room, abandoned Vietnamese agents kept sending pleading messages: "Please come get us, we're gonna die, we're gonna die." Although some agents were picked up, about 70 of them were holed up in a CIA hotel because the agent assigned to evacuate them had evacuated himself and left them at the hotel. After the takeover, the communists machine gunned most of the Vietnamese in that hotel.[97]

Shortly after midnight, Polgar, the station chief, burned all the CIA's files, cables, and codebooks. He then composed his farewell message: "THIS WILL BE FINAL MESSAGE FROM SAIGON STATION.... IT HAS BEEN A LONG FIGHT AND WE HAVE LOST.... THOSE WHO FAIL TO LEARN FROM HISTORY ARE FORCED TO REPEAT IT. LET US HOPE WE WILL NOT HAVE ANOTHER VIETNAM EXPERIENCE AND THAT WE HAVE LEARNED OUR LESSON. SAIGON SIGNING OFF."

He then blew up the machine that sent the message.[98]

Outside the walls, the situation was chaotic as people fought to get inside the compound. One Chinese man handed a Marine a paper bag filled with uncut gems in exchange for being let out of the country. The Marine returned the bag to him.

The landing zone for the big helicopters was in the parking lot of the embassy. There was a 70-foot vertical drop to get to the lot during which the bird was vulnerable. Normally it would move forward to gain some speed before ascending. Limited by trees and buildings, the bird had to ascend immediately and on a couple of occasions it failed to take off. The plane landed and dropped a few passengers and would try to lift off again. It hovered about six or seven feet before dropping again. A few more passengers had to be removed before the plane could finally take off. It would only need one helicopter crash to severely curtail the operation, for the roof helipad could only accommodate the regular 14-passenger helicopter.

The Marine pilots could not fly forever. And no decision was made as when to stop flying. Normally no helicopter flight was scheduled after 5 P.M. Flights, however, continued sporadically and no one could understand why. There was no communication contact between DAO and the embassy. The 2,500 people still remaining in the embassy compound were edgy as the minutes passed by—they were worried about being left behind. DAO was finally contacted and notified that DAO refugees had priority until midnight, after which all the flights would be switched to the embassy.

From midnight until 3:30 A.M., the choppers kept coming every ten minutes. If it was a big bird CH-53, 90 refugees were showed in. In case of a small one, the CH-46, then half went. No suitcases were allowed on the plane in order to accommodate as many people as possible. All the Vietnamese easily complied. There was a contingent of 50 men and women from the Korean Embassy. The ambassador, his secretary, the naval attaché, and the army attaché finally got into the chopper. Then came people carrying suitcases. The first one had his suitcase thrown into the bushes. The second suffered from the same fate. A lady pulling a heavy suitcase behind her came next. Captain Herrington, who was checking the passengers in, took the suitcase and threw it away. The lady crawled in the bushes and retrieved it. She walked back to the plane. The officer yanked it away from her again and threw it into the bushes. She went after her suitcase the third time and refused to let it go. Exasperated, he used the butt of an M16 gun to hit on her forearm until she let go. He then grabbed her and threw her into the chopper which then took off. That was the last chopper that left with civilians. Later it was learned that she was the ambassador's private secretary. Her suitcase contained all the valuables collected from the Korean community. It was explained to a Korean officer that if the captain had not done that, she would have been left behind and probably imprisoned in Hà Nội.

Late in the night, an order came from the president to pick up Ambassador Martin. The man relented. He was tired and did not have anything to say. He had worked 72 hours straight and was no longer young. He was 70 at that time. He took a few things from his office, carried the American flag and got aboard the plane. That moment officially marked the end of American involvement in Vietnam. It was about 4:47 A.M. on the 30th.

The Marines guarding the walls retreated back into the compound. In the courtyard, the 420 Vietnamese and TCN, realizing they were about to be abandoned, ran after them. The Marines locked the embassy door, sent the elevators to the sixth floor, and froze them there by cutting the power. They walked upstairs and closed the second and fourth floor grill gates behind them. They then moved to the rooftop where they settled down. All they had to do was to walk to the stairways to the rooftop landing zone.

Down below, 420 people were still waiting for a miracle that unfortunately would never come. Among them were a group of firefighters, a few Koreans, and a German priest. The firemen could have gone earlier, although they volunteered to stay behind. They told Herrington they would stay back to help out in case a fire broke out. They only asked their families to be sent out first, which was done. Among the Koreans was General Rhee Dai Young. They waited for a few more hours hoping a plane would come in, but then slowly dispersed home dispirited.

From the rooftop, the Marines took a last look at the city. Saigon was burning. There had been a lot of looting and trashing. Smoke billowed up in the air. A cavalcade of cars—it was Big Minh—passed by in front of the embassy before heading to the palace. In the distance, they could see the flashes of the NVA guns. They had two more hours to think about the whole situation. No regrets or bitterness were expressed at that time. They were sad and melancholic. They looked at all the waste and were moved by it. On the USS *Okinawa*, someone realized that a contingent of Marines were still left behind. They sent in another chopper which picked them up at 8 A.M. on the 30th.[99]

On the *Okinawa*, a reporter interviewed Colonel Summers and Herrington. Summers asked him, "Did you know what you just saw?" The reporter said, "The fall of Saigon." And Harry Summers said, "You saw betrayal of the worst order."[100]

Fox Butterfield, a *New York Times* reporter and an antiwar activist, realized during a trip to Hà Nội with Kissinger that he was dealing with a very authoritarian regime consumed with waging a war against the South. The North Vietnamese leaders were not "interested in economic development and the well being of their people; they were interested only in this goal of obtaining complete power." They were determined to pay whatever price was required to do that.

When Butterfield did not see any wounded soldier or amputee in Hà Nội, a Hungarian diplomat told him, "The Hồ Chí Minh trail is a one way street. People who were sent down the pike fight till they die or are just left down there. Nobody ever comes back." To be drafted by Hà Nội was a death sentence. There was a lot of draft resistance in the North, although it was never mentioned in the press. The average North Vietnamese was never particularly enthusiastic about the war.

Butterfield realized that a feeling of sadness pervaded Hà Nội, engulfing its people. The huge sacrifice they had made to the war had caused them to become lethargic. They had little to eat and were terribly poor. The NVA prisoners he interviewed later in the South were very unhappy kids. There was a lot of running away, a lot of desertion.

When he talked to Lê Đức Thọ and Phạm Văn Đồng about the American POWs, they asked, "What are you talking about? Two or three hundred men? Who gives a shit? We've lost 200,000 men going down south and never seen them again and who cares?" That very callous attitude on their part suggested a complete disregard for people's lives.[101]

Vietnamization had failed to provide the "RVNAF with enough time for an overall improvement." Had it started in 1965 instead of 1969, it might have worked. Built as a very expensive force, it was devoted primarily to static defense and was dependent on air support and fire power. It was not prepared to fight an insurgency war. It was shoved aside and told to watch the professionals work. The RVNAF therefore lost the "notion to be independent." Its rapid expansion lowered the quality and diluted the competence of the units and overtaxed the few good officers.[102]

"Vietnamization really meant Americanization.... It was not possible to return to a Vietnamese-style of war. It was going to be fought the American way." It meant surviving with greatly reduced American participation. The RVNAF failed to adjust and compensate for the departure of American troops and firepower.[103]

When the "friends" decided to abandon the struggle, the end result was the fall of Saigon and the demise of South Vietnam as a nation. Still, the South Vietnamese deserved a large part of the blame because they lacked the will to save themselves. T.E. Lawrence once said about assisting armies of other countries: "Better they do it imperfectly than you do it perfectly, for it is their country, their war, and your time is limited."[104]

The Saigon leaders realized that American aid came with strings attached: The Saigonese were not allowed to pursue their own ideas. When Diệm wanted a small army to fight insurgency, the U.S. told him to either have a conventional army or nothing. When he wanted to do things differently, they toppled him. When he wanted to suppress the Buddhist movement, the U.S. Embassy shielded Trí Quang. When Thiệu wanted to go his own way, Kissinger reminded him of the 1963 coup.

In the end, Saigon did not have the ally she needed in the most critical hours and "Saigon fell to a more brutal tyranny [North Vietnam] that was more effective, in part, because it was more brutal."[105]

10

Red Saigon
(1975–1988)

If the feud between royalists and Tây Sơn led to the 1782 Saigon massacre and the feud between Lê Văn Duyệt and Minh Mạng to the 1832 destruction of Saigon, then the fight between nationalists and communists resulted in the 1975 downfall of Saigon. Vietnamese never seem to forget to exact revenge on their fallen enemies.

April 30, 1975, marked the dawn of a new era. If anything looked unusual, it was the dark skies and a light drizzle of that morning, which seemed to portend darker days and years ahead. While streets were crowded with people, cars and motorbikes the day before, they were deserted on the 30th. Without warning, all merchants kept their stores locked as if they sensed something ominous or even sinister was about to happen.

April 30, 1975

A column of dirty T34 tanks rolling down Thống Nhứt Boulevard followed by Molotova trucks filled with bộ đội in their ill-fitting green olive uniforms and their nón cối (pith helmet), headed toward the presidential palace.[1] The small red flags dotted with a yellow star flying on their antennas denoted their origin. This was the first time in 21 years that a communist flag had been displayed with impunity on the streets of Saigon.

The appearance of soldiers in green olive uniforms and pith helmets took the rare few onlookers back two or three decades earlier. Leaves suddenly appeared to hang still on the tree branches. Time, people and even nature seemed to freeze in place at that moment except for the rumbling, slow-moving column of tanks. A morbid silence fell over the city, the dreaded silence before the big storm.

The Saigonese did not know how to react to these invaders against whom they had fought for decades. They silently and without expression looked at them: There was no hate, nor scorn on their faces, just the tired and grim expression of those who had fought a long and difficult war and lost. They were too shattered physically and psychologically to make any comment, let alone resist. They could only guess what was about to come and were prepared for the worst. Anxiously waiting for the verdict (for there was no victory without reprisal), they keenly remembered the Huế massacre[2] and other cruelties like the rocket firings into the city just a few days earlier. They were resigned to accept the worst outcome, although the worst they could think of was nowhere near the worst they would have to endure. They did not know it yet. They were too mellow, too free, and too respectful of the rule of law to figure it out. That was another reason why they lost the war. War is a matter of will and ruthlessness, not of intelligence. Ruthless people often manage to win wars.

The bộ đội, too, did not know what to expect. They looked bewildered and lost as they drove along the main boulevard through the heart of the city with its tall buildings, wide streets, neat villas, large cathedral, and the huge American Embassy compound. They were deeply indoctrinated and were told to "liberate" the brothers of the South who were dirt poor and lived in wooden shacks; the reality turned out to be different. At 11:10 A.M. on April 30, 1975, a T34 tank crashed through the gates of the presidential palace.

Tanks and bộ đội swarmed into the palace grounds, driving recklessly like conquerors over the well-manicured lawns and leaving behind gaping tracks of dislodged soil and grass. One bộ đội climbed the entrance steps trying to find his way to the top floor. Moments later, taking down the yellow southern flag, he hoisted the red communist flag up to the cheers of those below. The occupation of the city had formally begun. On the ground, the different units spread around to take control of the quarters.

Big Minh and his cabinet members had been waiting for them since early morning. The one-day-old president, who had announced the surrender, looked tired in his tie-less short-sleeved shirt. He had not shaved for a few days. When Colonel Bùi Tín, accompanied by Lt. Col. Bùi Văn Tùng, rushed into the room, President Minh is quoted as having said, "I have been waiting since this morning to turn over the government to you." The arrogant Bùi Tín snapped back, "You power has crumbled, therefore, you have nothing to turn over. You cannot surrender what you don't have."

The two sized each other up for a moment, not knowing what to say next. This was the first direct encounter in 21 years between the highest representatives of the two countries: South and North. Their paths from then on would diverge: one would savor victory and its entitlements, the other would fade into obscurity. History, however, is full of surprises. Who would have thought their paths would cross again 15 years later after both were exiled from the land they then represented? They ended up living as neighbors in the same district on the outskirts of Paris, both discarded by the Hà Nội government. Hà Nội had also erased Bùi Tín's name from the history's annals. He had by then fallen out of grace with the party and become a *persona non grata*. The April 28, 1991, issue of the *Quân Đội Nhân Dân* (People's Army), the Hà Nội's equivalent of *Pravda*, would then list Lt-Col. Tùng, not Bùi Tín, as the one who had accepted General Minh's surrender.[3]

A burst of gunfire that broke one of the windowpanes forced everyone in the room to duck. Bùi Tín broke the silence and said, "Our soldiers are only celebrating. You don't have anything to fear. Between all Vietnamese, there are no victors and no vanquished. Only the Americans have been defeated. The war for our country is over."[4]

To defuse the tension, he asked General Minh whether he was still playing tennis and probed him about his orchid collection—the general was known to have about 600 different species. He was then driven to the Saigon radio station to read the surrender statement written by Lt-Col. Tùng.

Bùi Tín left the room, roamed around the palace, and settled in the former President Thiệu's private office. He wrote, "April 30, 1975. I am writing this article while sitting at a desk on the second floor of the Presidential Palace in Saigon. The long war is over." After finishing his four-page report, he pulled out one of Thiệu's cigars from a drawer and lit it up. He put his feet up and began enjoying the delightful smell of the cigar. Later, he went to the U.S. Embassy a few blocks down the street and had his picture taken with a few comrades on its rooftop. He then headed to the airport. Finding the DAO telex destroyed, he ran over to nearby Camp Davis to send the message to Hà Nội. This was the first news coming out of Saigon that day since the telecommunication system had been cut off.[5]

Bùi Tín, the deputy editor of the *Nhân Dân*, was not supposed to be at the palace. On April 30, while in Củ Chi, he was advised to accept General Minh's surrender. He declined, arguing that he was only a correspondent, not an army commander, but in the end, he accepted the task.

At the CIO—the South Vietnamese equivalent of the CIA—four employees (three men and one woman) took out pistols, herded all the others out, and locked the building—thereby saving all the secret files that identified prisoners, defectors, and collaborators. The chief of the national police had failed to order their destruction.

At the AP office on Nguyễn Huệ Avenue, George Esper, after hearing the surrender message, handed a one-paragraph bulletin to the telex operator for transmission abroad. He then ran into the street to get the city's reaction. He met Lt. Col. Long, chief of the Saigon police department, who was in full regalia nervously pacing in front of the huge downtown statue commemorating the fallen soldiers. Visibly excited, Long continuously mumbled: "Fini. C'est fini." Being in charge of the counter-insurgency service, he expected no mercy from the VC. After giving a final salute to the monument, he drew out his gun, directed it to his temple and pulled the trigger. His body fell at Esper's feet and convulsed for a few seconds before lying still.[6] Bystanders rushed to give him resuscitation and then took his body to the Grall Hospital where he was pronounced dead on arrival.

The same tragic act repeated itself throughout the city as desperate high officials unable to escape or to save their families opted to kill themselves.[7] A middle manager corralled his wife and children into a room, gunned them down and killed himself. He could not bear to see them suffer under the new regime.

While the situation remained fairly calm in Saigon, pockets of fighting still continued. In Vũng Tàu, the children of the Trường Thiếu Sinh Quân (Junior Military Academy) continued to resist. On 29 April, the American adviser came by and took the commander, a colonel, with him. The second in command, a captain, gathered the boys and took them out of the town. Not knowing where to go next, he advised the kids to disperse. The older ones, about 50 of them, returned to the academy and vowed to fight the enemy. They barricaded themselves and fought against the VC until 2:30 P.M. The exasperated communists finally told them to surrender—otherwise they would fire a rocket and blast them out. They surrendered.[8]

In the Mekong Delta, the generals debated the future of the IV Corps.

General Nguyễn Khoa Nam (1927–1975), born in Da Nang, central Vietnam, graduated from the Thủ Đức Military Academy in 1953 as an Airborne officer. As a company commander of the 7th Airborne Battalion, he fought the Bình Xuyên in Saigon in 1955. He fought the VC around Saigon during the 1968 Tet offensive. He was one of the few generals who earned his ranks through hard work. During his career, he molded the 7th Division into one of the most efficient in the ARVN. His last assignment was that of a three-star general and commander of the IV military region (IVMR) which comprised the whole Mekong Delta. Well liked by his soldiers, he used to drop by to see them during their military operations. A vegetarian, he led a simple life and followed Buddhist rules closely. As a bachelor, he was not susceptible to bribery, which in Vietnam was usually channeled through officers' wives.

With the imminent fall of Xuân Lộc, he discussed plans with his deputy, General Hưng, about withdrawing their troops to a secret place in the delta in order to continue the fight. He even refused President Minh's pleas to order his soldiers to lay down their arms. Until the end, he requested every officer and soldier to remain at their post. When he became aware that the province chief of Kiên Giang had left his post on a boat, he ordered pilots to sink it with rocket and machine gun.[9]

Things were quiet in the MRIV and there was no immediate danger of being overrun by the enemy. When President Minh went on the radio on 30 April to announce his surrender to the communists, General Nam became obviously upset. He could not understand why Saigon had to surrender without putting up a fight. After conferring with General Hưng, he reluctantly went along with the president's decision. Both gathered their staff and saluted the

South Vietnamese flag one last time in the headquarters' court. They then bid farewell to the staff and to each other. He went to the Phan Thanh Giản Military hospital in downtown Cần Thơ, to comfort and bid farewell to the hospitalized soldiers there.[10]

When General Nam returned to the headquarters, he was told that General Hưng had taken his own life. At 11 P.M., he called Mrs. Hưng to offer his condolences. As a man of war, General Nam did not believe in surrendering to people he did not like and thought he could defeat. He locked himself in his office, put on his official white uniform along with his medals, sat at his desk and shot himself in the head. That incident occurred in the early hours of May 1, 1975. His body was taken to the morgue and buried at the Cần Thơ Military Cemetery among his peers. In 1994, his remains were exhumed and cremated. His ashes were stored at the Gia Lam Pagoda in Gia Định.

Two-star General Lê Văn Hưng (1933–1975) was born in the province of Gia Định, South Vietnam. He graduated from the Thủ Đức Reserve Officers School, class 5, in 1954. Respected for his bravery in combat, he was known as one of the five "tiger officers" of the army. He was made general commander of the 5th ARVN Division in 1972. At that time, North Vietnamese General Giáp had unleashed a three-pronged attack on Quảng Trị (I Corps), Kontum (II Corps) and An Lộc (III Corps). General Hưng and his 5th division held An Lộc for 95 days and defeated an overwhelming enemy force. Following the defeat of this bloody Eastertide campaign, General Giáp was relieved of his command and replaced by his deputy, General Văn Tiến Dũng. General Hưng was then promoted to the post of deputy to General Nam. In late April 1975, these two generals had been offered evacuation thrice, but they flatly declined the offer.

By 4 P.M. on 30 April, General Hưng was still proclaiming he would not surrender to the VC. He met with a delegation of the Cần Thơ city councilmen who urged him not resist lest the city be shelled by the VC with devastating results. He told them he would discuss the matter with General Nam.

He later met his wife and son and told her to be brave and to raise his son as a man. He gathered his soldiers and told them, "I will not abandon you in order to evacuate my family. I cannot surrender in this shameful situation. If I have yelled at you on occasions, when mistakes are made, please forgive me." He shook their hands and drove them out of his office, after which he locked himself in. A gunshot was later heard. His family and staff broke into the office and found the general, his arms outstretched, still convulsing, with blood all over his uniform. He had shot himself in the heart at 8:45 P.M. on 30 April, 1975.[11]

General Lê Nguyên Vỹ (1933–1975), born in Sơn Tây, North Vietnam, graduated from the Officers Candidate Course at the Regional Military School, MRII, at Phú Bài near Huế, class of 1951. He was a colonel at the battle of An Lộc in 1972. As the attack raged on and as the enemy got closer, he single-handedly took an M72 antitank gun to blast away a communist T54 tank. He became deputy commander of the 21st ARVN Division and in 1974 went to the U.S. for military training. On his return, he became commander of the 5th ARVN Division. When Saigon surrendered, he gathered his staff and bid them farewell. He locked himself in his office and shot himself with a Baretta 6.35. When the VC officer came to take over the military office, he calmly saluted the general and said, "This is how a general should behave."[12]

General Trần Văn Hai (1925–1975), then a colonel, had parachuted himself at the famous battle of Khe Sanh in 1968. He became commander of the 7th ARVN Division in 1974 and was known as a brave and clean officer who also cared for his soldiers. In April 1975, President Thiệu offered to take him out of the country, but he refused. He remained at his post and was notified of a heavy concentration of enemy troops across the border in Cambodia. He called the CIA person requesting air support to blow them away. "We have them in the open. Now is the time to get them.... I need help. Help me, CIA man." But the agent could not do anything and the general later watched hopelessly as the enemy crossed the border and overran his troops. General Hai committed suicide instead of surrendering to the enemy.

General Phạm Văn Phú, born in Hà Đông, North Vietnam, graduated from the Dalat Military Academy, class 8. He was the man who ordered the withdrawal from the II Corps under President Thiệu's insistence. Back in 1954, then–Captain Phú parachuted with his company in Điện Biên Phủ to reinforce the French troops. When Điện Biên Phủ fell, the Việt Minh held him prisoner, although they later released him. He vowed never to become prisoner of the communists again. He committed suicide on 30 April.

There were many more officers who committed suicide in the last days of the war. Colonel Lê Cầu, commander of the 47th Regiment, and Colonel Nguyễn Hữu Thong, commander of the 42nd Regiment, both from the 22nd Division, took their own lives instead of surrendering. Colonel Hồ Ngọc Cẩn, commander of the 15th Regiment 9th Infantry Division, refused to surrender to the enemy. He and his men fought until the end when he was captured before he could kill himself. He asked to salute his flag the last time before being shot to death by the enemy. Former Prime Minister Trần Chánh Thành, fearing falling into the hands of the communists he had deserted decades earlier, took poison.

These people had a very high sense of morality. They were ashamed of handing over the troops under their command to the enemy. They felt they were betraying "not their emperor, but a sovereign state that had ceased to exist long before, whose ideals they, as military officers, still respected."[13] Although South Vietnam had lost the war, the fact that five generals and scores of colonels and other officers took their own lives at the end of the war showed that there was something bigger and larger than defeat or victory. There was pride and belief that what they were fighting for—freedom, heroism, and dignity of human life—was worth more than life itself. By sacrificing themselves, they froze in history the bravery and courage of the RVNAF.

By nightfall, an eerie calm settled on Saigon as her anxious citizens worried about their future. Would there be another massacre? Would they be sent to jails? They holed up in their houses. There was no spontaneous welcoming reaction and no celebration because the victors came as conquerors not liberators.

For those who could not escape, the image of the tank crashing through the palace gates represented the failure of the U.S. to fulfill its promise to help South Vietnam and the betrayal of Hà Nội who broke its non-invasion promises. For those who were able to escape, the image of people lining on the stairs leading to the helicopter pad highlighted the painful loss of their homeland. For both, the demise of RVN on 30 April represented "the dusk of political pluralism, independent critique and free speech in Vietnam."[14]

Kissinger was unable to free American POWs without forcing Saigon to sign an agreement that led to the fall of Saigon. The 591 POWs released by Hanoi were exchanged for 17.5 million free South Vietnamese, making it the largest ransom deal in world history. General Homer Smith wrote, "The South Vietnamese, admittedly with many failings of their own, paid the ultimate price—their freedom as people and their existence as a sovereign nation."[15] Saigon's ambassador to the U.S., Trần Kim Phượng, said in an interview: "It is fatal to be allies of the U.S.... This is a conclusion that people in the world would draw."[16]

Life Under Communism

After General Minh announced the surrender, almost everyone in South Vietnam cried. They felt the humiliation of defeat and the end of a way of life. Had they known it, they probably would have cried more. The party's policy would be the same one that had been applied in the North in 1954: eradication of the middle class, nationalization of large enterprises, and abolition of property rights and freedom of speech. "On us the night is descending beyond which there is no dawn," Ambassador Trần Kim Phượng said.

The streets were empty and littered with soldiers' uniforms, guns, ammunitions, military hardware and trash. Smoke rose from vandalized houses and from materials people were burning. Anything that was related to the old regime was dragged out and burned.[17] Looters came out along with the Fifth Column (imbedded communist supporters) and the "30 April brigade." The latter were turncoats who at the last minute switched allegiance to the victors. They wore red armbands and started ordering people around. In order to win the confidence of the communists, they went out to greet them and notify them about what was going in the neighborhood.[18]

When Kim Vinh saw the northern troops coming, she rapidly changed into black clothes. She had heard rumors the day before that those who wore nice clothes would be killed. Her job was to burn all the photos and commendations her dad, a former ARVN soldier, had gotten from the government and the Americans.

The first day of May was a sad one. The electricity was out and the communists did not know how to fix it. On the radio, the loud and high-pitched voice of a northerner condemned America and those who followed her. He called them the "imperialist servants and dogs" because they had worked with the Americans against the communists.

The situation remained unstable the first few weeks because the VC did not have complete control of the city. People still had guns and stole things from others right in the streets. Hold ups were frequent as were break-ins. The few people who ventured outside carried a communist flag that served as a security pass to ward off unpleasant encounters.

Neighborhoods were divided into sections with a political adviser assigned to each block. The latter taught people about Marxism and Leninism, which were discussed at subsequent meetings. He made people criticize themselves, their neighbors and their parents. Kim Vinh said she "hated people like her parents who did what they did." She said that in order to survive.[19] People made up things and criticized and accused each other. Even if they did not know how to lie, they learned it on the spot in order to survive. Those who failed to master the basics of communism were deemed unrevolutionary and were banished to a new economic zone (NEZ).[20]

Loudspeakers installed at each neighborhood woke people up at 6 A.M. They were called to go outside and practice calisthenics to strange music. They were then forced to go to the countryside to build houses or repair roofs. If they refused, food and other rations were cut off. If children did not volunteer, the whole family would be sent to the NEZ.

Men were told to report to reeducation camps for ten days or four weeks. When that period had elapsed, anxious family members became disappointed not to see them back. They were not ready to come home, the police told them. People realized it was just a communist ploy to corral all military personnel. For Kim Vinh's father, four weeks became nine years. The police knocked at their door at 2 A.M. to search all over the house. Their real reason was to look for gold and money. When they could not find anything, they randomly criticized this or that. They forced Vinh's brother to enroll in the Youth Volunteers to build roads and to work in the jungle. But he had to sign a form stating that he volunteered.

In the end, people got tired of living under a government that tricked and cheated. To survive in such a society, the citizens also learned to trick and cheat. Vinh's brother pretended to have a broken arm during a fall. Her mother brought him to a nurse to have a cast placed on it. Another person was bribed to make sure that the neighbors knew about the story. The councilman was bribed so that the young man would not have to go to the NEZ.[21]

Schools reopened a few weeks later and teachers were ordered to return for retraining. For three weeks, they learned about the new policy, curriculum, and discipline. Gone were the old regime's rules and regulations. They were taught mostly politics—communism, the victory of the communists, and the defeat of the Americans—which they dutifully copied down word by word. If they turned in a paper that resembled what they had been taught, they would get a perfect score. They were also required to write an essay about why they "liked Hồ Chí Minh" and other kinds of lies.

The new semester began in July of 1975. They taught the new curriculum, attended meetings and studied politics, in addition to digging ditches and cleaning streets. They worked all day and often all night, and also on weekends. They also had to write up their biographies every so often so that the government could keep track of them. They had to teach students to curse and hate their fathers who had been officers in the old regime. They taught hostility and vengeance towards the U.S. and the former Republic of Vietnam.[22] Every other month on Sunday, they came to school to make sandals out of nylon strings. The products were shipped to Russia to earn foreign currency for the state. After the sandal project came the nylon hats, the nylon brooms, and thousands of other "wonderful" projects.[23]

Libraries were emptied. Books—even rare and precious ones—were brought outside and burned. They were replaced by books extolling the virtues of communism—books that just gathered dust on the shelves. More than 100 authors and thousands of books were banned. Jobs were reserved for Northerners and university slots for children of Northerners.[24] Children were classified from 1 to 14. Class 1 children were those of deceased communist soldiers: They received the best treatment as well as benefits. They would automatically go to university even if they did not have good scores. Children of ARVN soldiers who were sent to reeducation camps were classified 13. The last slot was reserved for children of traitors. Class 13 children were not allowed to go to universities except as agriculture majors.[25]

The liberating troops faced a plethora of goods: cassette tapes, radios, electronic watches, TV appliances, refrigerators, foreign-made cigarettes, and so on. They walked the streets with their eyes popping.[26] Dương Thu Hương, a northern communist, visited Saigon after the 1975 liberation. She saw goods and riches she had never seen before. Books were sold on the sidewalks— French, American, and others—which she never imagined could have existed. She bought lots of them. She reasoned that Hà Nội, by blocking all sources of information and keeping its people in the dark, must be an inhumane regime.[27]

Communist cadres spoke so fluently that everyone thought they were educated people. Their reading and writing, however, betrayed their limited education. Their lives reflected their poor knowledge and the material shortage in the North. They went to the market to buy purses, radio sets and watches with "windows" (the date) and "three pilots" (hands). Their eagerness to have pictures taken in South Vietnam kept photographers busy. Their money came from different sources. Some stole gas from tanks or military trucks. Others sold what they took from the South Vietnamese or military bases (barbed wire, tools, wood, steel, iron, aluminum sheets, cigarettes, etc.). Former civil servants helped their new communist bosses sell all the items they stole.[28]

While unemployed Southerners attempted to get rid of their belongings, Northerners became browsers, hagglers, and buyers. Communist generals' wives flew aboard military jets from Hà Nội to Saigon to buy antiques, jewelries, furniture, and high-end quality goods.[29] Small and large traders competed for these goods and shipped them north—especially cars, motorbikes, and other consumer goods. The South became a highly sought after post after the war.[30] The government, on the other hand, saw these goods as a threat to socialist authority because they shook people's confidence in the government. Over the years, Hà Nội had told them that the South did not have anything, needed everything and needed to be "liberated." All of a sudden, the flood of consumer goods that trickled northwards caused the people to question the veracity of Hà Nội's news. Hà Nội reacted by labeling these goods as poor in quality, the "bottom of the barrel." They were easily "outdated, inconvenient, and ugly." However, others worried about these commodities, which were "cruel, kill people without trembling and no one can avoid their claws and teeth."[31]

Hà Nội ordered two million people to unproductive or virgin areas they labeled as new economic zones (NEZ)—the civilian equivalent of the reeducation camps—to do cooperative farming. They were dropped in the wild and told to cut down trees, clear lands, and build their own huts. In some areas, they were provided with tools and seeds for a few months while they received no help at all in others. The main purpose of the NEZ was to remove dissident elements and to produce conformity through hard labor and confinement. ARVN officers released from reeducation camps were sent there. If workers were able to plant rice, most of the rice was stored in warehouses. Workers received only a small fraction of the harvest, with the rest going to the government and its representatives. They often labored from 5 A.M. until after dark, but still did not have enough to eat. If they spoke out against the mistreatment, they were beaten and jailed. They, therefore, escaped back to their hometowns[32] only to find out that their original homes had been confiscated and turned over to incoming North Vietnamese. They were forced to live outdoors or with friends or relatives.

The price of rice went up from 30 cents a pound to $2. Gasoline almost completely disappeared from the Saigon market. Overnight, people pulled out their old bikes and rode on them. Gas-powered buses switched to coal to keep running. Once in a while drivers would throw a few shovels of coal into the burner. If the engine stopped running, passengers had to get out and push to get it to start again. City streets that had previously been filled with cars and motorbikes became quiet as bikes replaced cars. Time had suddenly turned three or four decades backward.

Economically, all bank accounts were frozen and businesses and properties were nationalized. Gold, money, and objects of value that were confiscated often went into the bộ đội's pockets. South Vietnamese currency was abolished overnight and each family was allowed to only exchange a limited amount of money. Losing their saving accounts after having their businesses and properties confiscated caused people to kill themselves in despair. Everyone was affected. Lê Vân and his wife survived during the war by working as tailors. The new government banned the wearing of the traditional áo dài. Their income from sewing áo dài suddenly plummeted, forcing them to sell everything to survive: refrigerator, radio, and clothing. Only after the ban was lifted ten years later were they able to buy a new refrigerator, a TV and two motorbikes.[33]

Shortages of rice and food, which were common from 1975 to 1980, forced people to eat rice mixed with cassava to increase the bulk of their meal. Children failed to grow up normally because of malnutrition. They looked passive and lazy. Adults got sick and developed memory loss. Through a tight network of police and by controlling food distribution, the party kept people submissive and minimized their hostility to the government. Depressed and dispirited, people turned to smoking cheap domestic cigarettes to dissipate their worries. They also drank moonshine alcohol made of cassava dusted with insecticide powder. Not a few drinkers died after using this product.[34]

Hải Thuận, a southern VC, left his family and went North in 1954. When he returned to Saigon in 1975, he realized that his son, an ARVN soldier, had reported for reeducation. While his wife raised their son by herself during these war years, he, a communist cadre, could not even save him. The tormented Thuận wrote two letters to the Politburo requesting his son's release—citing his service to the government and the official policy of reconciliation. Receiving no response, he jumped to his death out of window of a tall building on Lê Lợi Street. He left two letters: one criticizing the party for their callous insensitivity and deceitfulness and the other asking his wife for forgiveness.[35]

Trương Như Tảng, a Saigon lawyer who joined the VC in the 1960s, returned to Saigon in 1975 as the minister of justice of the Provisional Revolutionary Government (PRG). His mother told him, "You have abandoned everything ... to follow the communists.... You will see. They will betray you, and you will suffer your entire life."[36] He even took his brothers Quỳnh and Bích, who had worked for the southern government, to reeducation camps—himself believing they would be released after four weeks. Thirty days, then 60 days passed without their release.[37] When he finally talked to Phát, the president of the PRG, the latter explained: It was "thirty days' worth of food and clothing," not 30 days of reeducation.[38] Tảng realized he had been betrayed by the communist system.

Tảng also witnessed "the army, local authorities, and security police" arresting anyone they wanted. There was no code of laws, no responsible authority for the decisions, and no protection for those seized. The prisoners could end up in jail forever. Arrests were more "kidnappings than legal apprehension." In the first year after liberation, 300,000 people were arrested—a number based on the number of people summoned for 30 days of reeducation.[39]

Đoàn Văn Toại was a communist sympathizer who, as a Saigon college student, led many demonstrations against Diệm and Thiệu.[40] On June 22, 1975, despite working for the PRG, the security police "mistook" him for another Toại and snatched him while he attended a concert at the Grand Theater in downtown Saigon. They threw him into the Lê Văn Duyệt jail, which was then ten times as crowded as under Thiệu's regime (2,000 in 1975 versus 200 before the revolution). The largest central jail, Chí Hòa was five times more crowded than before the revolution (40,000 compared to 8,000 inmates respectively).[41] Under Thiệu's regime, at least people had legal recourse, while after 1975, there was no legal system and no Red Cross to lean on. Inmates vegetated in jails until the administration decided to take a look at them. And it could take a long time. In the meantime, tortures, punishments, starvation and sometimes executions occurred almost daily.[42] Toại was finally released on November 1, 1977—exactly 863 days after his imprisonment. He was given a release form that left blank the reasons for arrest and release.[43]

The party saw itself as infallible and above the law. Its methods were brutal and unreasonable.[44] It imposed the will of an exclusive group of people (communists) over the whole society. Anyone who defied the party was taken down. It used fear as the motivating factor. It was fear that separated the bộ đội and the cán bộ from their humanity. It was fear that gave the revolution its steely resolve. To achieve its goals it had molded a machine of unearthly strength.[45]

Facing calls from Southerners for regulations for imprisonment, the party issued the 3/76 Law in March 1976, which defined jailable offenses and required formal charges to be filed. But if before 3/76 the communists arrested people arbitrarily without warrant, after that date they simply arrested people arbitrarily with a warrant. If a person was not a "reactionary, he was a pseudo-pacifist. If he was not a pseudo-pacifist, he was a bourgeois-pacifist. If not a bourgeois-pacifist, he was a decadent." These were all subtle forms of reaction, worthy of arrest.[46]

Under the communists, South Vietnam became a huge—if not the biggest—concentration camp in the world. Of its 20 million people more than one million—five percent—were sent to concentration camps or jails. Instead of "liberating" them, they simply sent them to jails.

Southerners lived like "hunted animals" or "fish in a fishbowl."[47] Discarded by the Americans, jailed by the communists, deprived of food and rations, shunned from governmental positions and even from schools, their private properties and belongings confiscated, they spent their days trying to make ends meet. They sold or traded belongings for food: these were their "darkest years." That period lasted for at least 13 years, until đổi mới policy was implemented. Of the 14 classes in the society—a supposedly classless one—Southerners fell into the last of the categories—the "condemned"—in their own land.

In the mid–1980s, Nick Sebastian noted that Southerners labored under terrible economic hardship and a repressive regime. "The people I met throughout the country accept their loss and in many cases unbelievable subsequent persecution with an equanimity, fortitude, strength of character, and will to survive that is awe-inspiring."[48]

Reeducation and Diaspora

At the end of World War II, Ratzinger, a defeated German soldier, was sent to a POW camp for three months and then sent home. The U.S. could have unleashed a full-blown revenge on him and Germany, but did not. Ratzinger went on to become Pope Benedict XVI and his generation was forever grateful to the U.S.[49] At the end of the Vietnam War, all southern officers and high-level officials were sent to re-education camps for two to 23 years. General Lê Minh Đạo, the hero of Xuân Lộc, for example, was sent to various northern concentration camps for a total of 17 years, during which he almost lost his life. By acting that way, Hà Nội deepened the political chasm between North and South and fulfilled the Lạc Long Quân-Âu Cơ curse that the two Vietnams would forever be divided socially, politically, and morally, if not geographically.[50] It has perpetuated the reality of the "two Vietnams" represented today by the socialist Vietnam in the old country and the "little Saigons" or the overseas Vietnamese community around the world.[51]

Cải Tạo was not the simple reeducation training one might think of. It carried a morbid and vicious meaning with its concealed goal and purposes. It was labeled as 10- and 30-day re-training, designed to give Southerners a taste of the suffering endured by the communists during the war. However, no one had expected that the majority would be locked up longer than three years, and many for more than 10 years. No one had expected that many would die of starvation, lack of medication and medical care, neglect, physical abuse, torture, confinement in tiny units, and recurrent psychological harassment. No one would have thought that many of them would disappear forever during their imprisonment without leaving a message or note. Unmarked mounds of earth with crude wooden tombstones or handmade crosses were the only reminders of their presence in the camps.

According to revolutionary language, the combination of two verbs, cải (to transform) and tạo (to create), conveys a threatening meaning: an attempt to "recreate" or completely "make over" sinful or incomplete individuals.[52] The goal was to transform Southerners with capitalist and democratic aspirations into inveterate communist believers. To achieve that goal, the communists used a four-pronged approach: indoctrination, physical punishment through labor, torture and confinement, behavioral modification through criticism and self criticism and strict surveillance. This was followed by banishment to the NEZ after release.[53]

The May 7, 1975, communiqué specified places and times at which ranking officers had to report, register, and turn in their weapons. On June 10, there was mention of "reforming and cleansing one's wrongdoings" in order to become a good citizen. Privates, lower-ranking officials, had to undergo three days of reeducation, after which they were sent home, except those serving in the intelligence—Marine, Airborne, and Ranger corps. On June 13, officers from lieutenant to major were ordered to report with a ten-day food supply. Then senior officers were told to report with a 30-day food supply. There was no legal justification needed for the reeducation. The short-term incarceration process turned out to be a ruse intended to mask the Politburo's policy, which was the incarceration of all southern officers and officials.[54]

One of the goals of reeducation was to remove individuals from the scene. Southerners were guilty because they belonged to the enemy camp. And the stigma of incarceration will forever be attached to them and their descendants. That was the power the police had in a communist country.

More than one million civilians and soldiers were incarcerated.[55] One Hà Nội official put the number at 1.2 million.[56] Jail conditions were primitive, sometimes brutalizing, with two parallel systems of camps: one run by the military and the other by the Công An (security police).

Dương Cụ, a 40-year-old supreme court justice, refused to be evacuated in 1975 in order to take care of his sick wife. Six weeks later, he was hauled into a reeducation camp. He underwent eight months of political lectures from teachers with minimal intellectual capacity who knew nothing about the outside world. After six years of reeducation, he was released because of bad health. He remained in Saigon, hoping for the best, and found work with an agency set up to attract investments for $5 per month and food stamps. As a southern "puppet," he was not allowed to use the telephone or contact foreigners. Like most educated Saigonese of his generation, his career was over.[57]

Professor Thông, dean of the Saigon University Law School was incarcerated at the Lê Văn Duyệt jail two days after the takeover. He did not want to leave Saigon, for he too had to care for his ailing mother. He thought that the communists would not bother a lawyer who had not been involved in politics. But, they accused him of being a CIA agent, sent him to jail, and tortured him because he refused to acknowledge he was a CIA agent. His left wrist was handcuffed to his right ankle and his right wrist to his left ankle.[58]

Reeducation camp inmates were not regular criminals. They were political detainees (politicals) or, more exactly, prisoners of conscience who fought to preserve their freedom from communism. They were brainwashed and forced to endure ten weeks of indoctrination during which they were taught about communism, socialism, the Labor Party, the American defeat, and the new economic zones. They had to discuss the topics between themselves and then recite verbatim the main points. At night, they had to do self-criticism and ask the party for forgiveness for having fought against the revolution. They then had to write autobiographies in which they detailed their "crimes." If they had not committed any crimes, they had to make them up. Killing a VC would be a crime from the revolution's side. Although they pretended to accept the new teachings, deep inside they saw a fatal inconsistency between communism and the South Vietnamese culture. Communism is a collective enterprise while the Vietnamese are highly individualistic in nature. Communism favors restriction of freedom and human rights while the Vietnamese believe in private property and ownership and civil rights.[59]

Inmates worked eight to ten hours a day, followed by three hours of political lecture and thought reform. They usually had to cut down trees with bayonets or dull knives, clear forests and hills to plant rice or corn, build new camps or lodging, and dig wells or irrigation canals. They had at their disposal no power tools, no machinery and not even hand saws. Everything had to be improvised. They were forced to pull the plough while one of them guided it (because of lack of buffaloes), and worse—to scoop cow dung or human waste with their bare hands for use as fertilizer for their fields.[60]

The A-30 Dã Bàn camp close to Tuy Hòa in central Vietnam was one of the South's largest concentration camps. It held 4,000 inmates at its peak. After cutting down trees, inmates had to move them from the forests to the camp. Since trucks or forklifts were unavailable, everything had to be done manually. The three-foot in diameter, 20-foot-long trunks had to be lifted by six people and carried from the work site to the river where they were rafted down the river. The work was dangerous because the river was wide—up to 60 feet in certain areas—and the current was swift. The mountain water was always cold and full of leeches and green-striped bloodsuckers. If inmates were not careful, they could be crushed between the big trunks, stabbed by branches, and pushed by the currents against big rocks.[61]

In the southern highlands, 660 inmates were ordered to clear 250 acres of forests in one month while building their own camps from scratch. Each was given a hoe and a bush knife.[62]

The bộ đội used food as a weapon with unequaled brutality and efficiency. They doled out the minimum nutrition required to survive. That minimum would be further reduced at the slightest infraction. The weekly regimen consisted of:

1 day: rice with salt
1 day: rice with fish sauce
1 day: rice with pork (1–2 morsels)
1 day: rice with fish (1–2 morsels)
3 days: rice with vegetables.

That regimen would provide at best 800 to 900 calories per day, though the laboring inmates would require 3,000 to 4,000 calories daily. They withered rapidly and within a month or two had lost half of their weight. They eventually lost their hair, their bones became brittle, their teeth decayed. Soon their legs and feet swelled due to béri béri, a nutritional disease linked to lack of Vitamin B1.[63]

Food was a drug. Once cut down sufficiently, people often reacted like addicts in withdrawal. They could do irrational things for a handful of rice. A former Diệm minister dishonored himself by trying to steal a spoonful of fish sauce from another prisoner. He was roughed up as a result. One engineer was caught taking someone else's share of rice. He was beaten up and thrown in isolation, after which he committed suicide.[64] A 25-year-old student was jailed following a failed escape attempt. He also fought for food in jail. He was sentenced to a two-month isolation at half ration and 30 blows with the cane. He died after receiving the 30th blow. The cell leader signed an affidavit stating that the prisoner had committed suicide by "swallowing his tongue."[65]

Hunger was so pervasive that prisoners thought only about food. It precipitated deliriums and caused them to do strange things—like snoop for the bộ đội (those who did were called "antenna") in exchange for food.[66] Others learned to control their hunger by eating anything that crawled: lizards, centipedes, mice, birds, snakes, grasshoppers. Rat meat, if available, was a delicacy. They were so aggressive in their hunting that rats and geckoes became extinct in many camps. They supplemented their meals with berries, cassava roots, corn, beans, and even grass they stole while working in the fields. They usually consumed these items "raw" because they would be punished when caught stealing.[67] Many unfortunately died after eating wild berries or toxic roots.

But what saved them was the food their families brought them. Without these supplies in the form of dry fish, dry meat, sugar, medicines, vitamins, and antibiotics, the majority would have died. They often shared their meager supply with less fortunate inmates. They were allowed to receive packages of food six months after their incarceration in the South and three years in the North.

There was no statute of limitations on reeducation. In the camps, ARVN officers found Catholics from the Quỳnh Lưu district who had been banished there for having incited rebellion in 1953 and also prisoners of the French Expeditionary Corps who had been incarcerated since 1954.[68]

The reeducation process was so beautifully perfected and methodically applied that it was in fact a combined psychophysical torture that left prisoners no room to maneuver. They either had to comply or die as a consequence of their opposition. Those who complied were still afraid of being punished because rules were not uniformly applied. Following all the orders did not guarantee immunity from punishment. A bad word or report from an antenna could result in a savage punishment even if one had not done anything wrong. This arbitrary pattern of treatment caused many to harbor nightmares years and even decades after their release from the camps: They would wake up in the middle of the night crying or breaking down. One former internee went into violent fits of rage, smashed furniture, got drunk or stared into the distance without uttering any word. Others were so afraid of being returned to the camps that even a scratch at the door would cause them to jump and look for a place to hide.[69] Many former inmates suffered from post-traumatic stress disorder (PTSD).[70] Those suffering from torture and traumatic head injury (THI) had thinner prefrontal-temporal cortices and a higher rate of depression (63 percent vs. 12 percent) than those without THI exposure. Trauma/torture events were associated with bilateral amygdala volume loss.[71]

The treatment in the camps was so inhumane that once released, prisoners attempted to escape rather than staying back. There were no charges, no hearings, and no sentences. No one knew when, if ever, they would be released. The power of their masters was total and totally arbitrary.[72] One former inmate recounted that when he returned home after years of being in concentration camps, he had changed so much for the worse—physically and mentally—that even his wife and children did not recognize him. They asked him who he was until he told them he was their husband and father.[73]

Having tasted hard labor, gnawing hunger, the constant pain and suffering of the reeducation camps, and psychological torture, prisoners just did not want to return to the camps a second time. Many had even tried to escape from Vietnam many times until they were successful or became broke. As a result of this effort, they became tame; they tried not to antagonize the authorities in order to avoid further retributions. Whether they remained inside or outside Vietnam, they had not yet mounted any effective political opposition to the Hà Nội regime since their release.

Zinoman remarked that after all was said and done, the "scope and intensity of the disciplinary power deployed by the colonial [French] state pale beside that of the movement that eventually dislodged and replaced it."[74]

Navy officer Trường Sa escaped to Guam after 1975. There, he had a change of heart. Along with 1546 other evacuees, he decided to return home on the fatidic *Vietnam Thuong Tin I* (Vietnam Commercial Bank), the boat many of them took to escape to Guam. From Vung Tau, they were escorted

Nha Trang, 100 miles north of Saigon. Instead of receiving a warm welcome, they were interrogated and confined to the former Korean Army installation. All the men were sent to the A-20 reeducation camp.[75] Women and children were sent home after a short incarceration period. Trường Sa was interned in many concentration camps for ten years before being released. He later escaped by boat and was relocated to Canada. His only comment was that returning to Vietnam was his biggest mistake.

The story of Commander Tran Dinh Tru of the *Vietnam Thuong Tin I* was no less brutal. He was subjected to three months of twice-daily interrogation and endless long sessions of "confession" writing. He was then sent to a camp that featured "rows of cottages, walls made of leaves, barbed wire, and watchtowers on the four corners." He slept on a reed mat placed on a bamboo bed and followed a strict and regimented schedule. He labored resiliently and obediently in the fields during daytime, endured nightly self-examination sessions, and subsisted on one yam for the morning, two yams or two ears of corn for noon, and two more for the evening. Eighteen months later he was trucked to a northern camp near the Laotian border, where conditions were worse than the first one. Late in 1978, he was moved to another southern camp for more years of imprisonment. His fourth camp was "run by animal-like hooligans trained in the art of intimidating, beating, and torturing inmates.... Days in this camp were the longest ever, and the pains here, the most excruciating." He was finally released on February 13, 1988 — 12 and a half years after returning home. Tru and his family applied for and were approved for immigration to the United States.[76]

As for the poet and musician Trúc Phương, he too tried to escape from Vietnam in 1979. Unfortunately, he was caught and jailed. Upon his release, he realized his wife had left him. Having no lodging, no family, and no work, he became destitute and lived day-by-day thanks to the charity of his friends. Talking about that time, he mentioned: "As for being hungry, I was not totally hungry. As for being full, I never had a full meal." At night, he slept on the ground at the bus station on a mat he could rent for one piaster. If he arrived early at night, he could find a decent place on the ground. The days he arrived late, he had to sleep near the latrines. His despair was recounted in one of his famous songs.[77]

The first wave of 130,000 people in 1975 landed in Guam, which became their gateway to freedom.[78] The exodus slowed to a trickle as the Vietnamese tried to adapt to the new regime. "By 1977, it became a flow—21,276; by the end of 1978, a flood—106,489, and in the first six months of 1979, a torrent—166,489."[79] Subsequent waves of refugees kept coming despite imprisonment by công an, traveling difficulties, piracy, storms, compassion fatigue, and so on.[80] This largest exodus in the world—eventually 3 million people settled in the free world, excluding the millions who perished at seas, in jails, or were victims of pirates—was the boldest and most visible indictment of the Hà Nội communist regime.

Economic and Cultural Resistance

The government controlled the distribution of rice, meat, fish, vegetables, and gasoline. Communications, transport, printing, hotels and rental housing, companies dealing with fertilizers and insecticides, pharmaceuticals, textiles and chemical products, were fully nationalized. However, small trade and manufacturing remained in private hands. There were 400 private factories and 15,000 small businesses and handicraft shops at the end of 1977. Hoarding and price speculation by private merchants were common.[81]

Farmers refused to sell their grain to the state at the low official price of one fifth of the free-market price. They kept about 600,000 tons of paddies off the market in 1977. In the early hours of March 28, 1978, all private shops were raided and an inventory of stocks was undertaken. The requisitioned goods were purchased by the state at cost plus 10 percent profit. Since the official price was well below the market price, and so many goods were purchased through black market channels, many businessmen were ruined.[82]

While the central and northern regions accepted collectivization, the South resisted it. Only 7 percent of households joined cooperatives in the South compared to 90 percent in the North. Farmers destroyed equipment and killed animals rather than hand them over to collective farms.[83] Of the 12,000 production collectives in the South, only half had worked with "collectivized production material." Coupled with bad weather, total food production was only 12.4 million tons in 1978.[84] All these subtle oppositions represented a "reaction" to the large presence of Northerners in positions of authority in the South as well as their propensity to treat the local population with contempt and arrogance.[85] Other causes included poor managerial techniques and lack of qualified technicians.[86]

Despite the threat of repression, southerners frequented their chợ trời (open-air market), which had been in existence for centuries in the South. Sellers did not have any rights because the gathering was illegal. They were at the mercy of the secret police, who descended on them like vultures to confiscate their wares. But like the tide, they would disperse only to reassemble later once the police was gone. This was a cat and mouse game between the police and these women. On one side, policemen did not want traders to be out of control or dismissive of the law. On the other hand, they received bribes from these women and tended to look the other way. A reporter noted what business was like before 1975: "The ordinary markets in South Vietnamese cities sell Hitachi or Sanyo electric fans, Olympic portable typewriters, Adidas sports shoes, Peugeot bicycles and Michelin inner tubes. Prices are about western level (therefore not affordable).... But someone must be buying them."[87]

The persistence of the markets two years after the end of the war worried the government which saw them as "fortresses of the capitalist business forces led by the comprador bourgeoisie." The latter conspired to "enslave people" and to attract them to buying the goods because of their availability and variety. While government stores often ran out of basic goods, the latter were available at the chợ trời. While customers were never treated nicely at government stores, they were welcome at the chợ trời.

By 1978, commercialism remained rampant. In response to the threat, communist officials conducted a full-scale "war" against these businesses and the southern mentality. Bulletins, billboards, posters, radio and TV ads were used to denounce the depravation of the old regime. They at the same time extolled the virtues of a communist society that valued not credit worthiness or commercial skills, but "revolutionary merit."

Escapees from the NEZ got involved in these chợ trời, which required minimal capital. Farmers smuggled their excess goods to these markets, where they got better prices than in government stores. Goods sent back by the Việt Kiều found their ways to the market. Even smuggled goods from Cambodia or Thailand ended up there. Therefore, instead of shrinking down, they kept expanding and supplied people with readily available and reliable commodities. This was the place where women got their supplies (medications, dry food, vitamins, and so on) prior to visiting their husbands in reeducation camps.

Soon, this non-compliant way of dealing with the government expanded to other areas and became a shift in national orientation.

Northerners who used art and music as tools to promote revolutionary ideas called southern music "yellow" (vàng). Southerners reacted by labeling northern music "red" (communist). Yellow music, with its languorous tone, was termed as lãng mạn (romantic), ủy mị (weakening), đồi trụy (depraved), kích dâm (lewd), đầu độc (poisonous), phản động (reactionary), and chống cộng (anti-revolutionary). One had to go back two centuries earlier to the Nguyễn dynasty to see such a condemnation of music. At that time, musicians and artists were cast outside the society. Their children were not allowed to go to school or apply for a governmental job.

Yellow music was banned from television, radio, public venues, and removed from repertoires. Cải lương, a southern classical opera, was described as adapted to the "lower tastes." Võ Văn Kiệt commented that southern music "after many centuries of a backward, feudal and a century of old and new colonialism ... had sunk into oblivion."

Yellow music imparted a "gloomy, embittered, impotent and cynical mood toward life ... a sensation of being drowned in a withered and desolate world." It was associated with "unwholesome" (không lành mạnh) lyrical themes of separation, loneliness, sadness and nostalgia. The extent of criticisms, as well as the implication that the U.S.–RVN era created melodies that were "quiet and interminable, like sad persistent drops of rain, sometimes bewailing one's lot," is intriguing. They commented that the style was a "sobbing, meltingly tearful way of singing, sounding like mourning or crying." They blamed the Saigon government for importing the refuse (rác rưới) and cast-offs (phế thải) of foreign music in an "undiscriminating and uncritical manner ... with the intention to poison and ruin the national culture." The comments only expressed the tortured mind of communist officials who did not understand or know how to handle music as the spontaneous "voice" of the people.[88]

They failed to recognize that unlike the communist government, Saigon did not hire musicians or artists to produce creations to enhance or bolster its regime. It probably should have but it did not. Southern music was mostly a private and personal creation. Without its spontaneity, it would not be natural, beautiful, or popular. There lay the difference between Hà Nội and Saigon. Saigon, although not a totally free regime, had a strong *laissez-faire* attitude about music. Only rarely did it interfere with artistic creation.

These melodies reflected the overall mood of the population, which was deeply traumatized by the communist invasion of the South and by the sufferings induced by the 21-year long war. People expressed their powerlessness and yearning for peace. It was a spontaneous search for some degree of healing by loudly expressing their worries and despairs and by attempting to convey and to share their personal feelings. Had they not loudly vented their feelings, they would have either become severely inhibited or suffered deeply from war-induced traumatic stress syndrome.

Religion and Human Rights

Vietnamese Buddhism—Mahayana, or Greater Vehicle or Wheel—was introduced into North Vietnam about the second century A.D. through China. It suggested social involvement, while Theravada—Smaller Wheel, introduced later in the South—proposed a purely religious way of practicing religion.

State religion since the 12th century in the North, it was slowly replaced by Confucianism under the northern Lê. The southern Nguyễn, on the other hand, adopted Theravada as its religion. Ngô Đình Diệm financed the construction of many pagodas and allowed free propagation of the faith. But some bonzes became vocal when Diệm restricted their rights. Their revolt caused the regime to fall. After 1964, the Mahayana and Theravada branches became unified and formed the United Buddhist Church (UBC).

After 1975, the communists launched a campaign of repression against all religions in Saigon. On November 2, 1975, 12 monks and nuns immolated themselves near Cần Thơ. In September 1976, 12 other monks and nuns burned themselves to death to protest against the repression.[89] All Buddhist organizations—cultural, social, and religious—were dismantled. Hundreds of bonzes were even sent to reeducation camps. Buddhist Thích Man Giác escaped from Vietnam in 1977. In 1978, the Venerable Thích Thiện Minh died in prison under torture. In 1982, as the UBC refused to back down, the Hà Nội government confiscated the Ấn Quan pagoda, home of the UBC, and installed the Vietnamese Buddhist Church (VBC) under the communist Patriotic Front. The Venerable Thích Huyền Quang, the leader of the UBC, was sent to Hà Nội under government control.

Under the đổi mới, religious control relaxed somewhat, although the UBC continued its fight. In May 1992, Thích Huyền Quang, after being under house arrest for ten years, informed Hà Nội of his desire to return to Saigon, stating he was innocent. A year later, he requested that all the Buddhist belongings be returned to UBC and that all the jailed bonzes be released. In November 1993, the Venerable Quang wrote directly from Saigon to Premier Võ Văn Kiệt an eight-page memorandum requesting freedom of speech and religion and the abolition of the monopoly of the communist party. In May 1994, more than 70 bonzes were sentenced from four years to life.[90]

In October 1994, the Venerable Thích Long Tri was arrested by the Saigon police. Interrogated for a whole day, he was relocated to Hoi An, about 500 miles north of Saigon. On November 6, the Venerable Thích Quang Độ, general secretary and number two man of the UBC, was jailed for having "disturbed religious peace" and having "profited from religious freedom, to torpedo state interests." He was sentenced to six years in jail. He went in and out of jail for the next ten years and was awarded the 2006 Rafto Prize.

Trần Ngọc Châu fought for the Việt Minh in the 1940s. Châu later joined the South Vietnamese military and rose to the rank of lieutenant colonel. In 1966, he won a seat on the Saigon National Assembly. In 1969, believing that the war could not be won, he advocated a settlement with the VC. He criticized his former friend President Thiệu for being harsh on the VC. The government reacted by accusing Châu of being a communist agent. It tried him in absentia and sentenced him to 20 years in jail. Although Châu remained imprisoned until 1975, he was treated with special consideration. He got newspapers, books and even a radio and television in his isolated prison cell.

In 1975 the communists deemed him dangerous for having switched sides and sent him to a reeducation camp north of Saigon. It was a barrack with iron sheets for a roof, corrugated sheets for walls, and bare cement floors. In the same camp were the elite of the South Vietnamese anti-communists: the Supreme Court Justice Trần Minh Triết, and hundreds of other judges, cabinet members, senators, congressmen, provincial governors, district chiefs, doctors, and professors. They endured six months of indoctrination before being sent to manual labor. Some people went crazy and committed suicide. Châu's roommate was found dead one morning of an overdose of sleeping pills. He was buried behind the barracks and his family was notified three months later.

Châu's wife told him that 25 members of his extended family who had worked for the communists during the war had petitioned for his clemency. His son, who had been admitted to the National Conservatory of Music, had been asked to withdraw because of his link to the former Saigon government. Châu was moved to the Thủ Đức camp in December 1977 and was ordered to write his biography detailing all his crimes against the revolution. Since he was knowledgeable about communist procedure in the 1940s, and since he had written three sets of biographies for them in 1975, he made sure he correctly repeated the same recitation of his "crimes." For 58 days, ten to 15 hours a day, he wrote an 800-page document following which he was interviewed by northern officials.

He was released in 1978 after being asked to write a letter of thanks to the communist government. A few weeks later, he was invited to join the Social Sciences Institute to study the former leaders of South Vietnam. He knew they wanted him to inform on his friends. Since he did not want to betray them, he wrote stories about those who had left Vietnam. He was finally able to buy false Chinese papers and to escape by boat.[91]

Father Nguyễn Văn Lý was jailed from 1977 to 1978, and then again from 1983 to 1992, for "opposing the revolution and destroying the people's unity." In 2001, he was sentenced to 15 years in jail for speaking out against the government, but was released in 2004. As a member of the pro-democracy movement, he was sentenced to eight years in jail in 2007. He tried to respond but was quieted by the communist police.

Dr. Nguyễn Đan Quế is an endocrinologist and human rights fighter. He was jailed in 1978 for criticizing the government. After his release, he continued to call for social reform, for which he was jailed from 1990 until 1998. He remained under "virtual house arrest" until 2003, when he was jailed a third time. His sentence was commuted in 2005. Dr. Quế was awarded the Robert F. Kennedy Human Rights Award in 1995.

Lý Tống is an "extreme anticommunist." He was a South Vietnamese Airforce pilot who was hit by a Soviet anti-aircraft missile during a combat flight in 1975. Jailed by the communists for five years, he escaped by way of Cambodia into Singapore where he petitioned the U.S. for political asylum. Arriving in the U.S. in 1984, he returned to Saigon where he dropped leaflets calling for the people to rise against the communists in 1992. He jumped out of the airplane and was caught. He was sentenced for 20 years but was soon released in 1998 under outside pressure. He returned to the U.S. and dropped leaflets over Havana in 2000, calling for a people's insurrection against Castro. He again dropped leaflets over Saigon in 2000 but was sentenced to eight years in a Thailand jail. Hà Nội requested he be extradited back to Vietnam. The Thai Appeal Court instead freed him, calling his action a political one.[92]

Đoàn Việt Hoạt, an American-trained English professor and deputy rector of Vạn Hạnh University, decided to stay in Vietnam in 1975 to help rebuild the country. He was, however, sent to various reeducation camps for 12 years. Released in 1988, he produced *Freedom Forum*, a newsletter calling for freedom of speech and democratic reforms. The fourth issue landed him and eight of his friends in jail. In 1993, he was sentenced to 20 years in jail for "attempting to overthrow the government."[93]

Nguyễn Khắc Viên, a French-trained pediatrician and long-time propagandist for the party, called for the Hà Nội leaders to resign and to introduce more political reforms because of their ineptitude: they had plunged the country into disorder and prevented all development.[94]

Đỗ Trọng Hiếu, a ranking party cadre in the South, was arrested in Saigon in June 1995 and sentenced to 15 months in prison. He once was a deputy in charge of religious affairs in Saigon after the war. He was expelled from the party in 1990 for having founded the Club of Former Resistance Warriors. Its goal was to fight for the political opening of the regime. Their newspaper, *Resistance Tradition*, railed against corruption and called for political openness.[95]

Lu Phương, a southern intellectual, challenged the party to give up its Marxist-Leninist ideology in 1994. A former culture ministry official argued that Hồ had used a Marxist theory to "turn intelligent people into foolish ones" and "bog down the nation in stagnation." Phương was expelled from the party because of his views.

At the same time, Hoàng Chính Minh, the former head of the Marxist-Leninist Institute of Hà Nội who fought for the rehabilitation of 60 "revisionist" party members, was also jailed from 1967 to 1972 and from 1981 to 1987.

On August 12, 1995, in Saigon, seven Vietnamese and two American Việt Kiều were condemned to from four to 15 years in jail for "violation of national integrity." They were only fighting for the establishment of democracy and pluralism in Vietnam.

The party did not want to hear anything about democracy and anyone who spoke about human rights or democracy can be subject to 15 years in jail.

Double Agents

Communist infiltration of the police had been going on for a long time. Right after the 1963 coup, Colonel Trần Bá Thành became deputy director of the national police. He released key VC prisoners, destroyed VC dossiers in police archives, and placed at least one known agent within the police structure. Although he was ousted when Khánh came to power, the national police took a long time to recover their anti-communist capabilities.

Colonel Phạm Ngọc Thảo was the director of the Việt Minh officer's training school in the Plain of Reeds in 1947. He was introduced to Điệm because of his strong Catholic roots. He rose to province chief of Kiến Hòa and at one time was in charge of the agroville system. After 1963, he was knowledgeable about every intrigue within the army and volunteered information to the embassy. He sowed discord and confusion within the military council before being tried and executed as a communist agent.[96]

The Saigon government was heavily infiltrated to the highest ranks with northern agents. Saigon, however, had only a few moles at the lower and middle levels in the NLF. VC General Trần Bạch Đằng pointed out four moles in the Saigon government: Đinh Văn Đệ, an ARVN colonel, Huỳnh Văn Trọng, and of course Phạm Xuân Ẩn.[97]

Congressman Đinh Văn Đệ, the chairman of the military committee in the Saigon Congress, also worked for the NLF. He headed a delegation to ask President Ford for additional military aid. When Đệ returned home, he sent his report to President Thiệu as well as a copy to Hanoi.

Huỳnh Văn Trọng, the special advisor to President Thiệu, was also a double agent. He met with Kissinger and Nixon while working for the NLF.

The biggest fish turned out to be Phạm Xuân Ẩn. In the late 1960s and early 1970s, Ẩn was the most trusted Vietnamese reporter working for western news agencies. He always delivered a detailed and accurate assessment. He frequently hung around at Givral, Saigon's upscale café, or next door at the veranda of the Continental Hotel.

He joined the resistance in 1945 and worked in the intelligence division. He worked for Caltex in 1952, and studied in the United States for two years before joining the U.S. Military Advisory Group as an adviser in Saigon in 1954. During the war, his contact was an old woman whose name he did not even know. Messages were passed from one to another at the Saigon Market or on Nguyễn Huệ or Lê Lợi streets written in invisible ink and hidden in biscuit tins or cigarette packs. Before the Tết offensive, the front asked him for a detailed report about the military installations around Saigon, the morale of the troops, and U.S. reaction to a potential attack. His reports were so accurate that General Giáp joked: "We are now in the U.S.'s war room."[98] His work therefore had affected many South Vietnamese and American lives and strategically altered the course of the war in direct or indirect ways.[99] Working for *Time* gave Ẩn access to classified information from briefings by generals Westmoreland and Abrams and by ambassadors Lodge and Bunker about strategies and operations for weeks in a row.[100]

He always held a modest but bourgeois lifestyle. He enjoyed songbirds and bet on fighting cocks. He helped save South Vietnamese spy Chief Trần Kim Tuyến on the last day of the war by contacting Southerland. Southerland then contacted officials at the U.S. Embassy who helped Tuyến get out of Saigon.

After the war, the communists did not trust him because by saving people like Tuyến, he proved himself to be a free spirit. He was recalled to Hà Nội and held under virtual house arrest for a year and a half. Promoted to general for his work, he was offered a job at the censorship department. He refused and was put out to pasture. The French intelligence uncovered his double life in 1978. Karnow tried to get him to write his memoirs, but he refused.[101] He was the "perfect spy," so good that even the CIA, foreign correspondents and Saigon's second bureau had no clue about his underground work. Instead of becoming suspicious about his broad knowledge, they came to him and treated him like the "information king."

He became disillusioned with the communists at the end of the war.[102] He said to DeVoss: "Why did we fight a war just to replace Americans with Russians? ... We called it a people's revolution, but of course the people were the first to suffer ... as long as the people sleep in the streets, the revolution was lost." He had also tried to smuggle his family out of Vietnam unsuccessfully twice and thought Hà Nội leaders were "more corrupt" than the old South Vietnamese regime. In 1997, he was denied an exit visa when he was invited to talk in the U.S. about Vietnam.[103] He died peacefully in September 2006. Although his rare American friends cited his "noble goals for Vietnamese nationalism,"[104] Southerners would counter that his betrayal of South Vietnam meant the death of 300,000 southern soldiers and untold numbers of others in reeducation camps and at seas. What kind of nationalism is that? In life and death, he continued to fool many unsuspecting Americans.

Of Casualties and Cemeteries

When the U.S. Civil War ended in 1865, General Ulysses Grant told his Union soldiers, "The rebels are our countrymen again." He sent General Lee's troops home and allowed them to keep their horses and side arms, thereby leaving their pride intact. He gave them food and forbid any retaliation against the defeated Southerners. With one bold and genial stroke, General Grant soothed the pains, angers, and resentment of the Southerners and brought long-term healing to the divided nation. If General Grant was remembered for his military feats, it was his spirit of reconciliation and forgiveness that catapulted him into the pantheon of great men.

One could not say the same thing about the Hà Nội leaders: by visiting their full wrath upon the South, they forever divided Vietnamese society. For them, the Southerners—who fought for their freedom and rights—did not deserve any pity. Those who surrendered were sent to reeducation camps and civilians were shipped to the NEZ where thousands would die in silence because of diseases, lack of food and medical care. Hà Nội confiscated Southerners' properties, houses, offices, and belongings, starved them, restricted their children's education, and drove them to the seas.

In the late 1960s, ARVN soldiers died at a rate of about 70 to 100 each day and civilian casualties ran about twice that rate. Cemeteries were filled to the brink and caskets overflowed the small office of the Hạnh Thông Tây military cemetery in Gò Vấp, north of Saigon. The shrieking and wailing of these slain soldiers' mothers or wives disturbed the quietness of the area, while some rolled wildly on the ground in deep grief. In the distance, helicopter-ambulances brought in many more dead soldiers tucked into dark body bags.

It was in this heartbreaking and painful environment that ARVN captain Nguyễn Thanh Thu, an artist by trade, attempted to conceive an idea for a sculpture to grace the front entrance of the new Biên Hòa National Cemetery. On one of these trips, Thu met a soldier who sat alone at a low table, drinking his sorrow away. He chastised his friend for having passed away and leaving him alone. He had two glasses: one for himself and the other for his ghost friend. He poured his soul out and talked to his imaginary friend. Empty cans of beer lay besides him. Thu tried to interrupt the sorrowful monologue but was waved away. The soldier handed Thu his wallet from which Thu got an address. From that encounter, he came up with the idea of the *Tiết Thương* (Remembrance) sculpture. Once the drawing was accepted, he hunted down the soldier and asked him to pose for the work. Eventually the sculpture was cast and hoisted at the front gate of the Biên Hòa cemetery. It received rave reviews from soldiers as well as their families and became the symbol of Saigon's remembering of its war deaths.

After the war, Thu was sent to a reeducation camp. When the VC realized he had conceived the sculpture, they threw him into a conex from which he was removed for interrogation. Nights were cold while days were hot like an oven. The air was especially suffocating at midday. He could have gotten out of this mess by denying his creation. But as a good and stubborn Southerner, it was unthinkable for him to reject his artistic creation. He was therefore returned to the conex. While others would have died after a few months in the container, Thu somehow stubbornly clung on to life. How he survived these months of brutal confinement is short of a miracle.

A political commissar flew down from Hà Nội to interrogate him. He was again given another chance to renege on his creation. As he once again refused, the commissar hit him hard enough to burst his eardrums. He was thrown back into his conex where he vegetated for a total of 22 months. One early morning, he was taken out of the container and led to an unknown area. The haggard, wobbly and markedly weakened artist thought he had met his destiny. But he no longer cared because he was too weak to think about anything else. The guards threw him into a room from which he awakened days later. He remained jailed for a few more years before being released. He came to the USA later through the Orderly Departure Program.[105]

Even the dead cannot rest in peace. The Biên Hòa cemetery, located about 20 miles northeast of Saigon, was the city's equivalent of the Arlington National Cemetery. It was opened in the late 1960s. The American press had raised the issue about its soldiers bearing the brunt of North Vietnamese attacks. Reality was quite different as the ratio of South Vietnamese/American casualties was 4:1 throughout the war. American reporters "spent 90 percent of their time covering the American aspects of the conflict, generally treating South Vietnam as something of a nonentity."[106]

Tables IV and V list the majority of U.S. casualties (58 percent) occurring from 1967 to 1969. The ARVN losses, on the other hand, averaged 18,000 to 20,000 per year during the 15-year period. For the four months of 1975, the losses during the highland withdrawal amounted to more than 40,000 people.

Table IV: Military Casualties

Year	United States	South Vietnam
1960	0	2,223
1961	11	4,004
1962	31	4,457
1963	78	5,665
1964	147	7,457
1965	1,369	11,242
1966	5,008	11,953
1967	9,377	12,716
1968	14,589	27,915
1969	9,414	21,833
1970	4,221	23,346
1971	1,381	22,738
1972	300	39,587
1973	237	27,901
1974	207	31,219
1975	(4 months)	40,000+ (estimate)
	46,370	294,256

Note: Modified from DL Anderson 2002: 290.

Table V: War Casualties

	Military Casualties	Civilian Casualties	Wounded
United States	58,000		300,000
South Vietnam	294,000	450,000	1,600,000
Viet Cong/North Vietnam	1,200,000 (est.)	70,000	

Note: Modified from DL. Anderson 2002: 289.

After the war, the *Tiết Thương* sculpture at the gate of the Biên Hòa National Cemetery was toppled. Graffiti was scrawled on headstones—many of which were knocked down. Graves were violated and headstones served as shooting targets. Grass grew everywhere, especially along the paths leading to the graves. Villagers from a nearby hamlet dug up the roads to sell the stones for house foundations. Soon all the paved roads became dirt roads that were invaded by weeds. No one was allowed to cut the grass or care for the cemetery. Lamb could do nothing but "[steam] about the desecration" of the cemetery:

> These were the faces and names of the vanquished.... For answering their government's call to duty—as nobly as Northern soldiers had answered Hanoi's—they had been dishonored by victors who desecrated their headstones and let the crabgrass run wild over their graves. In a country whose pride and dignity and sense of nationalism I had come to greatly admire, the cemetery stood as a symbol of national shame.[107]

Since that time, "a high cinderblock wall topped with rolls of barbed wire and overseen by watch towers" had been erected around the cemetery. More than 100 soldiers guarded it as a "military area. No picture allowed." Southerland wondered why the cemetery looked like an armed camp with its high walls and watchtowers. What did the government have to fear? Was it a prison for ghosts?[108] On the other side of the highway, lay a newly built cemetery for revolutionary soldiers. The headstones are "white, immaculate, and neatly marked. Some are adorned with flowers and urns containing sticks of incenses." The contrast could not be more glaring.

Saigon and South Vietnam not only lost the war, they lost close to 300,000 men and more than 450,000 civilians. The real number might be much higher since no 1975 ARVN statistics were kept after the war by any government.[109] There were also more than 1.6 million wounded civilians. ARVN veterans became the un-mourned and the neglected, for these losers had no future in Vietnam. They could not receive medical care, retirement or veterans' benefits and their widows received no pensions. They lived outside society, shunned by the victors and sometimes by their own families. They who once had dedicated their lives to the Saigon government suffered in shame, infamy, and poverty after the war.

Disabled southern war veterans were the ones who suffered the most. If they were glad to be alive, their disabilities became a long-term burden for themselves and their families. Northern paraplegics and those suffering from severe post-traumatic war symptoms were cared for at various northern rehabilitation centers. Disabled southern veterans, on the other hand, were left to fend for themselves.[110] Many were so distressed that they drank themselves to death.[111]

Taxes that Southerners paid covered the upkeep of northern cemeteries and the rebuilding of the North, with only a fraction coming back to the South. Northern cemeteries were "meticulously manicured, the grass carefully clipped, the gravel pathways spotlessly tidy." Mothers of northern soldiers killed in battle received "a one time payment of $272 and a life long monthly pension of $21 dollars, in addition to free medical care."[112] Mothers of southern soldiers got nothing.

Nguyễn Thị Lê had not mentioned her husband for 23 years. He, a then 25-year-old ARVN, was missing in action in 1973 when his unit was overrun by the VC. Her life had been over since that time. She had hoped he somehow would come back although he never did. She now lived in a two-bedroom, government-owned house with 12 children and grandchildren. She was two years in arrears of her $5 monthly rent and barely scraped enough together for daily meals. She would love to know how her husband had died, to search for her husband's remains and to give him a Buddhist burial, but could not afford the costs. Her husband was no traitor, she said, he loved Vietnam and served the country faithfully.

Hà Nội could have achieved reconciliation and healing after the war, but the paranoid leadership who wanted uniformity and control began instituting "unforgiving policies that would set Vietnam back thirty years or more." North Vietnamese troops were taught daily to "ignore the spirit of reconciliation, to ignore the warmth and passions among the remnants of this fallen, luxurious southern society. And especially to guard against the idea of the South having fought valiantly or been meritorious in any way."[113] Mothers of northern heroes have received medals and rewards, while mothers of southern troops bathe in humiliation.[114]

If the Americans had their Wall on the Mall in Washington, DC, their Arlington National Cemetery and the North Vietnamese their Đông Hà cemetery, the South Vietnamese had not had their moment of closure yet. They had no official place to mourn their dead. The Biên Hòa cemetery still lay in ruins three decades after the war, "an eerie stillness, populated only by the ghosts of the wartime past." Although the Hà Nội government talked about equality among all Vietnamese, the vivid contrast between the Đông Hà and Biên Hòa cemeteries reflects "the seeds of an unspoken conflict: reconciling North and South on a political level."[115] The gap is wide and has never been bridged. It reflects the continuing vindictiveness or arrogance of the northern government, a failure to forgive and to attempt to heal the wounds.

Former southern president, Nguyễn Văn Thiệu, once warned Southerners: "Do not believe what the communists say, but look at what they do." That advice stood the test of time. If a government could not officially dedicate a memorial to the 300,000 southern war-dead who had sacrificed their lives for freedom, it could not heal the deeper and longstanding war wounds. This arrogant attitude forces Southerners to live in limbo spiritually and emotionally. And although they are actively working under a communist government— either to pay their bills or to better themselves financially—they are far from embracing the communist philosophy or the invaders. They still feel like "foreigners" in their own country. Hồ Chí Minh, by importing a foreign theory, had become the divider instead of a unifier of the nation.

* * *

What the communists did to Saigon was worse than what Minh Mạng and the French had inflicted on the city. They stripped Saigon of its power, status, pride and wealth, and sent all males to prisons. They chased the elite out of the country, leaving only those who had nowhere to go. They hauled all Saigon's goods back to Hà Nội. The Saigonese were forced to lay low under the repression years. Having suffered during the 21-year war, they weathered the communist regime's vicious and unrelenting attacks and resisted them in three ways: escape, commercialization, and musical expression.

Private commerce was for many Southerners a way out of misery. It filled up their bellies, put their children through school, and allowed them to buy food and supplies for their jailed husbands. It gave them strength and a sense of direction and forced them to think for themselves. Private commerce, which began as a means of survival, became a way to deal with communism. It strengthened resiliency and resistance, opened the society up, and forced the Hà Nội government to liberalize the country. They soon realized that the communist system was broken and only free enterprise could lead to self-sufficiency.

Once the southern husbands returned home from reeducation camps, the savings generated gave them the means to escape abroad and to build a better world for themselves and their families. They built a new Saigon: Little Saigon in Orange County, CA, which would challenge Hà Nội's authority as the sole heir of the country. Although they do not live in Vietnam, they still influence the country's economy by sending home more than three billion dollars each year.

Southerners use their music as a way to express their emotions and feelings. Despite censure, yellow music thrives on. It reappears in cafes and restaurants in the South and spreads northwards, colonizing the eastern bloc where Vietnamese guest workers toil away from home.[116] Saigon and the South have managed to survive and thrive.

11

Resurgent Saigon
(1988–2010)

By 1986, after 21 years of war and 11 years of oppressive rule, the Vietnamese became weary and tired of the direction the Hà Nội government was headed. The government realized it had erred and slowly changed its rigid socialist policy. Thus was born đổi mới, or Vietnamese perestroika, a complete turnaround of the restrictive economic policy.

Reawakening

Efforts to convert the Saigonese to communist ideals fell by the wayside as the economy continued to go downhill. Right after the revolution, the *Tuổi Trẻ* (Youth) publication was filled with socialist themes of "heroism, resolute defense, collectivization of agriculture, elimination of the traces of the old regime." The Saigonese, however, charted their own course and a few years later all these "movements" became bankrupt.

This process was similar to the life of one of the *Tuổi Trẻ*'s editors. Born in central Vietnam, he registered at the Saigon's School of Pedagogy in the 1960s. Caught in a political demonstration, he was jailed. Once released, he went to the Tây Ninh jungle to join the resistance along with others like Trương Như Tảng. Confined to a small cubicle, he went through one year of training. Security was tight. He could not even see the other trainees and therefore, could not betray them if caught. He could only hear the instructor's voice. In 1978, he began to have second thoughts that led him to question the policies and directions of the communist government. He then realized that he had been blinded by communism, which had been his religion. He once "lived in a utopian paradise of Stalinism," but then had reawakened.[1]

The đổi mới reforms, passed at the 6th Party Congress in 1986, encouraged partial privatization and economic decentralization. Leaders admitted they "made mistakes ... and violated economic laws." But Hà Nội commented that the new policy was not a "conversion" to capitalism, but a "return" to a correct reading of the socialist classics. Kolko, however, did not buy this explanation. He wondered why it took a ruling party "fifty years to discover such inviolable rules in Marx' s writings." He denounced the policy flip-flop by asking why Hà Nội decided to fight a war that "cost millions of lives and caused immense suffering to drive 'out' foreigners only to turn around and appeal for aid from Americans, French, and Japanese."[2]

Lu Phương, a former party member and culture ministry official, had denounced neo-colonialism culture in the early 1980s. Following his reawakening in 1993, he criticized Hồ's adoption of socialism as a "simple-minded and ignorant choice and one that had been disastrous for the development of the nation." Marxism, he further added, was a doctrine that was not intended for Vietnam but had been applied in a "cynically pragmatic way to build up a repressive state." People were told to kowtow in front of their leaders as though they were monarchs from the past. The leaders then bestowed upon them a revolutionary theory which had been elevated to the level of "sacred political creed." They at the same time granted blessings to these people they looked upon as backward.[3]

Nguyễn Hồ was once one of the party's veteran soldiers in Saigon. In 1990, he resigned from the party and retired to the countryside. In 1994, he wrote in *My View and Life* that he felt free after leaving and no longer felt the iron pincers of the communist party:

> We have chosen the wrong ideology. Because more than 60 years on this revolutionary road, the Vietnamese people have endured incredible sacrifices yet achieved nothing in the end. The nation is still very poor, backward; the people are still without a comfortable, happy life, and have no freedom, no democracy. This is a shame![4]

VC General Phạm Xuân Ẩn remarked, "All that talk about liberation twenty, thirty, forty years ago, all the plotting, all the bodies produced this impoverished, broken down country, led by a gang of cruel and paternalistic half-educated theorists."[5]

Đổi Mới

When Lê Duẩn died in 1986 after being in power for 26 years, Vietnam was poorer than it had ever been. But Hà Nội leaders still thought of themselves as the center of the world and did not care about anything else. Almost all of the 6,000 state-run companies—heavy industries, hotels, grocery stores, beer halls—were losing money. Food and meat were rationed. Starvation was frequent and rice imports grew. Vietnam depended on Russia for survival and was as moribund economically as North Korea or Albania.

Following its failure to bring South Vietnam under its control, Hà Nội changed its policy and began recognizing the modernizing effects of the Republic of Vietnam on the delta. Nguyễn Khắc Viên, the northern doctor turned marxist chronicler, wrote that the South in the 1960s and 1970s, with U.S. help, had markedly improved machinery repair and agricultural expansion for peasants. It had created modern capitalistic centers that had improved wellbeing in the delta. He, however, suspected that the ultimate goal was to bring the South under the control of U.S. agribusiness.

President Thiệu's "land to the tiller program" eliminated big landowners and created a new class of middle peasants, who then constituted 70 to 80 percent of the peasant population. The middle peasant could have access to machinery, chemical fertilizers and new rice strains, and could adapt his production to market conditions. Unlike the poor peasant who just worked for subsistence, the middle peasant was opposed to any factor that could affect his income.[6]

By 1975, the majority of southern businessmen were small traders, with 8,132 enterprises in Saigon. They dealt with 45 countries in the world. Despite war, a small bourgeoisie had rapidly developed. South Vietnam had been a crucible of modernity and the southern peasant was noted to be a capable entrepreneur.

The đổi mới had been driven by the South, which rapidly broke out of the centralized subsidy economy and became the engine that drove the country into modernity. More recently Hà Nội had followed in Saigon's wake: selling lands, houses, building hotels, studying English. Although the North had caused a lot of upheavals and great losses, Saigon had resisted and survived.[7]

Three factors had been influential in Saigon and the South's recovery from socialism. First, the leadership in Saigon in the late 1970s allowed the director of state food to bypass the subsidy system and to buy rice directly from the delta for resale in Saigon. Second, the Long An party chief cancelled the voucher system, allowing people to buy and sell commodities at the market price. Third, Saigon allowed Southerners to receive money and goods from abroad, which then expanded the economy. The gold market began to grow.

Saigon's leaders responded to the needs of the population and politicians were flexible in interpreting socialism. They realized southern peasants did not want to participate in the collectivization of agriculture and industry. Opposition to socialism occurred in 1977 to 1980 when pressure from Hà Nội was the greatest. As the middleclass peasants resisted, the leaders felt the policies were unreasonable. Saigon could not be constrained by the economic policies of Hà Nội.

Saigon registered an upswing in commerce during the years 1989 to 1990, when Soviet bloc advisers were replaced by French and U.S. advisers. It saw a record rice export and became a home to seafood and freshwater fish industry.

Hà Nội realized that Southerners had unique personality traits: They were rustic and uncomplicated, generous to a fault, and prone to superstition but also fiercely nationalistic.[8] The farmers were industrious, patient, and creative in traditional wet rice culture; they could endure hardship. They could live in hamlets or isolated in their own fields. Living in a strange land and facing hardship, they had become united and mutually self supportive. They fought against wild beasts in dense forests and crocodiles in rivers, and an unfamiliar climate.[9] Having a pioneering spirit and a sense of adventure, they sought new horizons and were willing to defend their rights. Living in a bountiful land, they were less thrifty and mindful of the future than their northern counterparts.[10]

Saigon became an international hub in the '60s and '70s, although developments were negated by communist attacks. A commodity economy that had emerged in the 17th and 18th centuries was based on agriculture, ocean ports, and trade with foreign nations. This placed South Vietnam ahead of other regions in the country.[11] While pursuing the closed door policy, the Nguyễn allowed Saigon-Gia Định to continue its extensive overseas trade and opening of new lands. Private ownership and overseas trade allowed the South to become the granary of Vietnam.

When đổi mới was accepted in 1986 and implemented in 1990, the South had moved very far. Unshackled by regulations and agricultural collectivization, rice was produced in large quantities. Instead of just showing up for work to receive their quota of rice, farmers finally had the incentive to produce: the higher their production, the bigger their share. Production increased overnight: "lazy" farmers became motivated people. From being a rice importer, Vietnam became the second largest rice exporter in the world behind Thailand.

The bloated and uneducated Hà Nội bureaucracy began to worry about its future. The director of tourism might have excellent revolutionary credentials but she knew nothing about tourism. When journalists asked for interviews, she refused to grant any, which was unusual for a country that earned hard currency from that field.[12] While others thought about what they had to gain, Hà Nội leaders worried about what they had to lose and trod the đổi mới road with circumspection.

Foreign investors poured in capital right and left and paid two-year advances for a $5,000-a-month apartment. Hà Nội charged foreigners three times what the locals paid: It became the most expensive city to live in in the world. Coca Cola opened a plant outside the city, General Electric and General Motors, as well as many other industries, opened their offices there. Vietnam was expected to be the next Asian tiger.

By 1997, the bubble had burst because of a combination of corruption and reversal of the đổi mới policy. Conservatives, fearing for their loss of power, had outlasted the liberals and put a brake on the run. Someone once compared Vietnam to a turtle: sturdy but afraid to move forward. The only way to progress would be to stick out its neck and Hà Nội was not taking any risk. Investors began to pull out one after the other: Vietnam was a good place to live but not a good place to do business.

Despite the downturn, Saigon moved along while Hà Nội went back to the drawing board. Food production doubled between 1990 and 2000. Vietnam became the second rice and cashew nuts exporter in the world behind Thailand and India respectively, and the third largest coffee exporter behind Brazil and Columbia.

Coffee was planted in the highlands of the South. Introduced in 1920 by the French, it was highly appreciated by Southerners, especially the ca phe cứt chồn.[13] Everything Hà Nội put its hands on ended up in disaster. It even told farmers where to plant coffee although it knew close to nothing about coffee planting. The French grew the Arabica variety, a high quality plant that was extremely susceptible to disease and grew at a higher altitude (3,000 feet) than the coarser Robusta.

Coffee cultivation was modest between 1976 and 1986. People then switched to the Robusta variety and planted a million acres of plants between 1990 and 2000. Production soared and by 1994, Vietnam was among the ten largest coffee producers in the world. By 2000, it bypassed Columbia and only trailed Brazil. When frost damaged the Brazilian coffee crop in 1997, coffee prices soared and Vietnamese farmers prospered. By 2000, the coffee price came down and Vietnam was accused of flooding the market and upsetting balance between supply and demand. To eliminate the harsh Robusta flavor, marketers flavored coffee with hazelnut, French vanilla, and Irish coffee flavor. They also drenched the roasted beans in butter or fish sauce or passed the beans through the digestive systems of civets or lorises.

Success, however, has its downside. Lands were cleared and forests taken down, which increased soil erosion. Forest cover was reduced from 75 to 15 percent. There were also worries about unsustainable farming practices. The use of super-strong fertilizers destroyed the earth's nutrients and might "burn" the soil, affecting the livelihood of the next generation of farmers.[14]

The Rebuilding

The Lê Lai Hotel typified the bureaucratic dealings that went on within the communist government. Built in 1970, the hotel was nationalized by the government in 1975. In 1988, it came under the control of a powerful communist organization, Saigon Tourist. A year later, Saigon Tourist associated with Crystal Center Properties International to build a new hotel. By 1994, New World from Hong Kong jumped in to buy the rights of Crystal to build a 550-bed New World Hotel, a 25-story building with offices and a sports center.

Developers working in Vietnam needed patience in order to see projects through—a project could often take five years to complete. A developer would need to talk to a Vietnamese partner who was designated by the government, negotiate with him before proceeding with state negotiations, submit the paperwork with the State Committee for Investment and Cooperation, obtain a license, contact the contractors, import the necessary materials, deal with customs, accept sudden increases in prices from local vendors and landlords, deal with difficulties with transportation—and so on.

Since space was of prime importance, houses could not expand laterally. They went up two to three stories tall with a small base: tall, lanky buildings that rested on each other. By themselves they could easily topple down under the monsoon. People built everywhere without a thought to planning, aesthetics, or zoning. Three, four, or five stories could be raised on a foundation of 16 square meters.[15] Between the groups of buildings lay tiny three-to-four-feet sidestreets—wide enough for people to walk by or for a bike to get through. Behind the front buildings were more buildings that lodged more people—a growing population that Saigon needed to accommodate.

As the levels got higher, the terraces became larger—to the point that they were touching each other. At ten feet from the ground, a network of electrical wires of all sizes connected the houses to the main network. Denuded or connected together by cloth tapes, they formed loops, dropped drown because of their weight, mingled with others, and curved around the eaves before entering the buildings. Unauthorized wires were also used to divert electricity from the main network and caused a 50 percent loss of power. Electricity was cut twice a day between 20 to 60 minutes each.[16]

For the last 50 years, the war had caused the country to neglect the rebuilding or upgrading of the city's sewer system. The heavy monsoon rains rapidly overloaded the system, which regurgitated all its contents onto the streets. At the Tân Định market, rains could cause flooding with water rising up to two or three feet above street level. The sanitation crew attempted to clean up the debris, but the battle was usually unequal because the system built in the 1940s could not accommodate the overload.

This was also aggravated by the fact that industrial companies—rubber, chemical, pharmaceutical, textile, paper, concrete, garages, hospitals, hotels, markets—daily dumped 300,000 cubic meters of discharge into the river and canals. Two ecological disasters occurred on the Saigon River when two foreign ships accidentally discharged 200 tons of fuel and 1700 tons of diesel in 1994.

In the Chinese Arroyo and the Rạch Thi canal that bordered the southern end of the city and coursed through Chợ Lớn, the water is black, stagnant, with a constant bad odor.

Around the Thị Nghè Arroyo 300,000 people lived in huts on stilts without electricity and running water. Without sewer, they dumped everything into the arroyo. The government estimated there were 67,000 huts in that area in 1994 although the number could be higher. These are the city's poorest. They could not count on the state because many belonged to the "ghost village"—having no official residence papers, they lived on the margins of the society. They did not get any subsidy from the government, which practically ignored them.

Having no education and no training, they survived by taking on odd jobs. The best of them were masons, carpenters, or helpers in construction work. The rest worked as manpower for whatever industry needed them. They did the thousand menial jobs that no one wanted: selling newspapers, lottery tickets, carrying water, driving cyclo, gathering plastic bags, collecting bottles for resale to stores, tailoring, selling food and merchandise from one neighborhood to another, and so on. In the early 1990s, a few non-governmental organizations came by and taught the younger generation the basics of education and trade. The NGO's did not expect that these people would catch up with the rest of the Saigonese overnight, but they wanted to give them enough knowhow to lift them above the poverty line and to make them feel more human. The incidence of familial fights, alcoholism and violence seems to have decreased.[17]

The Embargo Is Lifted

On February 4, 1994, 19 years after the war ended, the U.S. lifted its embargo against Vietnam. A few hours later, Pepsi Cola distributed free cans of drinks on the streets of Saigon. Other countries had for some time invested heavily in Vietnam, rendering the embargo inefficient. In November 1994, Ford unveiled a car outlet with the following banner: "We are back."

The future middle class, who had been able to save some money, dollars or gold tael, began retrieving that money and injected it into the monetary system. The Bến Thành Market—the largest retail market in the region—found a new energy. This is where housewives from the neighborhood, the *nouveau riche*, and the bourgeois, came to shop—followed by a half-dozen mendicants trying to grab their attention.

Bến Thành Market sat on a square by itself. The main entrance at its southern end faced a huge roundabout. It was an indoor conglomeration of rows of stall—some small, others large—separated by narrow walkways. In one corner were rows of stalls dealing drapes, curtains and similar accessories. Close by were merchants of leather jackets, kitchen wares, clothing, watches, perfume, and so on. There were jeans of all kinds and colors, black, green, blue, from Lee Cooper or Levi Strauss, but made in China or in nearby factories. Shirts similar to those seen in New York, London or Paris hung in rows. Loud bargaining had become ritual—to the point that those who did not bargain were recognized as foreigners.

Outside the market on its northern end were set up stalls for flowers and fruit merchants. On the western side, farmers sitting on the ground sold their daily products in the open air. All around the square were stores that carried other types of merchandise. On the street pavement, small merchants sold soups, cigarettes, or advertised shoe repair. The market closed at 6 P.M. although activity continued all around it until 11 P.M.

In 1994, Lê Lợi Avenue still remained the main artery of downtown Saigon. It linked the roundabout of the Bến Thành Market to the municipal theater. Planted with trees at regular intervals, it was composed of a central avenue reserved for cars, flanked by two parallel streets, one on each side, reserved for two-wheeled motorcycles or bicycles. By 1994, there were only a few old cars traveling on Lê Lợi; the rest were bicycles. As one moved from the market to the municipal theater, one could find more and more upscale shops: cafés, ice cream shops, and lacquer and painting shops. Then the Rex hotel, which began as an automobile showroom in the 1960s, and the Abraham-Lincoln Commercial Center of the Americans of the 1970s.[18]

In April 1994, John Denver presented a musical concert at the theater: This was the first time for almost two decades that such a crowd was allowed to witness a show under the close watch of secret police. The crowd went crazy.

Chợ Lớn

Chợ Lớn is *the* wholesale market of Saigon, if not of the entire South. One can find fruit, flowers, peanuts, herbs, medicinal herbs, bamboo shoots, and rice: all the riches of the delta stop there before being shipped to other regions. Since 1986, commerce has returned to this city along with its cavernous storage hangars. One would be surprised to see so many riches in a country known as one of the poorest in the world.

Phước went into a 600-square-meter building where 4,000 wholesalers were conglomerated. In the center of the court was an empty pedestal where the stolen statue of Quách Đàm—a millionaire merchand—used to stand. He bought the market and built the building with his own money. The market was remodeled in 1982 by a group of Tawainese. This is where all the bargainings and transactions take place and where all the prices are fixed.

Imported products yield ridiculous margins that become important only because of the volume of the sale. Wholesalers fight for the exclusive right to a certain product which they can re-sell to distributors with a large profit. Success goes to those tenacious few who can bargain and maintain secrecy about the deal. However, yields are better with contraband goods that come from Thailand through Cambodia and elsewhere around the world. Whether perfume, mineral water, cigarettes, beauty products, or wine, one has only to look at what is sold at the market to realize more products are sold than imported. Without the excessive import taxes, these products could be sold below official prices with healthy margins.

Born to a Vietnamese mother and a Chinese father in 1931, Phước arrived in Saigon at the age of three. He went to Paris in 1953 where he graduated from the prestigious Sorbonne with a degree in economics and politics. In

1963, he gave advice to the South Vietnamese government about fixing the rice shortage. In 1966, Saigon turned to him again for advice against the rampant inflation. He liked to work behind the curtains rather than on stage. "Before 1975, life was easy. Everyone earned a lot and spent a lot," he said. "After 1975, everyone began to panic. We knew ... one week ahead that the communists would arrive in Saigon. People were afraid." He tried to stay calm while his mother burned his diploma to hide his past. He paid the police to prevent his two sons and his brother from being sent to the front. Phước stayed and tried to collaborate with the communists. In 1978, tensions between Hà Nội and Peking forced him to think about escaping: after failing 11 times and being confined to house arrest for seven months, he abandoned his attempts.

When the đổi mới was initiated in 1986, Chợ Lớn slowly reopened its business. Phước re-awakened and became the owner of a tourist agency. Collaborating with a Taiwanese "cousin," he opened a furniture store, which went belly-up. He lost again in a building construction venture. However, he still had 60 acres of land a few miles from Saigon and six factories in the Đồng Nai province.

He represented Pou Chen in negotiations with Biti, a Vietnamese firm, to build a shoe factory. To speed up the process, he asked Pou Chen to wire Biti 2.5 million dollars. Months later, there was still no land, although all the money had disappeared. Phước got mad and fought against Biti's chairman, another Chinese Vietnamese. Phước complained directly to Lê Đức Anh, the state president, and summoned the press to release a photocopy of the 2.5 million-dollar check endorsed by Biti. The fight had just begun.

The strength and vitality of the Chinese came from their overseas connections. The activity of Chợ Lớn was in the hands of powerful congregations—the center of which was located in China. The discreet Triều Châu are usually workers and craftsmen, while the proud and arrogant Cantonese are import-export merchants. The Fou Kien people grew tea and coffee and sold soup on mobile carts. These congregations built hospitals and schools, controlled the commerce and regulated social life. If one person behaved badly, he would be banished from the congregation, which was tantamount to excommunication.[19]

Chợ Lớn only had to wake up its dormant network. Today, as in the past, the stranglehold of the Chinese is strong, although not exclusive. They react faster than others when responding to commercial impulses. Their success is linked to their deep pockets, quietness and lack of interest in politics.

Unhealed Wounds

The story of Saigon lives in the stories of her inhabitants.

In February 1968, Lập, a 22-year-old law student, enrolled in a military academy. A year later as an aspirant, he was sent to Kampong Cham in Cambodia in 1971 to protect the Vietnamese living there from being massacred; his unit was ambushed and imprisoned by the North Vietnamese.

Prisoners underwent daily reeducation sessions during which they were considered traitors to the country. For the next four years, they were tied at night, two in a small hut, and un-tied in the morning so they could do community work. They cut or planted manioc during daytime, were interrogated regularly, and had monthly reeducation sessions. Before 1975, Lập was transferred to a northern camp. He was freed in 1976 and returned to Saigon to make room for new waves of prisoners.

All the shops in the city were closed or empty. The mood was sad and somber. Reporting neighbors to the police became the new game in town as good snooping was rewarded with a bag of rice. Poor people were sent to the NEZ. Lập did not have any choice because he had signed prior to his release to voluntarily move to a NEZ in Tây Ninh with his wife and son. They gave him a shovel and a pick to grow rice, potato, and manioc. The ground was dry, infertile and full of rocks. But everyone pretended not to see it. Unable to support his family, he escaped and became a fugitive.

Saigon two years after the liberation was a dead city. There was neither fuel nor cars on the streets. People lived on rations doled out by the state. Stores often ran out of products, leaving people hungry. Coffee and sugar, when available, were considered luxuries. The poor sold them to the rich or traded them for rice. Lập lived on the streets around groups of poor and homeless people since he could not afford to be seen at home. An escapee from a NEZ, he had fought for the South and was "re-educated" for five years: He had too many black marks. He sold old clothes to survive and lived in daily fear.

Caught in a police raid, he had to reveal his identity. Sentenced for three years to the Tổng Lê Châu reeducation camp near Sông Bé, he ended up serving five more years. By 1983, he had logged ten long years in communist jails. He became a cyclo driver, pedaling a three-wheeled bicycle with a seat in front for passengers. This was a hand-to-mouth job that required him to work almost every day. He had to rent the vehicle and pay a fee at the end of the day. The excessive fee, however, ate up the majority of his daily income.

In 1986, Lập applied for emigration to the U.S. through the ODP program. But since the four years he spent as a prisoner in the Cambodian forest did not count because the United States was not officially at war with Cambodia at the time, his request was rejected.

In 1990, a Swiss man asked him to serve as a guide around the city. Lập traded his daily job with that of a tour guide. He made a living for a while until the cafes organized minibus tours for their clients, stealing clientele away from him. His income went down.

Although he had been through a lot, Lập did not complain because he realized many officers ended up in worse situations than he. The whole city had gone through the same ordeal for two-and-a half decades. The dark years needed not be retold: They were forever suspended in history and fixed in the memory of the Saigonese.[20]

At age 55, Minh Hương was still unable to forget the past. Two of her brothers were sent to a reeducation camp. She even visited one of them in a northern camp. Every day, she used her old motorized bicycle to go to work. Although she hated the communists, *she needed to forget so she could live again.*

Before 1975, she was a schoolteacher with a promising career. Her aunt assisted her with building three apartments, which she rented out. After 1975, the communists had her come to the police department to sign away the apartments to the state. Her school was nationalized and her salary cut. Since her brothers were soldiers from the Saigon government, she was blacklisted. She survived with the money her brothers sent her from the U.S. Tired, she asked to emigrate to the U.S. but was turned down. The headmistress attempted to extort money from her. In the end, she resigned. She wanted to get out of the country but was afraid to escape by boat.

She continued to ask the government to return her properties. In the late 1980s, she learned that foreign languages would be taught again at school and contact with strangers allowed. In 1992, she finally got a certificate on the old property she lived in. This was a dilapidated building she did not have money to keep up and upgrade. The government would resell the other three apartments to finalize their status. Minh Hương was tired: She no longer wanted to fight against a brutal machinery that just kept irritating her. She had found work as a translator with foreign companies that paid her well, although her lifestyle still remained modest.

She turned to meditation and religion to get rid of all her troubles. She just wanted to be alone and detached from the worldly desires of this life. Her Buddhism is more than a collection of rites: It is a state of mind and a goodness of heart that need to be spread out to others.[21]

Hà Nội and Saigon

Life has always been easier and more secure in the southern part of the country. Southern villages have always been more open, less corporate, and more tolerant of initiative and cultural orthodoxy. When South Vietnam was a colony under French administration, it experienced more political freedom than did the rest of the country.[22]

When the communists took over Hà Nội in 1954, more than half of the Hanoians left their city for Saigon. The rest were sent out to the NEZ where they vegetated in misery. Hồ then filled Hanoi with his soldiers and peasants from the Nghệ Tịnh and Thanh Hóa regions. Therefore, these post–1954 Hanoians did not possess the distinctive Hanoian culture, language and voice tonality of the pre–1954 Hanoians.

The same population shift occurred again after 1975. When Saigon fell, most of the post–1954 Hanoians moved to Saigon to take the place of the Saigonese who had fled abroad. Another 500,000 to 1,000,000 Saigonese were displaced to the NEZ, although the majority came back to live on the fringes of the society. But the new arrivals never completely dislodged the old Saigonese because there were too many of them. Although they held the top administrative positions, they were assimilated by Southerners.

In 1985, the elegant French colonial buildings on Đồng Khởi Street (old Tự Do) looked badly run down. The old boutiques and bars of the 1974 to 1975 years were closed, some converted into gloomy state-run shops offering poor-quality merchandise. Men and women wore blue or white shirts outside dark trousers. By 7 P.M., most stores and restaurants had closed, and by 9 P.M., people were in bed. A year later, in 1986, a rebirth had begun with street ped-dlers hawking their wares. By the end of the 1980s, the city had regained its flashing neon lights and display windows. Shops on Lê Lợi, Nguyễn Huệ and Đồng Khởi reopened for business, served by cheerful sales clerks.[23]

If Saigon could be compared to New York with its up-tempo beat and economic clout, then Hà Nội is Boston. Hà Nội is smaller and more refined and austere than its southern sister-city. The Southerners think and do; the Northerners think and they think some more. The entrepreneurs live in Saigon, the poets in Hanoi.[24]

Saigon is driving Vietnam's economy. Her per-capita income is more than three times the national average of $1 per day. The city alone contributes one third of both the national budget and the national output. She accounts for two thirds of the nation's wealth and 80 percent of the tax revenues.[25] What Saigon symbolizes is an economy that rewards initiative, free enterprise, liberal ideas and frees itself from rigid government control.

Saigon had always been "an extraordinary *yin* city. It was considerably younger, bigger, richer, more diverse and lustier than Hà Nội or Huế. Bud-dhism, Taoism, and Catholicism joined with rampant secularism to dilute the rigid *yang* of its Neo-Confucian heritage."[26]

Saigon is the antithesis of Hà Nội. She is loud, aggressive, expansive, and market-oriented. Trained for centuries to be independent and resourceful, she has retained the entrepreneurial spirit of the old pioneers who shaped the history of the South.

Saigon and Hà Nội had a difficult relationship: separated, opposed and then reunited, they formed a strange pair of siblings. More than anything, they reflected the mood of their citizens. The North had won the power, the South claimed economic success and development. The gap in development is widen-ing between Saigon and the rest of the country. Saigon receives more tourists and businesspeople and has more deluxe hotels, more varied restaurants, and attractions than the jealous Hà Nội. Equipment and construction companies prefer Hà Nội, where the ministries are located. Saigon is vibrant, a city of enjoyment and attraction, open to the world and obsessed with consumerism, while Hà Nội is cold, suspicious, closed, and strongly influenced by communist ideology.[27]

Presidents Bush and Clinton—who both avoided serving in Vietnam—saw Hà Nội differently during their visits. Mr. Bush did not spend much time there: 15 minutes at the Joint Accounting Command that was looking for American MIA and no real interaction with the Hanoians. He attended Sunday mass at the French-built Cửa Bắc Cathedral to underscore the need for greater religious freedom. During this visit, the local police took activist Phạm Hồng Sơn into custody for eight hours and beat him up.

Thousands of people poured into the streets in 2000 to greet Mr. Clinton: They lined up from the Nội Bài International Airport to downtown to just catch a glimpse of him. This was a spontaneous outpouring of people, which made Mr. Clinton more popular than the Vietnamese head of state. He later toured the millennia-old Temple of Literature, mingled and took time to speak with Hà Nội students. He took the two sons of missing airman Lt. Col. Evert to a rice paddy north of the city to look for his bones; the airman's plane was shot down during the war and had landed on the field. Mrs. Clinton went to the city's Old Quarter—the requisite stop for all foreigners in Hà Nội—where she bought ten raw silk shirts for her husband. Ever since that time, the square collar of the men's silk shirt—which had been there for more than a millennium—has been renamed the "Bill Clinton collar."[28]

In Saigon, the reaction of the people was most lively. Clinton again mingled with the Saigonese and had lunch at Phở 2000. Phở—from the French pot au feu—is the Vietnamese traditional beef noodle soup, which started in Hà Nội in the 1920 to 1930s and later spread all over the country. Vietnamese cooks working for the French adapted the pot au feu recipe for their families. Instead of vegetables and beef, they used beef bones to preserve the smell and texture without the high cost of meat. In the cool northern climate, phở caught on like wildfire and became the traditional soup for the Vietnamese.

Northerners brought phở with them to the South in 1954. In the steamy, hot southern environment, phở lagged behind the other noodle soups: mì and hủ tiếu. It was only in the late 1960 to '70s that the modified phở—with the addition of bulky portions of beef and vegetables—took an upward swing.

In 1975, the Vietnamese brought phở to the U.S., which metamorphosed into something different from the native version. The noodle and beef portions took on gargantuan sizes. Phở then made its way back to Saigon through a Việt Kiều who opened a Phở 24 restaurant—open 24 hours a day—to serve foreigners. The place was also cleaner than other local phở restaurants. Phở 24 had also expanded to Hà Nội to cater to an increasing influx of foreigners.

This was how the phở formula, after circling the globe and being transformed through migrations and cultures and improved by various palates, returned to the city of its birth—to the bewilderment of the natives.

Mr. Clinton ordered a bowl of phở at Phở 2000, opened in 2000. He liked it so much that he ordered a second one. He then had a picture taken with the owner. Today, a large picture of Mr. Clinton and the owner presides over the dining place and the chair on which Mr. Clinton sat has been encased in glass and is displayed on the wall.[29]

Mr. Bush, on the other hand, just opened the Saigon Stock Exchange on 20 November and slipped out of town. The exchange began in 2000 with only two companies and two bonds. Today it has 56 stocks with a total capitalization of 3.5 billion dollars.

The Việt Kiều

The Saigon Tân Sơn Nhứt Airport is always full of returning Việt Kiều—especially close to the Tết season. On one side, elegantly dressed middle-aged men and women, children tagging along, pushed carts loaded with heavy luggage and gifts. And on the other side, groups of simple but neatly dressed Saigonese were excited and impatient about finally meeting their lost relatives. They then congregated outside the gate, two groups of people born on the same soil, separated after the war and finally reunited again amid floods of tears, hugging, sobbing, and hysterical laughing. They had not seen each other for the last two or three decades and could no longer contain their repressed emotions. The scene is unique to the Saigon airport because the diaspora was a uniquely southern phenomenon. Saigon had sent many of its best, brightest and most adventurous people abroad and they came home to reunite with their folks, to do business or try to improve the well-being of their people. And they came from all over the world—from America and California mostly—but also from Canada, France, England, Australia, Germany, Switzerland.

Kiệt is an engineer from France: He takes three weeks off in January to see his relatives and to reconnect with his childhood's neighborhood. During the Tết holidays, he and his cousins eat bánh chưng and bánh tét[30] and drink beer and rice wine until they become completely drunk. He goes fishing in the small pond beside the country house and watches young children riding on the backs of buffaloes. Although he likes the countryside, he feels estranged from this land where the communists are now the masters. As Vietnam moves backward, its lifestyle is different from the one he has experienced in France.

Only 30,000 Việt Kiều dared to return to Vietnam in 1990 and nine times more in 1995 due to the growing openness of the government. During the dark years, the money they sent back to Vietnam kept their relatives from sinking: 700 million dollars in the late '80s to more than four billion today. That money was used to buy motorbikes, a refrigerator, a TV set, which few local people could afford. It might also be invested in a store or a house. The packages they sent included cigarettes, socks, shampoo, creams, aspirin, cough products, and especially antibiotics.

However, the Việt Kiều do not form a uniform group. They went abroad in waves. First came the 1960s and early 1970s students who went abroad for study and never returned home. The 1975 wave of refugees consisted of highly-educated people or government officials who left the country right after the war. The 1980s and 1990s waves came more for economic than political reasons.

Văn considers himself a Frenchman. He studied in France in the late 1960s and married a French woman with whom he has two children. After 1975, he felt he could not be communist and opted to become a French citizen. He now returns to Vietnam mainly to do business for a French firm. Knowing the language and the customs is a big asset for him and his company.

His friends, however, had a different experience: They went back to Vietnam five or ten times before finally backing out in the face of the multiple barriers erected by the Hà Nội government. Hà Nội wanted to extract their knowledge and know-how but did not want to give anything back. They refused to accept them and to return their former assets and properties. They treated the Việt Kiều as foreigners as far as taxes were concerned. It was not until 1993 that Việt Kiều taxes were cut back compared to those of foreigners, allowing them to invest more easily in Vietnam. Việt Kiều, however, did not enjoy foreigners' political immunity if they got involved in local politics: A Việt Kiều would land in jail like any Vietnamese local. Lý Tống, a Vietnamese American, dropped leaflets over Saigon urging people to rise against the regime. He was caught and sentenced to 20 years of confinement in 1992 but was released in 1998 under outside pressure.

Mistrust has always been present between Hà Nội and the Việt Kiều. Hà Nội suspects them of fomenting dissension for the purpose of establishing democracy in Vietnam. It watches them closely and even sends police to check on them in the middle of the night. It slows down passport delivery, blocks their investments, and causes conflicts during discussions. When a group of Việt Kiều sent a million-dollar piece of equipment to improve the diagnostic capability of a hospital, Hà Nội quarantined it for years without explaining why. The machine sat idle in a hangar while patients waited for it. When another group sent thousands of dollars worth of medicine and engineering books, Hà Nội never released them, leaving students struggling with outdated books. When a local doctor decided to open up a new field of treatment for her patients and contacted her Việt Kiều friends in the U.S. for help, she told them to make any assistance program small so that it could pass under Hà Nội's radar—otherwise, it would incur the risk of being curtailed or cancelled.

Hà Nội loves to control everything, impose its position and will, and drag its feet—mostly because it does not know how to handle the situation. Recently opened to western business, its leaders, with their 18th-century minds, have difficulty adapting to the 21st-century world and to being open, transparent, and accountable. When religious groups in Saigon with monetary help from the Việt Kiều decided to open an orphanage, they just expanded their quarters and used the additional space to care for the children rather than seeking Hà Nội's approval or rejection for a new building. Dealing with Hà Nội has been more than difficult, as many foreigners can attest.

Besides, one can also detect a low-grade animosity or a jealous feeling from the part of the locals who, although they admire the Việt Kiều, do not like to see them come back and sit at the head of the table. Locals who could not get out in time suffered the most during the dark years, harassed and mistreated by the government, and now have to tolerate the newcomers. Some Việt Kiều indeed did not behave well in Saigon: They taunted their newly acquired wealth, flashed their cell phones and jewelry, talked loudly in public to let people know who they were, criticized the dirtiness of the streets, the poverty of the country, and occasionally behaved more outrageously than the Americans. They gathered themselves in small groups to sing American songs, and play jazz and golf instead of melting into the landscape. Not all Việt Kiều are like that—just a few bad apples that ruined the reputation of the rest of the group.[31]

The Việt Kiều—overseas Vietnamese—who escaped abroad at the end of the war scattered over more than 70 countries worldwide. They arrived worn out, dispirited, depressed, penniless, and did not even know the language of their host countries. In the U.S., the 130,000 first arrivals received a mixed reception.[32] Critics of the Vietnam War had minimal sympathy for the refugees. They complained that more than half of the refugees were low-level soldiers, bar girls, farmers, and people not at risk for political reprisals, while many who could not escape faced jail, reeducation camps and even death in Vietnam. Hawks (anti-war critics), however, thought refugees deserved American concern.[33] A backlash from the war, high unemployment in the late 1970s, and anti-immigrant sentiment made the adaptation to the new culture worse. With the same determination and drive to survive that guided them through the traumatic two-decade war, they rolled up their sleeves and began working. They spurned no job. A former senator sold fried chicken for a grocery store, a Supreme Court justice became a hotel watchman, doctors worked as nurses in a psychiatric hospital.[34] Hard work, family solidarity, pride and steadfast purpose gradually lifted the refugees up.

Thirty years later, everything had completely changed. The same risk-taking, courageous, and entrepreneurial spirit that drove the Việt Kiều to leave everything behind in Vietnam and to take tremendous risks during their escapes helped them succeed in the new countries.

They are now three million strong and most of them are achievers. In the

U.S., Việt Kiều hold important positions in research institutions, universities, hospitals, the computer industry, and on Capitol Hill. More than a dozen are CEOs of high-tech Silicon Valley firms.[35] Better educated than those who stayed back, they also have deep pockets. Hà Nội estimated that the "Việt Kiều economy" generated $20 billion a year. More than 300,000 overseas Vietnamese have been awarded university and post-graduate degrees in their adopted countries.

There are more Vietnamese medical doctors working abroad than in Vietnam. Almost all Saigon medical doctors who stayed back after 1975 were sent to reeducation camps. After the fall of Saigon, while Dr. A. vegetated in a reeducation camp doing hard manual labor, his physician-wife was shipped to a remote village to supervise the construction of outdoor communal latrines. This job could have been easily accomplished by a nurse-technician. But caught in a vindictive and misguided mood, the communists punished all Southerners and disregarded their qualifications while valuing only the fact that they belonged to a particular party. After two-and-a half years of hard manual labor (pulling a plough in place of a buffalo, digging canals, taking down trees, farming), Dr. A. was released. He and his wife eventually escaped on a boat using false identities.[36] After completing their residencies, they are now well-established practitioners in the mid–Atlantic region.

In communist Vietnam, to deal with the vacuum created by the lack of physicians, nurses without any medical training were promoted to the rank of physicians—with disastrous results. Doctors who returned from the camps were on many occasions not used according to their experience and training simply because they did not belong to the party.[37]

Việt Kiều who returned home did not feel welcome. They were treated as foreigners or as locals depending on Hà Nội's whims. In the 1990s, they not only required visas, but also had to be declared sane and sound by physicians before being allowed to land in Vietnam. No such psychological assessment was required of any other foreign visitor. They were charged foreigners' rates for hotels, transportation, and communications, along with a five percent tax on remittances they sent to their families in Vietnam. Every returnee was tracked by Hanoi's pervasive internal security agents. They had to stay in hotels and could only visit their families during the daytime.[38]

Thái, a Việt Kiều born and raised in California, went to study for a semester at the University of Hà Nội in 1995. After graduating from the University of Washington, he returned to Hà Nội with $700 and the goal of opening an outdoor coffee shop. When business prospered, his Vietnamese partners elbowed him out and kept the place for themselves. He became bankrupt and had only $3.50 left to spend. His mother who came to visit him cried. Her son had lost 15 pounds and lived in an apartment with only a mattress and chair as furniture. Thái was, however, a workaholic and an optimist. Within days, he leased the patio of a faded downtown villa and opened a new coffee shop, which he called Au Lac Café. This venture turned out to be a bigger success than the first one. He brought western concepts to an eastern setting to make the business work. He taught his young workers, all college students, about teamwork and long-term goals. He gave them a share of the profits. He went on to invest in a coffee plantation and a coffee export business. On the other hand, many investors lost hundreds of thousands of dollars and the chance to rebuild their businesses because the legal structure in Vietnam was primitive and written contracts were not enforceable.[39] Even large companies had folded in the past.

Younger Việt Kiều were the ones who returned first. They had fewer pre-conceived ideas than their parents. They, however, also had a few strikes against them. Local people resented them because they had not shared their suffering under the communist "Dark Years." They also envied them for their education and deep pockets. Hà Nội was also suspicious of their knowledge and Vietnamese roots: It saw them as potential adversaries.

The Việt Kiều represent a new way of being Vietnamese. Like Nguyễn Hoàng, who turned away from the old Thăng Long (Hà Nội) monarchy in 1600,[40] they too turned their backs to Hà Nội and the communists. Breaking free from the two-decade politico-military, they moved abroad, denying Hà Nội's control over their future and struggled to participate in a world of options and choices where talent and ability count more than dogmatism and party affiliation.[41]

The Lost Children

The living results of the war are still present on the streets of Saigon three decades later. Many have been severely injured or maimed by destructive bombs and mines; others, especially children, earn their living by themselves. Saigon may not only have more of these unfortunate people than other countries because of the long war, but also because authorities lack social programs and funding that would take care of them.

There are bilateral amputees who move around on skateboards displaying their stumps to strangers while asking for money, people with polio and their atrophied limbs, and women carrying their inert children on their backs. They all came out in the morning and disappeared in poor neighborhoods in the evening.

And then there are the children, age five to 15, who have skipped or never known school and have to fend for themselves at an earlier age than others. Public education, which is supposed to be free in a socialist country, has become a private paying system. Parents have to bribe the teachers to pay special attention to their children. Poor parents in the city, but especially in the countryside, have pulled their children out of school to help them with their work. In case both parents work, children are left alone and are free to roam the streets.

The socialist system, by decreeing that minors are state property, has significantly weakened familial bonds. Children are encouraged to criticize or report their parents. The animosity created markedly changes the fabric of the society. Other effects include an increase in the number of divorces, separations and concubinage.

Children arrive from the North and the highlands through the train station, attracted by the image of a wild and rich Saigon, which serves as a strong magnet. They mingle and work on passengers by pretending to help them out. When caught in the act, they are taken to the police station, punished for the day and then return to work the following morning. At the Saigon port where prostitution and contraband are common, they work under the supervision of adults. Their roles are either to check on the girls or pass contraband items. At the zoo, they follow visitors and look for the leftover meals. At Bến Thành market, they wake up at 3 A.M. to forage in the dumpsters prior to the arrival of the garbage trucks. They sell a bag full of recyclable objects for 60 cents. They can collect up to three bags on a good day.

The number of children on the streets is unknown. Some came with their mothers from the highlands. Ethnic highlanders who could not adapt to the communist assimilation program ran away from their homeland. They came to the cities looking for food and work. Adopted children freed themselves at age five or six. Others escaped from their families. They worked solo or in groups and slept under a tree, the eaves of a restaurant, or in a building under construction.

Those who work on Đồng Khởi Avenue concentrate on the rich, tender and naive travelers who frequent the hotels, diners and eateries of this neighborhood. They brush shoes, sell postcards, cigarettes, chewing gum, and newspapers. They sell pineapples, nuts, coconuts, or are pickpockets.

The children are afraid of the police who can put them in the famous School Number Three—renamed in 1994 as the Center of Education and Culture of the Children. It is a jailhouse from which children escape in the middle of the day because of lax surveillance and where food is scarce and treatment is harsh. If authorities are torn between strict discipline and simple education, children prefer the streets rather than School Number Three.[42] Some children live by scouring for food or items they can sell back to the market, like empty wine bottles and cans. They work in these unsanitary areas eight hours or more a day, breathing noxious fumes.

Corruption

Corruption in Vietnam has reached epidemic proportions. By writing its own rules, Hà Nội was able to legalize the seizure of houses, private properties and buildings belonging to Southerners prior to 1975—by taking them privately and selling them cheaply to party members.

A large business company that wants to import products into Vietnam has to acquire the services of a Vietnamese representative approved by the state. For a three percent fee on the contract, he will help the company navigate the bureaucratic hurdles. That amount has to be in cash, for cash is hard to trace to anyone in particular. In other countries, a similar thing occurs in the form of perks, cars or other products that can be easily written off as company expenses.

If in the beginning Hà Nội tried to hide these deviations, now it does not even attempt to hide the responsibilities of its officials. In the 1990s the privatization of Legamex, a model state enterprise, was delayed because of the arrest of its president for embezzlement of funds. In May 1995, the president of the People's Committee of Saigon-HCMC, Trương Tấn Sang, noted that corruption by city officials amounted to one million dollars and 824 gold taels, each worth $1,000. In 1996, national and local presses loudly complained about Dr. Trung, the Saigon health commissioner, for 20 years co-director of two foreign pharmaceutical companies and director in charge of importing medical equipment for the Saigon hospitals. The articles accused him of importing sophisticated equipment at overvalued prices. Some argued that the doctor was a genuine man of science who just wanted to help his country; others, including many foreign pharmaceutical companies, vilified him by calling him "Mister 15 percent."[43] By 1996, he was let go without having any charges filed against him.

To fight against corruption, in January 1995 the party gave Prime Minister Võ Văn Kiệt the power to approve all contracts worth more than 40 million dollars. Nine months later, the same power was reassigned to the newly formed State Committee on Cooperation and Investment. The shift merely underlined the weakness of the central government and its inability to impose its decisions on local organizations. The Socialist Republic acted like a feudal empire in which local officials could oppose or ignore any decision made by Hà Nội. One diplomat commented, "The power of the [Hà Nội] ministers stopped at the door of local officials who could modify any regulation without being held accountable."

The extent of the problem prevented the government from enforcing its rule without dismantling the whole structure. The innumerable section chiefs and department heads, armed with their threatening red stamps, had the power to hold up a procedure or plan in order to squeeze out a fee. They fought to preserve their turf and their share of the pie without thinking about public interest.

Officials, therefore, have the ability to squeeze out profits, but also to raise the costs of doing business in Vietnam. The rights to open a business— window representation—which costs $5,000 dollars, could double that amount if transactions dragged on for six or 12 months. A license to invest in an industrial project costs two million dollars. International assistance, which was plentiful by the end of 1993, ran against the slowness of the procedures and the inability of various departments, to coordinate the funds and to spread them out.

With any bidding, came an army of "consultants" comprised of important personalities, service chiefs, vice-ministers, ministers, and even members of the Assembly. It began with gifts for the lowly secretaries: small gifts of $100, 200, 400 dollars or jewelry at most. Each bidder gave something to the members of the subcommittees. As the process moved upward to the national level, money became bigger: A member of the committee received $10,000 dollars to move the right candidate ahead. Treason is frequent and Vietnamese consultants pay double agents who reveal opponent's projects and make entire files go missing. Within this environment one foreigner noted, "Vietnam is the only market where the price of the bidding counts. Technical details do not play an important role in the evaluation."

Poorly paid and unable to sustain their families, state officials and employees divert some of the circulating money into their pockets. While customs agents live in poverty, they see in front of them containers of expensive television sets and video sets. Two decades of an authoritarian system during which any official could lose his job to his boss' nephew has imprinted in the minds of many a tendency to think in the short-term.

There are so many ways for officials to make a living off their jobs. Padding additional costs or levying new local taxes is so common they have become official. Visits to merchants are used as a means to raise money. Two or three cops went into a local business pretending to check around and got to talk to the owner. The latter took them to lunch. A few hours later, they split up, smiles on their faces. When the Việt Kiều arrive or depart from Tân Sơn Nhứt airport, they face similar problems with customs agents. The latter might wave them by or even smile at them if visitors were to slip five- or ten-dollar bills into their passports. Otherwise they have to go through lengthy searches as well as other unnecessary procedures.

Every service rendered to an individual seems to require a fee in a poor country, especially in communist Vietnam. Besides the basic need to feed their families, that tendency can be traced to greed as well as the lack of discipline of leaders who condone it or do nothing to stop it. The depth and breath of this social disease propelled Vietnam into the group of most corrupt countries in the world.

Reliable institutions like religious groups have also been found guilty of funds embezzlement from humanitarian operations financed by foreign organizations. One Catholic priest, a deputy member of the National Assembly, was known for his high style of living. A founder of factories that were supposed to provide jobs for poor people, he later filed for bankruptcy, although he was never able to satisfactorily explain the disappearance of all the funds. A cursory review of his organization finances revealed that some of the money went to families that were not needy at all. University education has also suffered from corruption. The requirements for getting a degree from a state university include being able to sprint 100 meters and fire an AK-47.[44]

In a city deprived of goods and money since 1975, the sudden influx of large amounts of money has somewhat changed the concept of honesty. As communism has tossed aside familial piety and replaced it with allegiance to the party, it brushes aside the basic Confucian rules of decency.

Corruption has become part of the social fabric in communist Vietnam from North to South.[45] It is becoming worse and worse. An American Fortune 500 firm wanting to set up a plant in HCMC was told it would need $15,000 just to bring together the officials who would consider the application.[46] When the state owned everything and employed everyone, officials would pilfer cement, gasoline, or office supplies to sell them on the black market. Corruption was "worse under socialism than under the earlier feudal regime because moral values were no longer important."[47]

By making people poorer, communism has unleashed in them an uncontrollable urge and need for money that eventually leads them to perform dishonest acts. This is supported by recent studies documenting the fact that the mere sight of money can change human behavior. Students exposed to even trivial amounts of money, whether real or fake, tend to be less sociable and less generous than those who are shown neutral concepts.[48]

Vietnam is a society of two classes: the very rich and the very poor. The gap between the top and the bottom is getting wider. There is one set of rules for the rich and powerful and another for the poor.[49] The super-rich are the party members—nouveaux riches—who, after making money from other people, live in glamorous houses and drive fancy cars. The Communist Party elite are turning Vietnamese capitalism into a family business. One of Vietnam's richest men is Trương Gia Bình, CEO of a company called FPT, which started as a state-owned company called "Corporation for Food Processing Technology," is now the first Vietnamese IT firm. He was once married to a daughter of Võ Nguyên Giáp, war hero, one-time deputy prime minister. In the 1990s, any business that dealt with communication or construction had to see Giáp. The junior tier of this elite—provincial bosses, government officials—is called COCC or Con Ông Cháu Cha, literally, "son of father, grandson of grandfather." They can get away with anything, for their patrons outrank the police and the courts. The real elite is known as 5C or Con Cháu Các Cụ Cả, literally, "all children and grandchildren of the great grandfather." The Cụ here stand for the national president or the party secretary general. The 5C can get away with absolutely anything.[50]

Behind the glamour and glitz of fancy buildings, houses and cars, is the huge mass of disinherited and poor people who cannot afford education, food, housing or healthcare. Education and healthcare are no longer free. The patient has to pay in order to receive medical treatment. One of our friends, who was found to have Hodgkin's disease (a lymph node cancer), had to pay for his surgery and hospitalization. His friends in the U.S. sent him money so that he could receive his radiation treatment.

The Vietnamese and Saigonese are now running after money—they have always been commerce-oriented—more than before. They live day-by-day and do not think about the future. It is a philosophy of opportunism and the short-term. They want to grab as much as they can because the government and the công an (security force) could shake them any time. Very few people are thinking in the long-term. This is a society with weak laws that do not protect consumers. Therefore, they tend to bribe or settle to get away from fighting against the government or party members. According to Carl Thayer, Vietnam has 6.7 million công an out of a working population of 43 million. This suggests that one in six works either full or part-time for a security force.[51]

The Heritage Foundation/*The Wall Street Journal* placed Vietnam 144 out of 179 on the Index of Economic Freedom in 2010. In regards to press freedom, Reporters Without Borders placed Vietnam 166 out of 175 (2009). For corruption, Vietnam fell to 120 out of 180 (2009), again at the lower tier of the list. And the U.S. Commission on International Religious Freedoms included Vietnam among 11 worst nations in 2008.

Nguyễn Thị Châu Giang's painting *He is Inside of Me*, exhibited at the Rutgers-Camden Center for the Arts in September 2007, portrayed magnificently the mentality of the Saigonese. On the outside, they appeared to be happy or to even smile. But deep inside, they are not smiling and they pretend not to see what is going on under the communist regime (the woman in the painting has a patch on her right eye). Smiling used to be one of the characteristics of the Vietnamese, especially Southerners. They smile whenever they are happy or upset or embarrassed.[52] Even the French and the Americans never understood what that smile meant. The smile was often flashed as a sign of peace, for they did not want to deceive or disappoint other people. The absence of smile that was seen in this portrait or on Northerners' faces, therefore, indicates serious problems. Under a steely, oppressive, and unyielding regime, Southerners like cut flowers wilt away to present a saddened face that no longer smiles to the world.

2007

As of 2007, exports and investments continue to grow: Vietnam exported 1.2 billion dollars of rice in the first ten months of 2006.

Intel Corp, the world's largest chipmaker, has invested 1 billion dollars in Vietnam and built a 300-million-dollar plant in Saigon, which employs 1,200 workers. This is the largest single U.S. investment after the war.

Lotte Shopping Co., Korea's largest department store, opened its first store overseas in Saigon. The investment is worth 11.3 billions. APEC Asian Pacific Economic Cooperation has 5,681 projects with a total 41.7 billion in Vietnam.

Vietnam ranks just behind India as far as outsourcing is concerned. Vietnam has a five-billion-dollar trade surplus vis-à-vis the United States.

The old Saigon Tân Sơn Nhứt Airport built by the French in 1930 was upgraded to an international airport in 1956 with a 2,400 m runway. French, Japanese, and American military planes landed and took off from the airport during the Indochinese Wars. The Republic of Vietnam Air Force also maintained its squadrons there. During the war, it was one of the busiest airports in the world, handling not only passenger but also military airplanes. It was bombed and shelled by communist forces. A C123 carrying a load of orphans exploded on the runway after being hit by a communist missile in mid–April 1975.

Tân Sơn Nhứt saw many local and foreign leaders and investors come and go. It was an old and worn out airport that has sustained the life and business of the city and its people until today. The new international terminal of Tân Sơn Nhứt airport was opened for business on August 14, 2007. Formally inaugurated on September 2, 2007, it dealt with 34 carriers. The four-story terminal handled arrivals on its first floor and departure on its second floor. It could accommodate 10 million passengers annually and cost over U.S. $197.7 million to build. The old terminal is used exclusively for domestic airlines.

Located within the confines of the city, it would have difficulty expanding. Construction has begun on a second airport—Long Thành International Airport about 20 miles from the city. The first phase will be completed in 2010 with two parallel runways of 4,000 m—each capable of accepting the super jumbo jet A380. It would be able to handle 20 million passengers annually. The second phase, to be completed in 2015, will provide two additional runways and boost the total capacity of the airport to 80 to 100 million annually. By 2010, the Tân Sơn Nhứt Airport will be reserved for domestic flights.

Saigon is a city where past and present intertwine with each other, where the new is added to the old without ever destroying it, and where different philosophies, religions and political orientations grudgingly coexist for the survival of common people and the growth of the wealthy.

Saigon is about memories.

Different people hold different views about the city, for she represents something different for a Cham, a Khmer, a French, a Japanese, an American, a Russian, a South or a North Vietnamese.

The commemoration plaque in front of the Marie Curie high school clearly shows it. It lists the following chronology as the school came under different government—French, Japanese, South Vietnamese and communist—and bore the wounds of history.

1915	Construction began.
1918	Year completed. Named Ecole Superieure Francaise des Jeunes Filles (French high school for girls).
1941	Served as a hospital for the Japanese.
1942	Renamed Calmette high school.
1943–1945	Pupils studied in shelters as the Japanese bombed the city on May 1 and May 8, 1944, and January 1 and February 2, 1945.
1945	The Japanese overthrew the French government. The school became a concentration camp for French Navy personnel (March 9).
1946	Renamed Lucien Mossard high school.
1948	Renamed Marie Curie.
1970	Received schoolboys from Lê Quí Đôn high school (Jean Jacques Rousseau), which was turned over to the former Saigon government.
1975	Became a public high school under the communist government.
1997	Became a semi-private high school with classes in Vietnamese and French.

By 1997, it became bilingual again through the assistance of a French agency. Students had to pass the Vietnamese and French baccalaureates before graduation. They could then apply for undergraduate studies in French universities.

Despite all these changes, Saigon remains the one and only one city for the many people who have set foot there.

*   *   *

The two Vietnams, North and South, divided by two centuries under separate monarchs in the 17th and 18th centuries, by eight decades under the French and by two decades of war in the 20th century, could be no more different.

Vietnam below the 17th parallel, being more open, livelier, and less formal than its northern counterpart, is the North's antithesis. One can see people wearing baseball caps instead of pith helmets, colorful áo dài and dresses instead of dark outfits. Southern middle-aged people easily approach foreigners to try to practice their English, while Northerners shy away from strangers. Cafés, bars, and refreshment stands are seen everywhere in the South. The vọng cổ,[53] a reformed genre of classical opera, is often heard on radio or seen on TV. The most obvious difference would be karaoke cafés where people try to show off their singing talents. In the South, there is one karaoke café in every five houses where languorous songs dealing with separation, love loss, or nostalgia are sung everyday.[54]

Reunification did not change these differences overnight: it only exacerbated them because they are very striking. It is only after Hà Nội embarked on the đổi mới policy that the mood changed, the economy turned around, and that Saigon regained her vitality. The Saigonese went back to work to try to rebuild a modern city conducive to progress, economic expansion, and well-being—not only for Saigonese, but also for all Vietnamese. The goods and the riches of Saigon were shared by all other regions in the country.

Through the hard work, rebellious ingenuity, and unconventional approach of her citizens, Saigon has steered Vietnam toward economic recovery and well-being. By losing the war, she gained peace and prosperity for herself and the whole country.

Why then would the Saigonese continue to accept Hà Nội's ruling? Saigon has gone on her own way for quite some time and Hà Nội has agreed with reservation to give Saigon some breathing room. Hà Nội tries to slow down Saigon's inexorable march toward political freedom. It knows that freedom not only equates with riches but also with potential loss of power. It likes social and political changes to occur by slow evolution rather than abrupt revolution. The question is whether the Saigonese would want to wait forever for a change that might never come.

Saigon aims toward economic progress, tries to catch up with other Asian cities and erases the three decades of isolation and commercial torpor under the communist regime. Her inhabitants' income, though small by western standard, is three times higher than that of the rest of the country ($U.S. 4 a day). There seems to be a mutual and uneasy truce between the cities. Any momentous change that significantly alters the balance between the two cities could forever rattle the uneasiness that lurks beneath the surface and cause a breakdown between the two cities.

12

The Little Saigons

Philippe Franchini, Sr., a Corsican Frenchman who moved to Saigon to look for work, ended up marrying a Saigonese woman. His son, Philippe Jr. born in Saigon, felt nostalgic enough about Saigon to write two books in which he depicted the rise and fall of French Saigon: *Continental Saigon* and *Saigon 1925–1945. De la "Belle Colonie" à l'éclosion revolutionnaire ou la fin des dieux blancs* (From the "Beautiful Colony" to the Birth of the Revolution or the End of the White Gods). If a Frenchman could have strong sentimental bonds with the city, one wonders about those who were born there.

Nam Lộc was so sad about leaving Saigon on a refugee boat in 1975 that he wrote this song to remember the city. For him, the city was a lover that he would never forget. She would always be in his mind and he promised that he would be back there one day.[1] The song eventually became a hit and a rallying cry among the expatriate Vietnamese communities around the world.

Forced to flee their country, many refugees ended up in America, where they were purposely scattered to all 50 states in order to lessen the economic burden on some communities. They, however, tended to converge back to certain cities and states where jobs and housing, warmer climates, better social-welfare programs, and especially reunification with kin, friends and compatriots could be found. While only nine percent of Americans moved across state lines during 1975 and 1980, 45 percent of Indochinese refugees relocated to another state.[2] The most popular destination of this secondary migration was California.

They then tried to rebuild their lives, culture, and ways of living in ethnic enclaves called "little Saigons." Although the new life was entirely different from the old one because the old South Vietnam no longer existed, it helped them heal or at least stabilize the wounds of war. The past still haunts them and may haunt them for the rest of their lives. Most are, therefore, living in a country of "memory."[3]

One could arbitrarily categorize the little Saigons in three different groups based on the number of stores/businesses the community harbors; the bigger the community, the larger its little Saigon will be. The little Saigons in Westminster, California, and Houston, Texas, are the prototypes of the first group: They each have more than 600 stores. Westminster alone boasts 2,000 Vietnamese businesses; another 1,000 businesses are located in adjacent towns. The second tier comprises cities with 100 to 600 stores: The Virginia Eden Center and uptown Chicago are the primary examples. The smaller "little Saigons" comprise less than 100 stores each; such are the cases of Boston's Fields Corner and Indianapolis, Indiana.

Not every Vietnamese business district wants to be called little Saigon. The Falls Church, Virginia, community, known as the Eden Center, is happy with that designation. So is the uptown Chicago community, which does not even have a proper name.

Many people in San Jose, on the other hand, specifically wanted their Story Road retail area be called "Little Saigon" and went through tumultuous attempts to get it. On November 20, 2007, the San Jose city council voted 8 to 3 to name the area "Saigon Business District." By voting with the majority, council member Madison Nguyễn strangely voted against the "Little Saigon" appellation. She thought that "business district" was a good compromise for many non–Vietnamese merchants who shared space in the area and desired a less political name. She and the board had misunderstood the reaction of the local Vietnamese community. The vote resulted in an uproar that sparked repeated demonstrations and protests that were at times violent. Nguyễn was called a "traitor," although she has quite a few Vietnamese supporters.

Nguyễn was born in Vietnam in 1975 to a fisherman father. When she was four, her family escaped by boat and landed in the Philippines. After resettling for a while in Scottsdale, Arizona, they moved to Modesto, California, in 1990 in search for higher wages picking up fruit in the Central Valley. She worked in the fields alongside her father as a teenager. She was derisively called "banana"—yellow on the outside, but white on the inside because of her outspoken manner. She eventually graduated with a master's degree in social science from the University of Chicago. Elected in 2005 to represent the Story Road area, she became the first Vietnamese American San Jose council member.[4]

On March 5, 2008, the council, under pressure from the community, rescinded the "Saigon Business District" appellation and gave the Vietnamese the chance to name the retail area. After one year of wrangling, demonstrations, threats to recall Nguyễn, and even a hunger strike, the retail area was finally designated "Little Saigon." Some members of the community, upset over Nguyễn's initial opposition, gathered enough votes to force her recall even though she had apologized to the community. The recall vote took place on March 3, 2009. She survived it after a bruising campaigning process.[5]

Although it is too early to tell, the Nguyễn incident could signal the maturation of the Vietnamese political forces in the United States.

Little Saigon, California

Santa Ana in Orange County—ten miles southwest of Los Angeles—was in the mid–1970s a sparsely populated farming and agricultural area covered with orange groves and strawberry farms. The tens of thousands of Vietnamese who arrived at the Pendleton Camp near San Diego were sent to Santa Ana. Today, it is so crowded that it has been subdivided into five adjacent cities: Garden Grove, Westminster, Santa Ana, Fountain Valley, and Anaheim.

In the early days, oriental food stores and basic ingredients like soy sauce, fish sauce, hot sauce, oriental herbs and noodles, rice, and oriental vegetables were nowhere to be found. By 1977, a Chinese-Vietnamese opened the supermarket Hòa Bình. This was followed by a shipping store that mailed parcels to Vietnam: a real necessity at the time, when expatriates tried to help their relatives who remained there. By 1978, the Tú Quỳnh bookstore, the first Vietnamese restaurant, Thành Mỹ, and the Chinese drugstore Thúc Sinh opened their doors. If there were only a few stores in 1977, that number rose to 100 by 1982, and about 4,000 35 years later. In the 1970s, merchandise from Chinatown one hour away was brought back for sale to the community. Although expensive, some items disappeared from the shelves as fast as they were displayed. Arriving half-an-hour late could mean no ethnic food until the next shipment.[6] Over the years, the community has grown and expanded manifold. Although initially limited by four streets: Bolsa, Westminster, Brookhurst, and Magnolia, it has spread its tentacles to surrounding areas. In 1986, the town earned its designation as "Little Saigon," which was signed by Governor George Deukmejian.

Its geographic center, opened in 1986, is Phước Lộc Thọ or Asian Garden Mall. Although it is only a two-story, albeit large, complex, it holds a huge symbolism—much bigger than its size. It is the heart and center of the Vietnamese community. Although its intended use is purely commercial, it has become a target for politicians hoping to collect Vietnamese American votes. On September 13, 2000, presidential candidate George W. Bush talked to a crowd of 2,000 supporters in the mall parking lot. For a moment, Little Saigon became "proof" of the nation's commitment to diversity, freedom and democracy.

Local leaders have managed to transform a collection of storefronts into a cultural and political zone spanning the Vietnamese American community, city, county, state, nation, and globe.[7] They also helped to regulate the boundaries of place through commerce and through ideology, namely anticommunism. In 1999, when a local merchant exhibited an image of Hồ Chí Minh in his store, tens of thousands people demonstrated until he took it down. From that time onward, shopkeepers displayed the yellow flag with red stripes in front of their stores to mark the "yellowing" of the area in open opposition to the Hà Nội government. It was a way of framing one's sense of self and community in the face of the loss of homeland. In 2003, when California State

University–Fullerton displayed the red flag of the Socialist Republic of Vietnam at a graduation ceremony, Vietnamese students argued that only the yellow heritage flag should be flown because it represents not only the Vietnamese American community, but also freedom, democracy, and independence from communism and totalitarianism.[8] Through these protests, Vietnamese Americans intended to "remind themselves, and other Americans too, not to forget the old South Vietnam that they know and love."[9]

On May 11, 2004, Garden Grove passed a measure requiring the U.S. State Department to let it know two weeks in advance if any Vietnamese official should decide to visit the city. Westminster soon passed a similar measure. The timeframe would allow the local police to prepare and get ready for any massive protest. The cities also declared Little Saigon a "communist-free zone" by banning communists by declaration and demand.

The city of Westminster has in many ways been affected by Vietnamese Americans, not only by their affluence and businesses, but also by their memories. The Westminster War Memorial, dedicated in 2003, is also known as the "West Coast Statue of Liberty." Flanked by U.S. and South Vietnamese flags, it is comprised of an eternal flame, a fountain, and a three-ton, fifteen-foot bronze statue depicting two soldiers, American and Vietnamese, posing as war heroes. The design was carefully planned to deal with the omission of Vietnamese from the dominant collective memory. The monument, which occupies a park next to the Westminster City Hall, might not be there without the political and economic clout of Little Saigon.[10]

The Orange County Little Saigon has tried to preserve its Vietnamese roots and flavor of pre–1975 Saigon and refuses to be another Chinatown, although it includes quite a few Chinese-Vietnamese merchants and Taiwanese investors. The Vietnamese, therefore, shot down Jao's Harmony Bridge, which would be a bridge/shopping mall suspended over Bolsa Avenue, Little Saigon's main street. They argued that the bridge would make Little Saigon look like a Little Chợ Lớn.[11]

Uptown Chicago and Virginia's Eden Center

Uptown Chicago was a fashionable area between 1900 and 1920. Germans, Swedes, and Irish moved in succession into the area, followed by Jews. In the 1950s, its population gradually shrunk as whites moved out to the suburbs. Attempts to improve the area structurally and financially failed. Despite many attempts by investors to shore up the area, there were no takers. The area remained a "ghost town after dark ... dominated by pimps, prostitutes, and drug pushers who assembled on unlit, crumbling sidewalks."[12] By 1980, 48 percent of the residents lived below the poverty line, compared to 37 percent for the city as a whole.

The local government solved the problem by inserting newly-arrived Indochinese refugees—the first 2,500 arrived in Uptown between 1975 and 1978—who would find cheap rents, good transportation facilities, access to Lake Michigan, and education at a nearby community college. Having nowhere to go, they toughened up and tried to rebuild their lives. Economic security was the main goal at the time. They went to work during the daytime and holed up in their apartments after dark. Muggings and break-ins were common occurrences; broken windows, vacant, decrepit buildings, and unintelligible graffiti a common sight. Asian grocery needs were available 20 minutes away by car in Chinatown.

One business after another soon opened its doors. Buildings, streets, and sidewalks were spruced up one by one. Changes were slow and community security remained a concern. By the mid–1980s, with 10,000 Indochinese refugees living in uptown, newspaper headlines brashly proclaimed: "Vietnamese Reviving Chicago Slum." By the mid–1990s, more than 50 businesses—restaurants, boutiques, grocery stores, beauty salons, jewelry shops, and a bank—have opened their doors along Argyle, Wilson, and adjacent streets.[13] Asian refugees from nearby counties or states came by to stock up on goods and merchandise or to enjoy meals at the local restaurants. Traffic was so busy on weekends that visitors had difficulties finding a parking place.

Uptown remains an entry point, but not a permanent place, to stay for the majority of Asians who have moved to surrounding areas to be close to their work. They, however, have economically transformed uptown and at the same time revitalized and improved the area.

Eden Center (formerly Plaza Seven Shopping Center), near the crossroads of Seven Corners in Falls Church, Virginia, in the late 1970s was a destitute strip mall in a crime-ridden area. When the last American tenant moved out, the Vietnamese moved in and opened two restaurants and a grocery store. The latter was located in the back of a former American grocery store, and it occupied only one fourth or fifth of the space. One had to walk through a cavernous empty space with trashed paper and cardboard on the floor before reaching the actual Vietnamese store. The eerie feeling of the neighborhood was aggravated by the 9 P.M. store closing. Slowly, a few more businesses opened their doors. Once security was re-established and gangs were flushed out of nearby neighborhoods business picked up rapidly. By 1984, it has emerged as the Vietnamese American community of Northern Virginia, DC, and Maryland. Its name derives from the 1960 arcade Khu Eden in Saigon.

Today, it is home to 120 stores and is much more lively than decades earlier. It is jam-packed with cars on weekends when visitors from nearby states drive their friends in for dinners. Beside the usual grocery stores, travel agencies, food stores, carry-out places, hair and nail salons, tailoring shops, and even a Chinese pharmacy, the center has more than 30 restaurants.

The tall entrance gateway on Wilson Boulevard is adorned with two guardian lions. The tower clock on Eden Mall, the oldest interior mall of the complex, is a replica of that of the Central Market in Saigon, Vietnam. The parking place is divided into rows by streets, each carrying the name of renowned military persons or high officials of the Republic of Vietnam. In the center of the parking lot stands a tall flagpole adorned with American and South Vietnamese flags. The latter, with three red stripes on a yellow background, has proven to be an irritant to the Vietnamese Embassy located across the Potomac a few miles away. Rumor has it that the owner is willing to put the center up for sale and the Hanoi Embassy is more than willing to put its hands on the center and to hoist the communist flag up. Somehow, there was a stipulation that the Vietnamese community owns the right to keep the yellow flag flying for some time more. How long remains to be seen. The Vietnam War has become on the U.S. soil 35 years later a war of flags: a yellow flag symbolizing the freedom of the South Vietnamese expatriates vs. the red flag of the communists who wanted to control the expatriate community.

Joseph S. Wood once wrote, "Eden Center serves an 'epiphoric' function: it is more important and less tangible than itself.... Now it is a symbol with complex and contested meanings."[14]

Boston and Indianapolis

Although these mini little Saigons are not large enough to offer economic security, ethnic food variety, or cultural identification, they represent places where there thrives a modicum of Vietnamese-ness, which is enough to prevent Vietnamese Americans from completely losing their roots.

Indianapolis, Indiana, is a Midwestern city of 780,000 inhabitants with a tiny Vietnamese community of 2,000 people. As such, it has only a few Vietnamese businesses scattered all over town, but there was no localized little Saigon. Years ago, people living in that city used to drive to uptown Chicago about two hours away for their grocery or dining needs. Recently, Vietnamese from other states, especially California, have moved to Indianapolis, where competition is less stiff than in their states, to open businesses. This tertiary migration has helped expand Vietnamese businesses and culture and anchored Vietnamese tradition in the midwest.

In Boston, the small Vietnamese community was also scattered into four isolated neighborhoods. Slowly they have converged toward Field Corners where they bought homes to live in or rent out. Struggling through the 1980s, they have, by the 1990s, achieved a modicum of recognition. Due to their small size, they also serve other minorities: Puerto Ricans, Haitians, and recent Mexican immigrants, in order to survive. The shops do not sustain the city's Vietnamese American population in terms of jobs or goods and service.

The opening of a new two-story community center in 2002 helped to seal the Vietnamese imprint on this small Dorchester village, which eventually became a mini little Saigon—complete with restaurants, bakeries, groceries, hair and nail salons, and doctor's and dentist's offices. Only 30 businesses are documented in Fields Corner. Dorchester Avenue, which passes through the area, now represents a Vietnamese "Main Street."

The Việt Kiều

The Vietnamese overseas, or Việt Kiều—a special group of people—led a complicated life. Many characteristics have defined them:[15]

1. *They carry a lot of baggage*—physically and mentally—for having been through one of the longest wars in history, losing their country, and migrating from one country to another before reaching their final destination. Their lives are, therefore, painful, complex, and multidimensional—moreso than other immigrants to the States. This may also explain their fiery desire to succeed in this country.

Monique Trường's father was born in Vietnam and schooled in England and France. He married a Swiss woman with whom he had a daughter before returning to Vietnam. He later divorced his first wife and married a Vietnamese woman. He served in the ARVN before getting a job with a Dutch-owned oil company in Saigon. He escaped to the U.S. at the end of the war and lived in exile in North Carolina, and then Texas. He got an MBA degree and worked for an American counterpart of the former Dutch company. Forced to retire early, he went to work in Saudi Arabia, "too proud to sit still and too financially unsteady to stop bringing home a paycheck."[16]

Phước's childhood memories include: a home destroyed by war, a father taken prisoner by the communists, a horse-carriage ride in the middle of the night to see his imprisoned father, and a courageous mother who raised her children by herself while being harassed by the communists.[17] After graduating from medical school, he was assigned to the Phước Long Hospital where he took care of villagers and wounded soldiers. When the town was overrun by the communists in March 1975, he was taken prisoner with a foul smelling thigh wound all the way to the North where he was interned in a concentration camp for three years.[18] He successfully escaped abroad after many failed attempts.

2. *They are grieving* the loss of their country. It is a painful loss, even though it happened 35 years ago. Phan Bội Châu once said, "There is no greater loss than that of losing one's country." To this day, many are still carrying their unhealed war wounds with them.

Nguyễn Thị Thu Lâm, despite marrying an American and having a child with him, still feels attached to her birth country: "And for me and the Vietnamese of my generation, there will always be memories of another time and place, another life. I will forever remain an immigrant here. And even when I am happiest, I will remember my beloved Vietnam and the fate of its people. I am a child of war. I am a child of Vietnam."[19]

This is not a new phenomenon—the sociologist Georg Simmel once confronted it in the 1900s. He wrote about the immigrant, "*The stranger intends to stay, although he cannot ever become native.*" Born of Jewish parents in Berlin, Germany—his father later became a Roman Catholic and his mother a Lutheran—he never felt accepted by the German academia despite his talents. He was turned down from many vacant chairmanship positions before being elevated to full professor without Chair in 1901.[20] He, therefore, knew what it meant to be a "stranger" in a new land.

3. *They took risks* by escaping from the communists and crossing oceans to take refuge in other countries and to restart their lives anew.

4. *They embarked on the most amazing journey on earth.* This was a journey in search of freedom. Not only did they find freedom, they also built a new life. Who could imagine a rice farmer's son who only brought "seven oranges with him onto a crowded boat thinking they would last him the whole journey across the Pacific" is now an architect who helps design high rise buildings all over the globe?[21]

5. *The story of the Việt Kiều is about resiliency, hope, and healing*, although it is also about contributing to the new society. After having gone through war traumas, and the oppressive communist regime with its reeducation camps and new economic zones, they made harrowing escapes across oceans to reach refugee camps where they languished a long time before finding a third country that would accept them. They then had to restart anew with their lives under difficult conditions.

*   *   *

The purpose of the little Saigons is manifold, but they serve mostly to preserve Vietnameseness through community-building and place-making, rather than individual adaptation. The issue of "staying Vietnamese" is conceptualized in a social and spatial setting rather than in a personal and psychological one. It requires a constant shifting, changing, and adjustment in order to arrive at new ways of being Vietnamese in an American environment. Vietnamese Americans have to build new roots because the old ones have been disconnected. And these new roots have to be in some ways connected to themselves, their histories, and cultures.[22]

Epilogue

Hồ had decided a long time ago to take over the whole Indochinese peninsula. After engineering the takeover of Hà Nội in 1945, he ruthlessly suppressed all non-communist parties and took power for himself and the communist party. Forced by the Chinese and Soviets to accept the accords of 1954, Hà Nội lost the chance to reunify the country. Hồ—a fervent communist believer—was unlikely to desist from his grandiose ambition and switch over to democracy. Once he had embarked on the warpath, he used all means to get rid of other competitors, local and foreign. Therefore, the war he had initiated should be called the Communist War, not the Vietnam War, a neutral term used by the U.S., or the American War, as suggested by Hà Nội.[1] The South Vietnamese, on the other hand, have labeled it the "War against communist Aggression," for in the end, it was a war perpetrated against Saigon and the South Vietnamese; its "victims were primarily the South Vietnamese and its victors the North Vietnamese.[2] The war-makers "anesthetized themselves to the pain of battle in order to achieve their goals. The result was the dehumanization of everyone involved."[3]

A war "is a product of human agency, not blind fate."[4] The Communist War in Vietnam was shaped by powerful socio-political, economic, national and personal factors. On this warpath, Hồ faced President Harry Truman who threw his support behind the French in their effort to retake Indochina. That decision was followed by President Eisenhower's willingness to confront Hà Nội and to try to stop its ambitions. He was the first official to voice the theory of the "domino effect." The war could have ended right there, although neither side refused to back down. On one side was an ambitious warrior-politician who wanted to totally control Indochina, and on the other side stood the Americans who wanted to replace the French. The standoff led to the re-internationalization of the war. The first Communist War had been internationalized by Hà Nội, who fought against the French with the help of the Chinese. The second Communist War was a war of proxies: North against South Vietnamese with the assistance of 300,000 Chinese troops and a few thousand Soviets on one side[5] and more than 500,000 Americans and allies on the other side.

Had the Americans not intervened, Hồ would have simply taken over the South in 1955. Southerners would have been sent to reeducation camps as they were after 1975, because the highly suspicious communist regime would not tolerate any dissension.[6] It would have found any reason to purge real or imagined enemies, as it did during the 1954 Land Reform. Letting Hà Nội take over South Vietnam in the 1960s would not have "averted decades of warfare and the loss of millions of lives" as Appy has stated.[7] It would only have switched the burden of resisting the red tide to other states—Malaysia and Thailand— and a domino effect would have taken place. Because those countries were not prepared for total war, they would have gone through the same problems South Vietnam experienced in the 1960s and '70s. The U.S. would have to jump in to defend them unless they wanted to see one Asian country after another fall to the communist tide.

Saigon and South Vietnam lost the war for various reasons. They pursued their cause half-heartedly and their (imposed) strategy was mainly defensive. A war has rarely been won by just fending off attacks. They were not unified: The cacophony of voices (pro-war, anti-war, Buddhists, generals, politicians, students) was enough to drown out the political will of the newly-emerging state. They were too immature politically to define themselves as a nation. This attitude can be traced to a lack of moral discipline and/or respect for the office of the government. It has been said that "if one puts two Vietnamese in the same team, they manage to work well together. Add a third one, and dissension [will] occur," as no one would listen to the other. This sad reality is not new, as has been suggested by a Vietnamese saying:

> One becomes a king, if one wins,
> One causes trouble, if one loses.[8]

Vietnamese history is replete of rebellions, insurgencies, wars as those who were governed had tried to topple or disrupt the established government: the Tây Sơn in 1773 (capture of Qui Nhơn) and the communists in 1945 are two of the examples.

Southern nationalists also lacked good leaders. This is not to say that communists are good leaders—they are not, but they did manage to do better through their ruthlessness. Southerners did not know how to mobilize popular support, except after the Tết offensive, or to keep the people focused on the war effort. They were not self-sufficient: Dependence on America eventually proved fatal when the U.S. opted to pursue its own goals.[9] They were too gullible: generals trusting the Americans, Buddhists believing in neutrality and communists, politicians in third force. Coming off a heavily-contested fight during which they wrestled their freedom from the French, they did not have the political will or wisdom to withstand a lengthy war, a will that would blend all the differences and personal preoccupations into a steely resolve to defend freedom and their country.

After 1954, the South Vietnamese had hoped for freedom, independence, and peace, but instead found revolution, war, and misery. And even after the war had ended in 1975 and all foreigners had gone home, the misery still persisted. The whole process was a tragedy of epic proportions.

Although responsible for their freedom, they did not actively fight for it and were not able to master the forces that had shaped South Vietnamese history. The French would not grant them independence until 1955, nine years after Hà Nội had won its independence—a critical interval thus lost.[10] The communists then sought to impose class-warfare in the South, causing the Americans to intervene and take over the fight. Caught between these forces, Vietnamese nationalists were not able to assume their responsibilities and control their destiny.

The U.S. had failed because of its limited vision of the nature of the war and the requirements for victory—failure to assess vital interests and capabilities.[11] They could have assisted in stabilizing the battlefield by sealing off the DMZ and the HCM trail, and the South Vietnamese could have taken over from there. Had the South Vietnamese failed, it would have been their own fault. But the U.S. had decided to fight the big war their own way, only to lose the will to fight on. Thiệu helped to stabilize the country. Had he had a few more years, he could have, if not won the war, at least stabilized the country. After 1968, the Viet Cong were decimated and the South—a pluralistic ferment—had shown a predilection for change and development. Time, however, ran out on them. And they lost their country to a chilling police state.

Saigon and the South have been and remain a different entity and region than the rest of the country since the early days of 1600 when Nguyễn Hoàng began establishing his southern "kingdom."[12] Being an outpost away from the direct control of the court, a melting pot of various nationalities, an economic powerhouse with a frontier mentality, Saigon and the South have always followed the beat of their own drum.

Saigon has come a long way: from a village in the forest, she has become a large, cosmopolitan city—the largest in Vietnam, bypassing the former capital cities: Hà Nội and Huế. She has undergone tremendous change and passed through many hands: the Khmers, the Chinese, the Nguyễn, the Tây Sơn, the French, the Japanese, the British, the Ngôs, the Americans, and the communists. She has gone through bloody revolutions from the battles against the Khmers, the Thais, the Tây Sơn, to the Lê Văn Khôi revolt, the Nghĩa Quân revolt, the Tết Offensive, and the fall of Saigon.

Christians and Buddhists have died there. Khmers, Chinese, Vietnamese, Thais, Chams, French, Americans, other foreigners, nationalists, and communists have fought there to lay claim to this city and economic region. Well-known heads of state and officials have passed away in this corner of the land: Lê Văn Duyệt, Phan Thanh Giản, Phan Chu Trinh, Tạ Thu Thâu, Ngô Đình

Diệm, and Ngô Đình Nhu, along with scores of others. The bishop of Behaine was once laid to rest here dressed in a mandarin gown far away from his native land. They all defended or fought for the control or freedom of Saigon and the country or to raise their names in this corner of the world.

Wars have brought down buildings and monuments, forcing new monuments to be erected and taken down in the future. There are probably few cities in the world that have witnessed that many battles involving that many diverse entities, armies and countries. The Nguyễn first wrested these lands from the Khmers, who had fought against the Chams for similar reasons. The Tây Sơn fought to expand their lands, the Nguyễn to retain the last jewel of their crown. Bishop de Behaine fought to spread Christianity among the Vietnamese. The French and the Japanese fought to use Saigon as a beachhead to expand their conquests, the Americans to expand their worldwide influence. The locals fought to regain their cherished freedom. Life is cyclical in this corner of the land. People come and go, but Saigon remains.

Saigon lies at the crossroads of many civilizations, which is why the French coined for it the name of Indo-China. This is the land where all the various religions converged: Mahayana and Theravada Buddhism, Catholicism, Taoism, Confucianism, and Islam. This is where communism and capitalism came head to head and had their biggest fight. This is where socialism tried to expand its reach, only to succumb to fatigue and overextension.

Saigon has always rebounded anew even while conquerors are still in town. She remains vibrant and adaptable. She is there and ready to take on another challenger or invader. People come and go but only she remains in place to serve her people's needs. She is the engine of the country and the soul of the South Vietnamese.

Saigon was neither Huế nor Hà Nội. She was not always the capital of the country or the "chosen" capital of princes or kings. She temporarily served as Nguyễn Ánh's capital in his time of despair, only to be pushed aside once he had regained his throne. She was the capital of Lê Văn Duyệt, Lê Văn Khôi, Phan Thanh Giản, of the rebels, the South Vietnamese government and the French. These were the people who trusted her and made her their hometown. Saigon opened her arms to the destitute, the poor, and the fallen. As a mother, she is always available and ready to comfort, nurture, reenergize, and rebuild. Unlike Huế and Hà Nội, her uniqueness lies in her modernity and commercial ventures. She came of age at the time when southeast Asian states began trading with each other in the late 17th and 18th centuries before international commerce was taken over by the Europeans. She did not go along well with people with entrenched ideas—for modernity and adaptability can only thrive with minimal conformity and regulation.

Hồ's ironic claim, "There is nothing more important than freedom" rings hollow as freedom was non-existent under communism. Was there any freedom under a one-party-rule? Freedom when opposition was not allowed to voice its opinion? Freedom when a dissenter like Father Lý was shut up right in the middle of a court session in full view of the people and world press? Freedom at a time when Catholics, Buddhists, Hòa Hảo, and other intellectuals are still jailed 35 years after the end of the war? Freedom when Southerners are treated as second-class citizens and when southern cemeteries are still desecrated? Freedom when a Lenin statue still stands in Hà Nội while most Lenin statues have been taken down elsewhere?[13] Freedom when political opposition is not allowed and when mail and writings are still censored?

To this day, the communists have not acknowledged their invasion and the killing of hundreds of thousands of South Vietnamese. They fail to acknowledge having improperly seized houses, offices, buildings, businesses, lands, and properties of the South Vietnamese and installed themselves as owners of South Vietnam, forcing the South Vietnamese to escape for their lives. They are now trying to lure the expatriates back by suggesting that the "American policy ... destroyed our nation and caused the separation of our people," and that expatriates can "heal the wounds of war."[14]

Saigon is a city of many memories—good and bad—and one that exemplifies the "easy-going-ness," the resilience, and combativeness of the South Vietnamese. Although Saigon is lost, it will not be forever lost.

Saigon, Huế and Hà Nội, the three main Vietnamese cities, could not be more different. If Saigon is a frantic, commercial and intellectual center that embraces modernism and capitalism at its core, she also has her romantic side—a side that millions of Việt Kiều still long for. She is not like Hà Nội, a colonial city frozen in time with its century-old French buildings and its sedated, mercurial communist atmosphere, or the imperial Huế, which still resonates with the sweet and decadent perfume of the last Vietnamese emperors. Saigon's history is anchored in the future through her connection with the global market and world. She has to play catch-up with the other Asian commercial cities because of the time lost under communist control. The day she stops experimenting and modernizing will be the one that marks her real demise.

Saigon has changed hands on many occasions throughout history. Although her masters have come and gone, she has remained steady, unbowed and undeterred. Having fallen to her knees in 1975, she rebounded economically a decade later. She has regained some of her former image by becoming entrepreneurial, bustling, and vibrant. Like a rebellious child, she writes her own story and charts her own course. She has her own brand of culture, heroism, nationalism, and a unique spirit of independence that helps her survive her conquerors.[15]

Saigon is about resilience. If in the 1960s and 1970s, the U.S. failed to rebuild her to their image, the communists also failed to transform her into a communist colony in the 1980s and 1990s. Saigon will never be a drab communist city no matter which rules have been imposed on her. Sooner or later, she will free herself from all yokes, for she is a free city-state.

Although Saigon has lost her name, Southerners still call her Saigon, a rebellious and free-spirited city; a mistress on the Mekong River that thrives on adversity and re-emerges anew and vibrant after each defeat: RESILIENT, INDESTRUCTIBLE, ADAPTABLE.

Appendix

Saigon Street Names
According to Periods
in History

Under the French	Before 1954	After 1975
Albert Premier	Đinh Tiên Hoàng	Đinh Tiên Hoàng
Amiral Roze	Trương Công Định	Trương Định
Armand Rousseau, Jean-Jacques Rousseau	Trần Hoàng Quân	Nguyễn Chí Thanh
Arras	Cống Qùynh	Cống Qùynh
Aviateur Garros, Rolland Garros	Thủ Khoa Huân	Thủ Khoa Huân
Barbé	Lê Qúy Đôn	Lê Qúy Đôn
Blancsubé, rue Catinat prolongée	Duy Tân	Phạm Ngọc Thạch
Bonard	Lê Lợi	Lê Lợi
Carabelli	Nguyễn Thiệp	Nguyễn Thiệp
Catinat	Tư Do	Đồng Khởi
Champagne	Yên Đỗ	Lý Chính Thắng
Charner	Nguyễn Huệ	Nguyễn Huệ
Chasseloup Laubat	Hồng Thập Tự	Nguyễn Thi Minh Khai
Chemin des Dames	Nguyễn Phi	Lê Anh Xuân
Colonel Boudonnet	Lê Lai	Lê Lai
Dixmude	Đề Thám	Đề Thám
Đỗ Hữu Vị, Hamelin	Huỳnh Thúc Kháng	Huỳnh Thúc Kháng
Douaumont	Cô Giang	Cô Giang
Ducos	Triệu Đà	Ngô Quyền
Duranton	Bùi Thị Xuân	Bùi Thị Xuân
Espagne	Lê Thánh Tôn	Lê Thánh Tôn
Eyriaud Des Vergnes	Trương Minh Giảng	Trần Quốc Thảo
Frédéric Drouhet	Hùng Vương	Hùng Vương
Frère Louis	Võ Tánh	Nguyễn Trãi
Frères Guillerault	Bùi Chu	Tôn Thất Tùng
Gallieni, rue des Marins	Trần Hưng Đạo, Đồng Khánh	Trần Hưng Đạo
Garcerie	Duy Tân	Phạm Ngọc Thạch

Under the French	*Before 1954*	*After 1975*
Général Lizé	Phan Thanh Giản	Điện Biên Phủ
Georges Guynemer	Võ Di Nguy	Hồ Tùng Mậu
Huỳnh Quan Tiên	Hồ Hảo Hớn	Hồ Hảo Hớn
Jaccario	Tản Đà	Tản Đà
Jauréguiberry	Ngô Thời Nhiệm	Ngô Thời Nhiệm
La Grandière	Gia Long	Lý Tự Trọng
Lacaze	Nguyễn Tri Phương	Nguyễn Tri Phương
Lacote	Phạm Hồng Thái	Phạm Hồng Thái
Larégnère	Đoàn Thị Điểm	Trương Định
Legrand De La Liraye	Phan Thanh Giản	Điện Biên Phủ
Léon Combes	Sương Nguyệt Ánh	Sương Nguyệt Anh
Mac Mahon, De Lattre De Tassigny, Gen. De Gaulle	Công Lý	Nam Kỳ khởi nghĩa
Marins	Đồng Khánh	Trần Hưng Đạo
Miss Cavell	Huyền Trân Công Chúa	Huyền Trân Công Chúa
Nancy	Cộng Hòa	Nguyễn Văn Cừ
Nguyễn Tấn Nghiệm, rue de Cầu Kho	Phát Diệm	Trần Đình Xu
Nguyễn Văn Đướm	Nguyễn Văn Đướm	Nguyễn Văn Nghĩa
Ohier	Tôn Thất Thiệp	Tôn Thất Thiệp
Paul Blanchy	Hai Bà Trưng	Hai Bà Trưng
Pavie, Hui Bôn Hoả	Lý Thái Tổ	Lý Thái Tổ
Pellerin	Pasteur	Pasteur
Phan Thanh Giản	Ngô Tùng Châu	Lê Thị Riêng
Pierre Flandin	Bà Huyện Thanh Quan	Bà Huyện Thanh Quan
Pierre Pasquier	Minh Mạng	Ngô Gia Tự
Place Eugène Cuniac	C. Trường Quách Thị Trang	C. Trường Quách Thị Trang
Place Maréchal Joffre	Công Trường Quốc Tế	Hồ con Rùa
Richaud	Phan Đình Phùng	Nguyễn Đình Chiểu
Somme	Hàm Nghi	Hàm Nghi
Testard	Trần Qúy Cáp	Võ Văn Tần
Thévenet	Tú Xương	Tú Xương
Tổng Đốc Phương	Tổng Đốc Phương	Châu Văn Liêm
Trương Minh Ký, Lacant	Trương Minh Ký	Nguyễn Thị Diệu
Verdun, Thái Lập Thành, Gen. Chanson, Nguyễn Văn Thinh	Lê Văn Duyệt	Cách mạng tháng 8
Ypres	Nguyễn Văn Tráng	Nguyễn Văn Tráng
11è R.I.C.	Nguyễn Hoàng	Trần Phú

Chapter Notes

Preface

1. Champa: a Hinduized culture that flourished from the seventh to the 14th centuries in present-day central Vietnam. The people of Champa are called the Chams (see chapter 1).

2. Khmer: a Hinduized culture that flourished from the ninth to the 14th centuries and once occupied present-day Cambodia, Thailand and South Vietnam (see chapter 1).

3. Chúa is equivalent to the western "prince" or "lord," or the Japanese "shogun."

4. Fall, 15. While the Nguyễn conquered the Mekong Delta, the Dutch and Spaniards were in the Spice Islands, the French and British in India, and the Portuguese throughout Southeast Asia—even in Laos.

5. Dengue fever is transmitted by *Aedes egypti* and malaria by *Anopheles*. Even today, two million people die of these diseases despite prevention and advances in medical treatment.

6. The southern colony was called Cochinchina, and the central and northern parts were known as Annam and Tonkin.

7. Nghia M. Vo, "The Duality of the Vietnamese Mind," in *The Sorrows of War and Peace*, by Nghia M. Vo et al., 111–122. There are major social, cultural, historical, economic, and political differences between southerners and northerners.

8. Christina's comment on file.

9. http://en.wikipedia.org/wiki/Saigon.

10. Diem and Chanoff, *In the Jaws of History*, xiii.

11. Pelley, *Post–Colonial Vietnam*, 13, 40, 236. Since 1954, Hanoi had been rewriting Vietnamese history to fit a Marxist view—imposing revolutionary ideas and excluding the views of southern historians. It took Hanoi historians 20 years to complete the first volume of the *History of Vietnam* (from

prehistory to 1854, published in 1971), and 30 years to finish the second (from 1854 to 1945, published in 1985).

12. Fitzgerald, *Fire in the Lake*, 5–15.

13. Templer, *Shadows and Wind*, 17.

14. Ibid., 18.

Chapter 1

1. Reid, *Southeast Asia in the Early Modern Era*, 4. Cambodia (Khmer) and Champa, with its center at Phan Rang (present-day central Vietnam), were declining powers by the 17th century.

2. The kapok tree is a tropical tree that produces a silky fiber used as padding in pillows and mattresses; it is also called a cotton tree.

3. Cham and Khmer are two Hinduized cultures that once thrived in what are now known as Vietnam, Cambodia, Thailand and part of Malaysia. The Khmer empire was the precursor of Cambodia.

4. Po Dharma, "The History of Champa," in *Hindu-Buddhist Art of Vietnam*, edited by Emmanuel Guillon, 15–17. Chams and Khmers fought against each other constantly. The Chams beat the Khmers in 1074 and 1080. The Khmers in turn defeated the Chams in 1145. The Chams again defeated the Khmers in 1171, who took their revenge in 1190.

5. Reid, *Southeast Asia in the Age of Commerce*, 19, 60. A map on page 60 of Reid's book shows a well-developed and active sea-land-river trade connecting the various Southeast Asian countries and the "markets" of the Mekong Delta up to Phnom Penh from the 15th to the 17th centuries. Because the Chinese banned trading with Japanese "pirates," Southeast Asian ports became necessary entrepôts where Japanese silver was

exchanged for Chinese silk and Southeast Asian spices, sugar, and deerskin. See Anastasia Edwards, *Saigon*, 2.

6. Malleret, *A la Recherche de Prei nokor*, 26–33. Had Baigaur/Prey Nokor been a political or administrative center instead of a commercial site, we would have found more artifacts from this era.

7. Edwards, *Saigon, Mistress on the Mekong*, 2.

8. Wook, *Southern Vietnam*, 19–20. Another unlikely explanation suggests that Gia Định comes from the Chinese "gia" (pretty or happy) and "định" (to decide or to pacify).

9. Thanh Khoi Le, *Le Vietnam*, 268.

10. The new south was a fluid and evolving region that did not have a name at that time: it was only known the prefecture of Gia Định. Vietnam was later divided into three distinct regions: Miền Nam (south or Cochinchina), Miền Trung (center or Annam), and Miền Bắc (north or Tonkin). Đàng ngoài corresponds to Bắc Bộ while đàng trong comprises Nam Bộ and Trung Bộ (see table II). Although regional overlap existed between these different appellations, they mostly represented the same geographic areas, which in turn corresponded to different ethnic and cultural groups.

11. Vương, *Saigon Năm Xưa*, 90.

12. http://en.wikipedia.org/wiki/Saigon

13. Vương, *Saigon Năm Xưa*, 71; Crawfurd, *Journal of an Embassy*, 223.

14. Crawfurd, 542.

15. Li Tana, "The Water Frontier," in *Water Frontier*, edited by Cooke and Tana, 9.

16. A "học" is a Vietnamese measure that corresponds to five liters.

17. Li Tana, "The Late 18th and Early 19th Century Mekong Delta," in *Water Frontier*, edited by Cooke and Tana, 81. Some rich Vietnamese families possessed up to 300 to 400 oxen and buffalo each.

18. Vương, *Saigon Năm Xưa*, 99.

19. Petrus Ky, "A Painting of Old Saigon," in *Saigon, Mistress on the Mekong*, by Edwards, 44.

20. Vương, *Saigon Năm Xưa*, 95.

21. Franchini, *Saigon 1925–1945*, 48.

22. Roland Dorgeles, "The Mandarin Route," in *Saigon, Mistress on the Mekong*, by Edwards, 119.

23. Petrus Ky, "A Painting of Old Saigon," in *Saigon, Mistress on the Mekong*, by Edwards, 42–43.

24. John Thomson, "Choquan Sorcerer," in *Saigon, Mistress on the Mekong*, by Edwards, 68–69.

25. Vương, *Saigon Năm Xưa*, 97.

26. Pirogue made with three planks (two sides and one bottom) glued or nailed together: see Hồng Sén Vương, *Saigon Năm Xưa*, 90.

27. P. Peycam, "Saigon, des Origines à 1859," in Quang Ninh Le and S. Dovert, 37. These southern characteristics had already been noted in 1773: individualism, sense of adventure, and trade-oriented behavior.

28. Keith W. Taylor, "Surface Orientation," 966–967.

29. Choi Wook, 21.

30. P. Peycam in *Saigon: Trois Siecles de Developpement Urbain*, by Quang Ninh Le and S. Dovert, 41.

31. Hoành is the region around present-day Huế. That newly acquired land formed a buffer zone between the Chams in the south and the Vietnamese in the north, where convicts or poor people were sent to populate and cultivate the land. Moving down there was, for Nguyễn Hoàng, a sort of banishment rather than a social elevation. It took a lot of courage for him to abandon the Hà Nội court, his dream to succeed the Lê and to make the move south. By moving south, he created the đàng trong (south) and abandoned the đàng ngoài (north).

32. Tana, *Nguyễn Cochinchina*, 11.

33. Thành Khôi Lê, *Le Vietnam*, 247–251. The Trường Đức wall was three meters high and ten kilometers long, while Lũy Thây was six meters high and 18 kilometers long. Free labor was recruited from villagers who also brought their own food with them. The wall was only breached once during the Tây Sơn War.

34. Cooke and Tana, eds., *Water Frontier*, 147. One thousand Vietnamese lived in Phnom Penh by 1623.

35. Taboulet, *La Geste Francaise en Indochine*, 95; "Dharma," in *Hindu-Buddhist Art of Vietnam*, by Emmanuel Guillon, 20–25. Wook gave the number of 40,000 Vietnamese by 1698; see Choi Wook, *Southern Vietnam*, 39.

36. Coedes, *The Indianized States of Southeast Asia*, 236–237.

37. P. Peycam, in *Saigon*, by Quang Ninh Lê and S. Dovert, 27–29.

38. Y. Sakurai, "Eighteenth Century Chinese Pioneers," in *Water Frontier*, edited by Nola Cooke and Li Tana, 40–42.

39. P. Peycam, in *Saigon*, by Quang Ninh

Lê and S. Dovert, 33. Nguyễn Đình Dậu suggested the rampart was 15 miles long. See note 79 below. That rampart eventually became the last line of defense against the French in the 19th century.

40. Ibid., 25.

41. Tana, *Nguyễn Cochinchina*, 27–28.

42. Taboulet, *La Geste Francaise*, vol. 1, 67.

43. Tana, *Nguyễn Cochinchina*, 38.

44. Barrow, *A Voyage to Cochinchina*, 284.

45. Tana. *Nguyễn Cochinchina*, 102.

46. Li Tana, *Nguyễn Cochinchina*, 108.

47. Thế Anh Nguyễn, "The Vietnamization of the Cham Deity Pô Nagar," in *Essays into Vietnamese Pasts*, edited by Keith W. Taylor and John Whitmore, 44.

48. Philip Taylor, *Goddess on the Rise*, 66, 75, 109, 206, 265, 267. The Lady of the Realm (or Bà Chúa Sứ) is the Cham Thiên Y A Na, the Chinese Tiên Hầu, a local Khmer woman, a Thai woman, an existential creditor, spiritual banker, and reliable partner. While Thien Y A Na drowned in the sea, the Lady of the Realm died by the side of the hill. Presently, she takes on a nurturing maternal role at the center of an autonomous feminine realm.

49. Tana, *Nguyễn Cochinchina*, 113.

50. Tana, *Nguyễn Cochinchina*, 131. In the delta, the ceremony took place in lunar March in the open air with three bowls of offerings to three local deities.

51. Quang Ninh Le and S. Dovert, *Saigon*, 164–165.

52. Ibid., 166–169.

53. George Hickey, "The Vietnamese Village through Time and War," *The Vietnam Forum* 10, (1987): 18.

54. Philip Taylor, *Fragments of the Present*, 91, 93, 103.

55. Cristoforo Borri, *Cochinchina*, translated by Olga Dror and K.W. Taylor. In *Views of Seventeenth Century Vietnam*. Ithaca, NY: Cornell University Southeast Asia Program, 2006, 114.

56. Jamieson, *Understanding Vietnam*, 299–300.

57. Tana. *Nguyễn Cochinchina*, 12–13, 109–110; K. W. Taylor, "Nguyễn Hoàng," in *Southeast Asia in the Early Modern Era*, edited by Anthony Reid, 64; Nghia M. Vo, *The Bamboo Gulag*, 7–9; Nghia M. Vo, "The Duality of the Vietnamese Mind," in *The Sorrows of War and Peace*, by Nghia M. Vo, Chat V. Dang, and Hien V. Ho, 111–122. Geographical, political, cultural, and religious forces have differently shaped North and South Vietnamese and determined their reaction to war and peace. Southerners have been compared to Italians and northerners to Germans.

58. Po Dharma, "The History of Champa," in *Hindu-Buddhist Art of Vietnam*, edited by Emmanuel Guillon, 14–15.

59. Coedes, *The Indianized States of Southeast Asia*, 65–70. Funan peaked from the first to the sixth centuries CE. Chenla peaked from 550 to 630 CE.

60. Ibid., 65, 111–122, 169–176.

61. Lê Thành Khôi, *Le Vietnam*, 267.

62. Peycam, in *Saigon*, by Quang Ninh Le and S. Dovert, 29–31; Thanh Khoi Le, *Le Vietnam*, 267; Vương, *Saigon*, 22–23, 26; Huỳnh Tấn of the Mỹ Tho clan killed Dương Ngạn Dịch, the Biên Hòa's clan leader. He then rebelled against the Huế court. The Vietnamese army stepped in, killed Huỳnh Tấn, and stabilized the situation.

63. Wook, "The Nguyễn Dynasty," in *Water Frontier*, edited by Nola Cooke and Li Tana, 85.

64. Li Tana, "The Water Frontier: An Introduction," in *Water Frontier*, edited by Nola Cooke and Li Tana, 5–6.

65. Dutton, *The Tay Son Uprising*, 198–99.

66. Ibid., 200–203.

67. Cooke and Tana, eds., *Water Frontier*, 7.

68. Nola Cooke, "Water World: Chinese and Vietnamese on the Riverine Water Frontier," in *Water Frontier*, edited by Nola Cooke and Li Tana, 139–156. The local network in South Vietnam connects the towns of Saigon, Cần Thơ, Châu Đốc, Hà Tiên, Rạch Giá, Cà Mau, and Bạc Liêu.

69. "Spain," *Catholic Encyclopedia*, http://www.newadvent.org/cathen/14169b.htm.

70. McLeod, *The Vietnamese Response*, 3–4; Sellers, *The Princes of Ha Tien*, 65.

71. Taboulet, *La Geste*, 12–13.

72. Taboulet, *La Geste*, 14–20. Father de Rhodes did not exactly "invent" the quốc ngữ. The Romanization of the Vietnamese language was the collaborative work of fathers de Pina, Bori, Gaspar de Amaral, and Antoine Barbosa. What de Rhodes did was to document, codify, and publish the quốc ngữ. In the early 17th century, Đàng Trong comprised part of present central Vietnam. It did not include South Vietnam, which was still under Khmer control.

73. Ibid., 38–39. In 1770, barely 40 years after the arrival of the missions étrangères, there were 40 Vietnamese priests in both Tonkin (North) and Cochinchina (South Vietnam).

74. McLeod, *The Vietnamese Response*, 4–5.

75. Dutton, *The Tay Son*, 177. Missionaries forbade their followers to contribute to the performance of rituals of ancestor worship and the construction of temples that they regarded as superstitious. They forbade sacrifices to village deities and condemned polygamy.

76. Y. Sakurai, "Eighteenth-Century Chinese Pioneers," in *Water Frontier*, edited by Nola Cooke and Li Tana, 45.

77. Sellers, *The Princes of Hà Tiên*, 9–12.

78. Cooke, "Water World," in *Water Frontier*, edited by Nola Cooke and Li Tana, 27–30.

79. Đinh Dậu Nguyễn, *From Saigon to Ho Chi Minh City*, 18–19. Built in 1772, the Nguyễn Cửu Đàm earthen rampart, according to Dậu, measured 15 miles long from Cát Ngang in the South to Lào Huế Bridge (Phú Nhuận).

80. Cooke and Tana, eds., *Water Frontier*, 61–64.

81. Sakurai, "Eighteenth-Century Chinese Pioneers," in *Water frontier*, edited by Nola Cooke and Li Tana, 46–47.

82. Although the Vietnamese could have lived or done business in and around Prey Nokor as far back as 1600, a tax collecting post was not established there until 1623.

Chapter 2

1. Dutton, *The Tây Son Uprising*, 37. When Lord Nguyễn Phúc Khoát died in 1765, Loan, who was the regent and Khoát's maternal uncle, forged an edict allowing him to imprison Crown Prince Hưng Tổ. He then appointed the 12-year-old Duệ Tôn as the new chúa and promoted himself as chief adviser and minister of civil affairs—positions that gave him control over state tax collection.

2. Tana, *Nguyen Cochinchina*, 142–144. Two other Nguyễn generals refused to save Hà Tiên when the latter was invaded by the Siamese in 1771.

3. Crawfurd, *Journal of an Embassy*, 511.

4. Tana, *Nguyen Cochinchina*, 146–148.

5. Ibid., 154. It was in Saigon that Nguyễn Ánh reorganized the southern administration, militarily and administratively controlled the provinces, and expanded rice culture and riverine and overseas trade.

6. Dutton, *The Tây Sơn Uprising*, 39. Records hint that Nhạc had gambled away tax money, although another author suggested that he was not able to collect taxes because of the underlying economic woes.

7. Tana, *Nguyễn Cochinchina*, 147.

8. The leader Nguyễn Nhạc was delivered to the Qui Nhơn province chief by his men in a cage. At night, he got out of his cage and opened the citadel door, allowing his men to come in and capture the citadel.

9. Sellers, *The Princes of Hà Tiên*, 69–73.

10. Ibid., 86.

11. Dutton, *The Tây Son Uprising*, 202–203. The Saigonese feared the Tây Sơn so much after the massacre that they dared not do anything—not even bury the dead.

12. White, *A Voyage to Cochinchina*, 234; http://books.google.com.

13. Dutton, *The Tây Son Uprising*, 45–46.

14. Ibid., 58. The Tây Sơn spent so much time waging wars that they did not have the time to administer the country. The people were exhausted, and the country and economy were in ruins after they left the stage.

15. Ibid., 116–17, 121.

16. Ibid., 133–36.

17. Quoted in Dutton, *The Tây Son Uprising*, 112.

18. Sellers, *The Princes of Hà Tiên*, 101.

19. Southern rulers called themselves chúa or lords—one level below the king—in reverence to the northern king Lê, although militarily and economically, they were the equals of the Lê. They administered a country larger than the North and even received allegiance from the kings of Laos and Cambodia.

20. Sellers, *The Princes of Hà Tiên*, 77–70.

21. Daughton, "Recasting Pigneau de Behaine," in *Borderless Histories* by Nhung T. Tran and Anthony Reid, 294.

22. Sellers, *The Princes of Hà Tiên*, 104–105.

23. Wook, *Southern Vietnam*, 24–26.

24. Ibid., 21. They included Lê Quang Định, Phạm Đăng Hưng, Trịnh Hoài Đức, Ngô Tùng Châu, and Ngô Nhân Tĩnh.

25. Dutton, *The Tây Son Uprising*, 204–205.

26. Quoted in Cooke and Tana, eds., *Water Frontier*, 86. Iron, lead, and sulfur were not naturally found in South Vietnam.

27. Sellers, *The Princes of Hà Tiên*, 111–113.

28. Li Tana, "The Water Frontier," in *Water Frontier*, edited by Nola Cooke and Li Tana, 5.

29. Đình Dậu Nguyễn, *From Saigon to HCMC*, 22–25.

30. Ibid., 29.

31. McLeod, *The Vietnamese Response*, 10–11; Sellers, *The Princes of Hà Tiên*, 116–117.

32. Taboulet, *La Geste Francaise*, 232–233.

33. Moyar, *Triumph Forsaken*, 5.

34. Sellers, *The Princes of Hà Tiên*, 121. Methodical was the name of the game for Nguyễn Ánh, who did not want to gamble away his chances. That was why it took him two and a half decades to win back his throne. That was why he chose to return to his Confucian roots instead of becoming an enlightened leader.

35. Barrow, *A Voyage to Cochinchina*, 283.

36. Despite being an independent state, Vietnam recognized Chinese suzerainty as Imperial China was too big a force to be ignored. Diplomatic relations at that time were based on the theory that all rulers in the world derived their power from the emperor of China.

37. Sellers, *The Princes of Hà Tiên*, 124–6.

38. Nghia M. Vo, *The Bamboo Gulag*, 169. Of the more than one million detained ARVN (Armed Forces of the Republic of Vietnam) soldiers, 250,000 to 300,000 were kept in concentration camps for over one year. See Văn Cảnh Nguyen, *Vietnam Under Communism*, 197–198. Hanoi official Nguyen Co Thach mentioned that 2.5 million people had been incarcerated: See Desbarats, "Repression in the Socialist Republic," in John N. Moore, *The Vietnam Debate*, 196.

39. Grant, *The Boat People*, 80–81; Wain, *The Refused*, 212–213, 256. By 1981, more than 1 million refugees had been resettled in 31 countries worldwide.

40. Chin, "The Junk Trade," in *Water Frontier*, edited by Nola Cooke and Li Tana, 62.

41. Reid, *Southeast Asia in the Age of Commerce*, 60.

42. Li Tana, "Mekong Delta," in *Water*

Frontier, edited by Nola Cooke and Li Tana, 77.

43. Cooke and Tana, eds., *Water Frontier*, 136.

44. Vietnamese sailboat.

45. Li Tana, "Mekong Delta," in *Water Frontier*, edited by Nola Cooke and Li Tana, 80.

46. Chin, "The Junk Trade," in *Water Frontier*, edited by Nola Cooke and Li Tana, 63–64.

47. One picul (a Chinese measure) equals 60 kg or 133 pounds.

48. Wood from a tropical tree that yields a red dye.

49. Li Tana, "The 18th Century Mekong Delta," in *Vietnam: Borderless Histories*, by Nhung T. Tran and Anthony Reid, 149.

50. A "can" equals 0.6 kg in weight.

51. Cooke and Tana, eds., *Water Frontier*, 10.

52. Reid, "Chinese Trade and Southeast Asian Economic Expansion," in *Water Frontier*, edited by Nola Cooke and Li Tana, 27.

53. Li Tana, "The Water Frontier," in *Water Frontier*, edited by Nola Cooke and Li Tana, 3.

54. Crawfurd, *Journal of an Embassy*, 542.

55. Li Tana, "The 18th Century Mekong Delta" in *Vietnam: Borderless Histories*, by Nhung T. Tran and Anthony Reid, 155.

56. White, *A Voyage to Cochinchina*, 235.

57. Li Tana, "Ships and Ship Building in the Mekong Delta," in *Water Frontier*, edited by Nola Cooke and Li Tana, 122.

58. Ibid., 124.

59. Ibid., 119.

60. Ibid., 121.

61. Chanta is from the Sanskrit "Chandra," meaning moon; buri is from the Sanskrit "Puri," meaning city or town. Chantaburi therefore signifies Moon City. The town is located on the Gulf of Siam close to the Cambodian border. Chantaburi has a large Vietnamese population; the first group came in the 1830s following Minh Mạng's persecution of the Catholics and the Lê Văn Khôi's rebels; the second group arrived in the 1920s to 1940s from French Indochina, and the third group came following the fall of Saigon in 1975.

62. Li Tana, "Ships and Ship Building," in *Water Frontier*, edited by Nola Cooke and Li Tana, 129.

63. McLeod, *The Vietnamese Response*, 7–9.

64. Li Tana, "The Water Frontier," in *Water Frontier*, edited by Nola Cooke and Li Tana, 1–12.

65. Ibid., 4.

66. Ibid., 11.

67. Marr, *Vietnamese Anticolonialism*, 22–25.

68. K. W. Taylor, "Nguyen Hoang," in *Southeast Asia in the Early Modern Era*, by Anthony Reid, 64.

69. K. W. Taylor, "Surface Orientation," 949–978.

Chapter 3

1. By combining words from the names of the cities Gia Định and Thăng Long (Hanoi), the former southern and northern capitals, and using them as his reigning name, Nguyen Anh wanted to stress the re-unification of the country under his rule.

2. Intersex people were previously known as hermaphrodites, a word which derives from the combination of Hermes (Greek god of male sexuality) and Aphrodite (Greek goddess of beauty and love). A hermaphrodite is a person born with both female and male genitals. Because of sexual ambiguity, the child could be raised as a girl or a boy. See "Born True Hermaphrodite," http://www.angelfire.com/ca2/BornHermaphrodite/. Since an intersex person is sterile, he can be compared to a eunuch or a surgically castrated male. Many eunuchs in the past have served as military commanders, ministers, advisers, musicians, and guards for the kings' harems of wives.

3. Wook, *Southern Vietnam*, 52. The army following the Chinese system was comprised of five divisions: front, back, left, right and center. Commanders of the left and center divisions were the most powerful figures in the South.

4. Woodside, *Vietnam and the Chinese Model*, 284–285; Taboulet, *La Geste*, 325.

5. Wook, *Southern Vietnam*, 57–58.

6. This is fortunately or unfortunately one of the characteristics of the South Vietnamese: They are straight to the point and blunt. It is said that they wear their hearts on their sleeves.

7. Wook, *Southern Vietnam*, 59. The two generals tendered their resignations, but they were not accepted.

8. Taboulet, *La Geste*, 295.

9. Wook, *Southern Vietnam*, 56–57.

10. Taboulet, *La Geste*, 325.

11. White, *A Voyage to Cochinchina*, 233.

12. Taboulet, *La Geste*, 327.

13. Woodside, *Vietnam and the Chinese Model*, 286.

14. Ibid., 288–289.

15. Thanh Khoi Le, *Le Vietnam*, 366.

16. McLeod, *The Vietnamese Response*, 21–23. As a Confucian monarch, Gia Long feared that prohibiting Catholicism during the early years of his reign would be seen as an act of betrayal to friends who had helped him in difficult times. He was also irritated by the continuous demands of missionaries who requested that Catholicism be granted a special status in his land.

17. Wook, *Southern Vietnam*, 68–69.

18. Wook, "Nguyen Dynasty's Policy Toward Chinese," in *Water Frontier*, edited by Nola Cooke and Li Tana, 87.

19. White, *A Voyage to Cochinchina*, 234.

20. Brown, *Cochinchina and My experience of It*, 198–199.

21. Wook, "The Nguyen Dynasty's Policy," in *Water Frontier*, edited by Nola Cooke and Li Tana, 88–89.

22. Ibid., 88.

23. White, *Voyage to Cochinchina*, 265.

24. Wook, *Southern Vietnam*, 69–81.

25. Cooke and Tana, *Water Frontier*, 80.

26. Cooke and Tana, *Water Frontier*, 93.

27. Vương, *Saigon Ngày Xưa*, 82–84. To thank Southerners for their help during the war, Nguyễn Ánh granted the governor of the South huge privileges. As viceroy, the latter governed the South as well as controlled Cambodia.

28. Taboulet, *La Geste*, 327–328. Priests were said to teach a religion that disrespected Buddha and ancestors. Converts were given the chance to give up the religion.

29. Wook, *Southern Vietnam*, 85–88

30. Taboulet, *La Geste*, 331. The tomb was chained and then flogged 100 times. See note 33, below. Not only was his tomb desecrated, 16 members of his family were executed.

31. Wook, "The Nguyen Dynasty's Policy," in *Water Frontier*, edited by Nola Cooke and Li Tana, 96; Taboulet, *La Geste*, 331.

32. Wook, 95.

33. Wook, *Southern Vietnam*, 96–97. Official records mention that Duyệt's tomb was "flattened." It is difficult to reconcile what was done to Duyệt's tomb because the procedure had rarely been performed in the past and had not been well described.

34. McLeod, *The Vietnamese Response*, 30.

35. Quoted in Wood, *Southern Vietnam*, 102. As Minh Mạng had noticed, southerners had moved so far away from the norms of Confucianism that they were no longer recognizable to government officials. But instead of seeing these differences as riches that needed to be nurtured and cultivated, he saw them as abnormalities that needed to be suppressed.

36. Vo, "Confucianism and Communism," in *The Men of Vietnam*, by Nghia M. Vo et al., 111–137.

37. Wook, *Southern Vietnam*, 103.

38. Ibid., 112–115. In an endowed land, Southerners were more oriented toward commerce and trade than learning the basics of Confucianism.

39. Ibid., 152–153.

40. Ibid., 195–197.

41. Đình Dầu Nguyễn, *From Saigon to HCMC*, 48.

42. Ibid., 23–24, 48–50.

43. White, *A Voyage to Cochinchina*, 236.

44. Ibid., 234.

45. Ibid., 234.

46. Why a thousand generations? This allegorical expression was used to stress the severity of the sentence. In the eyes of Minh Mạng, Lê Văn Duyệt had committed such a heinous crime that only a thousand-generation sentence could erase it.

47. Le and Dovert, *Saigon*, 69.

48. Dang, "General Lê Văn Duyệt," in *The Men of Vietnam*, edited by Vo et al., 55–71. Over the years, and especially during major festivities, people came to pray at the mausoleum, which eventually became a worshiping place. Nguyen An Ninh's father brought him to the mausoleum before his trip to France to ask him to swear never to forget his duty to his country (see Nguyen An Ninh in main text, page XXX). As favors had been fulfilled, Lê Văn Duyệt was acknowledged to be a "responsive deity," which, in turn, brought in a larger number of worshipers. During the Diệm and Thiệu years, the mausoleum became a busy place of worship where crowds came to pray, ask for favors, and to solemnly celebrate the New Year. Young people flocked the shrine to gather leaves and flowers (hái lộc) for happiness and luck. The place was shut down in 1975 when the communists arrived, until the 1990s when authorities allowed its restoration. The shrine again regained its status as the most popular place of worship in Vietnam.

49. Nam kỳ lục tỉnh: the six provinces of the South. In 1861, the French conquered these provinces and called the region Cochinchina.

50. Cooke and Tana, *Water Frontier*, 12.

Chapter 4

1. Sellers, *The Princes of Ha Tien*, 66. The first missionaries met the Khmers in South Vietnam in the 16th century, while the French (arriving later in the mid–18th century) saw and baptized newly-arrived Vietnamese. The Khmers, strongly influenced by Buddhism, converted to Catholicism to a lesser degree than did the Vietnamese. Less than two percent of Cambodians are Christians compared to ten to 15 percent of Vietnamese.

2. Opium from British India was smuggled by traders into China, which prohibited the use and trade of opium. Open warfare ensued from 1839 to 1842, with China being forced to cede Hong Kong to Britain. A second war from 1856 to 1860, opened many more Chinese cities to westerners through unrestricted trade. See http://www.wsu.edu:8080/~dee/ching/opium.htm.

3. McLeod, *The Vietnamese Response*, 35.

4. Tucker, *Vietnam*, 28; McLeod, *The Vietnamese Response*, 36. French officers Lapierre aboard the *Gloire* and Rigault de Genouilli aboard the *Victorieuse* gave the order to open fire on Da Nang—knowing full well that all missionaries had been released.

5. Borer, *Superpowers Defeated*, 22.

6. McLeod, *The Vietnamese Response*, 42–43. Since even the Dutch and Portuguese had their own Asian colonies, the French, who were eager to have their share, exerted heavy pressure on Napoleon III.

7. Dommen, *The Indochinese Experience*, 4–5.

8. Pallu de la Barriere, *Histoire de l'Expedition de la Cochinchine de 1861*, 30–31, http://www.archive.org/stream/histoiredelexpd00barrgoog#page/n45/mode/1up.

9. McLeod, *The Vietnamese Response*, 41–44. While Đà Nẵng held on for more than five months, Saigon fell in two days. This suggested how weak the resistance was in Saigon.

10. Barrelon, *Cities of Nineteenth Century Colonial Vietnam*, 19. One wonders what had happened to the Vietnamese Navy, one of the best in Asia in 1800, which had allowed

Nguyễn Ánh to re-conquer his throne. Six decades later, it could not resist a few French warships, forcing its commander to take his own life. It is hard not to assume that Minh Mạng, by tearing down Saigon in 1835 to bring her under his control, had so weakened the South that it could not offer much resistance to the French.

11. Ibid., 16.

12. Pallu de la Barriere, *Histoire de l'Expedition*, 32.

13. Thomazi, *La Conquete de l'Indochine*, 34–39. http://en.wikipedia.org/wiki/Siege_of_Sai gon. The French in 1859 only controlled the partly-destroyed Saigon citadel and the shores of the Saigon River. It was only in 1861, after the fall of the Kỳ Hòa fort, that Saigon was totally controlled by the French.

14. Pallu de la Barriere, *Histoire de l'Expedition*, 34–35.

15. Ibid., 36–37.

16. Haley, "1861 French Conquest of Saigon," http://www.historynet.com/1861-french-conquest-of-saigon-battle-of-the-ky-hoa-forts.htm. The French had 1,200 men of the 3rd and 4th infantry regiments, 600 men of the 2nd infantry battalion, 200 artillery men, 800 sailors and 100 others, along with 270 Spanish troops, as well as the contingent left in Saigon; Pallu de la Barriere quoted a number close to 4,000 soldiers (Pallu de la Barriere, *Histoire de l'Expedition*, 15–16). http://www.archive.org/stream/histoiredelex pd00barrgoog#page/n30/mode/1up.

17. Pallu de la Barriere, *Histoire de l'Expedition*, 65–66.

18. Ibid., 76–77; a trou-de-loup is a five-foot-deep conical pit with a vertical stake at its center. A cheval-de-frise is an obstacle composed of barbed wire or spikes attached to a wooden frame. These kinds of obstacles might have been useful in 1800, but not in 1861 when the firing power of firearms and cannons easily overwhelmed defenders.

19. Ibid., 86–87.

20. McLeod, *The Vietnamese Response*, 45–46.

21. Borer, *Superpowers Defeated*, 23.

22. McLeod, *The Vietnamese Response*, 50–51. Lê Duy Phụng's army was defeated only in 1864.

23. Ibid., 47.

24. McLeod, *The Vietnamese Response*, 46–49.

25. Ibid., 52–53. The chu hoa group grew larger with time and soon won the king's sup-

port. During the same period, the court faced the Le rebellion in the North. That second military front may have tipped the scale toward the chu hoa's side.

26. Taboulet, *La Geste*, vol. 2, 474–6; McLeod, *The Vietnamese Response*, 54–55. Tu Duc's reaction was ambivalent and controversial at best. Although he publicly lambasted his negotiators after the signature of the 1862 treaty, he kept them in their positions and even allowed them to negotiate further with the French. It is also unlikely that Phan Thanh Gian and Lam Duy Hiep, who were high court officials and faithful Confucians, would voluntarily dare to disobey their master. When Phan Thanh Gian ceded the three remaining southern provinces in 1867, Tu Duc's reaction was the same. He chastised Gian publicly but did not repudiate the concessions. Gian, who was 71 at that time, had on many occasions submitted his retirement, but took the position at the insistence of Tu Duc. He had probably realized that this was a losing proposition. Had he waged the war against the French, his soldiers would have been massacred. Had he surrendered, as in this case, he would have been condemned by the court. In the end, as a true Confucian he accepted his responsibility, returned all his titles and medals to Tu Duc, and committed suicide in 1867.

27. Quoted in Jamieson, *Understanding Vietnam*, 47. "Nghia" can best be translated as righteousness. It implies duty, justice, and obligation. In the eyes of Tu Duc, if even wild animals, crocodiles and tigers could follow these rules and respect a righteous person, people would too.

28. Jamieson, *Understanding Vietnam*, 47.

29. Quoted in McLeod, *The Vietnamese Response*, 56–57. McLeod has suggested that Tu Duc had probably instructed his emissaries to grant France the substantial privileges mentioned in the treaty. See McLeod, 59.

30. Marr, *Vietnamese Anticolonialism*, 32.

31. Huynh, *An Anthology of Vietnamese Poems*, 85–89. Nguyen Dinh Chieu suggested spending time to enjoy the riches of nature instead of cooperating with the French. He reminded people that if a horse remembers its old home, should men forget the country of their birth?

32. Jamieson, *Understanding Vietnam*, 44.

33. Marr, *Vietnamese Anticolonialism*,

30–31. Thủ Khoa Huấn was the top cử nhân graduate of the 1852 regional examinations.

34. Pallu de la Barriere, *Histoire de l'Expedition*, 229. The correct term would be Cochinchinese rather than Annamese, because most of the fighters were from the South: Cochinchina. At that time there was no clear distinction between Annam and Cochinchina.

35. Buu Lam Truong, *Patterns of Vietnamese Response*, 73–74.

36. Ibid., 11.

37. Pallu de la Barriere, *Histoire de l'Expedition*, 226, 231. Minh Mang believed so in moral Confucian authority that he thought even wild animals listened to Confucian rules.

38. McLeod, *The Vietnamese Response*, 65.

39. Ho Tai, *Millenarianism and Peasant Politics*, 68–69.

40. Ibid., 44–48.

41. Ibid., 52–57.

42. Ibid., 69–75.

43. Jamieson, *Understanding Vietnam*, 45. The key ministries were: justice, finance, defense, and rites. The Ministry of Rites—a combination of department of the interior and foreign affairs—was the dominant one.

44. Marr, *Vietnamese Anticolonialism*, 28.

45. Buu Lam Truong, *Patterns of Vietnamese Response*, 20.

46. Quoted in Buu Lam Truong, *Patterns of Vietnamese Response*, 20. The funeral oration engraved on the king's tombstone, usually written by a king's successor, was written by Tự Đức himself in 1867.

47. Jamieson, *Understanding Vietnam*, 42, 45. One should not blame Tự Đức only—Gia Long and his successors could have corrected their course at any time before 1862 and probably averted the disaster.

48. Thanh Khoi Le, *Le Vietnam*, 365.

49. Buu Lam Truong, *Patterns of Vietnamese Response*, 18.

50. Thanh Khoi Le, *Le Vietnam*, 363–364. Tộ was considered to be a moderate and well-meaning reformer who wanted to leave monarchy in place but wanted also to remove the mandarinate system because he believed mandarins were corrupting the system.

51. Borer, *Superpowers Defeated*, 24–25. The heavy-handed Hue Treaty was never ratified by the French government and was replaced by the Patenotre Treaty on June 6, 1884.

52. Tainturier, "Architectures et Urbanisme sous l'administration Francaise," in

Saigon, by Le and Dovert, 75–78. Bonnard is spelled with two "n's" in French books and only one "n" in American books.

53. Barrelon, *Cities of Nineteenth Century Colonial Vietnam*, 14.

54. Ibid., 20–21.

55. Tainturier, "Architectures et Urbanisme," in *Saigon*, by Le and Dovert, 75–78.

56. Cooper, *France in Indochina*, 44–45.

57. Baudrit, *Extraits des Registres*, vol. 2, 7–9, 15.

58. Ibid., 33. The governor still remained powerful and governed by decree, although the council had assumed some powers.

59. Ibid., 45–52. Although the work of building a whole new town from scratch could be overwhelming in the face of limited resources, the council appeared to be very conservative by trying to delay one project after another instead of being more aggressive in their goals and planning.

60. Ibid., 41.

61. Baudrit, *Extraits des Registres*, vol. 1, 79.

62. Ibid., 80–81.

63. Ibid., 97–99, 102–103. There was not enough new regenerating water feeding into the tank and the well.

64. Ibid., 145.

65. Tainturier in *Saigon*, by Le and Dovert, 79–81.

66. Wright, *The Politics of Design*, 185.

67. Baudrit, *Extraits des Registres*, vol. 1, 14–16, 21.

68. Ibid., 31.

69. Ibid., 40–41. Of course, council members were at the same time working on other projects like the sanitation of the Boresse marsh, the opening of new streets, and the location of the new My Tho-Saigon train station.

70. The Saigon River is affected by maritime tides, which could reach flood levels swamping Saigon and its environment even today. See: http://english.thesaigontimes.vn/Home/business/environment/2010/.

71. Baudrit, *Extraits des Registres*, vol. 2, 89–90.

72. Ibid., 101.

73. Le and Dovert, *Saigon*, 104–105. According to Baudrit, the exact date of the beginning of the work was not mentioned in the June 27, 1898, minutes of the city deliberations. See Baudrit, *Extraits des Registres*, vol. 1, 300–301.

74. Baudrit, *Extraits des Registres*, vol. 1, 318–333.

75. Ibid., 340–342. There was no mention in the minutes about whether the city council had tried to recover the money from Ruffier.

76. Tainturier, in *Saigon*, by Le and Dovert, 85–87.

77. Baudrit, vol. 2, 163–165. The majority of people at the time died of infectious diseases (lack of antibiotics) rather than heart disease, high blood pressure, obesity, diabetes, which are diseases of the modern age.

78. Tainturier, in *Saigon*, by Le and Dovert, 91–93.

79. Morice, *People and Wildlife In and Around Saigon*, 1–9.

80. Ibid., 29–30.

81. Thanh Khoi Le, *Le Vietnam*, 373–374. Francis Garnier was the captain who conquered North Vietnam and then Tonkin in 1873.

82. Guillaume, "Saigon or the Failure of an Ambition (1858–1945)," in *Colonial Cities*, by Ross and Telkamp, 185–193.

83. http://www.omniglot.com/writing/chunom.htm.

84. Jamieson, *Understanding Vietnam*, 68.

85. Bouchot, *Petrus Truong Vinh Ky*, 73.

86. Jamieson, *Understanding Vietnam*, 69–71.

87. Barrelon, *Cities of Nineteenth Century Colonial Vietnam*, 35–37.

88. Ibid., 39–42.

89. McLeod, *The Vietnamese Response*, 90–93.

90. Templer, *Shadows and Wind*, 211.

91. The French figure of 6,000 people in 1860 seems low compared to the Vietnamese figure of 20,000 to 30,000. The discrepancy may stem from the fact that native soldiers, government officials, their families and neighbors might have left town following the French takeover of Saigon.

92. Quach Thanh Tam Langlet, "Saigon, Capitale de la Republique du Sud-Vietnam ou une Urbanization Sauvage," in *Peninsules Indochinoises*, by P. B. Lafont, 186, 193.

Chapter 5

1. Vo, "Roots of Southern Nationalism," in *The Sorrows of War and Peace*, by Nghia M. Vo et al., 35–73. One could argue about the exact date of the emergence of Vietnamese nationalism. It was there all along throughout the millennia. Whereas before the arrival of the French it was attached to a central authority, e.g., the king, in the 20th century it was linked to ideas of freedom, individual liberty, and rights. The South Vietnamese concept of nationalism had its roots during their southern migration when they felt free to develop new lands, to farm, practice their religion, and trade with other nations with minimal control by the central government. The religious sects, which reflected the pioneers' spirit, never mentioned the king.

2. McHale, *Print and Power*, 7.

3. Smith and Williams, *Pre–communist Indochina*, 116–119. The predominance of spirits with French identities (Victor Hugo, Jeanne d' Arc) is due to the strong cultural influence of France.

4. Ibid., 131–136. The three Eras are associated with the three Buddhas: Amitabha (past), Sakyamuni (present), and Maitreya (future).

5. Ibid., 143.

6. "Bửu Sơn Kỳ Hương" (Strange Fragrance From the Precious Mountain) refers to a religious tradition practiced by the mystic Đoàn Minh Huyên (1807–1856) in the Mekong Delta and later expanded by Huỳnh Phú Sổ. Huyên, the Buddha Master of Western Peace (Phật Thầy Tây Ân), was known for his supernatural abilities to heal and cure the sick and the insane, especially during the big cholera epidemic of 1849. See http://en.wikipedia.org/wiki/Buu_Son_Ky_Huong.

7. Nam Thiếp is the Buddha Master's second disciple. He led various peasant rebellions against the French before renouncing violence at the age of 50 to become a village chief who protected his village with magic. Nguyen and Pivar, *Fourth Uncle in the Mountain*, 136–138.

8. For the Hòa Hảo, the terms "communist" and "Việt Minh" were interchangeable. In the 1940s, in the absence of a strong nationalistic party, Vietnamese nationalists flocked to the Việt Minh's side to fight the French. They soon realized that the Việt Minh was just a front for the communist party.

9. Ho Tai, *Millenarianism and Peasant Politics in Vietnam*, 116–144.

10. Buttinger, *Vietnam: A Dragon embattled*, 33–34.

11. Ibid., 62–65.

12. The South Vietnamese called him Phan Châu Trinh and the North Vietnamese, Phan Chu Trinh.

13. Marr, *Vietnamese Anticolonialism*, 129. Therefore, they were not privy to any world affairs, foreign cultures, or modernity. Minh Mang's bế quan tỏa cảng policy (close off the country) to prevent priests and thus foreigners from entering the country had also shut off cultural exchanges with the rest of the world.

14. Marr, *Vietnamese Anticolonialism*, 136, 143. Under the influence of Trương Vĩnh Ký, quốc ngữ had achieved some intellectual respectability by the end of the 19th century in Cochinchina. Native Catholics had also used quốc ngữ for centuries.

15. Jamieson, *Understanding Vietnam*, 91, 72.

16. Marr, *Vietnamese Anticolonialism*, 238–240.

17. Turner, *Vietnamese Communism*, 8–10; Marr, *Vietnamese Anticolonialism*, 260. The price tag was between 100,000 to 150,000 piasters.

18. Marr, *Vietnamese Anticolonialism*, 156–157, 191. Huỳnh Thúc Kháng was caught for having fomented a rebellion in 1908 in Hội An. He spent 13 years in a Poulo Condore jail. For having expressed vague approval of rumors about demonstrations somewhere else, Trần Quý Cấp was found guilty of treason and was executed by being chopped in half at the waist in 1908.

19. Although there was a school reserved for princes and children of high officials, there was no public school for common people. The curriculum, which included a few classic Confucian texts, resulted in the formation of men of letters who were geared toward perpetuation of the system—of which they were a part—rather than improving the well-being of people or changing the status quo.

20. Marr, *Vietnamese Anticolonialism*, 164–167. A private, tuition-free school open to young and old, male and female, rich and poor, beginners or advanced students. It was opened in 1907 and closed a year later by the French because of its revolutionary curriculum.

21. Jamieson, *Understanding Vietnam*, 56–58.

22. Marr, *Vietnamese Anticolonialism*, 198–201.

23. Ibid., 169–170; Jamieson, *Understanding Vietnam*, 59–60. Actually, the Vietnamese originally wore their hair in buns and were told to shave their heads, leaving only a ponytail.

24. Marr, *Vietnamese Anticolonialism*, 170; Jamieson, *Understanding Vietnam*, 60.

25. It is interesting to note that hair could serve as a symbol of revolt. While haircutting was used in Vietnam, letting hair and beards grow long was the symbol of resistance for the hippies in western societies in the 1950s.

26. Quoted in Jamieson, *Understanding Vietnam*, 61.

27. Marr, *Vietnamese Anticolonialism*, 188–193. The poison plot occurred at a boarding house/restaurant where colonial soldiers mingled with local cooks. During a banquet, poison was introduced into the food, but due to improper dosage, the soldiers became ill but were not killed. After dropping the poison, one of the cooks got cold feet and confessed to a priest who relayed the news to the French. Thirteen participants were executed and four received life imprisonment.

28. Marr, *Vietnamese Anticolonialism*, 242. The island was also called Côn Sơn in the South.

29. Marr, *Vietnamese Anticolonialism*, 182–183. All the official paperwork at the time was written either in Han Chinese or nôm, which the common people could not read or write. By introducing and teaching the quốc ngữ to the masses, Trương Vĩnh Ký and others had provided them with a means of communication and a tool for education, as well as a bonding for future endeavors. Without the spread of the quốc ngữ, there would probably have been no revolution at all.

30. Marr, *Vietnamese Tradition on Trial*, 24–31.

31. Hemery, "Saigon la Rouge," in *Saigon 1925–1945*, by Franchini, 163–66; Marr, *Vietnamese Tradition on Trial*, 47.

32. Marr, *Vietnamese Tradition on Trial*, 37–38.

33. Ibid., 222–226.

34. Smith and Williams, *Pre–communist Indochina*, 148–149.

35. Ibid., 151.

36. Marr, *Vietnamese Anticolonialism*, 262.

37. Ibid., 265, 268.

38. Smith and Williams, *Pre–communist Indochina*, 158–160.

39. Marr, *Vietnamese Tradition on Trial*, 19–23; Ho Tai, *Millenarianism and Peasant Politics in Vietnam*, 158–60.

40. Marr, *Vietnamese Anticolonialism*, 275.

41. While the two Phan were trained and

did most of their work in the North, Ninh worked exclusively in Saigon. If the Phans were the last bastions of the Confucian tradition, Ninh was a modernist who was trained in Paris and exposed to leftist French thinkers. Southern landlords were important benefactors for the revolutionary movement. They contributed lodging to revolutionaries who came to the south and funds to send students abroad for study. Being an intellectual loner was the common link between Ninh and Trinh. See Marr, *Vietnamese Anticolonialism*, 268.

42. Ho Tai, *Radicalism*, 72–73, 130–131.

43. Ibid., 82–84, 143.

44. Ibid., 152–153.

45. Ho Tai, *Millenarianism*, 82–83.

46. Hemery, in *Saigon 1925–1945*, by Franchini, 188.

47. McHale, *Print and Power*, 18, 24–25.

48. Ibid., 31.

49. Ibid., 145, 149, 159.

50. Jamieson, *Understanding Vietnam*, 5.

51. Marr, *Vietnamese Anticolonialism*, 261.

52. Jamieson, *Understanding Vietnam*, 93–97.

53. Vo, "Confucianism and Communism," in *The Men of Vietnam*, by Nghia M. Vo et al., 116–117.

54. Jamieson, *Understanding Vietnam*, 106–107.

55. Ibid., 159. They could be, however, very individualistic if they got involved in politics. There were almost as many political parties as people under the Thieu regime in the 1960s and 1970s. At least 20 different candidates vied for the presidency during that period. Back in 1942, when they were invited by the Chinese to attend the Liuchow meeting, there were 20 leaders from various and competing groups and parties. See Jamieson, 179.

56. Under the Vietnamese Confucian regime, the wife of a man was known by her husband's title. Mrs. Judge or Mrs. Teacher would refer to the wife of a judge or a teacher, even though she might not have any education at all.

57. Jamieson, *Understanding Vietnam*, 117–125.

58. Ibid., 135–146.

59. Ibid., 93, 171.

60. Phạm Quỳnh suggested retaining the best of that which is Eastern, acquiring the best of that which is Western, and synthesizing the two cultures. Nguyễn Tường Tam ad-

vised a complete break with the past and traditional culture as described in *Breaking the Ties*.

61. Hemery, in *Saigon 1925–1945*, by Franchini, 172–73.

62. Follower of Leon Trotsky, a Russian revolutionary theoretician. He was a leader of the 1917 Bolshevik revolution and was expelled from the Communist Party (1927) and banished (1929) for opposing Stalin's authoritarianism. He was murdered at the behest of Stalin while in exile in Mexico in 1940.

63. Marr, *Vietnamese Tradition on Trial*, 6.

64. Hemery, in *Saigon 1925–1945*, by Franchini, 174–188.

65. Huynh, *An Anthology of Vietnamese Poems*, 120–121.

66. Zinoman, *The Colonial Bastille*, 10–11.

Chapter 6

1. South Vietnam had only become part of đàng trong by the mid–18th century.

2. Jamieson, *Understanding Vietnam*, 214–215. The Cao Đài use almost the same hierarchical structure as the Catholic Church. The highest priest is, therefore, called "pope."

3. Dommen, *The Indochinese Experience*, 53–63.

4. Lockhart, *The End of the Vietnamese Monarchy*, 65, 69, 82, 87, 92.

5. Diem and Chanoff, *In the Jaws of History*, 31.

6. Dommen, *The Indochinese Experience*, 83–89.

7. Fall, *The Two Vietnams*, 206; Diem and Chanoff, *In the Jaws of History*, 35. The erudite Kim did not have the Machiavellian sophistication of Hồ, the politician.

8. Diem and Chanoff, *In the Jaws of History*, 43, 46.

9. Fall, *The Two Vietnams*, 207.

10. Dommen, *The Indochinese Experience*, 103–112. The transfer being invalid, the Hà Nội government was illegitimate.

11. Goodwin, *No Way Out*, 125.

12. Jamieson, *Understanding Vietnam*, 185.

13. Việt Minh or communist. Later called Việt Cộng (VC). Bảo Đại had already declared the independence of Vietnam on March 11, 1945.

14. Jamieson, *Understanding Vietnam*, 198–199.

15. VNQDD: Vietnam Quốc Dân Đảng or Vietnam Nationalist Party. Similar to the Chinese Kuomintang. Đại Việt is the Greater Vietnam Party.

16. Dommen, *The Indochinese Experience*, 153–54.

17. Jamieson, *Understanding Vietnam*, 210–211.

18. Dommen, *The Indochinese Experience*, 184–86; Fall, *The Two Vietnams*, 210. These murders sealed the end of the non-communist coalition.

19. The French would not turn over the Norodom-Saigon Palace to Bảo Đại.

20. Fall, *The Two Vietnams*, 204–205, 215; Diem and Chanoff, *In the Jaws of History*, 64–66. Bảo Đại obtained greater formal independence from the French in two years of hard bargaining than Hồ had asked for in his most extreme demands of 1946; he had also gained international recognition for the country, although he could not command the loyalty and affection of the Vietnamese people. North Vietnam's treatment of the peasants was even worse than South Vietnam's. While Britain gave independence to Burma in a four-page document, the transfer of autonomy from France to Vietnam filled a thick 258-page book (Fall, 216).

21. Jamieson, *Understanding Vietnam*, 228–231.

22. Diem and Chanoff, *In the Jaws of History*, 78–80.

23. Dommen, *The Indochinese Experience*, 226–230.

24. Summers, *Historical Atlas of the Vietnam War*, 58–59, 120–121. Diện Biên Phủ is located 180 miles from the French bases at Hà Nội, astride supply lines to Laos. Khe Sanh, located 14 miles south of the DMZ and four miles from the Laotian border, allowed the monitoring of infiltration troops through the HCM trail.

25. Dommen, *The Indochinese Experience*, 209, 231–232.

26. Karnow, *Vietnam*, 214–217.

27. Bảo Đại was born in 1913, the 13th and last monarch of the Nguyễn dynasty. He ruled from 1926 to 1944 as king of Annam and emperor of Vietnam from 1944 to 1945. He married Nguyễn Hữu Thị Lan, a commoner from a wealthy southern Catholic family, in 1934 in Huế, and they had five children. She was renamed Empress Nam Phuong (Southern Perfume). He also had four other wives, three of whom he wed during his marriage to Nam Phuong. He wed Phú Anh, a cousin, in 1935; Hoàng a Chinese woman, in 1946; and Bùi Mộng Điệp in 1955. In 1972, he married Monique Baudot, a French citizen who was renamed Empress Thái Phượng. He died in 1997 and was buried in Paris. The following are a few quotes from this emperor.

When the Japanese colonel decided to take measures to ensure his safety against a possible Viet Minh coup in 1945, he simply declared, "I do not wish a foreign army to spill the blood of my people."

About his abdication in 1945, he said, "I would prefer to be a citizen of an independent country rather than Emperor of an enslaved one."

28. Dommen, *The Indochinese Experience*, 237–38; Diem and Chanoff, *In the Jaws of History*, 85–86.

29. Jamieson, *Understanding Vietnam*, 233.

30. Noppe and Hubert, *Art of Vietnam*, 185.

31. Cooper, *France in Indochina*, 46.

32. Ibid., 51–52. This was a definite break from the past when the "white town" was reserved for colonists and was architecturally and administratively different from the indigenous town. It was a town-park planted with 22,500 trees; see Franchini, *Saigon 1925–1945*, 31–35.

33. Tổng đốc is the chief of province.

34. Pham, *Two Hamlets in Nam Bo*, 66–68.

35. Dommen, *The Indochinese Experience*, 242–54.

Chapter 7

1. This was the most thoughtful remark that any foreigner has ever made about Vietnam. In the end, it was a fight of ideologies: communism against capitalism, oppression against freedom, internationalism against nationalism. Despite the "fog of war," it was obvious that the communists fought for hegemony over Indochina and the spread of communism around the world. They could be nationalistic, but they were more internationalist than nationalistic. It was in fact a fratricidal war pitting Vietnamese against Vietnamese.

2. There was only one university in Hà Nội throughout Indochina under the French. South Vietnamese, Laotians, and Cambodians wishing to obtain a college degree at that

time had to go either to Hà Nội or to France. The Saigon University was founded in 1954 by many Hà Nội faculty members who fled the communists.

3. Jacobs, *America's Miracle Man in Vietnam*, 25–26. Diệm was one of the most popular non–communist nationalists Vietnam had ever had. Although he stood for a free, independent, non–communist Vietnam, he did not have a real political base. He therefore turned to Nhu, his brother and right-hand man, to whom he owed his rise and demise.

4. Jamieson, *Understanding Vietnam*, 234. He was also stubborn, self-righteous, and a complete stranger to compromise. As a Confucian leader, he felt he was morally superior and needed to be obeyed.

5. He should be counted more as a mandarin, a good and virtuous administrator, and a man of principle like Minh Mạng, than a revolutionary or innovator like Phan Bội Châu or Phan Chu Trinh.

6. These were some of the tasks facing him in office. Yet for a man who had not worked for two decades, he deftly solved them one after the other. He managed to absorb one million refugees into a country that was almost broke, without causing further economic turmoil.

7. Karnow, *Vietnam: A History*, 216–7.

8. Catton, *Diem's Final Failure*, 6. By promoting his cause and ideas to U.S. politicians and decision-makers, he had secured a spot to lead his country in the future. His "third way" was widely praised by U.S. politicians. However, Diệm became premier more by default than by design on the part of the U.S.

9. Jacobs, *America's Miracle Man in Vietnam*, 52–57.

10. Catton, *Diem's Final Failure*, 9.

11. Jacobs, *America's Miracle Man in Vietnam*, 175. The Hall of Mirrors was reputedly the world's largest brothel. *Newsweek* called the Pearl of Orient the "most sinful city … and it is all legal."

12. Moyar, *Triumph Forsaken*, 21; Jacobs, *America's Miracle Man*, 214–215.

13. Hinh, a French Air Force lieutenant-colonel, was promoted general and chief of staff of the South Vietnamese Army by Bao Dai. The SVA, according to *Time*, although 120,000 man-strong, had only 560 lieutenants and sub–lieutenants, 76 majors and captains, and four colonels. See *Time Magazine*, April 28, 1952. In 1954, Hinh returned to the French

Air Force at his former colonel rank before becoming a general under De Gaulle.

14. Jacobs, *America's Miracle Man*, 172–173. Diem not only had to fight against the various sects, armies, the French, the Viet Minh, and Bao Dai, but also against the U.S. Ambassador who was plotting to have him replaced. This was heterogeneous Saigon and Vietnam in 1954—a cacophony of voices, a disorganized, rebellious collection of religious sects and political parties—that needed to be restrained and homogenized. These forces and new ones would rebel against Diem and topple his regime later on.

15. The Nùng or tribal highlanders were trusted because they were apolitical.

16. Jacobs, *America's Miracle Man*, 206. Saigon suffered worse damage in terms of casualties and property damage in 1954 than they would after the Tet Offensive in 1968.

17. Ibid., 210–215.

18. Although Diem's definition of democracy was different from that of the U.S., it was well within Vietnamese norms of the times and was much better than the illegal communist seizing of power of the North in 1947. Edward Miller, "Grand Designs: Vision, Power, and Nation Building in America's Alliance with Ngo Dinh Diem." PhD diss., Harvard University, 2004, 208.

19. Dommen, *The Indochinese Experience*, 281–298.

20. Vo, *The Vietnamese Boat People*, 17–30. The 1954 refugees included 800,000 Catholics and 133,276 Buddhists. Also included were intellectuals, Chinese, landowners, but also fishermen and peasants.

21. Frankum, *Operation Passage to Freedom*, 204.

22. Ibid., 88, 112, 126, 160, 202.

23. Tom Dooley, *Deliver Us from Evil*, 34.

24. Fisher, *Dr. America*, 37–38.

25. Vo, *The Vietnamese Boat People*, 32–34; Frankum, *Operation Passage to Freedom*, 205.

26. Frankum, *Operation Passage to Freedom*, 90.

27. Ibid., 69, 75. They were met by a band, an honor guard, and American, French, and Vietnamese officials under a downpour. They were given food and drinks by the Vietnamese Red Cross.

28. Vo, *The Vietnamese Boat People*, 17–41. It was remarkable that Premier Diệm, who had just taken office and did not have his own bureaucratic infrastructure, had been able to smoothly relocate a million refugees.

29. Larsen and Tran, *Shallow Graves*, 188.

30. Ibid., 189.

31. Frankum, *Operation Passage to Freedom*, 205.

32. Ibid., 201.

33. Wiesner, *Victims and Survivors*, 14–18.

34. Higgins, *Our Vietnam Nightmare*, 168.

35. Jamieson, *Understanding Vietnam*, 235–236, 256–257.

36. Catton, *Diem's Final Failure*, 26–34.

37. Higgins, *Our Vietnam Nightmare*, 166.

38. Catton, *Diem's Final Failure*, 35–39.

39. Masur, "Hearts and Minds," 77, 87, 90.

40. Ibid., 141, 143–145.

41. Ibid., 223.

42. Vo, "The Duality of the Vietnamese Mind," in *The Sorrows of War and Peace*, by Nghia M. Vo et al., 111–122.

43. Nhân can be translated as benevolence, compassion, or love of one's neighbor, while diệu indicates softness, moderation in feeling or views in order to achieve harmony within a system or group.

44. Jamieson, *Understanding Vietnam*, 290–291.

45. Vo, "Synopsis of the War," in *War and Remembrance*, by Nghia M. Vo et al., 167.

46. He was a member of the Resistance before bolting out because of his disillusionment with the party's dogmatic ideological regimentation in 1950. He moved South in 1954 and wrote that he had pity for the northern men who were burdened with hatred.

47. Jamieson, *Understanding Vietnam*, 324.

48. Ibid., 327–329.

49. Philip Taylor, *Fragments of the Present*, 39–40. "Yellow music" has been called phản động (reactionary), chống cộng (anticommunist), đầu độc (poisonous), and ủy mị (weakening), among other things.

50. Hoang Lac, "Blind Design," in *Prelude to Tragedy*, by Neese and O'Donnell, 70.

51. Berman, *Perfect Spy*, 148–149. Thảo's role was destabilization and coup-plotting against the Ngo regime. Coming from an anti-communist Catholic family, Thảo was recommended by his parents to Ngô Đình Thục, then bishop of Vĩnh Long. Thục referred him to his brother Nhu, and then Diệm. Thảo convinced Diệm to move quickly rather than slowly in the strategic hamlet program, thereby elevating hostility and alienating the peasants.

52. Catton, *Diem's Final Failure*, 119–140.

53. Ibid., 185–186.

54. Ibid., 193–208.

55. Dommen, *The Indochinese Experience*, 501–502.

56. Nhu Tang Truong, *A Viet Cong Memoir*, 63–80.

57. Diem and Chanoff, *In the Jaws of History*, 96.

58. Dommen, *The Indochinese Experience*, 505.

59. Berman, *Perfect Spy*, 147–150. The role of Tuyến remains to be elucidated. He trained and directed two big moles, Ba Quốc and Ấn, and was a friend of Thảo. Since all three of them worked for the CIO (Central Intelligence Organization), it was unlikely he did not know about their activities. If he was aware of their roles, why did he tolerate rather than unmask them? Was he also a double agent? Ấn refused to discuss Tuyến's activities (Berman, 150).

60. Higgins, *Our Vietnam Nightmare*, 181, 191–92.

61. Dommen, *The Indochinese Experience*, 524–37.

62. Ibid., 538–547.

63. Ibid., 547–55.

64. Ibid., 556–58; Jacobs, *America's Miracle Man*, xi.

65. Topmiller, *Lotus Unleashed*, 5.

66. Ibid., xi, 7. Vietnamese Buddhists are split into many groups: the radicals, led by Tri Quang; the moderates, led by Thích Tam Châu; the Hòa Hảo; Chinese Buddhists; Vietnamese Theravada Buddhists; Khmer Theravada Buddhists; Hinayana Buddhists; and the Buddhists of the Mekong Delta. While the radical Trí Quang wanted a share and/or total control of the political power in Saigon, the moderates tended to go along with the government. Neither group had an influence on the Hòa Hảo or the large number of Buddhists who lived in the Mekong Delta. One could say that Trí Quang did not represent the Vietnamese Buddhist community in general.

67. Ibid., 65

68. Fitzgerald, *Fire in the Lake*, 136–137.

Chapter 8

1. Moyar, *Triumph Forsaken*, 281. Almost everyone who was part of the Diem administration was either fired or demoted, although many were outstanding citizens or loyal officers.

2. Topmiller, *Lotus Unleashed*, 12–13. Only Topmiller believed that Buddhists "had formed a realistic appraisal of the dangers of a coalition government" (no proof was given) and that "given that communists threatened American treasure and power, the U.S. had to combat to preserve U.S. affluence." Although the Tri Quang-led Buddhists were just one of the many Buddhist groups, Topmiller still argues that they represented the views of the Vietnamese Buddhist community. It should be remembered that the larger Thich Tam Chau-led group was pro-government and strongly anticommunist.

3. Nhu Tang Truong, *A Viet Cong Memoir*, 268. "The Provisional Revolutionary Government was always simply a group emanating from the DRV."

4. Moyar, *Triumph Forsaken*, 282–287.

5. Ibid., 295.

6. Topmiller, *Lotus Unleashed*, 19.

7. Moyar, *Triumph Forsaken*, 296–297; Topmiller, *Lotus Unleashed*, 18.

8. Topmiller, *Lotus Unleashed*, 23.

9. Browne, "You Could Smell the Burning Flesh," in *Patriots*, by Christian Appy, 72.

10. Diem and Chanoff, *In the Jaws of History*, 122.

11. Dommen, *The Indochinese Experience*, 620–631; Moyar, *Triumph Forsaken*, 340–349.

12. Moyar, *Triumph Forsaken*, 350.

13. Ibid., 351–352.

14. Diem and Chanoff, *In the Jaws of History*, 127. Like many other southern leaders, Quat was imprisoned after the communist takeover of Saigon in 1975. He died in one of their jails in 1981, leaving behind no notes.

15. Moyar, *Triumph Forsaken*, 364–366.

16. Carter, *Inventing Vietnam*, 154.

17. Diem and Chanoff, *In the Jaws of History*, 131–132.

18. Ibid., 134.

19. George Barmann, "Did Nixon Mull Chance in Vietnam?," *Plain Dealer*, 14 November 1971.

20. Moyar, *Triumph Forsaken*, 402–403.

21. Topmiller, *Lotus Unleashed*, 38.

22. Dommen, *The Indochinese Experience*, 653; Topmiller, *Lotus Unleashed*, 71–91.

23. Topmiller, *Lotus Unleashed*, 128–129.

24. Dommen, *The Indochinese Experience*, 635–648.

25. Ibid., 658–659.

26. Chairman's Memo, "Impressive Achievements in South Vietnam," *The Em-Kayan*, December 1966, 1.

27. Paul Harder, "Long Binh: New Military City in Vietnam," *The Em-Kayan,* June 1967, 3–5.

28. Carter, *Inventing Vietnam*, 192–194.

29. Paul Harder, "Tan Son Nhut: a Modern Jet Port for Saigon," *Power Parade*, 1967, 12–14.

30. It should be remembered that Hanoi initiated the war by sending their troops to "liberate" the South.

31. Hedrick Smith, "More Health Aid for Saigon Urged," *New York Times*, 22 September 1967. Although the social picture was bad during the war years, medical treatment was free for all citizens. Therefore, it was no worse than under today's socialist system where patients had to pay for their healthcare needs. One Vietnamese doctor in 2004 had to rely on his overseas classmates' remittances to pay for chemotherapy treatment.

32. Larsen and Tran, *Shallow Graves*, 19.

33. Whitfield, *Historical and Cultural Dictionary*, 29. Ca dao are folksongs that are a vital part of the oral literature of Vietnam. Most are written in the (six-eight) lục bát form. Ca Dao reflect the soul of the common people of a given period.

34. Larsen and Tran, *Shallow Graves*, 21.

35. Ibid., 28.

36. Ibid., 90.

37. Ibid., 33. VD stands for venereal disease.

38. Ibid., 35.

39. Ibid., 46.

40. Ibid., 80.

41. Chicken bred in the U.S. for their white meat have plump feet. See, "Chinese Tax on U.S. Chicken Feet," http://www.sandiegorestaurants.com/article.cfm/article/355/Chinese-Tax-on-US-Chicken-Feet.

42. Larry Berman, in *The Tet Offensive*, by Gilbert and Head, 43.

43. Kamm, *Dragon Ascending*, 173. The author has confirmed this fear in numerous conversations with the Vietnamese who expressed fear and contempt for the communists.

44. Ibid., 179.

Chapter 9

1. Diem and Chanoff, *In the Jaws of History*, 210. The size disparity between the two allies, the feeling that the Vietnamese were ineffective or corrupt, ingrained Asian "pas-

sivity," and the tendency to avoid direct confrontation (the last two being offshoots of the Confucian culture), are some of the physical and psychological factors that forced the U.S. to take over the war. However, the Americans failed to understand war psychology: The Vietnamese needed to win their own war in their own land to have a permanent victory. Elbowing them aside and waging a defensive and limited war had a detrimental effect on their war effort and morale and ultimately led to their downfall.

2. John Prados, "The Warning That Left Something to Chance," in *The Tết Offensive*, by Gilbert and Head, 145–151.

3. Ibid., 161–162.

4. Robert McG. Thomas Jr., "Nguyen Ngoc Loan, 67, Dies," *New York Times* 18 July, 1998; Eddie Adams, "Eulogy: General Nguyen Ngoc Loan," *Time*, 27 July, 1998.

5. Smith and Williams, *Pre-Communist Indochina*, 202.

6. Oberdorfer, *Tet*, 229–230.

7. Ibid., 197.

8. Smith and Williams, *Pre-Communist Indochina*, 253; Oberdorfer, *Tet*, 232.

9. Nam, "An Underreported Tragedy: The Hue Massacre," in *The Sorrows of War and Peace*, by Nghia M. Vo et al., 159–165. Lê Văn Hảo, the provisional "mayor" of Hue, and other traitors fled with the communists to the jungles after the offensive and returned to the city after 1975. Hao, who had since fled to France, denied his culpability during that period. So did Hoàng Phú Ngọc Tường. Only Lê Minh, the NVA field commander, acknowledged in his diary: "There were those who were unjustly sentenced in the situation at hand.... The responsibility of such injustice must belong to the leadership, part of which is mine. The task of the revolution is ... to make amends to the children of those unjustly killed." The Hanoi government has yet to this day to acknowledge its role in the Hue massacre.

10. Dommen, *The Indochinese Experience*, 661–668; Smith and Williams, *Pre-Communist Indochina*, 230–231; Wiest, *Vietnam's Forgotten Army*, 271.

11. http://en.wikipedia.org/wiki/Tet_offensive

12. Spector, *After Tết*, 162–164. That brutality against the Saigon citizenry had rarely been reported by U.S. news.

13. Sorley, *A Better War*, 24.

14. Lamb, *Vietnam, Now*, 148.

15. Diem and Chanoff, *In the Jaws of History*, 227–228. The main goal of the Paris talks for the Americans was to extricate themselves from the war without suffering further casualties and without being blamed for having lost the war.

16. Dommen, *The Indochinese Experience*, 673–692.

17. Ibid., 707–711.

18. Ibid., 754–755. Kissinger had talked about a "decent interval" of eight years between an American withdrawal and a Saigon takeover as early as 1966. By 1968, the decent interval had decreased to two to three years. There was even suggestion of overthrowing Thiệu if he opposed the settlement.

19. Nguyen and Schecter, *The Palace File*, 33.

20. Ibid., 40.

21. Dommen, *The Indochinese Experience*, 758–760.

22. Diem and Chanoff, *In the Jaws of History*, 272–274.

23. Dommen, *The Indochinese Experience*, 761–765.

24. Ibid., 786.

25. Karnow, *Vietnam*, 631.

26. Nguyen and Schecter, *The Palace File*, 82.

27. Snepp, *Decent Interval*, 14.

28. Diem and Chanoff, *In the Jaws of History*, 249.

29. Summers, *Historical Atlas*, 174–179. The communists attacked on three fronts: Quảng Trị (I Corps), Kontum (II Corps), and An Lộc (III Corps). They took over Quảng Trị, which was brilliantly retaken by General Ngô Quang Trưởng in September 1972. Kontum and An Lộc defenders held the cities and turned back the communists. The NVA took more than 100,000 casualties.

30. Dommen, *The Indochinese Experience*, 792–806.

31. Nguyen and Schecter, *The Palace File*, 83–84.

32. K. Beech, "Christ Almighty, How Can They Do This?" in *Tears Before the Rain*, by Engelmann, 185–190.

33. Dommen, *The Indochinese Experience*, 807–811.

34. Asselin, *A Bitter Peace*, 111.

35. Dommen, *The Indochinese Experience*, 822–823.

36. Ibid., 849–853.

37. Ibid., 867, 891. The cutoff of U.S. aid was worsened by the 1973 oil crisis and the Arab-Israeli War. Saigon could no longer pursue the type of war it was trained to do.

38. Diem and Chanoff, *In the Jaws of History*, 325–328.

39. Asselin, *A Bitter Peace*, 188–190.

40. Van Don Tran, *Our Endless War*, 149.

41. Brigham, *ARVN*, 3–6.

42. Ibid., 14–17.

43. Ibid., 40. It was hard for Saigon to articulate a positive and optimistic military policy and to boost the morale of its fighting soldier when it was forced to only wage a *defensive* war.

44. Ibid., 41; Masur, "Hearts and Minds," 85–86.

45. Ibid., 62. Although food shortage was also noted on the VC side, the bộ đội never witnessed its effect on their families because they were sent South a thousand miles away from home. ARVN soldiers saw with their own eyes the misery, poverty, and suffering of their relatives.

46. Ibid., 74.

47. Ibid., 80, 83, 89, 93.

48. Ibid., 114–130.

49. Andrew Krepinevich, *The Army and Vietnam*, 196.

50. Maguire, "The World Was Coming to an End," in *Patriots*, by Appy, 444.

51. Sorley, *A Better War*, 164.

52. Wiest, *Vietnam's Forgotten Army*, 55.

53. Ibid., 127.

54. Langguth, "I Think They Pictured It as a Kind of Huge Bamboo Pentagon," in *Patriots*, by Appy, 382–384.

55. Hosmer et al., *The Fall of South Vietnam*, 32–36.

56. Wiest, *Vietnam's Forgotten Army*, 236–242, 268.

57. Ibid., 150.

58. Ibid., 121.

59. Ibid., 90.

60. Ibid., 118–119.

61. Ibid., 166.

62. Ibid., 169–174.

63. Sorley, *A Better War*, 194.

64. Wiest, *Vietnam's Forgotten Army*, 220–224.

65. Ibid., 251–272.

66. Ibid., 275–281.

67. Ibid., 303. Wiest has argued that a more cooperative military and better political structure (better military and political leaders) might have led to victory; others have found that the ARVN had made so much progress that if they were given more time and if the U.S. and ARVN had followed a different military strategic course from the beginning, they could have turned the corner and won the war.

68. Snepp, *Decent Interval*, 186–188.

69. Dawson, *55 Days*, 58.

70. Snepp, *Decent Interval*, 193–195.

71. Dawson, *55 Days*, 72.

72. Dommen, *The Indochinese Experience*, 901–904. Kissinger was the manipulator who undermined Thieu and the 25 million South Vietnamese people. Even Johnson was at times upset with him. Granted that he worked for the U.S. government, he did not have to pull the plug for the sake of pulling the plug. All he did was try to complete his work in time so that he could go out with a winning legacy. Although the Paris Accords were just a gimmick, as everyone knew—a save-face for Washington, they meant the end for Saigon and her 25 million people. For Kissinger, all these people who sacrificed their bodies, blood, and sweat to fight along with the U.S. meant nothing. When time came for him to receive the Nobel Peace Prize, he accepted it with a grin on the back of millions of dead South Vietnamese. At least Le Duc Tho, the Nobel Prize co-winner who knew too well the Accords were worth nothing more than a piece of scrap paper was truthful enough to refuse the honor.

73. Snepp, *Decent Interval*, 209–212, 221–222.

74. Summers, *Historical Atlas*, 200.

75. Dawson, *55 Days*, 234–239, 267, 284–285.

76. Herrington, *Peace with Honor?*, 177–78.

77. Le Khac Ly, "Only I Am Left to Tell You the Story," in *Tears Before the Rain*, by Engelmann, 233.

78. Branson, "A Planned Program of Terrorism," in *Tears Before the Rain,*, by Engelmann, 216. The evacuation plan called for: first priority, use commercial airlift as long as possible; second, use military fixed wing as long as possible; and in the last resort, option four or Operation Frequent Wind, which was the helicopter lift.

79. Ly Tong Ba, "There Was a Kind of General Sickness," in *Tears Before the Rain*, by Engelmann, 241–245.

80. Diem and Chanoff, *In the Jaws of History*, 5–10.

81. Wolf Lehmann, "American Embassy," in *Tears Before the Rain*, by Engelmann, 40–43.

82. Neil, "I'm Dreaming of a White Christmas," in *Tears Before the Rain*, by En-

gelmann, 198. This excerpt gives details about what was happening in the last hours and minutes of the U.S. radio station in Saigon.

83. Kashiwahara, "The Bus Ran over the Baby" in *Tears Before the Rain*, by Engelmann, 159–167.

84. Do and Kane, *Counterpoint*, 195–199.

85. Ibid., 209.

86. Ibid., 210–211.

87. Ibid., 215–216.

88. Page and Pimlott, *Nam*, 562–563. Secretary of State Kissinger and Ambassador Martin frustrated evacuation plans until it was too late. Kissinger sought a diplomatic compromise with Hanoi while Martin, fearing an even faster collapse, tried to maintain the illusion of support for South Vietnam. Many important people were left behind. Success of the operation was due to General Homer Smith, who organized illegal "black flights."

89. John Degler, "To Hell with What You Say, We're Coming Right Now," in *Tears Before the Rain*, by Engelmann, 168–169.

90. Ibid., 171.

91. Mike Marriott, "American Traitor," in *Tears Before the Rain*, by Engelmann, 173.

92. Le Van Hai, "It Was a Nice Day," in *Tears Before the Rain*, by Engelmann, 247–249.

93. Mai Lien, "Shadow of the Past," in *Remembering Saigon*, by Nghia M. Vo et al., 145–150.

94. Vo, *The Vietnamese Boat People*, 74–75.

95. Nguyen Ngoc Bich, "Absolutely Hell," in *Tears Before the Rain*, by Engelmann, 265.

96. Neil, "I'm Dreaming of a White Christmas," in *Tears Before the Rain*, by Engelmann, 198–206.

97. Snepp, "There Was Classified Confetti All Over the Trees," in *Patriots*, by Appy, 501–502.

98. Weiner, *Legacy of Ashes*, 343.

99. Kean, "There Has to Be a Better Way," in *Tears Before the Rain*, by Engelmann, 120–137.

100. Herrington, "Không ai sẽ bị bỏ lại. Đừng lo," in *Tears Before the Rain*, by Engelmann, 93–106.

101. Butterfield, "Turn Out the Light at the End of the Tunnel," in *Tears Before the Rain*, by Engelmann, 176–180.

102. Willbanks, *Abandoning Vietnam*, 276–82. In reality, the RVNAF was forced to assume the role of two armies—its own and that of the vacating Americans. Short of manpower, firepower, and ammunitions, it collapsed on itself.

103. Ibid., 283–86.

104. Ibid., 287–88.

105. Lind, *Vietnam: The Necessary War*, 245.

Chapter 10

1. Nón cối: pith helmet, a relic of the French colonial time. While the South Vietnamese had a long time ago discarded the pith helmet, the North Vietnamese hung on to that colonial vestige.

2. Nam, "An Underreported Tragedy: the Huế Massacre," in *The Sorrows of War and Peace*, by Nghia M. Vo et al., 159–166; Bacsy Nguyen Lê Hiếu, "The Tết Offensive: My Story," in *The Sorrows of Peace and War*, by Vo, 87–109. Many thousands of people—civilians and soldiers, were massacred during the Huế attack and their bodies dumped into collective graves; many of them had their hands tied behind their backs while others had their skulls cracked.

3. Tín, *Following Hồ Chí Minh*, 84–85. Lt. Col. Bùi Văn Tùng, political commissar of the 203rd Tank Regiment, and Nguyễn Văn Hản, chief of security, were the only high-ranking officers stationed close to Saigon on 30 April. As Col. Bùi Tín, a war correspondent, happened to be around, Tùng urged him to talk to Big Minh and accept Saigon's surrender. Fifteen years later, Bùi Tín defected while attending a meeting in Paris. He was stripped of his Party membership in March 1991. Big Minh was allowed to move to Paris in 1990.

4. Karnow, *Vietnam: A History*, 669.

5. Tín, "I Became a Man of War and I Never Wanted That," in *Tears Before the Rain*, by Engelmann, 300–301.

6. Lamb, *Vietnam*, 85–88.

7. Vo, *The Vietnamese Boat People*, 86.

8. Nguyễn Phúc Hậu, "Yes. We Fought," in *Tears Before the Rain*, by Engelmann, 256.

9. Dawson, *55 Days*, 8.

10. Hoàng Như Tùng, "Remembering General Nguyễn Khoa Nam," in *The Men of Vietnam*, by Nghia M. Vo et al., 23–33.

11. Dommen, *The Indochinese Experience*, 921–924.

12. Vo, *The Bamboo Gulag*, 18–21; Vo,

"Tự Sát (War Suicide) in Vietnam," in *The Men of Vietnam*, by Nghia M. Vo et al., 35–53. This study reveals a high number of Tự Sát in Vietnam. Tự Sát seems to be a tradition unique to southern Vietnam, akin to the Japanese harakiri or seppuku.

13. Dommen, *The Indochinese Experience*, 923.

14. Philip Taylor, *Fragments of the Present*, 5.

15. Dommen, *The Indochinese Experience*, 940.

16. Ibid., 921.

17. Ha, *Stormy Escape*, 18; Berman, *Perfect Spy*, 244. "Everything was burned after the fall of Saigon—medical books, government documents—now they regret it. Everything (is now) from Russia—so naive" (Berman).

18. Trần Thị Mỹ Ngọc, "They are Ants Encircling Us," in *Tears Before the Rain*, by Englemann, 294–295.

19. Vũ Thị Kim Vinh, "We Cried When We Realized It Was Over," in *Tears Before the Rain*, by Englemann, 285–289.

20. A NEZ was most likely a virgin, forested area where people had to take down trees, shrubs, build their huts from scratch, and cultivate the land for living.

21. Vũ Thị Kim Vinh, "A Picture We Could Look At and Dream," in *Tears Before the Rain*, by Engelmann, 336–341.

22. Hà, *Stormy Escape*, 21, 24.

23. Nguyễn Thị Kim Anh, "We Tried to Forget Most of the Bad Things," in *Tears Before the Rain*, by Engelmann, 329–332.

24. Cargill and Huynh, *Voices of Vietnamese Boat People*, 137.

25. Ibid., 107–108.

26. Doan and Chanoff, *The Vietnamese Gulag*, 186–187.

27. Kamm, *Dragon Ascending*, 145–162; Templer, *Shadows and Wind*, 184–185. Hương appalled at the corruption and the ineptitude of party leaders, wrote *Beyond Illusions, Paradise of the Blind*, which satirized government officials who were removed from circulation in Vietnam. She was expelled from the party, jailed, kept under close watch and presently lives in exile in France.

28. Pham, *Two Hamlets in Nam Bo*, 164–166.

29. Karnow, *Vietnam: A History*, 37.

30. Philip Taylor, *Fragments of the Present*, 33–34.

31. Ibid., 34–35. All the goods owned by South Vietnamese were either sold to or confiscated by the victors and found their way northwards. Northerners, who had been deprived of basic goods for more than two decades, rushed to acquire them.

32. Cargill, *Voices of Vietnamese Boat People*, 68–70.

33. Lamb, *Vietnam, Now*, 89–90, 107–110.

34. Pham, *Two Hamlets in Nam Bo*, 180–181. Poor and destitute, they could only afford to buy cheap cigarettes and booze, which, when consumed, adversely affected their health.

35. Nhu Tang Truong, *A Viet Cong Memoir*, 277–278. Viet Minh is short for Vietnam Độc Lập Đồng Minh Hội or League for the Independence of Vietnam. This is a communist organization, which in South Vietnam took the name of Viet Cong.

36. Ibid., 260.

37. Ibid., 273; Dommen, *The Indochinese Experience*, 945. Quỳnh was the director of the Saigon General Hospital and adviser on health policy to the Nationalist Party, and Bích was head of the foreign exchange division of the National Bank. Quỳnh would be jailed in various northern camps for a total of 12 years. Tảng resigned from his post of minister of justice in 1976 and escaped abroad by boat in August 1977.

38. Ibid., 275.

39. Ibid., 279, 282. This number does not account for those called for the ten-day reeducation and the unknown number of civilians jailed in city and county jails, which came under the prerogative of the Security Police. The total number of inmates, which amounted to 1.2 million, was the largest held by any government in Vietnamese history.

40. Doan and Chanoff, *The Vietnamese Gulag*, 13, 74, 105, 108, 112.

41. Ibid., 210.

42. Ibid., 214–215, 218, 238, 241, 257. There was more or less respect for the law under the Saigon government while it was non–existent under the communist regime.

43. Ibid., 311, 313. The revolutionary government could thus claim it was not responsible for the arrest.

44. Ibid., 231.

45. Ibid., 249. Bộ đội is a soldier while cán bộ is the cadre or officer. Fear was the glue, the motivating factor that kept uniformity within the bộ độis' rank. The bộ đội were grouped in cells of three, each one watching and reporting the other; there was no place to hide since each knew the other through the daily self-criticisms. Still, about

250,000 bộ đội turned themselves over to Saigon's side during the war: They were called chiêu hồi. ARVN soldiers did not switch sides in such a great number; when they decided to go AWOL, they usually returned to their villages to do farming.

46. Hùynh, *To Be Made Over*, 199. Using that "logic," any citizen was worthy of arrest and incarceration. The South Vietnamese called it luật rừng, the law of the jungle.

47. Cargill and Huynh, *Voices of Vietnamese Boat People*, 14.

48. Sorley, *A Better War*, 388.

49. Israely Biema, "The American Pope," *Time*, 14 April 2008, 48.

50. Vo, "Duality of the Vietnamese Mind," in *Sorrows of War and Peace*, by Nghia M. Vo et al., 111–122. According to legend, King Lạc Long Quân wed fairy Âu Cơ who gave him 100 children. Both considered to be the ancestors of the Vietnamese nation, they later split up; taking 50 children, he settled along the coastal area and founded the Vietnamese nation (the Kinh make up 85 percent of today's population) and she took the other 50 children to the mountains, and these became the highlanders. The first documented "divorce" in world history implies a physical, geographical, and moral division between the Vietnamese—in this case highlanders vs. lowlanders. This division made way for a north-south division that occurred between 1600 to 1802 (202 years), 1859–1954 (95 years), and then 1954–1975 (21 years).

51. Vo, "The Two Vietnams," presented at the Second Annual SACEI Conference, Tysons Corner, VA, September 25, 2010. By frequently demonstrating against visiting officials of the Vietnamese socialist government to the U.S., Australia, and Europe, and by flying the yellow flag, the overseas Vietnamese community expresses their political and moral split with Hanoi.

52. Hùynh, *To Be Made Over*, x.

53. Wives and even inmates were tricked into signing for the NEZ as a way to get out of the reeducation camps early.

54. Như Tang Trương, *A Viet Cong Memoir*, 274–275.

55. Jamieson, *Understanding Vietnam*, 363.

56. Dommen, *The Indochinese Experience*, 945.

57. Lamb, *Vietnam Now*, 77–79.

58. Doan and Chanoff, *The Vietnamese Gulag*, 23. The shortcut at that time was to accuse educated Southerners of being CIA agents.

59. Vo, *The Bamboo Gulag*, 143–148.

60. Thanh, *The Inviting Call of Wandering Souls*, 82. In this communist society, buffaloes were more valuable than human beings.

61. Ibid., 74–77.

62. Tri, *Prisoner of the Word*, 87. Lack of tools was a common feature for all these camps and could be explained by the sudden imprisonment of a million inmates. In addition to the lack of legal reason to jail them, the criminality of the process had to do with the fact that Hà Nội continued to imprison these people despite the fact that they did not have the means to feed, clothe, keep them healthy, or to provide tools for them to do their work.

63. Vo, *Bamboo Gulag*, 117–120.

64. Doan and Chanoff, *The Vietnamese Gulag*, 257.

65. Ibid., 259–261.

66. These snoopers acted like antennae—registering everything before reporting it to the communists.

67. Vo, *Bamboo Gulag*, 121–126.

68. Freeman, *Hearts of Sorrow*, 239.

69. McKelvey, *A Gift of Barbed Wire*, 6, 67.

70. M. C. Smith-Faawzi et al., "The Validity of Screening for Post Traumatic Stress Disorder and Major Depression among Vietnamese former Political Prisoners," *Acta Psychiatrica Scandinavia* 96 (1997): 87–93. An unpublished report by T. Pham found that 51 percent of prisoners reported having been beaten; 39 percent reported having been placed in a sack, box, or container; 86 percent reported having witnessed others being tortured; and 10 percent reported having experienced a mock execution.

71. R.F. Mollica et al., "Brain Structural Abnormalities and Mental Health Sequelae in South Vietnamese Ex-Political Detainees," *Archives of General Psychiatry* (Nov. 2009): 1221–1232. Neuro-imaging studies in patients with THI have reported that reduced volumes of the prefrontal cortex and hippocampus were associated with development of depression and psychiatric symptoms.

72. Jamieson, *Understanding Vietnam*, 365.

73. Chuong Trinh. Comment made at the Second Annual SACEI Conference, The Fall of Saigon, Tysons Corner, VA, September 25, 2010.

74. Zinoman, *The Colonial Bastille*, 302.

75. Thanh, *The Inviting Call of Wandering Souls*, 142.

76. Thompson, *Refugee Workers*, 72–73.

77. Asia Videotape, Westminster, CA, 2007.

78. Vo, *The Vietnamese Boat People*, 65–78.

79. Grant, *The Boat People*, 54.

80. Vo, *Vietnamese Boat People*, 142–172.

81. Duiker, *Vietnam Since the Fall of Saigon*, 33.

82. Ibid., 34, 38.

83. Templer, *Shadows and Wind*, 57. This attitude reflected the free spirit of southern peasants who were used to being independent and had never sided with the revolution, except under the barrel of guns during the war.

84. Duiker, *Vietnam Since the Fall of Saigon*, 41–43, 47–48.

85. Ibid., 19.

86. Ibid., 31. By 1975, the South was more advanced than the North in the industrial, commercial, economic, and medical sectors. On the medical side for example, a northern nurse could expect to become the equivalent of an osteopath or a physician in five or ten years respectively without medical training. The lack of adequate training therefore impacted the performance of nurses and doctors. Many of the latter eventually treated and operated on party members with disastrous results. After the war, Northerners used Southerners to train them as engineers and doctors in an attempt to replace them in the future.

87. Philip Taylor, *Fragments of the Present*, 36.

88. Ibid., 39–42.

89. Khong, *Learning True Love*, 206–208. This was the largest number (24) of self-immolations recorded in South Vietnam in protest against the Hà Nội government. While the Diệm regime fell with a lower number of immolations, the repressive communist regime remained unshaken and further tightened its grip on all religions.

90. Lauras, *Le Chantier des Utopies*, 25–27.

91. Chau, "The Curriculum Was Designated to Detoxicate Ds," in *Patriots*, by Appy, 475–480.

92. http://en.wikipedia.org/wiki/Ly_Tong.

93. Hiebert, *Chasing the Tigers*, 186–187.

94. Ibid., 197–199.

95. Lauras, *Le Chantier des Utopies*, 148–151.

96. Dommen, *The Indochinese Experience*, 635.

97. Trần Bạch Đằng, "We Believe in Forgiving and Forgetting," in *Tears Before the Rain*, by Engelmann, 306–307.

98. Berman, *Perfect Spy*, 14.

99. Ibid., 17.

100. Ibid., 180. By having access to *Times'* classified information, Ẩn transformed *Times* correspondents to inadvertent spies for Hà Nội. General Trần Văn Đôn was also Ẩn's long-time secret. See Berman, *Perfect Spy*, 222.

101. Lamb, *Vietnam Now*, 81–85.

102. Berman, *Perfect Spy*, 246, 253.

103. Ibid., 279.

104. Ibid., 13.

105. Vo, *Bamboo Gulag*, 209–213.

106. Lamb, *Vietnam, Now*, 98.

107. Ibid., 100.

108. Southerland, "Honoring the Dead," http://www.rfa.org/english/features/blogs/vietnamblog/205/7/15/blog4_vietnam_south erland

109. Vo, "Vietnam and the Vietnamese," in *The Men of Vietnam*, by Nghia M. Vo et al., 12–13.

110. Lamb, *Vietnam, Now*, 262.

111. Mai Lien, "Shadow of the Past," in *Remembering Saigon*, by Vo et al., 145–150. These people's bravery had never been acknowledged before.

112. Lamb, *Vietnam, Now*, 93–94, 97.

113. Ibid., 105–106.

114. Hiebert, *Chasing the Tigers*, 122.

115. Lamb, *Vietnam, Now*, 101.

116. Philip Taylor, *Fragments of the Present*, 52–53.

Chapter 11

1. Philip Taylor, *Fragments of the Present*, 56–58. After 1975, the whole country had only two newspapers, *Tuổi Trẻ* (Youth) and *Nhân Dân* (The People), both government-owned and geared toward spreading party news and indoctrinating the people with communist ideals. Southerners who had lived more or less freely for more than two decades under the Diệm and Thiệu regimes, gradually looked for ways to survive, while southern communist officials began to "reawaken" (a Buddhist term that stressed the importance of the process) to the reality that communist policies had led the country on a downhill course. They stopped implementing Hà Nội's economic policies in the South, spearheading changes that led to a successful southern economic recovery. Hà Nội gradually back-

tracked and accepted the idea of đổi mới before making it official throughout the country.

2. Ibid., 59–62. Gabriel Kolko, a Hà Nội supporter, asked whether "it was worth fighting a war which cost millions of lives and caused immense suffering to drive out a foreign imposed society, only to reproduce it in a superficially different form and even appeal for aid from those Americans, French and Japanese who once tormented them" ("Vietnam Since 1975: Winning a War and Losing the Peace," *Journal of Contemporary Asia* 25, 1995, 3–49).

3. Ibid., 68–69. The question was: Why did Hồ and his communists wage a war to impose a repressive state on Vietnam?

4. Ibid., 70.

5. Sorley, *A Better War*, 99, 384.

6. Philip Taylor, *Fragments of the Present*, 76–77. During the đổi mới, Hanoi distinguished the big landowners, the middle peasants (who represented the middle class), and the poor peasants.

7. Ibid., 82.

8. Vo, "The Duality of the Vietnamese Mind," in *The Sorrows of War and Peace*, by Vo et al., 111–122; Philip Taylor, *Fragments of the Present*, 91. Southerners in general are trustful, easygoing, gullible, and pragmatic. They are more open socially and politically and more tolerant of religious differences than Northerners. Southerners have been compared to Italians and northerners to Germans.

9. Philip Taylor, *Fragments of the Present*, 93.

10. Ibid., 94.

11. Ibid., 97–98.

12. Lamb, *Vietnam, Now*, 117–118.

13. Templer, *Shadows and Wind*, 75. This is the rarest coffee in the world, and is also the first case of "wet processing" of coffee beans by an animal. The fox selected the best and ripest beans and fermented them in his gut. The beans emerged in long strings which were then washed and roasted to produce a sensuous, rich, and aromatic coffee.

14. Lamb, *Vietnam, Now*, 124–126.

15. Lauras, *Le Chantier des Utopies*, 36.

16. Ibid., 37.

17. Ibid., 39–42.

18. Ibid., 44–56.

19. Ibid., 66–82.

20. Ibid., 84–92, 187–189. This case illustrates the drama of ARVN soldiers who fought for Saigon, ended up in reeducation camps during or after the war, and were later neglected by Hanoi because they were on the losing side. For them, it was a double betrayal.

21. Ibid., 27–28, 93–96. This is another tragic story of a southern schoolteacher who was victimized twice by Hanoi, which seized her apartments and sold them and denied her a professional career because her brothers had once served Saigon.

22. Jamieson, *Understanding Vietnam*, 5.

23. Hiebert, *Chasing the Tigers*, 112–113.

24. Lamb, *Vietnam Now*, 18.

25. Ibid., 70.

26. Jamieson, *Understanding Vietnam*, 236.

27. Lauras, *Le Chantier des Utopies*, 231–232.

28. D. Sanger and H. Cooper H. "Unlike Clinton, Bush Sees Hanoi in a Bit of a Hurry," *New York Times*, 19 November 2006.

29. Vo, "A Short History of Pho," in *The Sorrows of War and Peace*, by Vo et al., 129–133.

30. Bánh chưng and bánh tét are, respectively, northern and southern cooked rice cakes stuffed with pork meat and mung beans; these are served during the Tết holidays.

31. Lauras, *Le Chantier des Utopies*, 84–107. Since revolutionaries were rarely intellectuals, they often had trouble dealing with administrative duties after they won the elections or a war. Governing became difficult because of their narrow-mindedness and lack of vision.

32. Vo et al., *The Lands of Freedom*, 37–54.

33. Schultzinger, *A Time for Peace*, 113, 119.

34. Vo, *Boat People*, 181–188. The Vietnamese faced rough economic and social times in their early years in the U.S. Most were not fluent in English and had trouble adapting to a competitive system.

35. Lamb, *Vietnam Now*, 211–213.

36. Interviewed in July 2003.

37. Ngo, "My Life as a Zombie," in *Remembering Saigon*, by Vo et al., 69–79. Under the strictly regimented and controlled communist society, people felt like zombies. Everything had been dictated to them—how much they could eat, what they could say and do, and how far they could go.

38. Lamb, *Vietnam, Now*, 213.

39. Ibid., 216–218.

40. Taylor, "Nguyễn Hoàng and the Be-

ginning of Vietnam's Southward Expansion," *Southeast Asia in the Early Modern Era*, by Anthony Reid, 64–65. By turning their backs to Hanoi and the communists, they found freedom, choice, new opportunities, and riches. This does not mean, however, that they have completely forgotten their countrymen; they are sending money home each year, $8 billion in 2009 alone.

41. Vo, "The Two Vietnams," presented at the SACEI Conference on The Fall of Saigon, Tysons Corner, VA, September 2010.

42. Lauras, *Le Chantier des Utopies*, 119–128.

43. This implies that he will take a 15-percent commission.

44. Hayton, *Vietnam*, 13.

45. Lauras, *Le Chantier des Utopies*, 178–201.

46. Hiebert, *Chasing the Tigers*, 135–136.

47. Ibid., 201.

48. Schmid, *Seeing Money Can Change Behavior*. http://news.yahoo.com/s/ap/2006 1116/ap_on_bi_ge/show_me_the_money

49. Hayton, *Vietnam*, 164.

50. Ibid., 22–23. The current president, Nguyễn Minh Triết, rose to power from the Bình Dương province. He was promoted boss of HCMC, and then head of state. His nephew has taken over as provincial boss and Triết's "umbrella" shelters his family and network in Bình Dương.

51. Ibid., 73.

52. Vo, "The Lotus Pond," in *The Vietnamese Mayflowers*, by Chat V. Dang et al., 39–48.

53. Nguyen Luu Vien, "South Vietnamese Traditional Music and Vọng Cổ," in *The Men of Vietnam*, by Vo et al., 195–99.

54. Philip Taylor, *Fragments of the Present*, 23–24.

Chapter 12

1. Nam Lộc is a songwriter, singer, and emcee for Asia Video Production in Westminster, California.

2. Robinson, *Terms of Refuge*, 132.

3. Aguilar-San Juan, *Little Saigons*, 68.

4. http://en.wikipedia.org/wiki/Madi son_Nguyen. It is remarkable that her father—a fisherman with nine children—could put her through school all the way to college, where she got a master's degree. Had she remained in Vietnam, the best she could have aimed for would have been to be a fisher-

man's wife with at most a high school degree. In this socialist society, schooling is not free and parents often take their children out of secondary school because they cannot afford the tuitions.

5. Vo, "The Generational Cultural Divide," in *The Lands of Freedom*, by Vo et al. 75–78.

6. Vo, *The Boat People*, 175–177.

7. Aguilar-San Juan, *Little Saigons*, 7–9.

8. Ibid., 84.

9. Việt Thanh Nguyễn, *Orange County Register*, 2003.

10. Aguilar-San Juan, *Little Saigons*, xvi, 78–79. City council member Frank Fry, who once opposed the idea of the statue, is now a strong supporter.

11. Ibid., xxiii–xxv, 106–108.

12. *New York Times*, 2 January 1985.

13. Hein, *From Vietnam, Laos, and Cambodia*, 54–58.

14. Wood, "Vietnamese American Place-Making," 70.

15. Vo, *The Việt Kiều in America*, 201–207.

16. Monique Truong, "My Father's Vietnam Syndrome," *New York Times*, 18 June 2006.

17. Phuoc, "The Bong Son Mother," in *Faces of the War*, by Vo et al., 105–113.

18. Phuoc, "A Yam in Yen Bai," in *Faces of the War*, by Vo et al., 93–103.

19. Thị Thu Lâm Nguyễn, *Fallen Leaves*, 23–24, 65–67.

20. http://en.wikipedia.org/wiki/Georg_ Simmel. Accessed 8–29–2010.

21. Lam, *Perfume Dreams*, 13.

22. Aguilar-San Juan, *Little Saigons*, xxvii.

Epilogue

1. Vo, "Confucianism and Communism," in *The Men of Vietnam*, by Vo et al., 111–129. There are many misconceptions about this tripartite Vietnam War and each side has advanced its own theories and justifications. Voices from all three sides should be heard before a final conclusion is made.

2. Gardner, "Hall of Mirrors," in *Why the North Won the Vietnam War*, by Marc Gilbert, 240. The war was initiated by the communists with the goal of taking over the whole of South Vietnam. The presence of northern military divisions and tanks slam-

ming the gates of the Saigon Independence Palace was the ultimate and unequivocal proof of this invasion and conquest.

3. Rotter, "The Role of Economic Culture in Victory and Defeat in Vietnam," in *Why the North Won the Vietnam War*, by Gilbert, 211.

4. Appy, *Patriots*, 35.

5. Herring, "Fighting without Allies," in *Why the North Won the Vietnam War*, by Gilbert, 85. The Chinese helped to maintain the vital supply route from China to Vietnam besides contributing more than 300,000 soldiers to Hà Nội's side. By spreading the international communist banner all over Indochina, the North Vietnamese proved to be more "nguy" (puppet) to their Chinese and Soviet masters than the South Vietnamese to the Americans.

6. Reeducation camps are the creation of communist leaders whose goals were to reform society. They began with the gulag camps in the Soviet Union, spread to Communist China, and were refined by Hồ and his acolytes in Vietnam.

7. Appy, *Patriots*, 38. Knowing the Vietnamese communists as they were throughout the 1954 Land Reform, the lengthy and bloody war, and the reeducation camps, it seems strange that some, like Appy, still believe in cohabitation and appeasement of the communists.

8. "Ăn làm vua, thua làm giặc." Having lost a battle or cause, losers try to topple the established government by causing insurrections and disturbances.

9. North Vietnam was not self-dependent either. It depended on military aid and advisers from the Soviet bloc and China. To this day, it is still repaying the debt it owed during the war by ceding to China portions of northern territory and the Paracel Islands.

10. During this period (1945–1954), the North Vietnamese built up and refined their political system, eliminated the remaining opponents to their ideology, and strengthened their army. The South Vietnamese never recovered from that lost interval.

11. Gilbert, *Why the North Won the Vietnam War*, 188.

12. Vo, "The Two Vietnams," presented at the Second Annual SACEI Conference. Tysons Corner, VA, September 25, 2010.

13. Hiebert, *Chasing the Tigers*, 127; Templer, *Shadows and Wind*, 97. Lenin may have been discredited in his country, but in Hà Nội he lives on. According to Hiebert, a giant, five-meter-high-statue of Lenin—the only one left anywhere on the planet—still towers over a park close to Ho's mausoleum.

14. Thi Binh Nguyen, "The Longest Peace Talks in History," in *Patriots*, by Appy, 465–467.

15. Vo, "Roots of Southern Nationalism," in *Sorrows of War and Peace*, by Vo et al., 35–73. As explained throughout this book, Southerners have their own social, religious, political, and economic particularities, which make them different from Northerners. These differences have been present since 1600, when Nguyễn Hoàng decided to build a "southern" empire.

Bibliography

Aguilar-San Juan, Karin. *Little Saigons: Staying Vietnamese in America.* Minneapolis: University of Minnesota Press, 2009.

Appy, Christian. *Patriots: The Vietnam War Remembered by All Sides.* New York: Viking, 2003.

Asselin, Pierre. *A Bitter Peace: Washington, Hanoi, and the Making of the Paris Agreement.* Chapel Hill: University of North Carolina Press, 2002.

Barrelon, Pierre, Jules Brossard de Corbigny, Charles Lemire, and Gaston Cahen. *Cities of Nineteenth Century Colonial Vietnam.* Paris: 1860. Reprint, Bangkok, Thailand: White Lotus, 1999.

Barrow, John. *A Voyage to Cochinchina in the Years of 1772 and 1773.* London: 1806. http://books.google.com.

Baudrit, André. *Extraits des Registres de Deliberations de la Ville de Saigon, 1867–1916.* Vols. 1 and 2. Saigon, Vietnam: Imprimerie Testelin, 1936.

Berman, Larry. *Perfect Spy.* New York: HarperCollins, 2007.

Borer, Douglas A. *Superpowers Defeated: Vietnam and Afghanistan Compared.* New York: Frank Cass, 1999.

Borri, Cristoforo. *Cochinchina.* London, UK: 1633. Reprint, New York: 2006.

_____. *Views of Seventeenth-Century Vietnam.* Ithaca, NY: Cornell Southeast Asia Program, 2006.

Bouchot, Jean. *Petrus Truong Vinh Ky. Erudit Cochinchinois.* Saigon, Vietnam: Imprimerie Ardin, 1925.

Brigham, Robert. *ARVN. Life and Death in the South Vietnamese Army.* Lawrence: University Press of Kansas, 2006.

Brown, Edward. *Cochinchina and My Experience of It: A Seaman's Narrative of His Adventures and Sufferings During a Cap-tivity among Chinese Pirates on the Coast of Cochinchina, and Afterwards During a Journey on Foot Across That Country, in the Years 1857–1858.* Taipei, Taiwan: Ch'eng Wen, 1971.

Buttinger, Joseph. *Vietnam: A Dragon Embattled.* New York: Praeger, 1967.

Cargill, Mary T., and Jade Ngoc Quang Huynh. *Voices of Vietnamese Boat People: Nineteen Narratives of Escape and Survival.* Jefferson, NC: McFarland, 2000.

Carter, James M. *Inventing Vietnam: The United States and State Building, 1954–1968.* Cambridge, UK: Cambridge University, 2008.

Catton, Philip. *Diem's Final Failure.* Lawrence: University Press of Kansas, 2002.

Coedes, George. *The Indianized States of Southeast Asia.* Honolulu: University Press of Hawaii, 1968.

Cooke, Nola, and Li Tana, eds. *Water Frontier: Commerce and the Chinese in the Lower Mekong Region, 1750–1880.* Lanham, MD: Rowman & Littlefield, 2004.

Cooper, Nicola. *France in Indochina: Colonial Encounters.* New York: Oxford, 2001.

Crawfurd, John. *Journal of an Embassy from the Governor General of India to the Courts of Siam and Cochin China.* London: 1830. Reprint, Kuala Lumpur, Malaysia: Oxford University Press, 1987.

Dang, Chat V., Hien V. Ho, Nghia M. Vo, An T. Than, and Anne R. Capdeville. *The Vietnamese Mayflowers of 1975.* Charleston, SC: Book Surge, 2009.

Dawson, Alan. *55 Days: The Fall of South Vietnam.* New York: Prentice Hall, 1977.

Diem, Bui, and David Chanoff. *In the Jaws of History.* Bloomington: Indiana University Press, 1999.

Do, Kiem, and Julie Kane. *Counterpoint.*

Annapolis, MD: Naval Institute Press, 1998.

Doan, Van Toai, and David Chanoff. *The Vietnamese Gulag*. New York: Simon & Schuster, 1986.

Dommen, Arthur J. *The Indochinese Experience of the French and the Americans. Nationalism and Communism in Cambodia, Laos, and Vietnam*. Bloomington: University of Indiana Press, 2001.

Dooley, Thomas A. *Deliver Us from Evil*. New York: Farrar, Straus and Cudahy, 1962.

Duiker, William. *Vietnam Since the Fall of Saigon*. Athens: Ohio University Press, 1985.

Dutton, George. *The Tay Son Uprising: Society and Rebellion in Eighteenth-Century Vietnam*. Honolulu: Hawaii University Press, 2006.

Edwards, Anastasia. *Saigon, Mistress on the Mekong*. New York: Oxford University Press, 2003.

Engelmann, Larry. *Tears Before the Rain: An Oral History of the Fall of South Vietnam*. New York: Oxford University Press, 1990.

Fall, Bernard. *The Two Vietnams: A Political and Military Analysis*. 2nd edition. New York: Praeger, 1967.

Fisher, James T. *Dr. America: The Lives of Thomas A. Dooley, 1927–1961*. Amherst: University of Massachusetts Press, 1997.

Fitzgerald, Frances. *Fire in the Lake: The Vietnamese and the Americans in Vietnam*. New York: Little, Brown, 1972.

Franchini, Philippe. *Saigon 1925–1945*. Paris: Editions Autrement, 1992.

Frankum, Ronald B. *Operation Passage to Freedom: The United States Navy in Vietnam, 1954–1955*. Lubbock: Texas Tech University Press, 2007.

Freeman, James S. *Hearts of Sorrow: Vietnamese American Lives*. Stanford, CA: Stanford University Press, 1989.

Gilbert, Marc. *Why the North Won the Vietnam War*. New York: Palgrave, 2002.

_____, and William Head. *The Tet Offensive*. New York: Praeger, 1996.

Goodwin, Jeff. *No Way Out: States and Revolutionary Movements, 1945–1991*. Cambridge, UK: Cambridge University Press, 2001.

Grant, Bruce. *The Boat People: An "Age" Investigation*. New York: Penguin, 1979.

Guillon, Emmanuel. *Hindu-Buddhist Art of Vietnam*. Trumbull, CT: Weatherhill, 1997.

Hà, Kim. *Stormy Escape: A Vietnamese Woman's Account of her 1980 Flight*. Jefferson, NC: McFarland, 1997.

Haley, J.M. "1861 French Conquest of Saigon: Battle of Ky Hoa Forts." *Vietnam Magazine* (12 June, 2006). http://www.historynet.com.

Hayton, Bill. *Vietnam: Rising Dragon*. New Haven, CT: Yale University Press, 2010.

Hein, Jeremy. *From Vietnam, Laos, and Cambodia: A Refugee Experience in the United States*. New York: Twayne, 1995.

Herrington, Stuart A. *Peace with Honor? An American Reports on Vietnam*. Novato, CA: Presidio, 1983.

Hiebert, Murray. *Chasing the Tigers. A Portrait of the New Vietnam*. New York: Kodansha, 1996.

Higgins, Marguerite. *Our Vietnam Nightmare*. New York: Harper & Row, 1965.

Ho Tai, Hue-Tam. *Millenarianism and Peasant Politics in Vietnam*. Cambridge, MA: Harvard University Press, 1983.

_____. *Radicalism and the Origins of the Vietnamese Revolution*. Cambridge, MA: Harvard University Press, 1992.

Hosmer, Stephen T., Konrad Kellen, and Brian M. Jenkins. *The Fall of South Vietnam: Statements by Vietnamese Military and Civilian Leaders*. New York: Crane Russak, 1980.

Huỳnh, Sanh Thong. *An Anthology of Vietnamese Poems*. New Haven, CT: Yale University Press, 1996.

_____. *To Be Made Over: Tales of Socialist Reeducation in Vietnam*. New Haven, CT: Yale Southeast Asia Studies, 1988.

Jacobs, Seth. *America's Miracle Man in Vietnam*. Durham, NC: Duke University Press, 2004.

Jamieson, Neil L. *Understanding Vietnam*. Berkeley: University of California Press, 1993.

Kamm, Henry. *Dragon Ascending: Vietnam and the Vietnamese*. New York: Arcade, 1996.

Karnow, Stanley. *Vietnam: A History*. New York: Viking, 1983.

Khong, Chan. *Learning True Love: How I Learned and Practiced Social Change in Vietnam*. Berkeley, CA: Parallax, 1993.

Krepinevich, Andrew F. *The Army and Vietnam*. Baltimore, MD: John Hopkins University Press, 1988.

Lafont, P. B. *Peninsules Indochinoises*. Paris: L'Harmattan, 1991.

Lam, Andrew. *Perfume Dreams: Reflections*

on the Vietnamese Diaspora. Berkeley, CA: Hey Day Books, 2005.

Lamb David. *Vietnam, Now: A Reporter Returns*. New York: Public Affairs, 2003.

Larsen, Wendy W., and Thi Nga Tran. *Shallow Graves: Two Women and Vietnam*. New York: Harper & Row, 1987.

Lauras, Didier. *Le Chantier des Utopies*. Paris: Autrement, 1997.

Le, Quang Ninh, and S. Dovert. *Saigon: Trois Siecles de Developpement Urbain*. Ho Chi Minh City, Vietnam: Nha Xuat Ban Tong Hop TP, 2004.

Le, Thanh Khoi. *Le Vietnam*. Paris: Maisonneuve, 1955.

Lind, Michael. *Vietnam: The Necessary War*. New York: Free Press, 1999.

Lockhart, Bruce McFarland. *The End of the Vietnamese Monarchy*. New Haven, CT: Yale Southeast Asia Studies, 1993.

Malleret, Louis. *A la Recherche de Prei nokor; note sur l'emplacement presumé de l'ancien Saigon Khmer*. Saigon, Vietnam: Bulletin de la Societé des Etudes Indochinoises, 1942.

Marr, David G. *Vietnamese Anticolonialism, 1885–1925*. Berkeley: University of California Press, 1971.

_____. *Vietnamese Tradition on Trial: 1920–1945*. Berkeley: University of California Press, 1981.

Masur, Matthew. "Hearts and Minds: Cultural Nation-Building in Vietnam, 1954–1963." PhD diss., History, Ohio State University, 2004.

McHale, Shawn F. *Print and Power: Confucianism, Communism, and Buddhism in the Making of Modern Vietnam*. Honolulu: University of Hawaii Press, 2004.

McKelvey, Robert. *A Gift of Barbed Wire. America's Allies Abandoned in South Vietnam*. Seattle: University of Washington Press, 2002.

McLeod, Mark. *The Vietnamese Response to French Intervention, 1862–1874*. New York: Praeger, 1991.

Miller, Edward. "Grand Designs: Vision, Power, and Nation Building in America's Alliance with Ngo Dinh Diem." PhD diss., Harvard University, 2004.

Mollica, Richard F., et al. "Brain Structural Abnormalities and Mental Health Sequelae in South Vietnamese Ex-Political Detainees Who Survived Traumatic Head Injury and Torture." *Archives of General Psychiatry* 66 (November 2009): 1221–1232.

Moore, John N. *The Vietnam Debate: A Fresh Look at the Arguments*. Lanham, MD: University Press of America, 1990.

Morice, A. *People and Wildlife In and Around Saigon, 1872–1873*. Paris: 1875. Reprint, Bangkok, Thailand: White Lotus, 1997.

Moyar, Mark. *Triumph Forsaken: The Vietnam War, 1954–1965*. New York: Cambridge University Press, 2006.

Neese, Harvey, and John O'Donnell. *Prelude to Tragedy: Vietnam 1960–1965*. Annapolis, MD: Naval Institute Press, 2001.

New York Times. "Vietnamese Reviving a Chicago Slum." *New York Times*, 2 January 1986.

Nguyễn, Đình Dậu. *From Saigon to Ho Chi Minh City*. Ho Chi Minh City, Vietnam: Science and Technics Publishing House, 1998.

Nguyen, Quang Van, and Marjorie Pivar. *Fourth Uncle in the Mountain: A Memoir of a Barefoot Doctor in Vietnam*. New York: St. Martin's Press, 2004.

Nguyễn, Thị Thu Lâm. *Fallen Leaves: Memoirs of a Vietnamese Woman from 1940 to 1975*. New Haven, CT: Yale SEAS, 1989.

Nguyễn, Tiến Hưng, and Jerold L. Schecter. *The Palace File*. New York: Harper & Row, 1986.

Nguyễn, Văn Cảnh. *Vietnam under Communism, 1975–1982*. Stanford, CA: Stanford University Press, 1983.

Nguyễn, Việt Thanh. "Behind Flag Fight, Deep Pain." *Orange County Register*, 17 August 2003.

Noppe, Catherine, and Jean-Francois Hubert. *Art of Vietnam*. New York: Parkstone Press, 2003.

Oberdorfer, Don. *Tết: The Turning Point of the Vietnam War*. New York: DaCapo Press, 1971.

Page, Tim, and John Pimlott. *Nam: The Vietnam Experience 1965–75*. New York: Mallard Press, 1988.

Pallu de la Barriere, Leopold. *Histoire de l'Expedition de Conchinchine en 1861*. Paris: Hachette, 1864.

Pelley, Patricia M. *Post-Colonial Vietnam: New Histories of the National Past*. Durham, NC: Duke University Press, 2002.

Pham, David Lan. *Two Hamlets in Nam Bo: Memoirs of Life in Vietnam*. Jefferson, NC: McFarland, 2000.

Reid, Anthony. *Southeast Asia in the Age of Commerce, 1450–1680*. New Haven, CT: Yale University Press, 1993.

_____. *Southeast Asia in the Early Modern Era: Trade, Power, and Belief.* Ithaca, NY: Cornell University Press, 1993.

Robinson, Courtland. *Terms of Refuge: The Indochinese Exodus and the International Response.* New York: Zed Books, 1998.

Ross, Robert, and Gerard Telkamp. *Colonial Cities: Essays on Urbanism in a Colonial Context.* New York: Springer, 1985.

Schultzinger, Robert. *A Time for Peace: The Legacy of the Vietnam War.* New York: Oxford, 2006.

Sellers, Nicholas. *The Princes of Ha Tien.* Brussels, BE: Thanh-Long, 1983.

Smith, Ralph B, and Beryl Williams. *Pre–Communist Indochina.* New York: Routledge, 2009.

Snepp, Frank. *Decent Interval.* New York: Random House, 1977.

Sorley, Lewis. *A Better War: The Unexamined Victories and Final Tragedy of America's Last Years in Vietnam.* New York: Harcourt Brace, 1999.

Spector, Ronald H. *After Tét.* New York: Vintage, 1993.

Summers, Harry. *Historical Atlas of the Vietnam War.* New York: Houghton Mifflin, 1995.

Taboulet, Georges. *La Geste Francaise en Indochine.* Vol. 1. Paris: Adrien-Maisonneuve, 1955.

Tana, Li. *Nguyen Cochinchina. Southern Vietnam in the Seventeenth and Eighteenth Centuries.* Ithaca, NY: Cornell University SEAP, 1998.

Taylor, Keith W. "Surface Orientation in Vietnam: Beyond Histories of Nation and Region." *The Journal of Asian Studies* 57, 4 (November 1998): 949–978.

_____, and John K. Whitmore. *Essays into Vietnamese Pasts.* Ithaca, NY: Cornell University Press, 1995.

Taylor, Philip. *Fragments of the Present: Searching for Modernity in Vietnam's South.* Honolulu: University of Hawaii Press, 2001.

_____. *Goddess on the Rise: Pilgrimage and Popular Religion in Vietnam.* Honolulu: University of Hawaii Press, 2004.

Templer, Robert. *Shadows and Wind: A View of Modern Vietnam.* New York: Penguin, 1998.

Thanh, Lu Van. *The Inviting Call of Wandering Souls.* Jefferson, NC: McFarland, 1997.

Thomazi, Auguste. *La Conquete de l'Indochine.* Paris, France, 1934.

Thompson, Larry Clinton. *Refugee Workers in the Indochina Exodus, 1975–1982.* Jefferson, NC: McFarland, 2010.

Tín, Bui. *Following Hồ Chí Minh. Memoirs of a North Vietnamese Colonel.* Honolulu: University of Hawaii Press, 1995.

Topmiller, Robert. *Lotus Unleashed.* Lexington: University Press of Kentucky, 2002.

Tran, Nhung T., and Anthony Reid. *Vietnam: Borderless Histories.* Madison: University of Wisconsin Press, 2006.

Trần, Văn Đôn. *Our Endless War: Inside Vietnam.* Novato, CA: Presidio Press, 1978.

Tri, Le Huu. *Prisoner of the Word: A Memoir of the Vietnamese Reeducation Camps.* Seattle: Black Heron Press, 2001.

Truong, Buu Lam. *Patterns of Vietnamese Response to Foreign Intervention, 1858–1900.* New Haven, CT: Yale University Southeast Asia Studies, 1967.

Trường, Monique. "My Father's Vietnam Syndrome." *New York Times*, 18 June 2006.

Trương, Như Tảng. *A Viet Cong Memoir.* New York: Vintage Books, 1985.

Tucker, Spencer. *Vietnam.* Lexington: University Press of Kentucky, 1999.

Turner, Robert F. *Vietnamese Communism: Its Origins and Development.* Stanford, CA: Stanford University Press, 1975.

Vo, Nghia M. *The Bamboo Gulag: Political Imprisonment in Communist Vietnam.* Jefferson, NC: McFarland, 2004.

_____. "The Two Vietnams." Presented at the Second Annual SACEI Conference "The Fall of Saigon," Tysons Corner, VA, 25 September 2010.

_____. *The Viet Kieu in America: Personal Accounts of Postwar Immigrants from Vietnam.* Jefferson, NC: McFarland, 2009.

_____. *The Vietnamese Boat People, 1954 and 1975–1992.* Jefferson, NC: McFarland, 2006.

Vo, Nghia M., Chat V. Dang, and Hien V. Ho. *Faces of War.* SACEI Forum # 7. Denver: Outskirts Press, 2010.

_____. *Lands of Freedom.* SACEI Forum # 5. Denver: Outskirts Press, 2009.

_____. *The Men of Vietnam.* SACEI Forum # 4. Denver: Outskirts Press, 2009.

_____. *Remembering Saigon.* SACEI Forum # 1. Denver: Outskirts Press, 2008.

_____. *The Sorrows of War and Peace.* SACEI Forum # 2. Denver: Outskirts Press, 2008.

_____. *War and Remembrance.* SACEI Forum # 6. Denver: Outskirts Press, 2009.

Vương, Hồng Sén. *Saigon Năm Xưa*. Saigon: 1960. Reprint, Ho Chi Minh City, Vietnam: Nhà Xuất Bản TP, 1991.

Wain, Barry. *The Refused: The Agony of the Indochina Refugees*. New York: Simon & Schuster, 1981.

Weiner, Tim. *Legacy of Ashes: The History of the CIA*. New York: Doubleday, 2007.

White, John. *A Voyage to Cochinchina*. London: Longman, Hurst, Rees, Orme, Brown and Green, 1824.

Whitfield, Danny J. *Historical and Cultural Dictionary of Vietnam*. Metuchen, NJ: Scarecrow Press, 1976.

Wiesner, Louis. *Victims and Survivors*. New York: Greenwood Press, 1988.

Wiest, Andrew. *Vietnam's Forgotten Army*. New York: New York University Press, 2008.

Willbanks, James H. *Abandoning Vietnam: How America Left and South Vietnam Lost Its War*. Lawrence: University of Kansas Press, 2004.

Wood, Joseph S. "Vietnamese American Place Making in Northern Virginia." *Geographical Review* 87, no. 1 (1997): 58–72.

Woodside, Alexander B. *Vietnam and the Chinese Model*. Cambridge, MA: Harvard University Press, 1971.

Wook, Choi B. *Southern Vietnam Under the Reign of Minh Mang (1820–1841): Central Policies and Local Response*. Ithaca, NY: Cornell University Southeast Asia Program, 2004.

Wright, Gwendolyn. *The Politics of Design in French Colonial Urbanism*. Chicago: University of Chicago Press, 1991.

Zinoman, Peter. *The Colonial Bastille*. Berkeley: University of California Press, 2001.

Index